Honey Hunt

4 story and art by Miki Aihara

Honey Hunt 4

CONTENTS

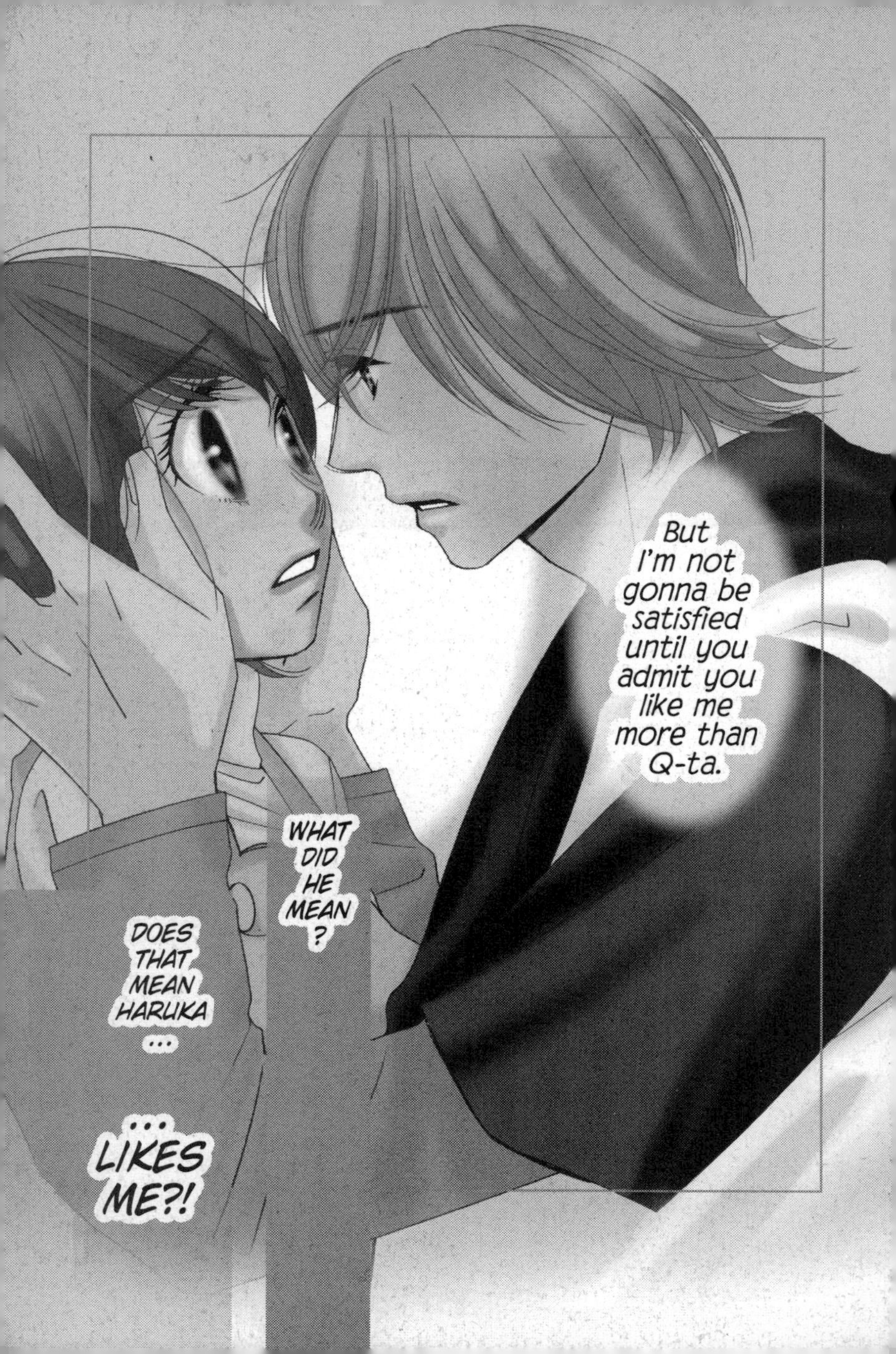
But I'm not gonna be satisfied until you admit you like me more than Q-ta.
WHAT DID HE MEAN?
DOES THAT MEAN HARUKA...
...LIKES ME?!

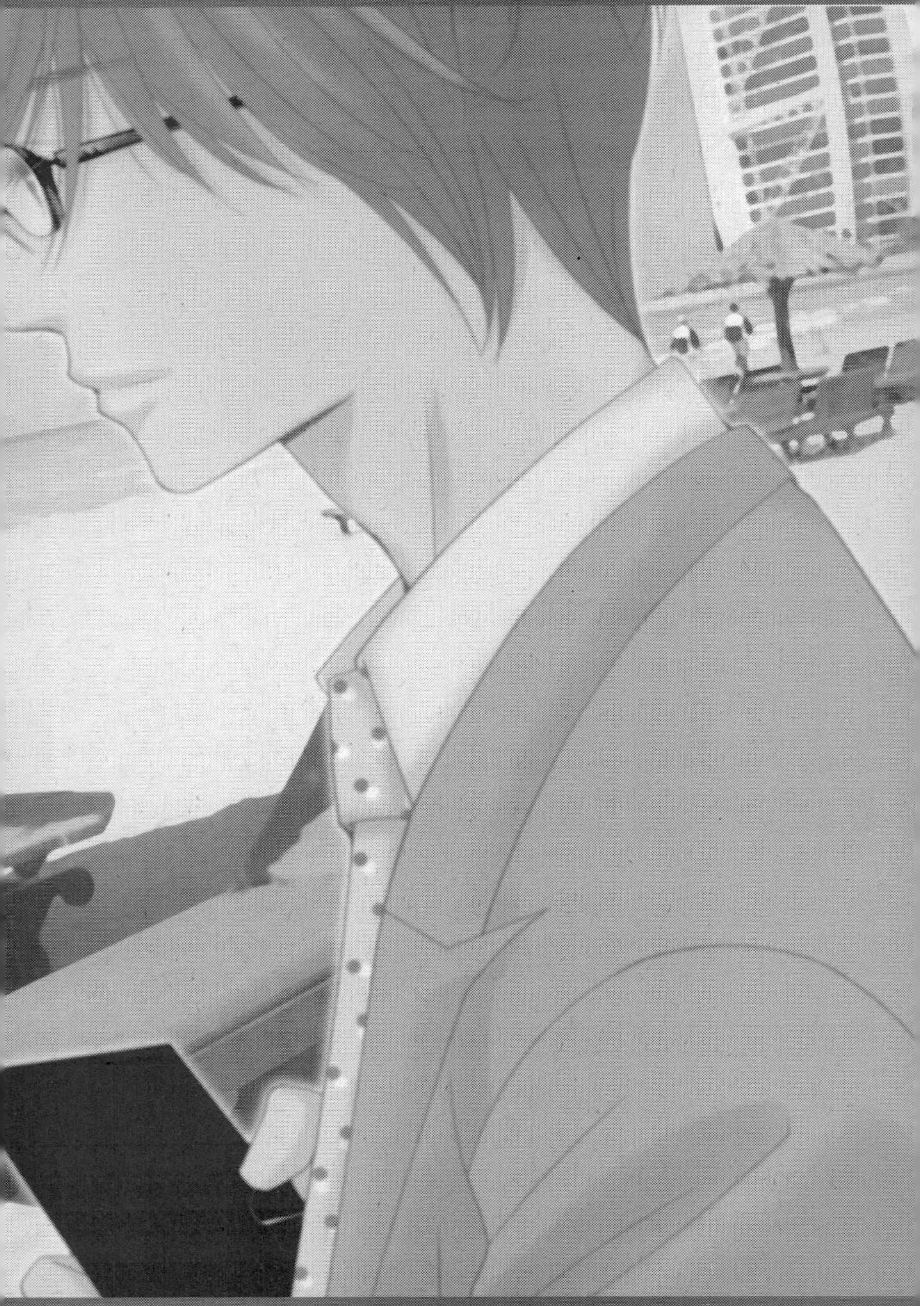

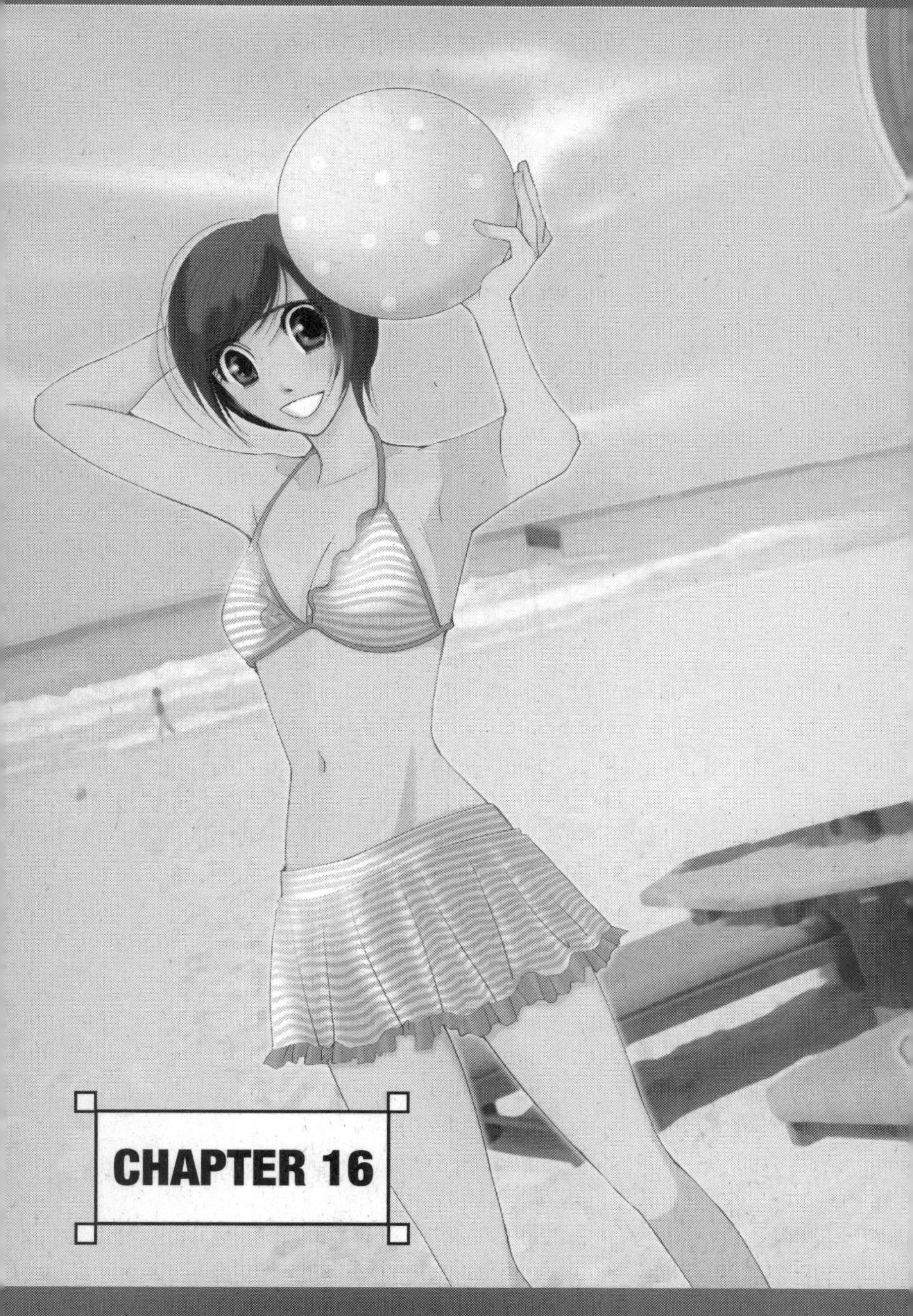
CHAPTER 16

CHARACTERS

YURA ONOZUKA ★
The only child of celebrity parents. She is a surprisingly average, ordinary girl, considering her father is a world-famous musician and her mother is an award-winning actress.

KEIICHI MIZOROGI ★
President of the entertainment company Meteorite Productions. He scouted Yura and became her manager.

Q-TA MINAMITANI ★
The singer of popular music group Assha (also known as "h.a."). He likes Yura.

HARUKA ★
A member of the pop idol group KNIGHTS. Q-ta's twin brother and rival.

Honey Hunt 4

STORY

★ Yura knows that growing up as the only child of famous parents isn't as glamorous as it would seem. Because of their busy schedules, Yura was often left home alone. Yura has always been sensitive about being compared to her parents because, unlike them, she is plain, shy and painfully normal.

★ When her parents' love affairs become public, they announce that they will divorce, leaving Yura with no place to go. What's worse, Yura discovers that her mother's lover is her childhood friend Shinsuke.

★ Fed up with how her parents overlook her, Yura decides to start acting in order to compete with her mother. Keiichi sees promise in the unpolished Yura and invites her to stay at his house and work with him. Here she will begin her new life.

★ When Yura is chosen as the lead actress in the "Noodle Girl" project, she finally finds herself a working actress. She also finds herself developing a crush on Q-ta. But she worries that the only reason Q-ta is interested in her is to get closer to her father, whom he respects more than anyone.

★ Q-ta is currently in London recording his newest album. While Yura waits for him to return, Haruka makes his move, holding her close and telling her how he feels...

Honey Hunt 04

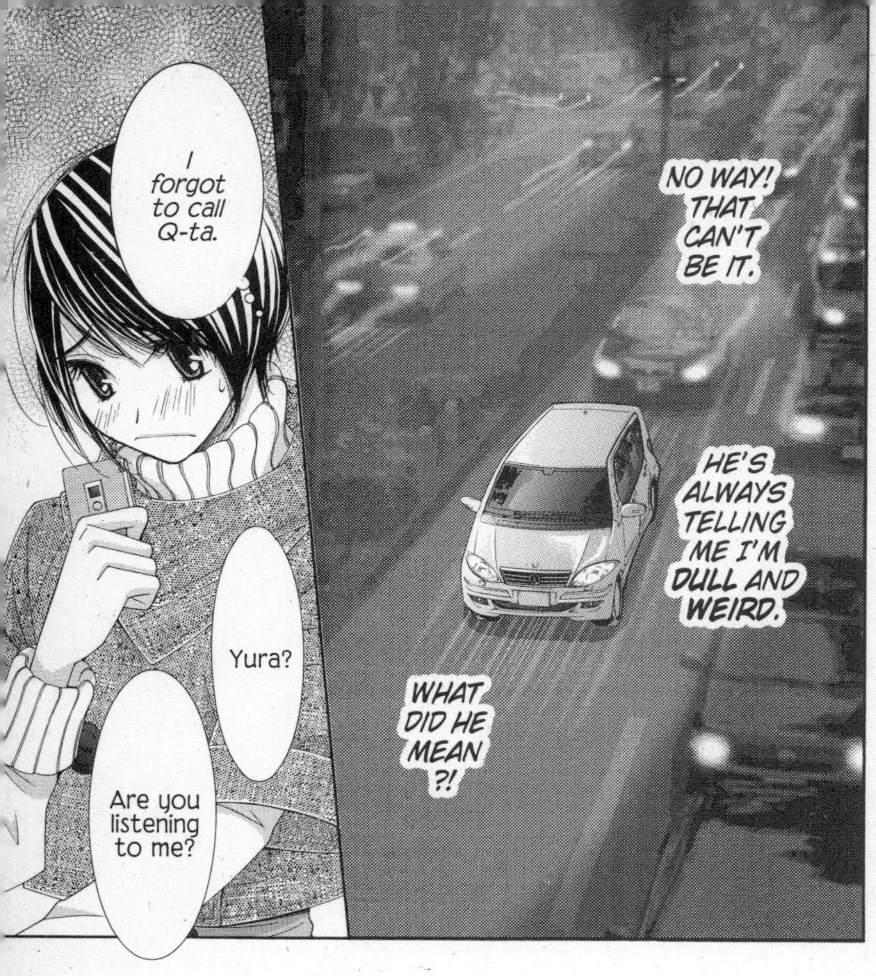
NO WAY! THAT CAN'T BE IT.
HE'S ALWAYS TELLING ME I'M DULL AND WEIRD.
WHAT DID HE MEAN?!
I forgot to call Q-ta.
Yura?
Are you listening to me?

Honey Hunt

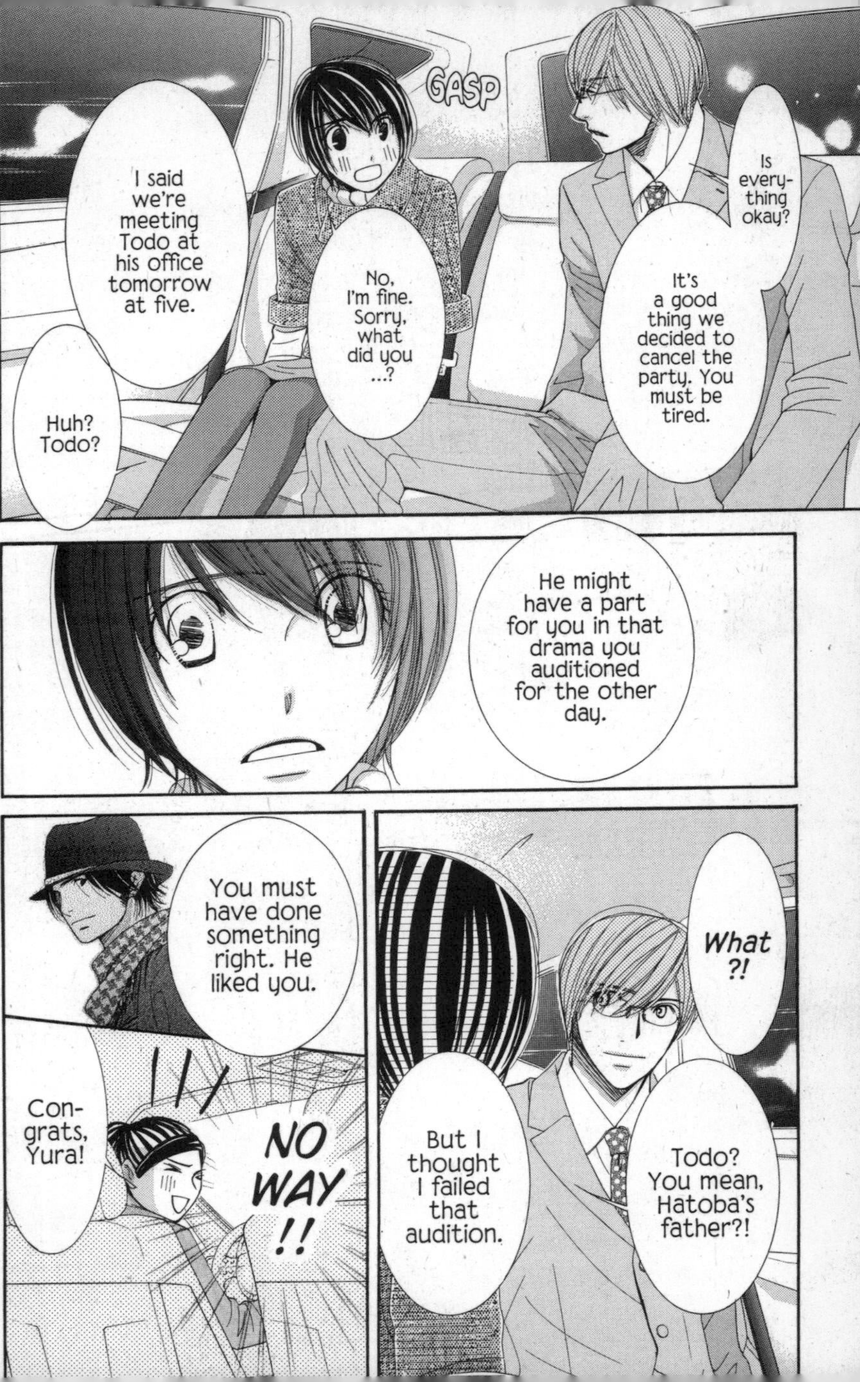
Is everything okay?
It's a good thing we decided to cancel the party. You must be tired.
GASP
No, I'm fine. Sorry, what did you ...?
I said we're meeting Todo at his office tomorrow at five.
Huh? Todo?
He might have a part for you in that drama you auditioned for the other day.
What?!
Todo? You mean, Hatoba's father?!
But I thought I failed that audition.
You must have done something right. He liked you.
Con-grats, Yura!
NO WAY!!

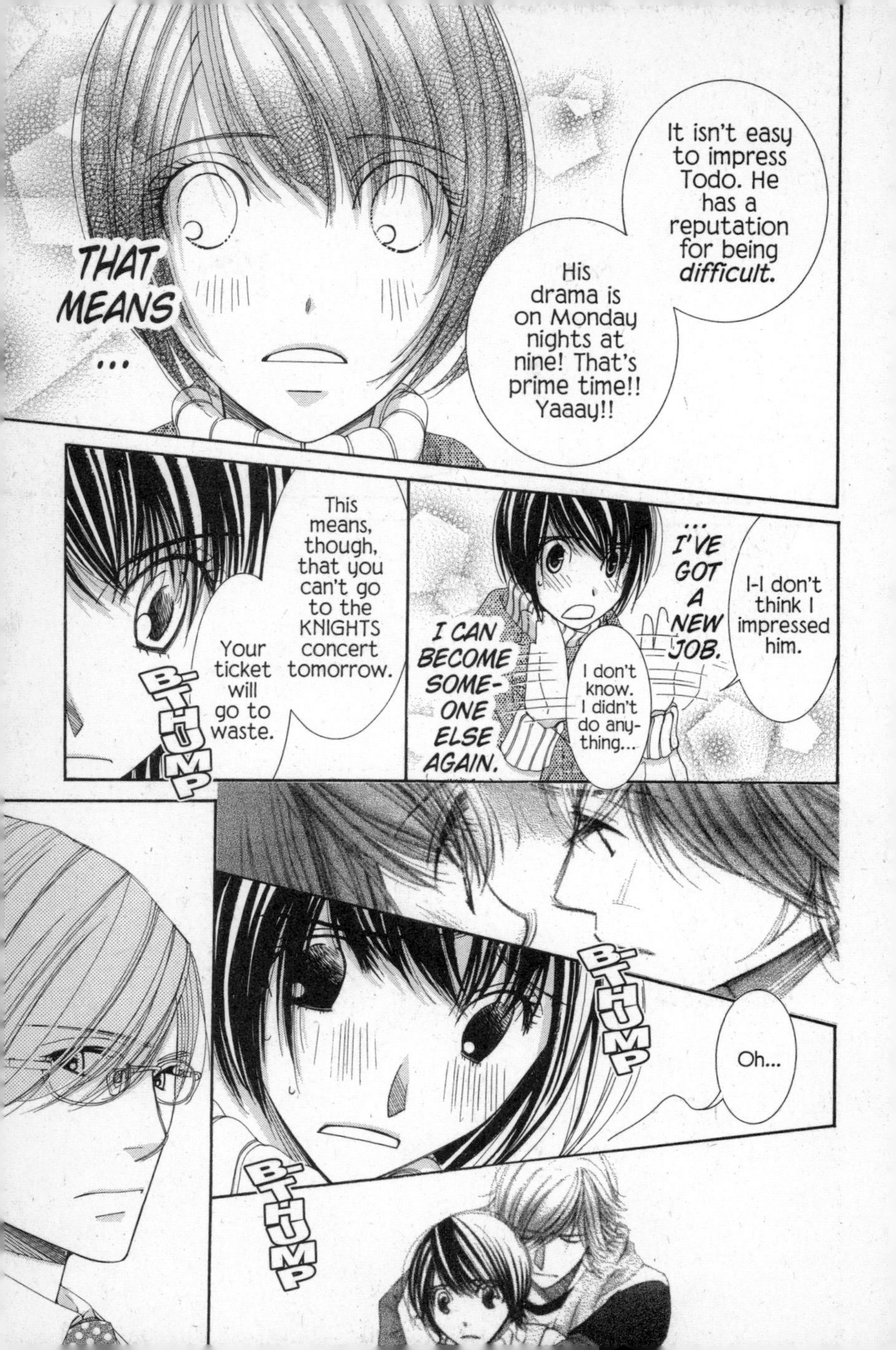
It isn't easy to impress Todo. He has a reputation for being *difficult.*
His drama is on Monday nights at nine! That's prime time!! Yaaay!!
THAT MEANS ...
I-I don't think I impressed him.
... I'VE GOT A NEW JOB.
I don't know. I didn't do any-thing...
I CAN BECOME SOME-ONE ELSE AGAIN.
This means, though, that you can't go to the KNIGHTS concert tomorrow.
Your ticket will go to waste.
B-THUMP
Oh...
B-THUMP
B-THUMP

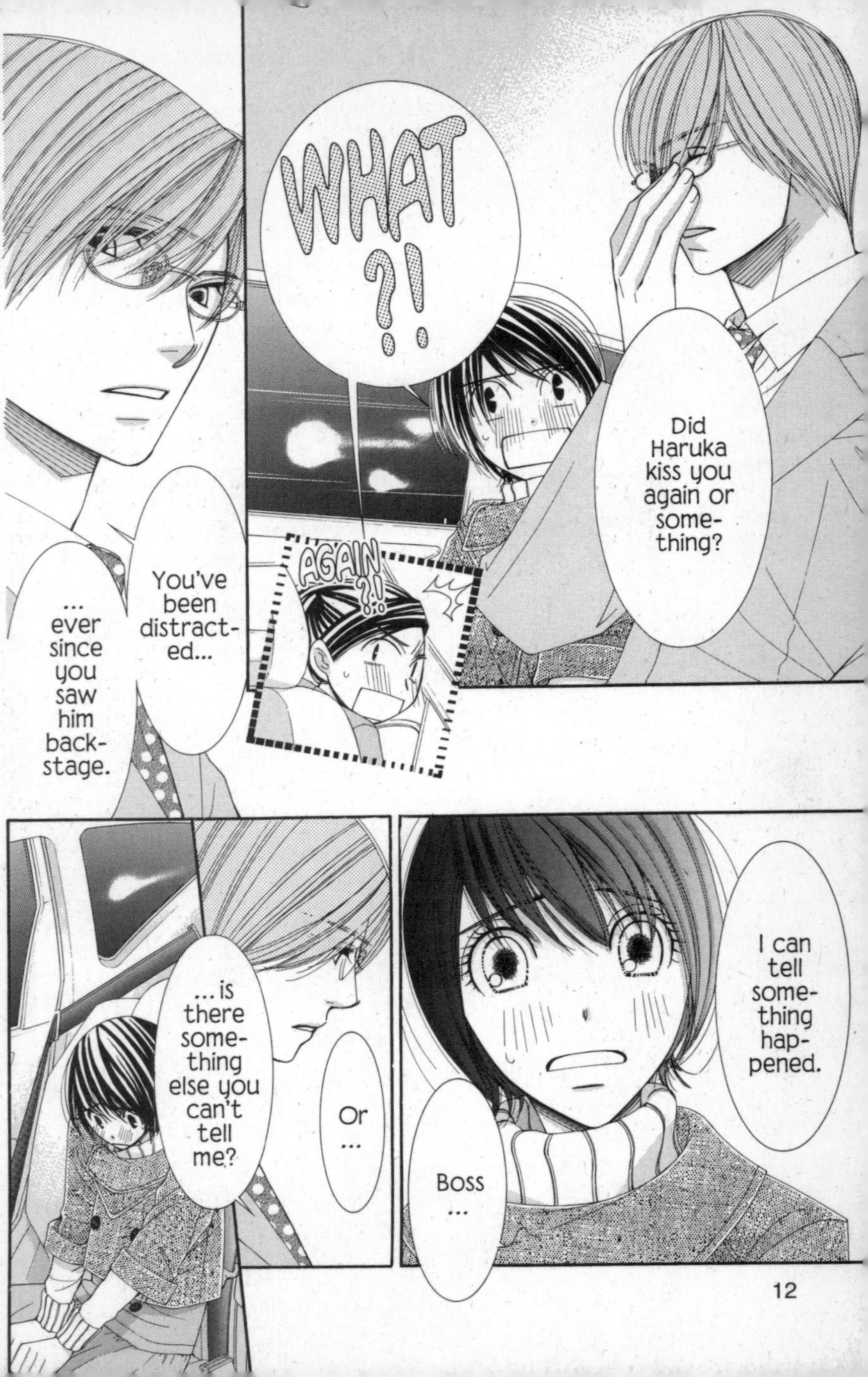

Did Haruka kiss you again or something?
WHAT ?!
AGAIN ?!
You've been distracted...
... ever since you saw him backstage.
I can tell something happened.
Boss ...
Or ...
... is there something else you can't tell me?

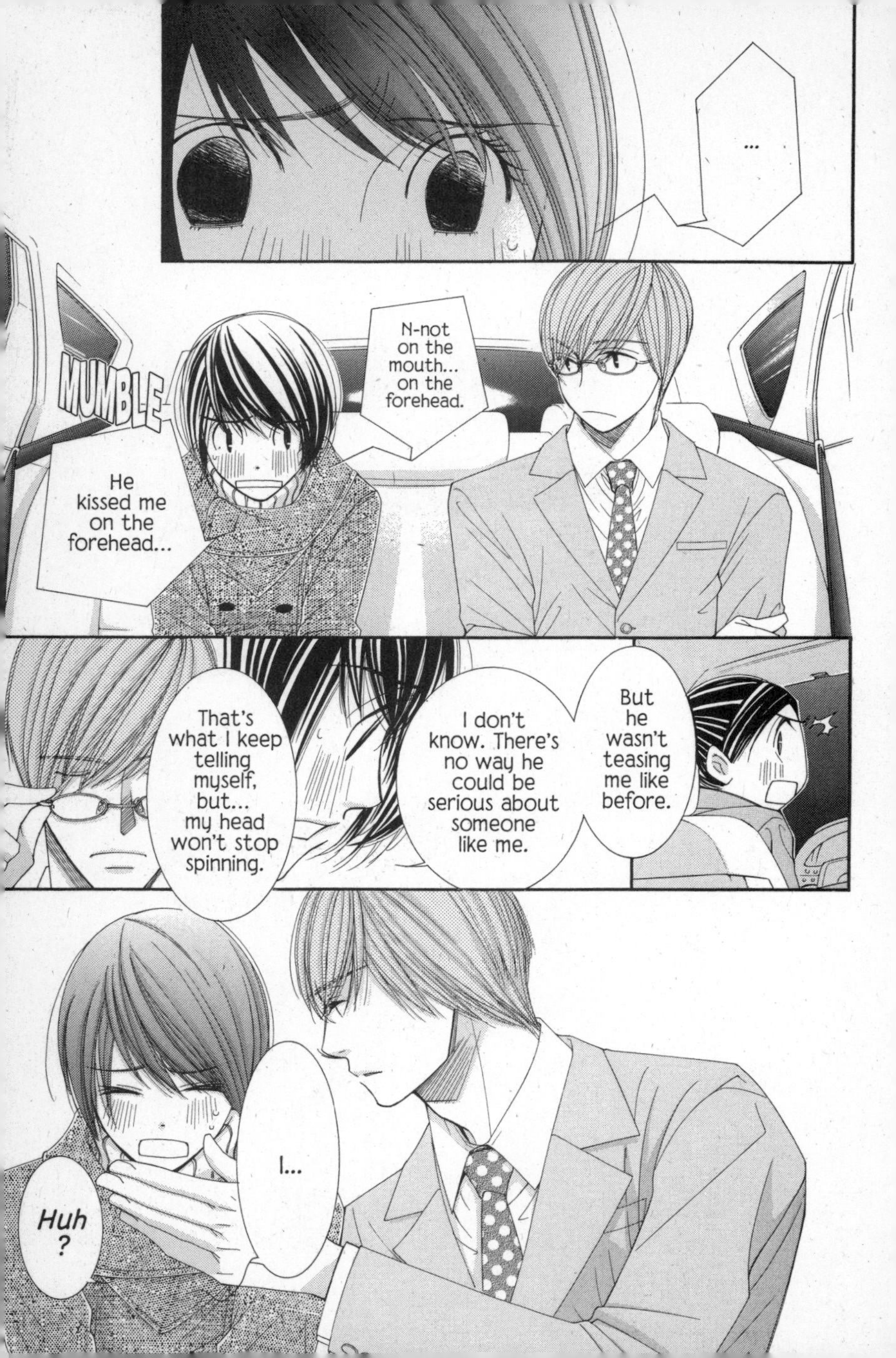
...
N-not on the mouth... on the forehead.
MUMBLE
He kissed me on the forehead...
But he wasn't teasing me like before.
I don't know. There's no way he could be serious about someone like me.
That's what I keep telling myself, but... my head won't stop spinning.
I...
Huh?

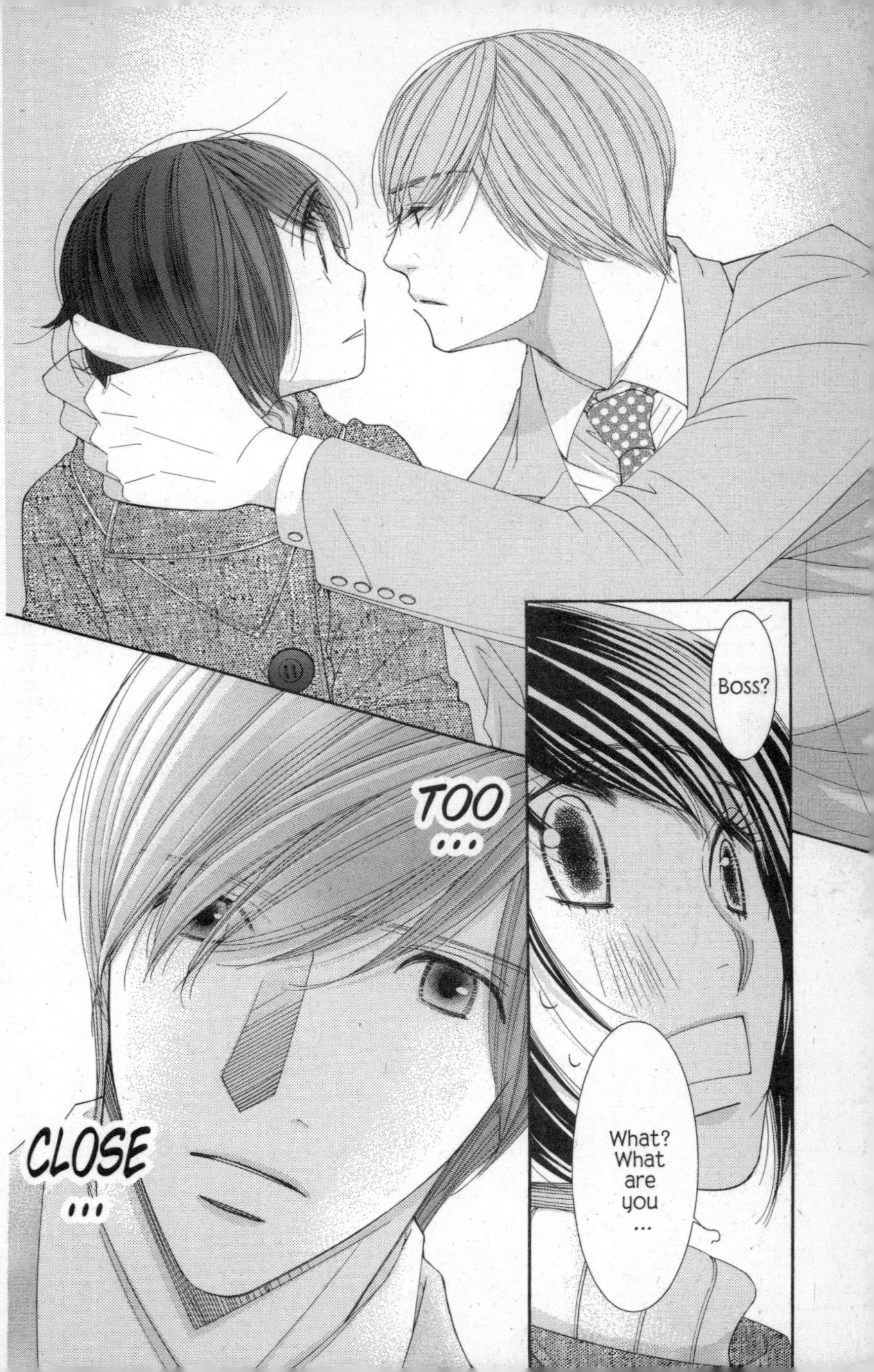
Boss?
What? What are you ...
TOO ...
CLOSE ...

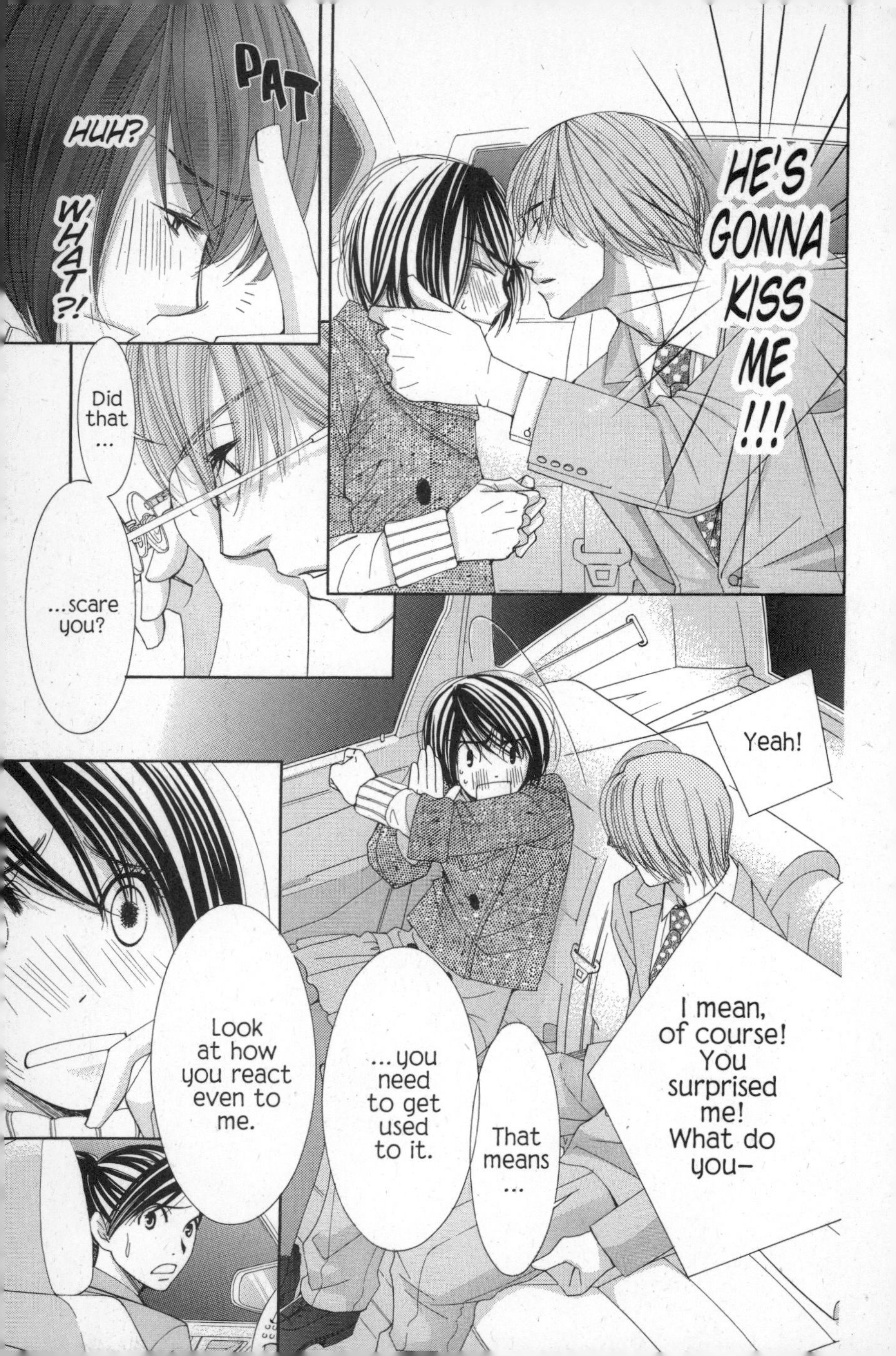
HE'S GONNA KISS ME !!!
PAT
HUH?
WHAT?!
Did that ...
...scare you?
Yeah!
I mean, of course! You surprised me! What do you–
That means ...
...you need to get used to it.
Look at how you react even to me.

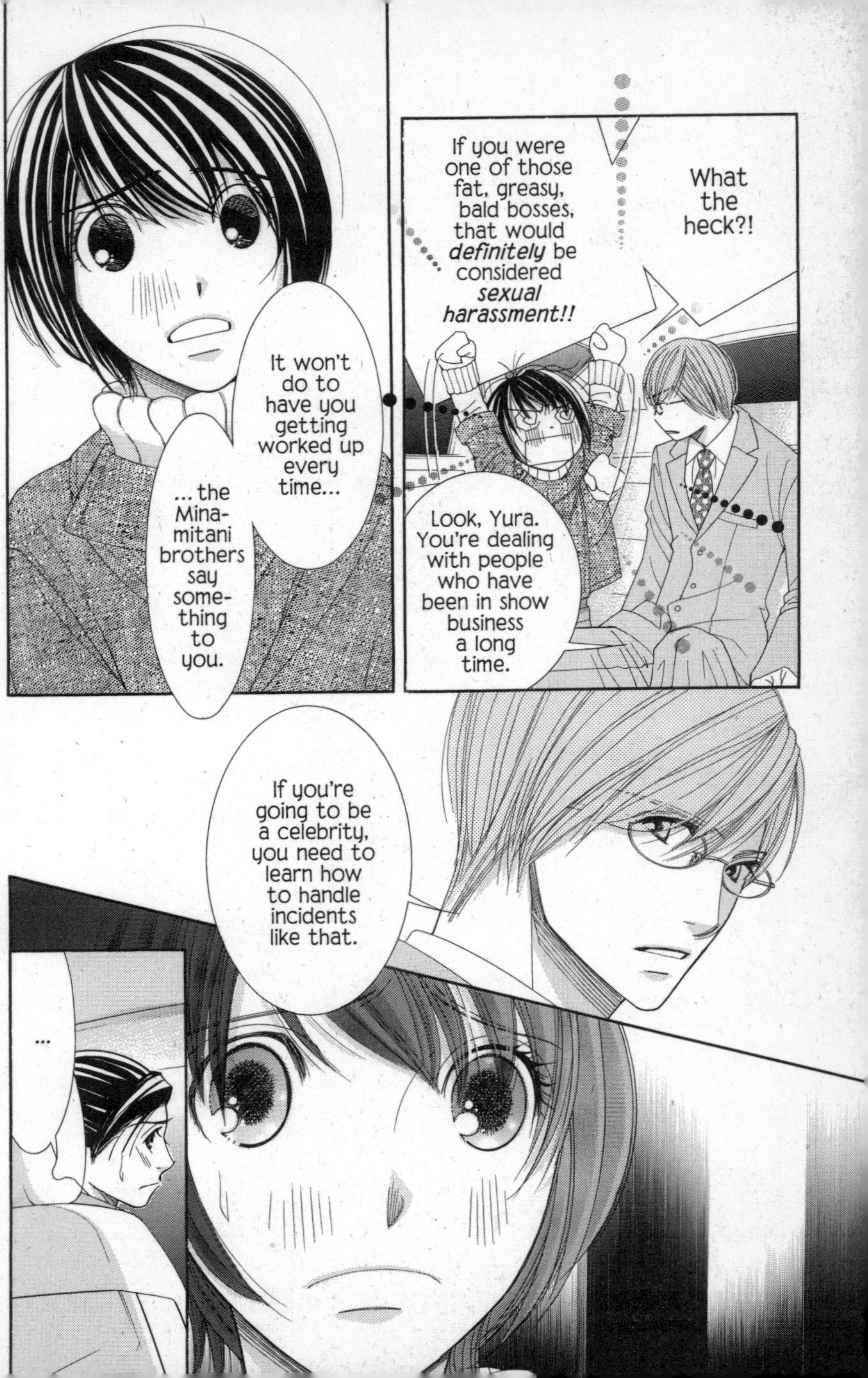
What the heck?!
If you were one of those fat, greasy, bald bosses, that would *definitely* be considered *sexual harassment!!*
Look, Yura. You're dealing with people who have been in show business a long time.
It won't do to have you getting worked up every time...
...the Mina-mitani brothers say some-thing to you.
If you're going to be a celebrity, you need to learn how to handle incidents like that.
...

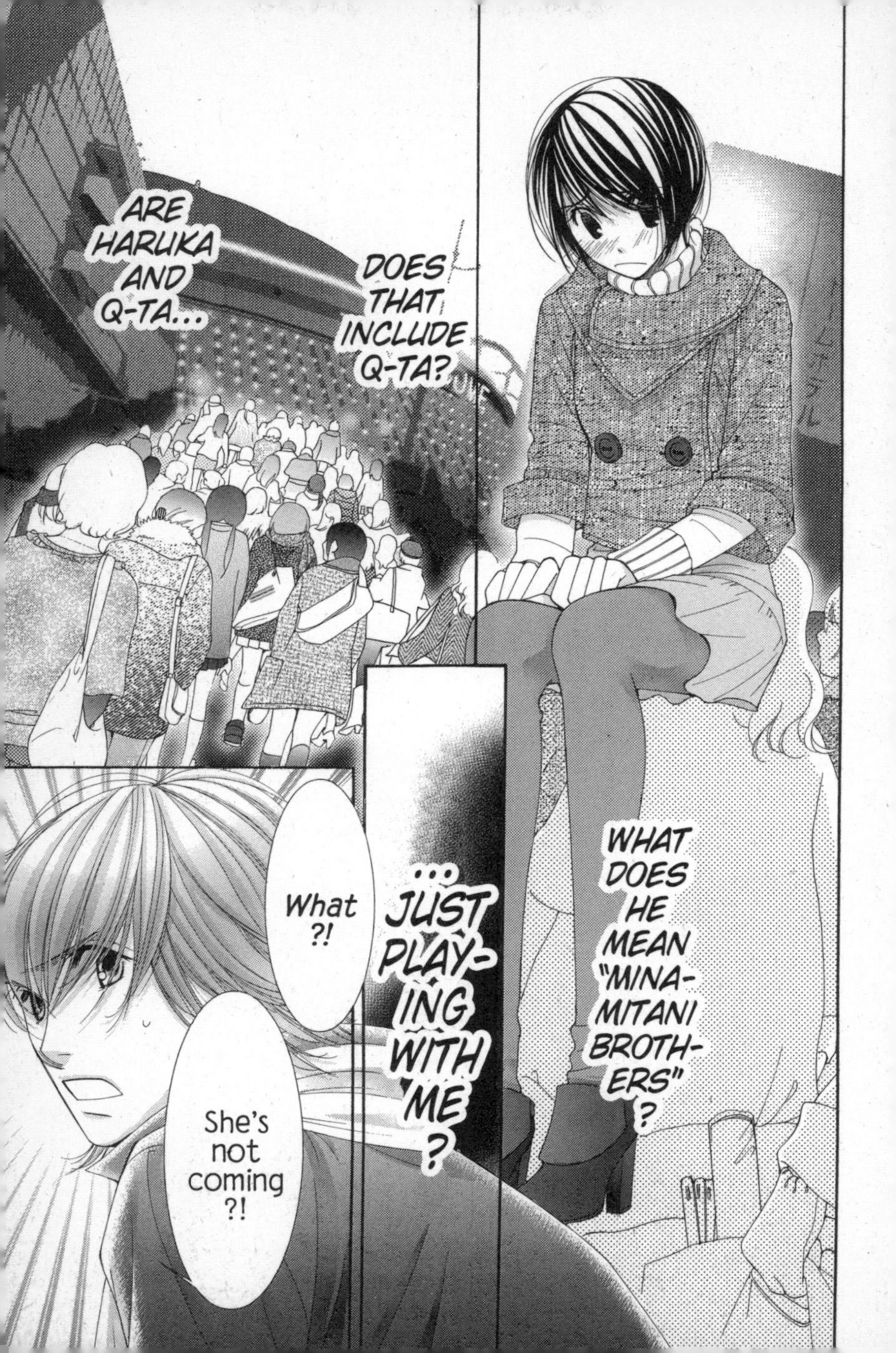

WHAT DOES HE MEAN "MINAMITANI BROTHERS"?
DOES THAT INCLUDE Q-TA?
ARE HARUKA AND Q-TA...
...JUST PLAYING WITH ME?
What?!
She's not coming?!

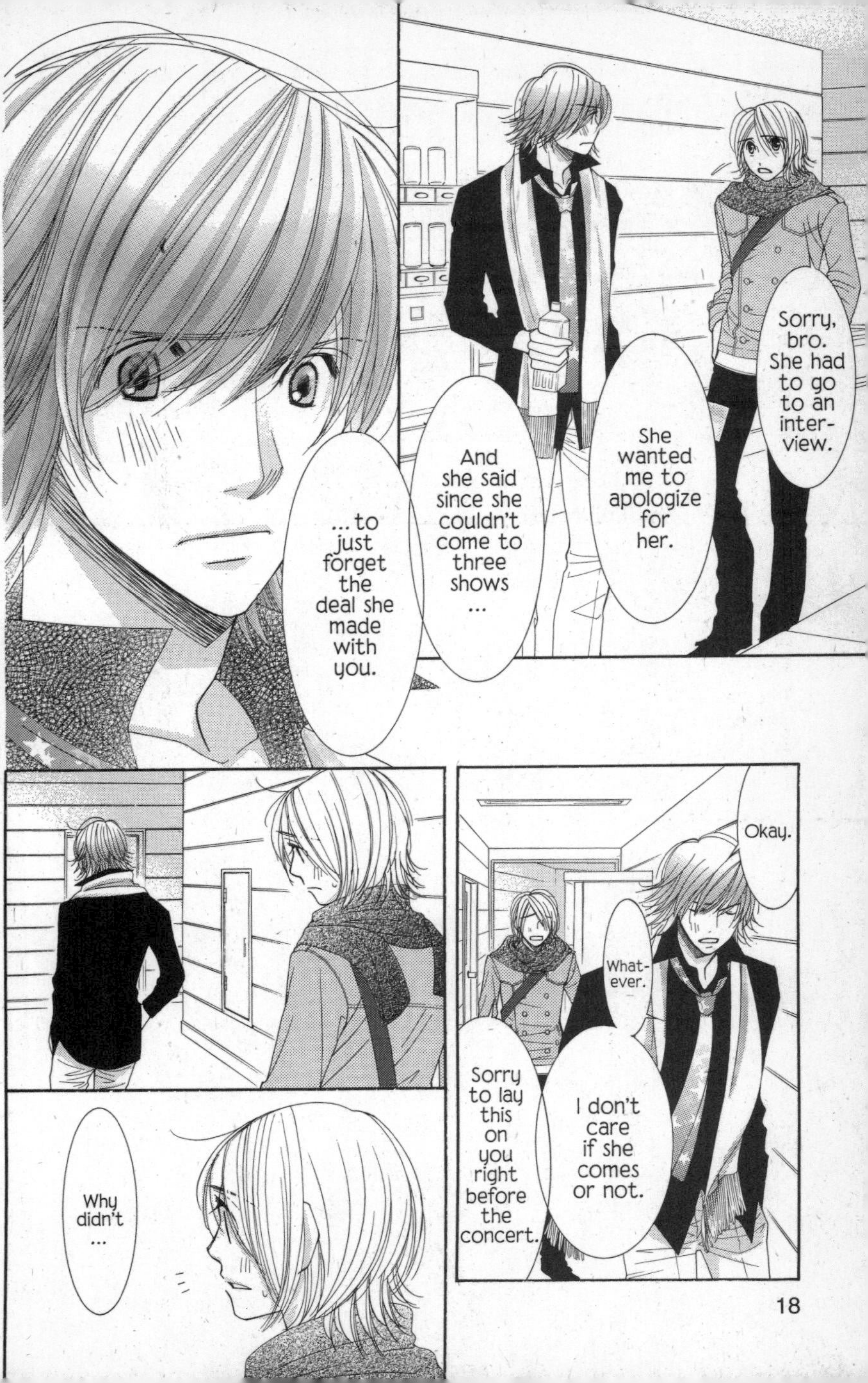
Sorry, bro. She had to go to an interview.
She wanted me to apologize for her.
And she said since she couldn't come to three shows ...
...to just forget the deal she made with you.
Okay.
Whatever.
I don't care if she comes or not.
Sorry to lay this on you right before the concert.
Why didn't ...

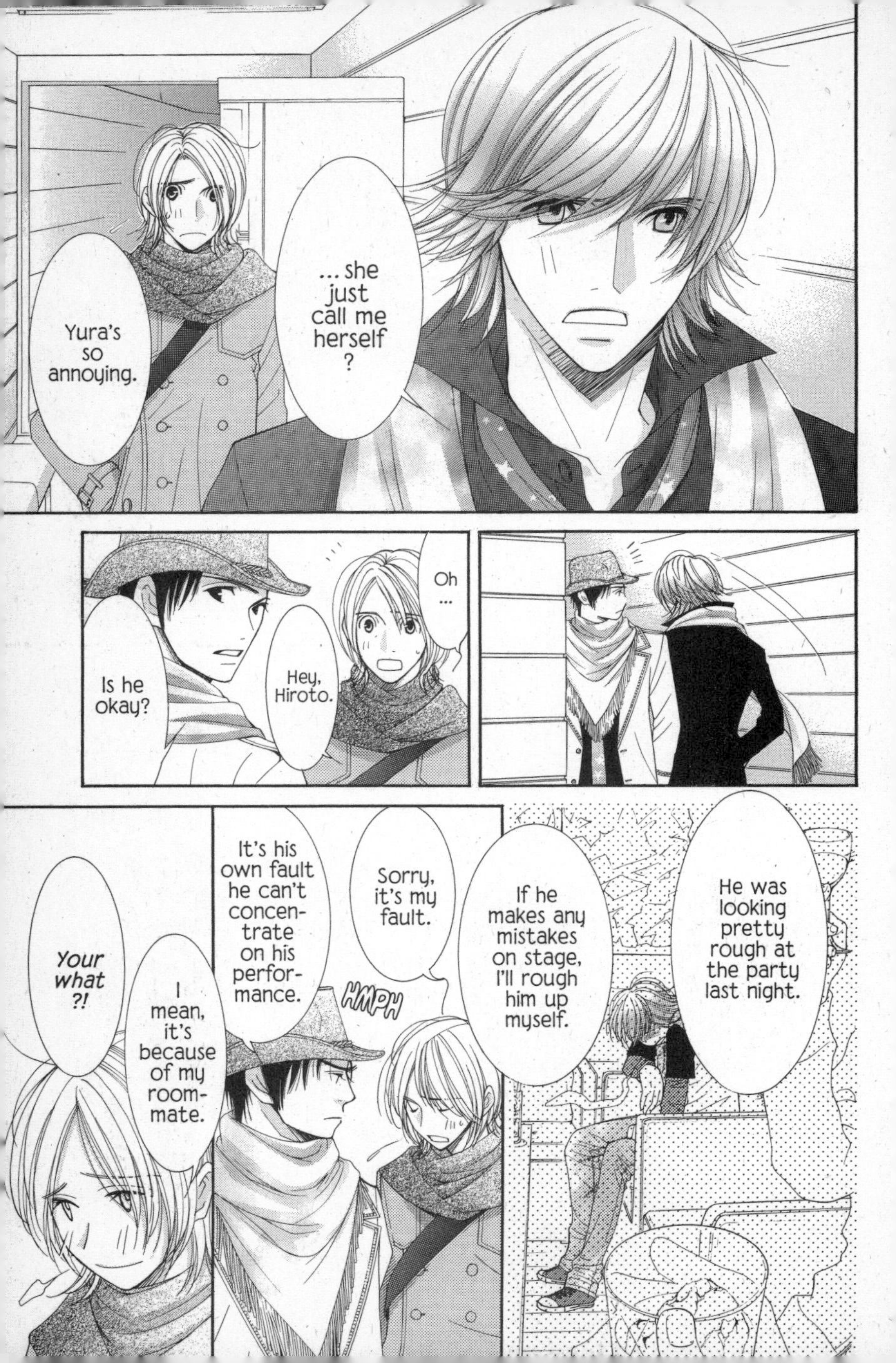

... she just call me herself?
Yura's so annoying.
Oh ...
Hey, Hiroto.
Is he okay?
He was looking pretty rough at the party last night.
If he makes any mistakes on stage, I'll rough him up myself.
Sorry, it's my fault.
HMPH
It's his own fault he can't concentrate on his performance.
I mean, it's because of my roommate.
Your what?!

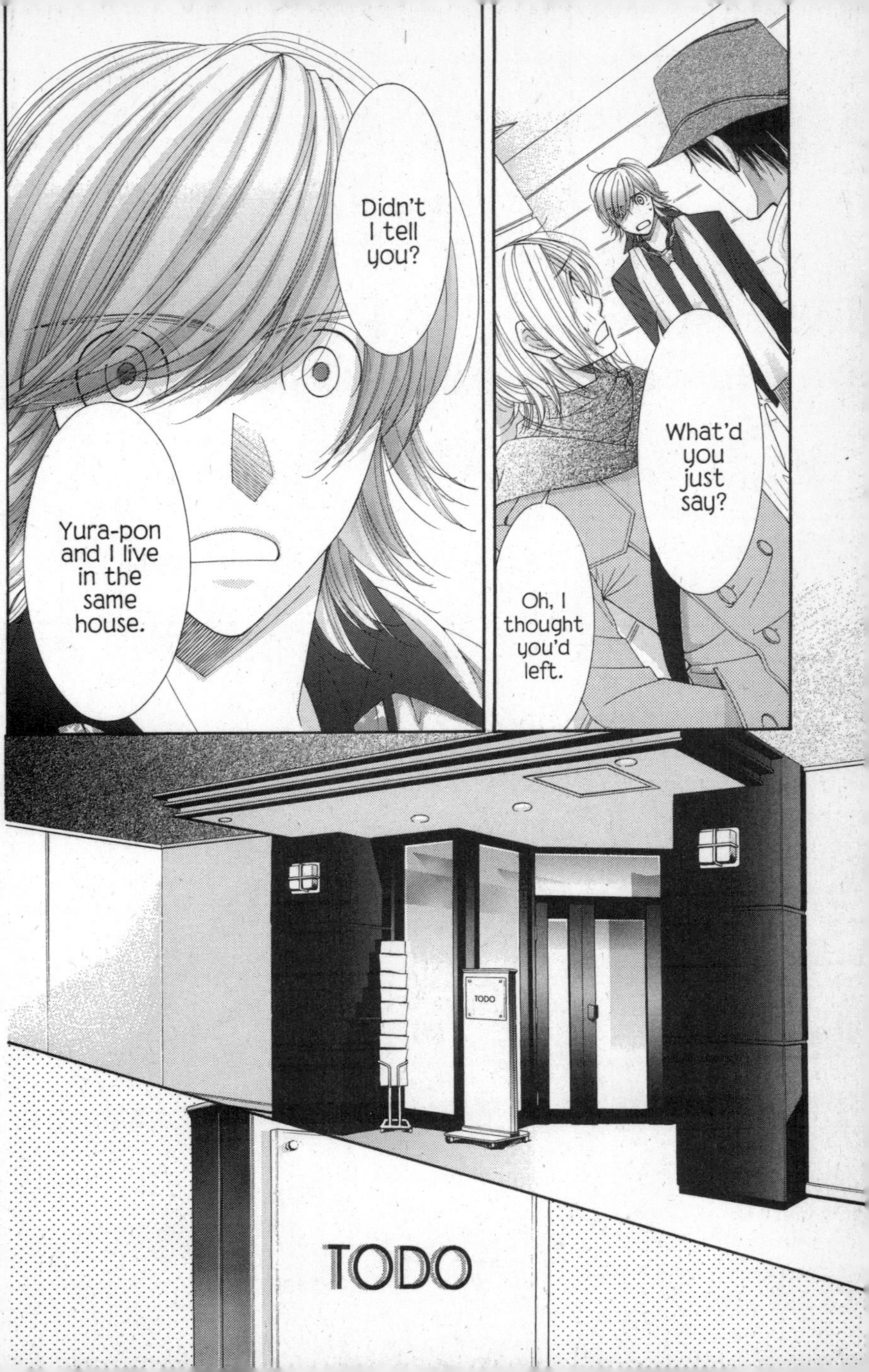
What'd you just say?
Oh, I thought you'd left.
Didn't I tell you?
Yura-pon and I live in the same house.
TODO
TODO

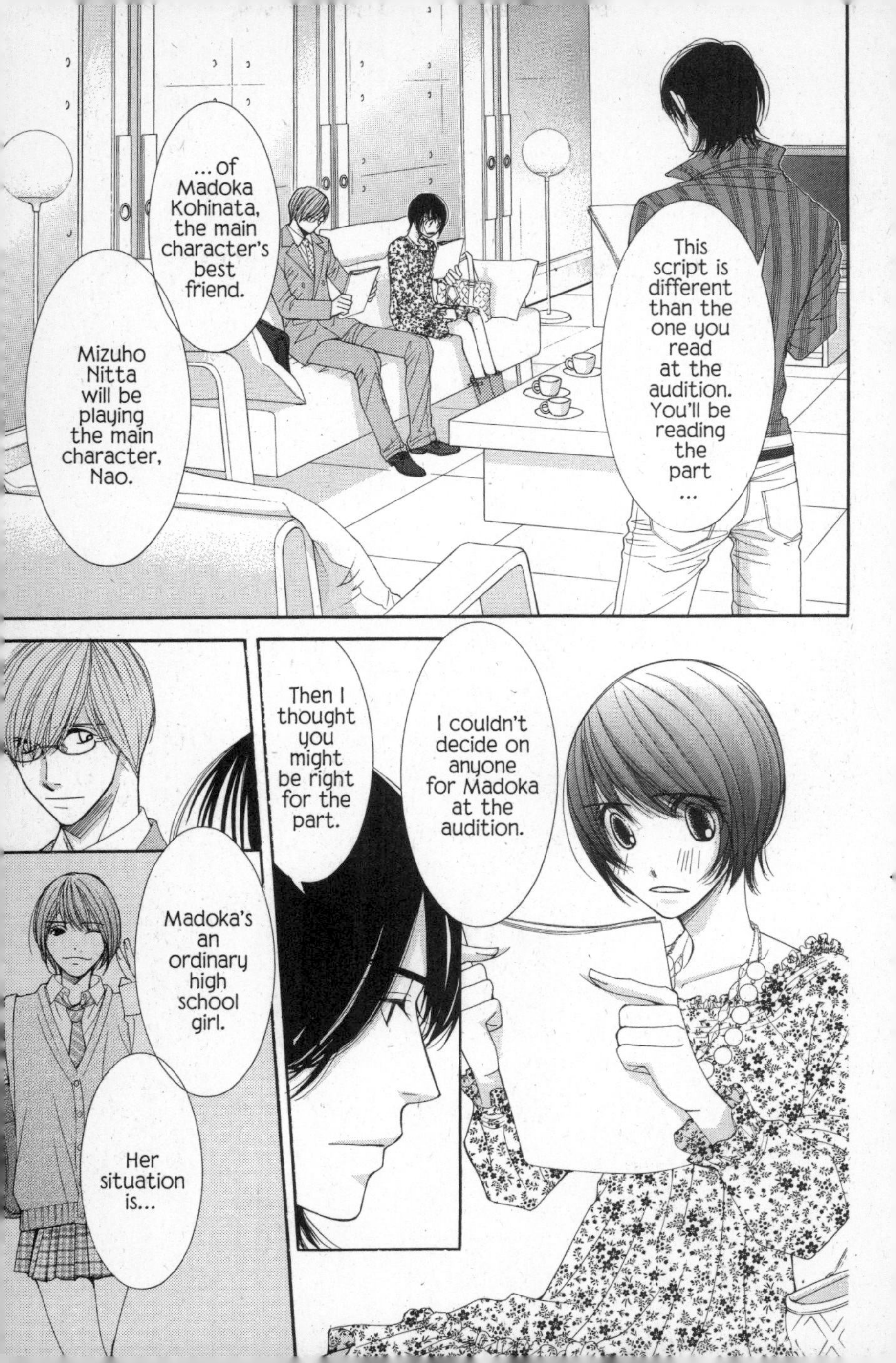
This script is different than the one you read at the audition. You'll be reading the part ...
...of Madoka Kohinata, the main character's best friend.
Mizuho Nitta will be playing the main character, Nao.
I couldn't decide on anyone for Madoka at the audition.
Then I thought you might be right for the part.
Madoka's an ordinary high school girl.
Her situation is...

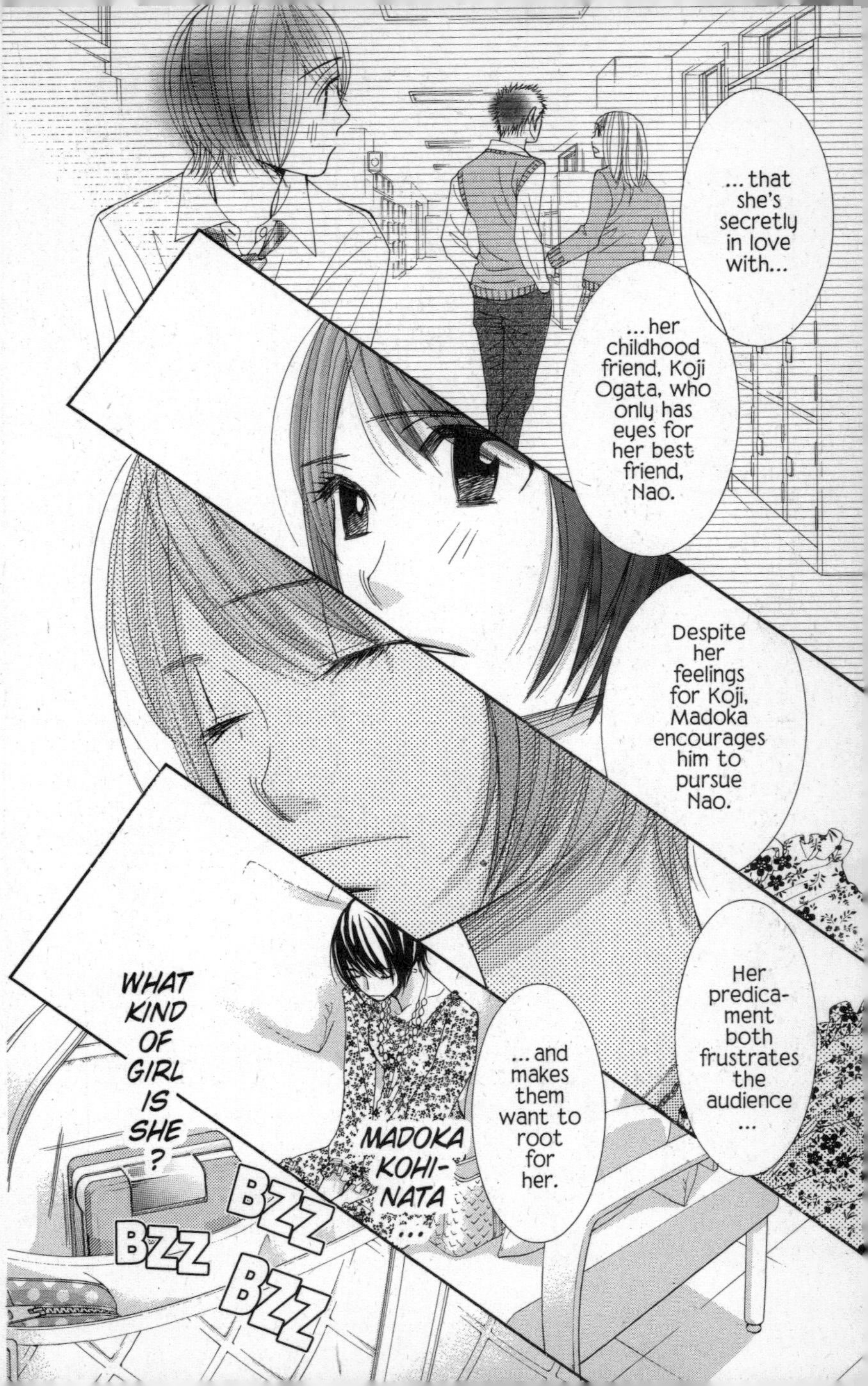
...that she's secretly in love with...
...her childhood friend, Koji Ogata, who only has eyes for her best friend, Nao.
Despite her feelings for Koji, Madoka encourages him to pursue Nao.
Her predicament both frustrates the audience ...
...and makes them want to root for her.
MADOKA KOHI-NATA...
WHAT KIND OF GIRL IS SHE?
BZZ
BZZ
BZZ

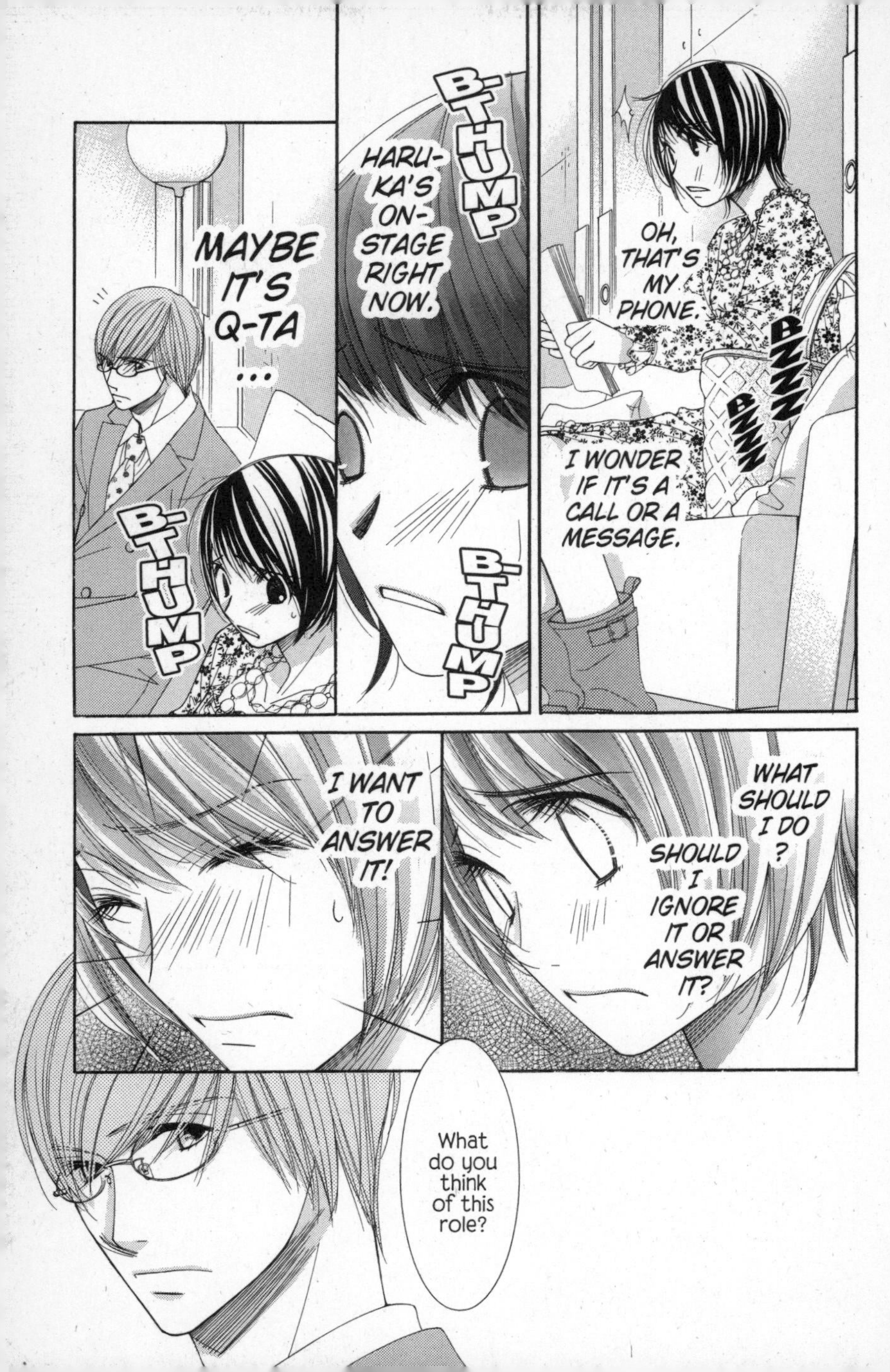
OH, THAT'S MY PHONE.
BZZZ
BZZZ
I WONDER IF IT'S A CALL OR A MESSAGE.
B-THUMP
HARUKA'S ONSTAGE RIGHT NOW.
B-THUMP
MAYBE IT'S Q-TA...
B-THUMP
WHAT SHOULD I DO?
SHOULD I IGNORE IT OR ANSWER IT?
I WANT TO ANSWER IT!
What do you think of this role?

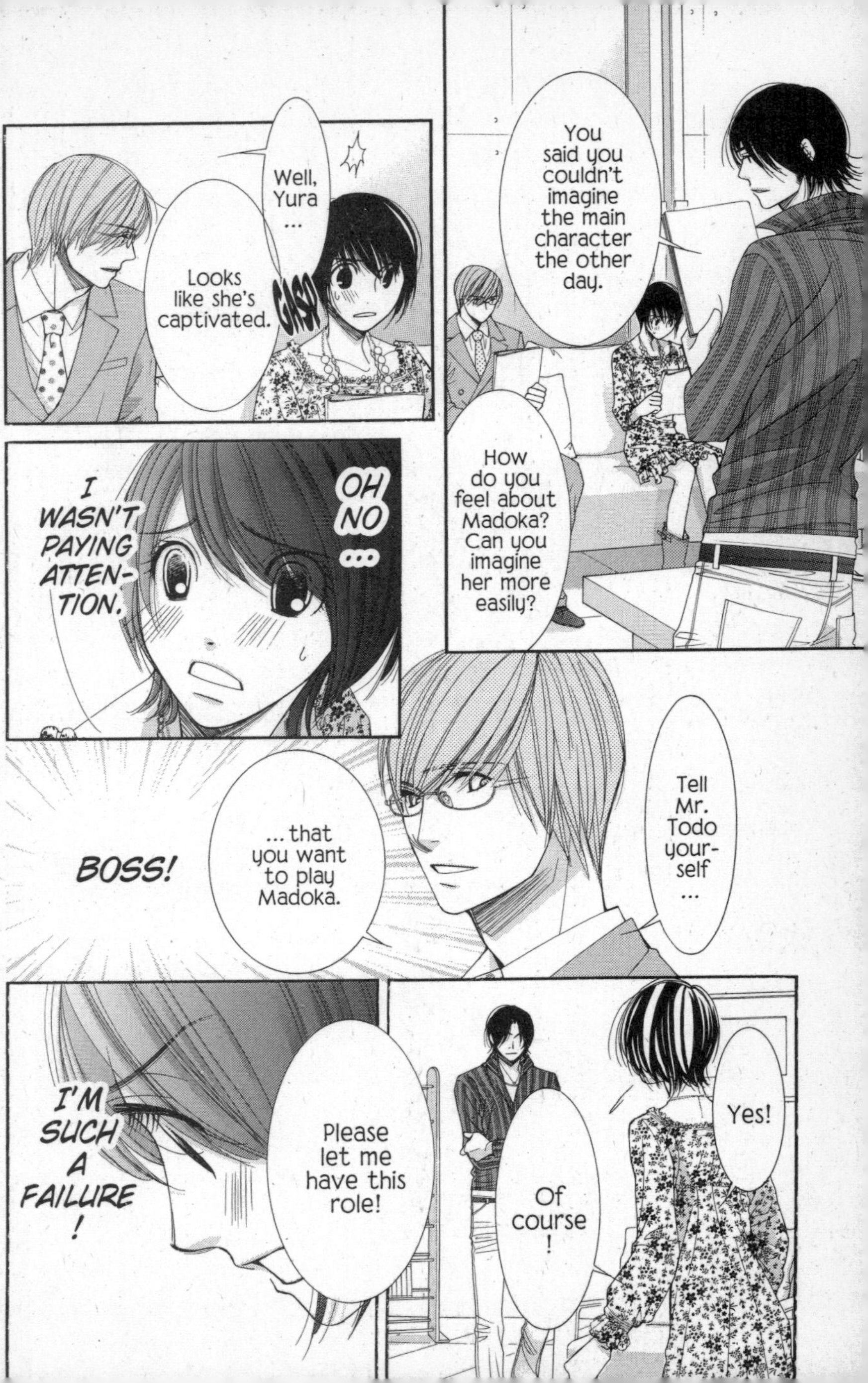

You said you couldn't imagine the main character the other day.
How do you feel about Madoka? Can you imagine her more easily?
Well, Yura ...
GASP
Looks like she's captivated.
OH NO ...
I WASN'T PAYING ATTEN-TION.
Tell Mr. Todo your-self ...
... that you want to play Madoka.
BOSS!
Yes!
Of course!
Please let me have this role!
I'M SUCH A FAILURE!

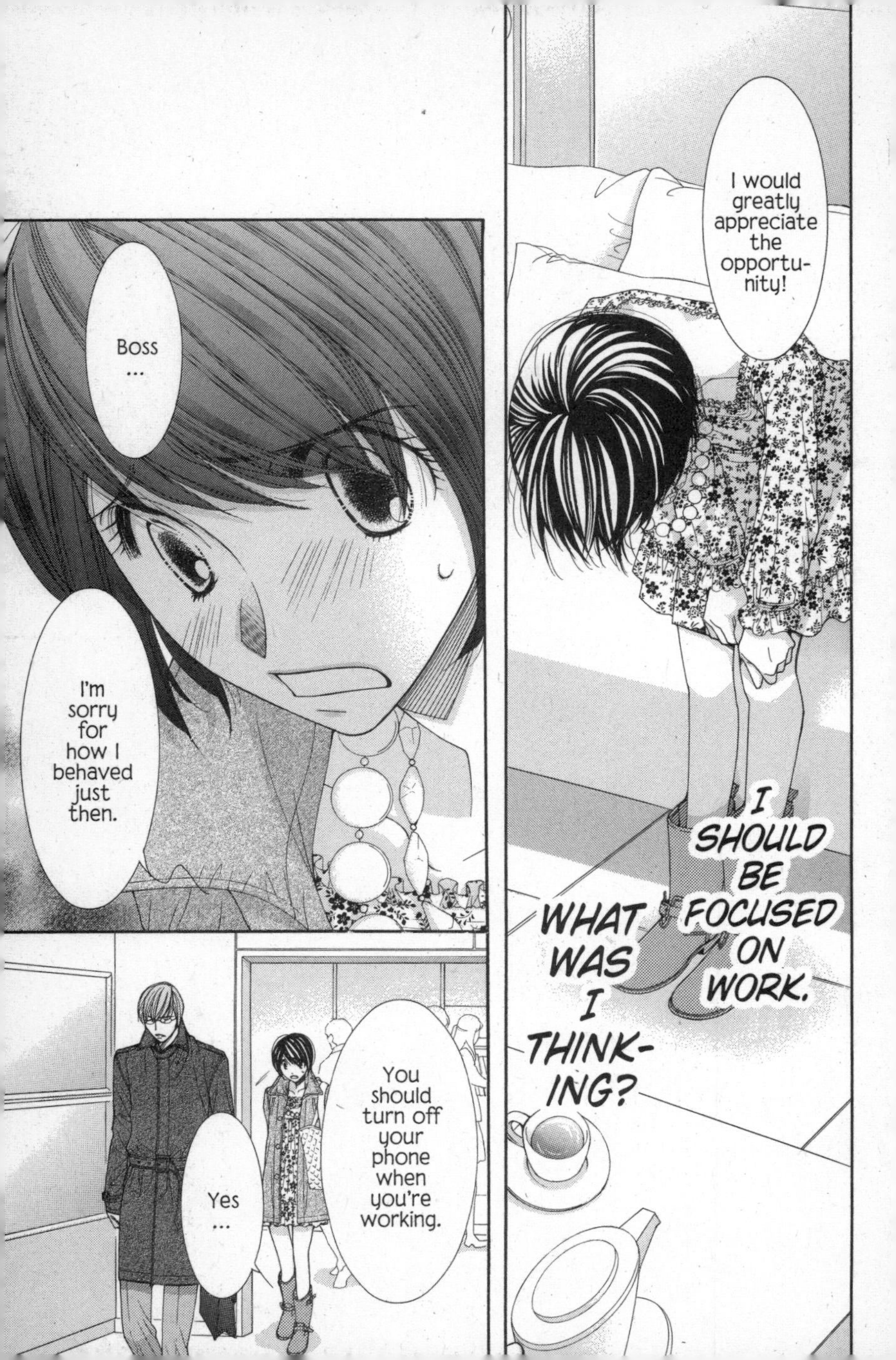
I would greatly appreciate the opportu-nity!
I SHOULD BE FOCUSED ON WORK.
WHAT WAS I THINK-ING?
Boss ...
I'm sorry for how I behaved just then.
You should turn off your phone when you're working.
Yes ...

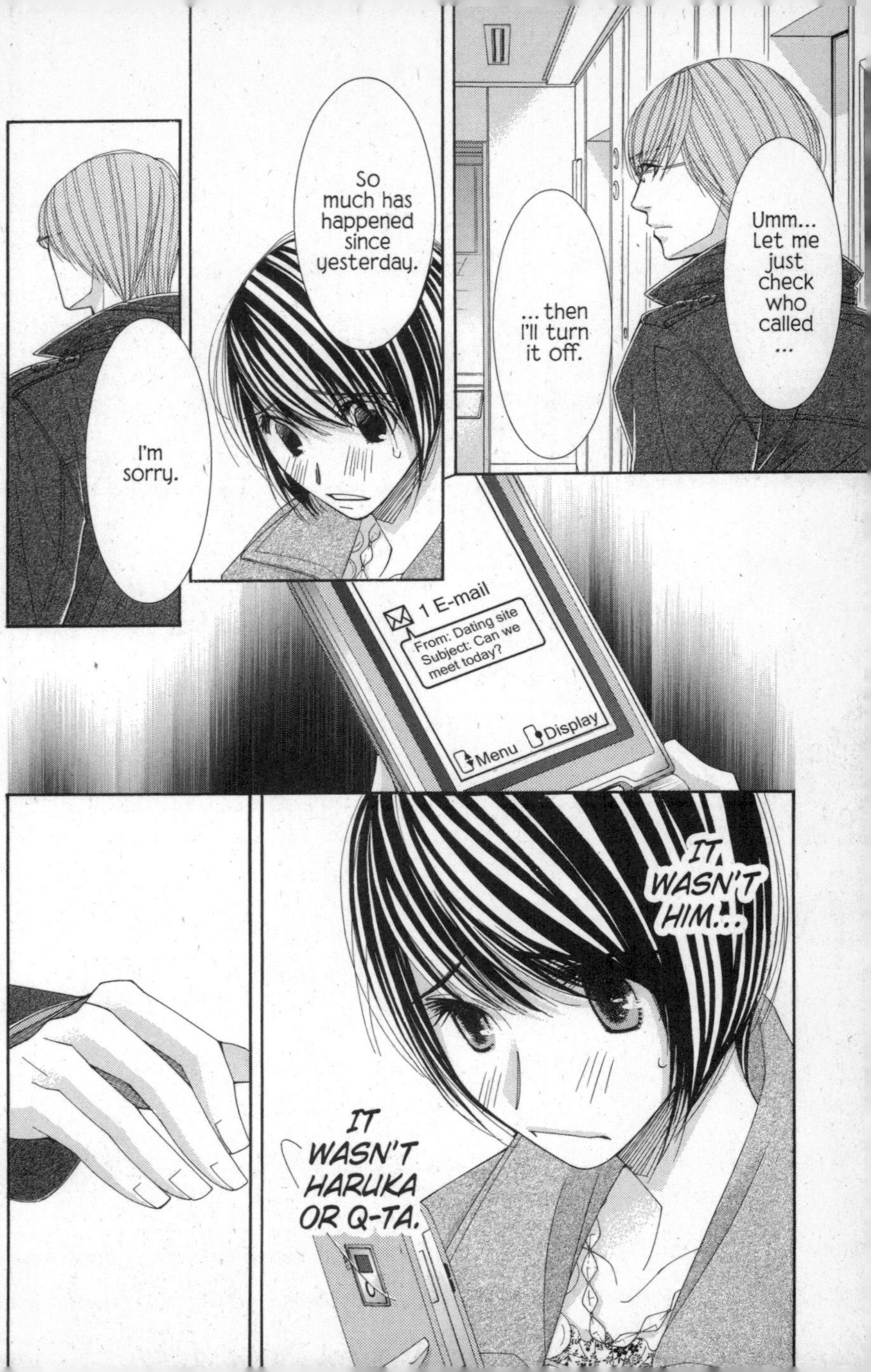
Umm... Let me just check who called ...
... then I'll turn it off.
So much has happened since yesterday.
I'm sorry.
1 E-mail
From: Dating site
Subject: Can we meet today?
Display
Menu
IT WASN'T HIM...
IT WASN'T HARUKA OR Q-TA.

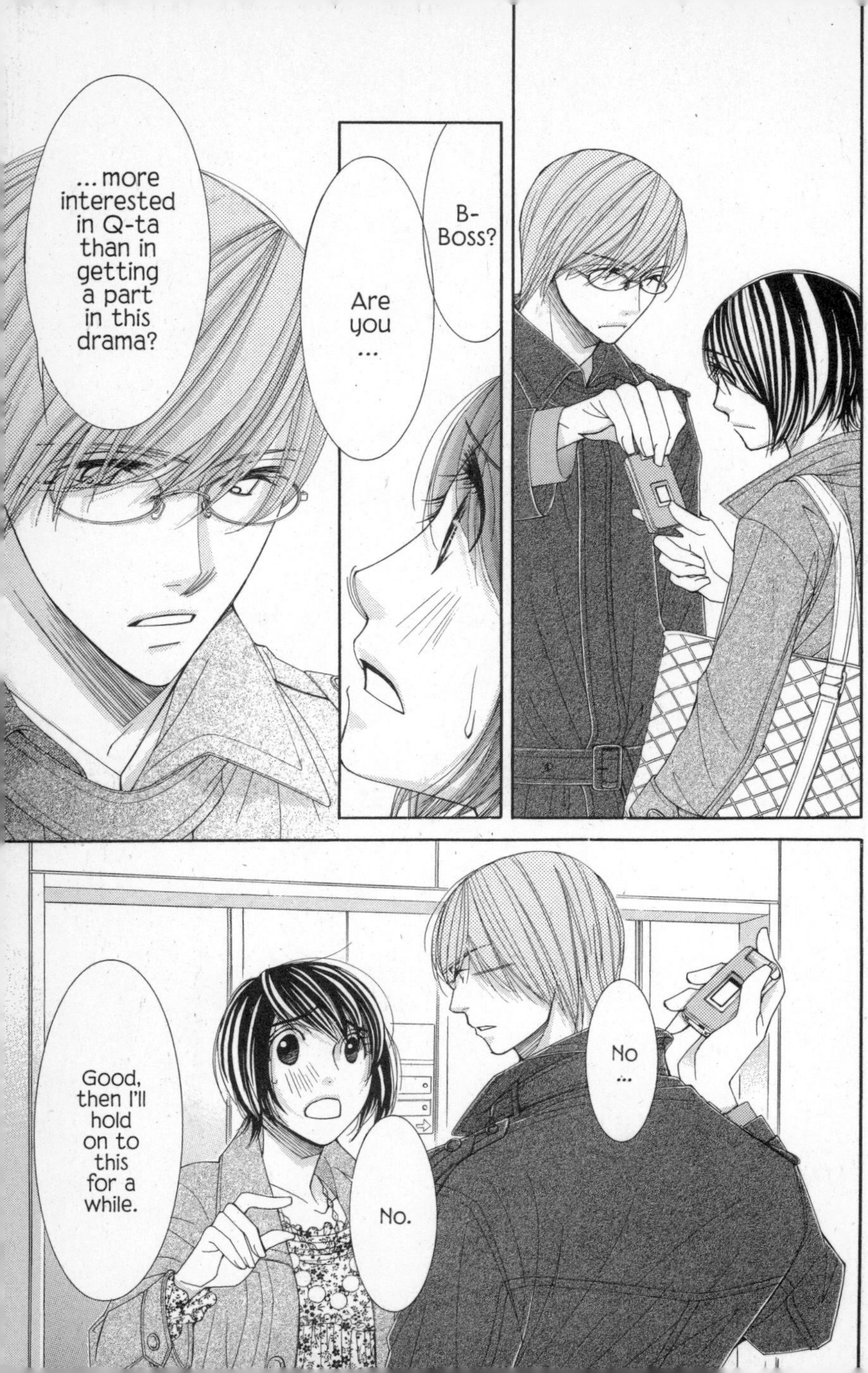
B-Boss?
Are you ...
...more interested in Q-ta than in getting a part in this drama?
No ...
No.
Good, then I'll hold on to this for a while.

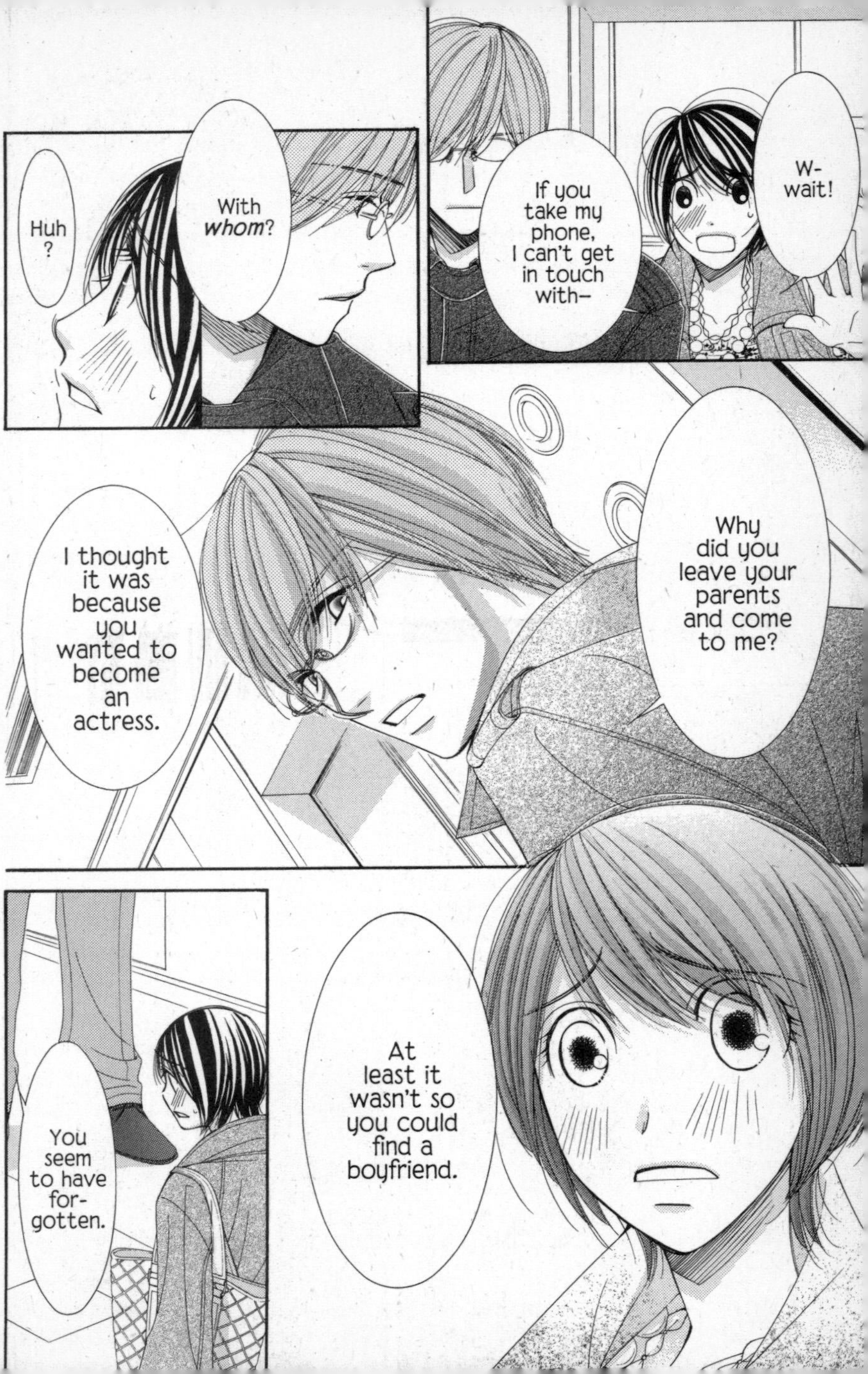
W-wait!
If you take my phone, I can't get in touch with–
With *whom*?
Huh?
Why did you leave your parents and come to me?
I thought it was because you wanted to become an actress.
At least it wasn't so you could find a boyfriend.
You seem to have forgotten.

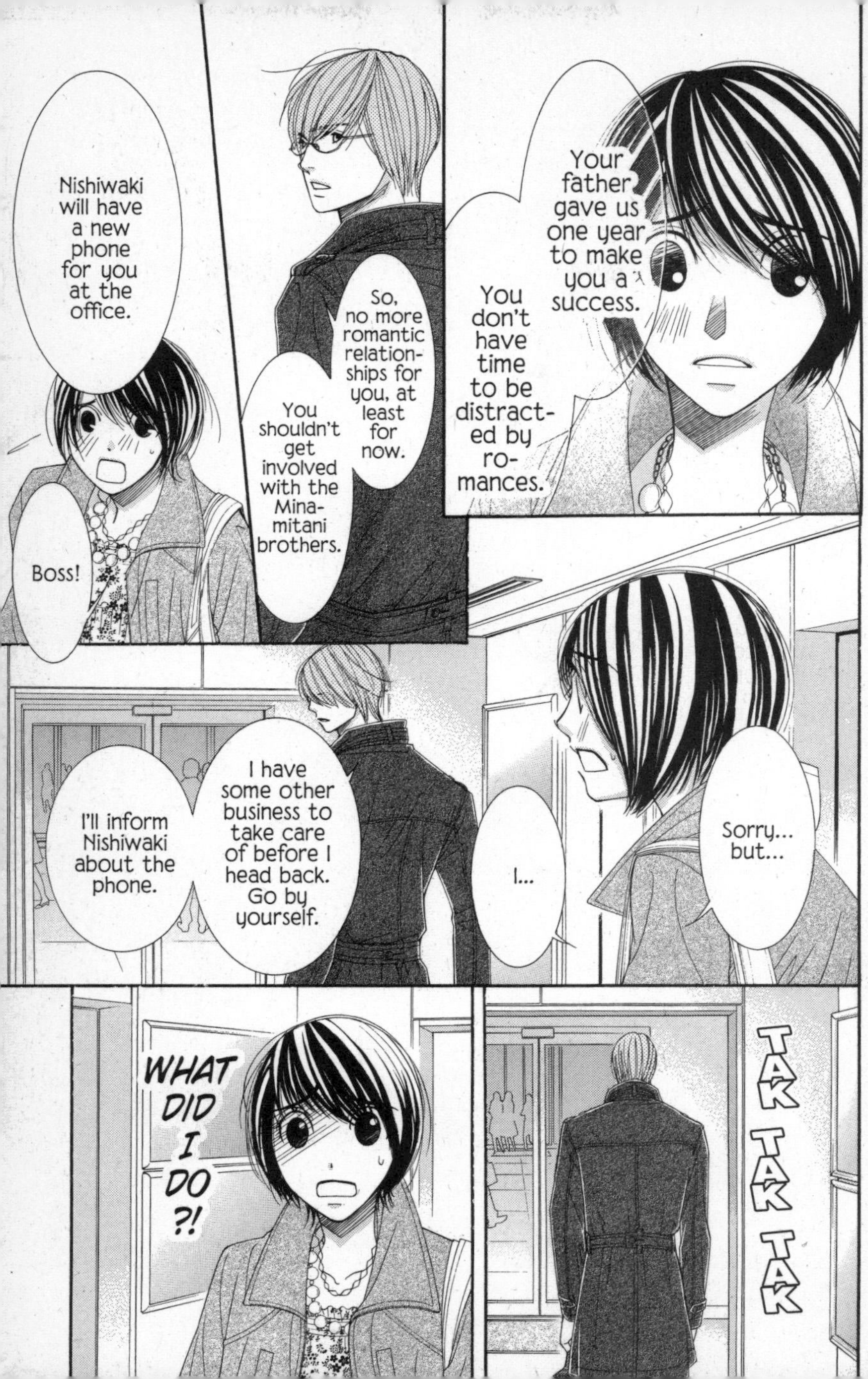
Your father gave us one year to make you a success.
You don't have time to be distracted by romances.
So, no more romantic relationships for you, at least for now.
You shouldn't get involved with the Minamitani brothers.
Nishiwaki will have a new phone for you at the office.
Boss!
Sorry... but...
I...
I have some other business to take care of before I head back. Go by yourself.
I'll inform Nishiwaki about the phone.
TAK TAK TAK
WHAT DID I DO?!

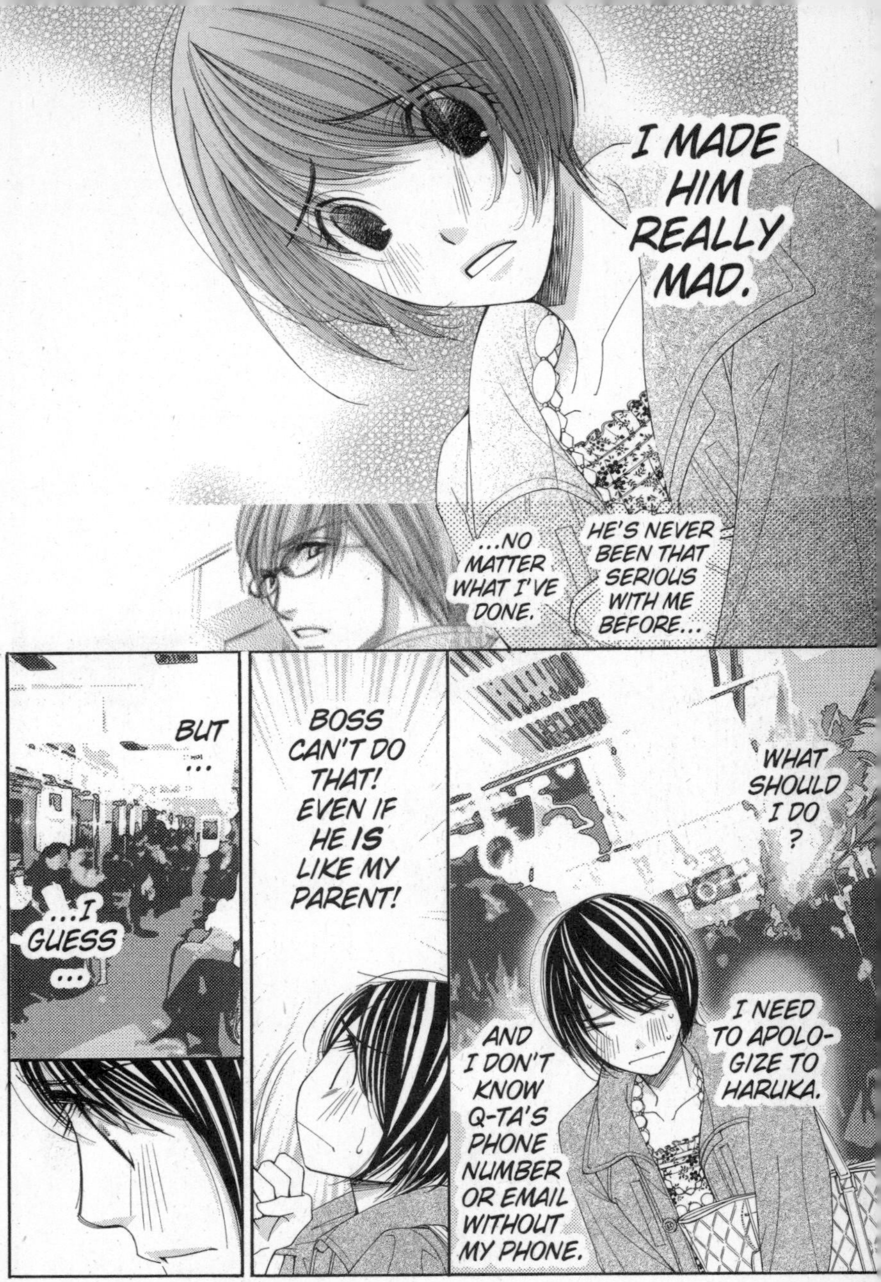
I MADE HIM REALLY MAD.
HE'S NEVER BEEN THAT SERIOUS WITH ME BEFORE...
...NO MATTER WHAT I'VE DONE.
WHAT SHOULD I DO?
I NEED TO APOLOGIZE TO HARUKA.
AND I DON'T KNOW Q-TA'S PHONE NUMBER OR EMAIL WITHOUT MY PHONE.
BOSS CAN'T DO THAT! EVEN IF HE IS LIKE MY PARENT!
BUT ...
...I GUESS ...

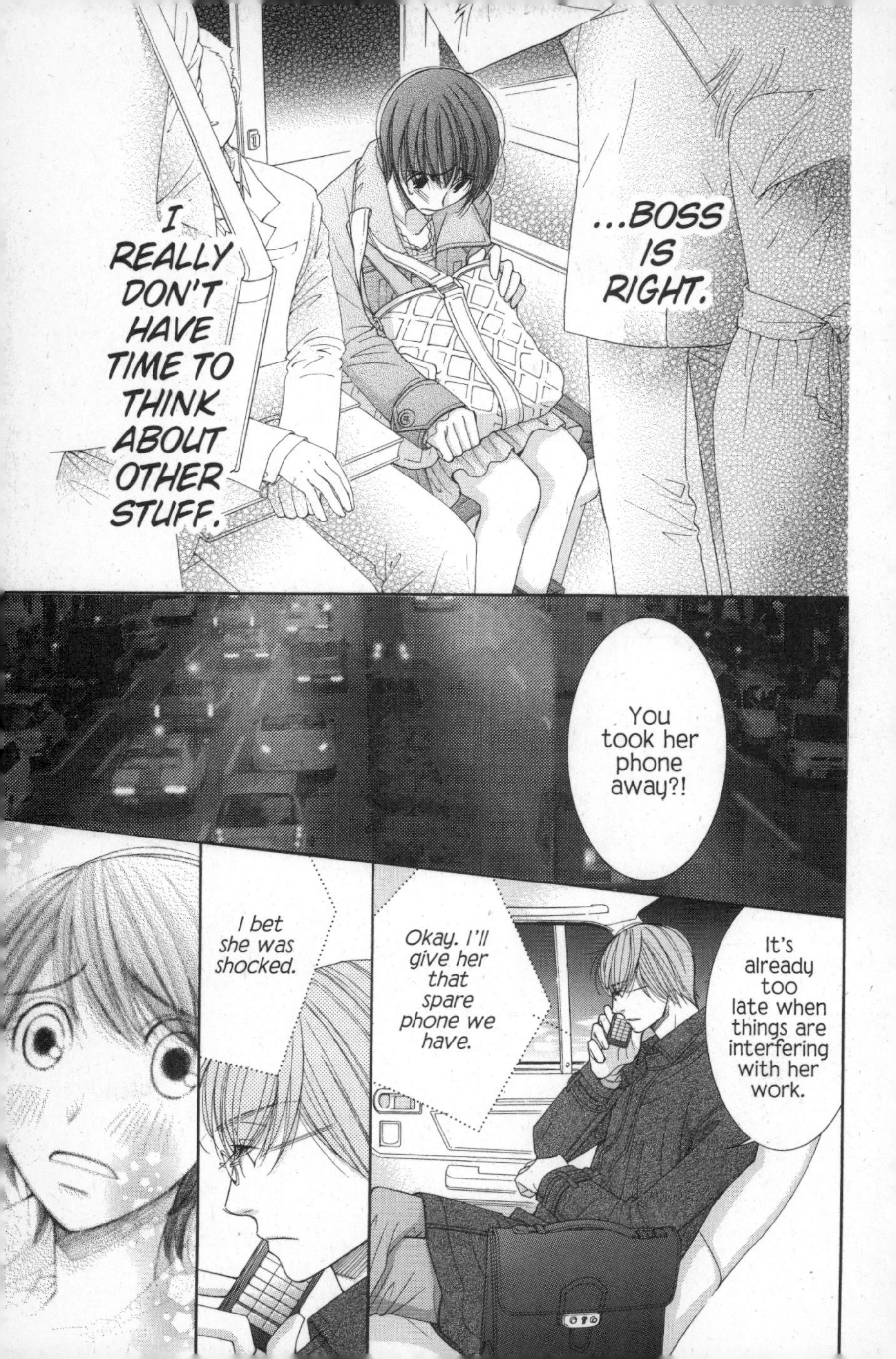
...BOSS IS RIGHT.
I REALLY DON'T HAVE TIME TO THINK ABOUT OTHER STUFF.
You took her phone away?!
It's already too late when things are interfering with her work.
Okay. I'll give her that spare phone we have.
I bet she was shocked.

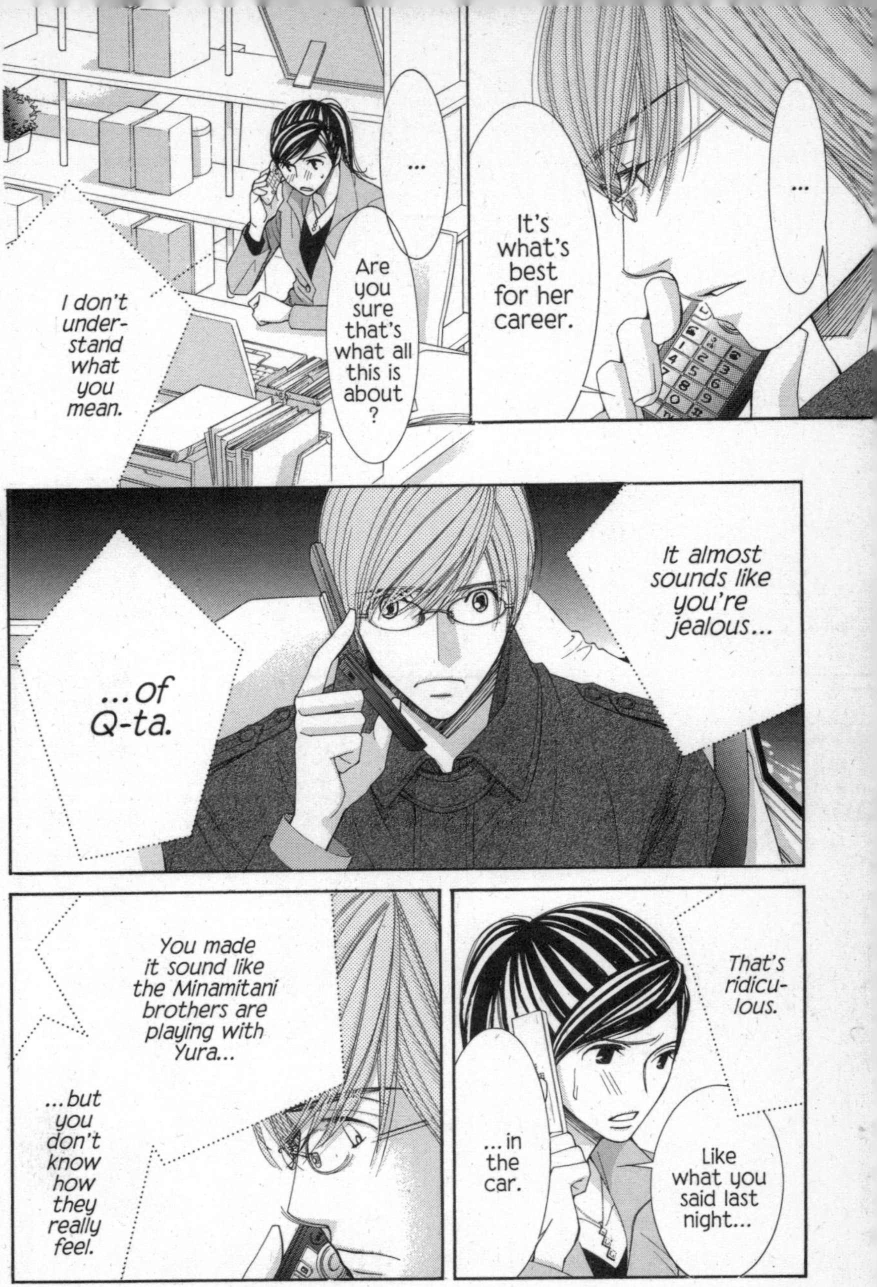
...
It's what's best for her career.
...
Are you sure that's what all this is about ?
I don't understand what you mean.
It almost sounds like you're jealous...
...of Q-ta.
That's ridiculous.
Like what you said last night...
...in the car.
You made it sound like the Minamitani brothers are playing with Yura...
...but you don't know how they really feel.

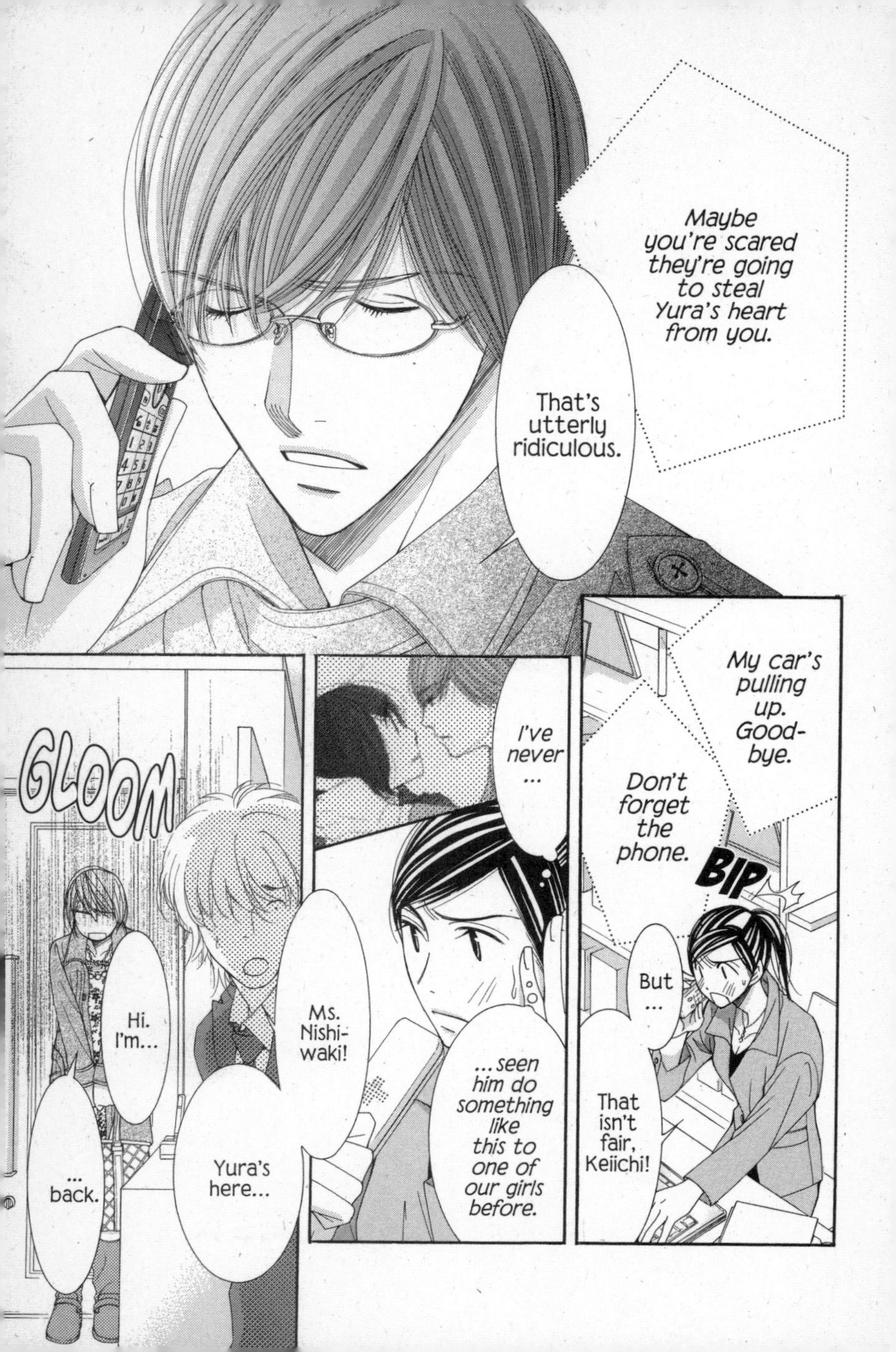
Maybe you're scared they're going to steal Yura's heart from you.
That's utterly ridiculous.
My car's pulling up. Good-bye.
Don't forget the phone.
BIP
But...
That isn't fair, Keiichi!
I've never...
...seen him do something like this to one of our girls before.
Ms. Nishi-waki!
Yura's here...
GLOOM
Hi. I'm...
... back.

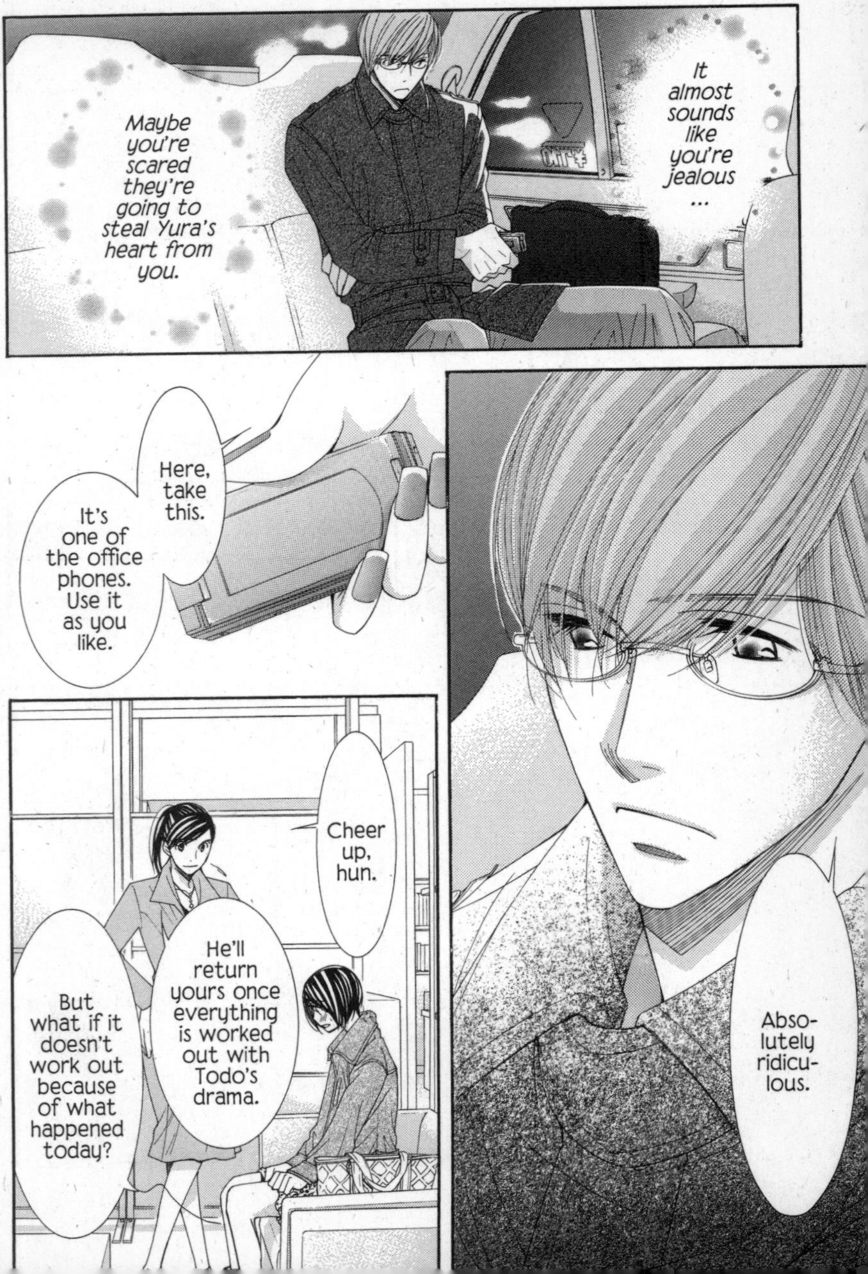
It almost sounds like you're jealous ...
Maybe you're scared they're going to steal Yura's heart from you.
Absolutely ridiculous.
Here, take this.
It's one of the office phones. Use it as you like.
Cheer up, hun.
He'll return yours once everything is worked out with Todo's drama.
But what if it doesn't work out because of what happened today?

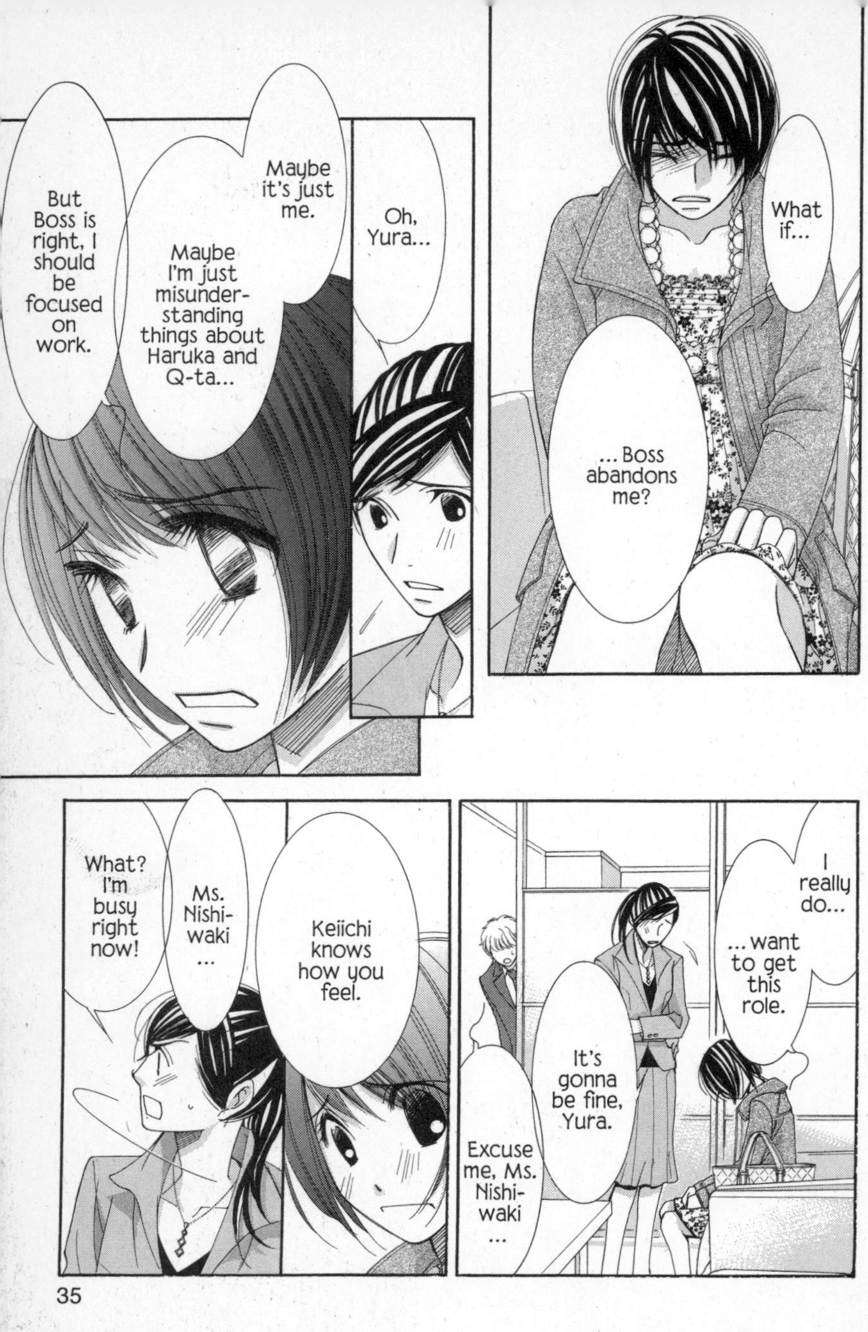
What if...
... Boss abandons me?
Oh, Yura...
Maybe it's just me.
Maybe I'm just misunder-standing things about Haruka and Q-ta...
But Boss is right, I should be focused on work.
I really do...
... want to get this role.
It's gonna be fine, Yura.
Excuse me, Ms. Nishi-waki ...
Keiichi knows how you feel.
Ms. Nishi-waki ...
What? I'm busy right now!

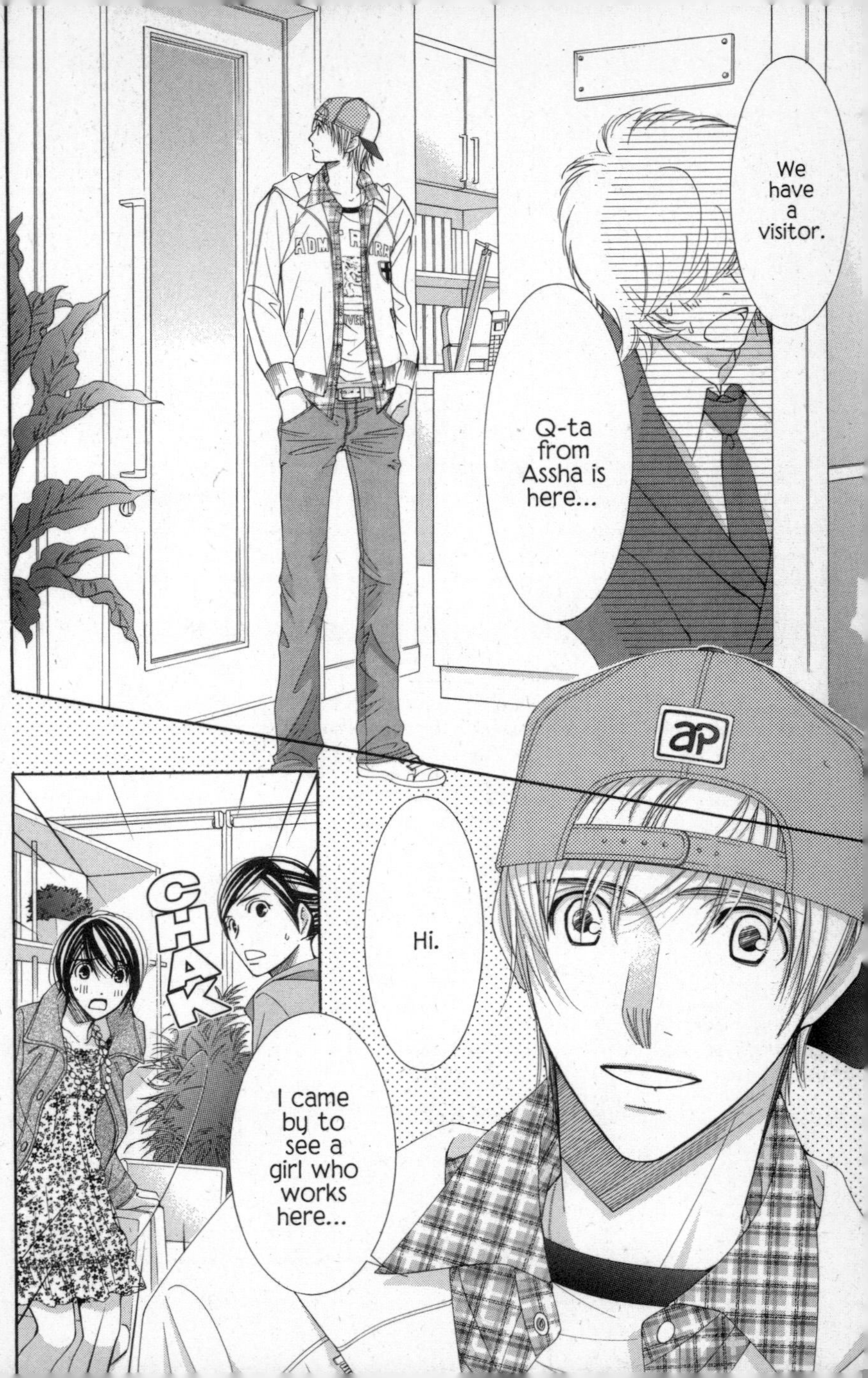
We have a visitor.
Q-ta from Assha is here...
Hi.
I came by to see a girl who works here...
CHAK

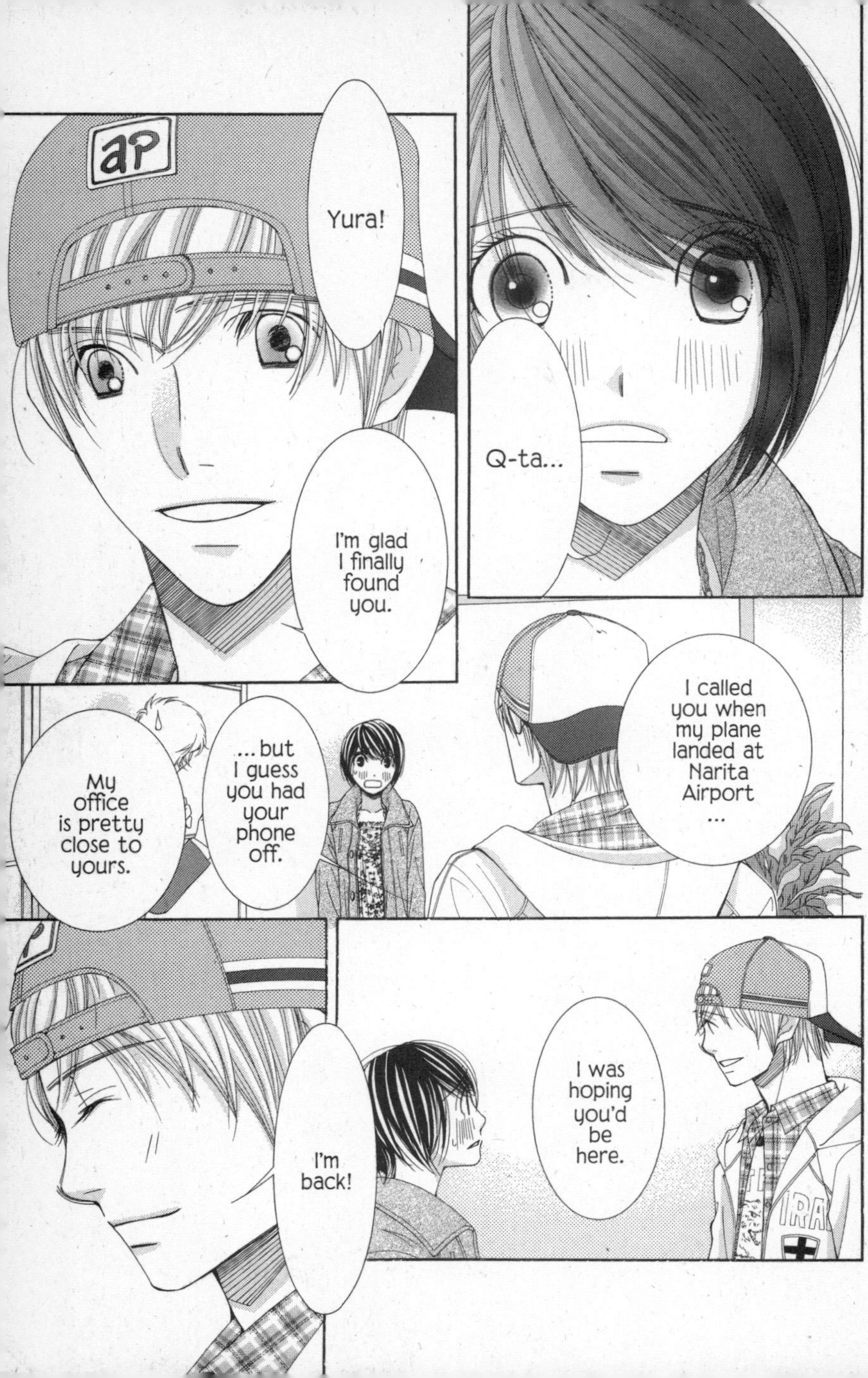
Q-ta...
Yura!
I'm glad I finally found you.
I called you when my plane landed at Narita Airport ...
...but I guess you had your phone off.
My office is pretty close to yours.
I was hoping you'd be here.
I'm back!

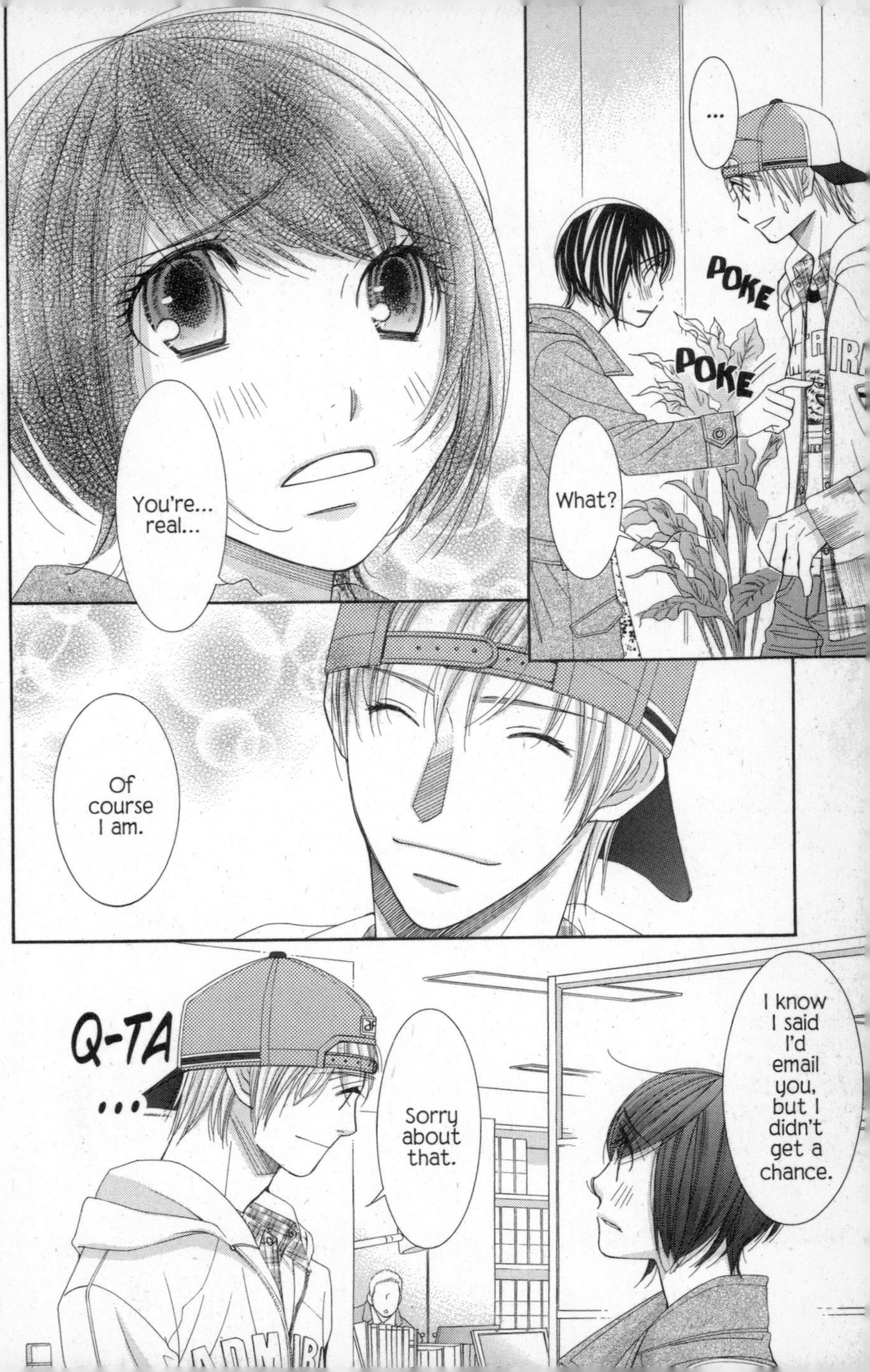
...
POKE
POKE
What?
You're... real...
Of course I am.
I know I said I'd email you, but I didn't get a chance.
Sorry about that.
Q-TA...

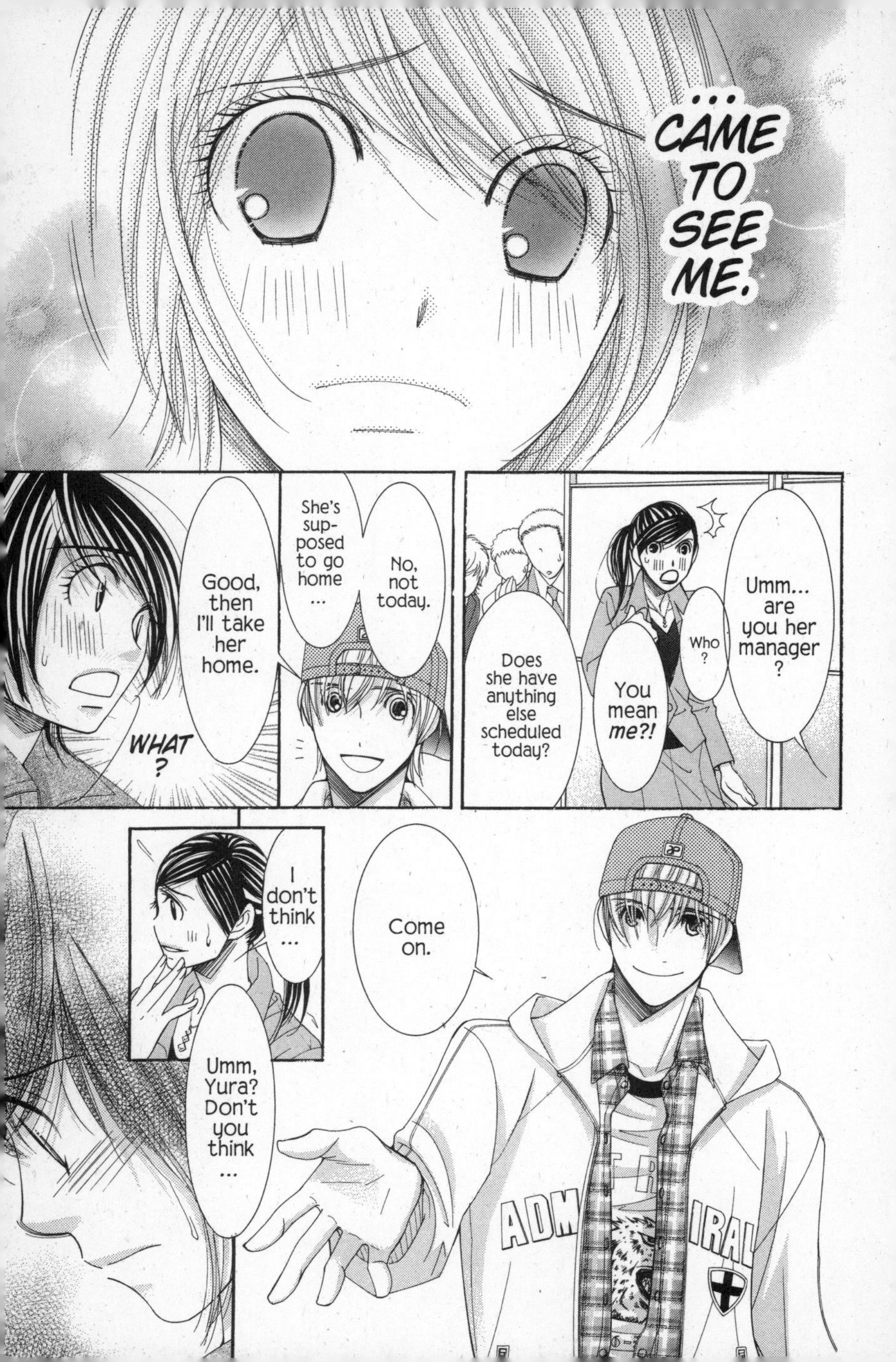
... CAME TO SEE ME.
Umm... are you her manager?
Who?
You mean me?!
Does she have anything else scheduled today?
No, not today.
She's sup-posed to go home ...
Good, then I'll take her home.
WHAT?
Come on.
I don't think ...
Umm, Yura? Don't you think ...

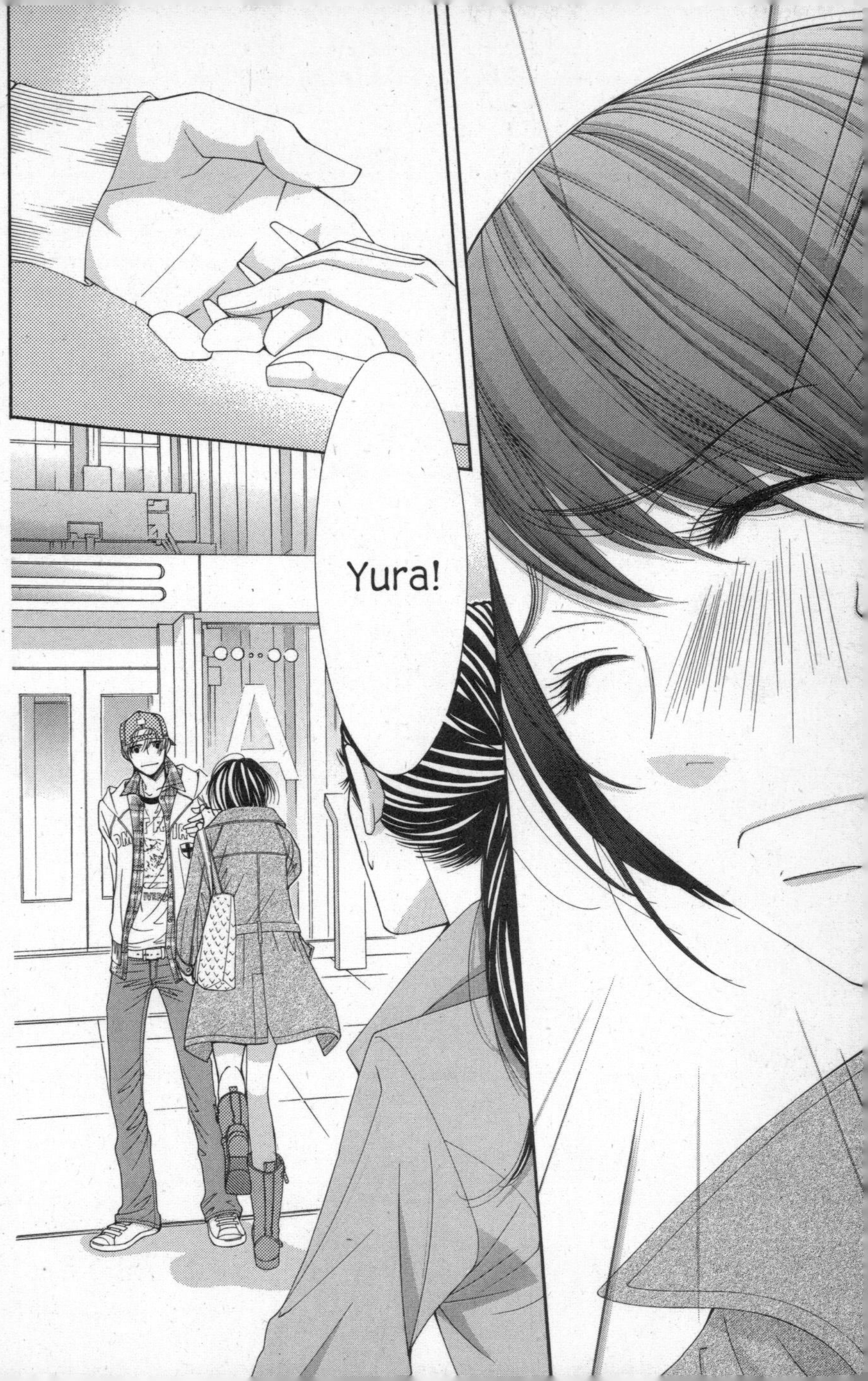
Yura!

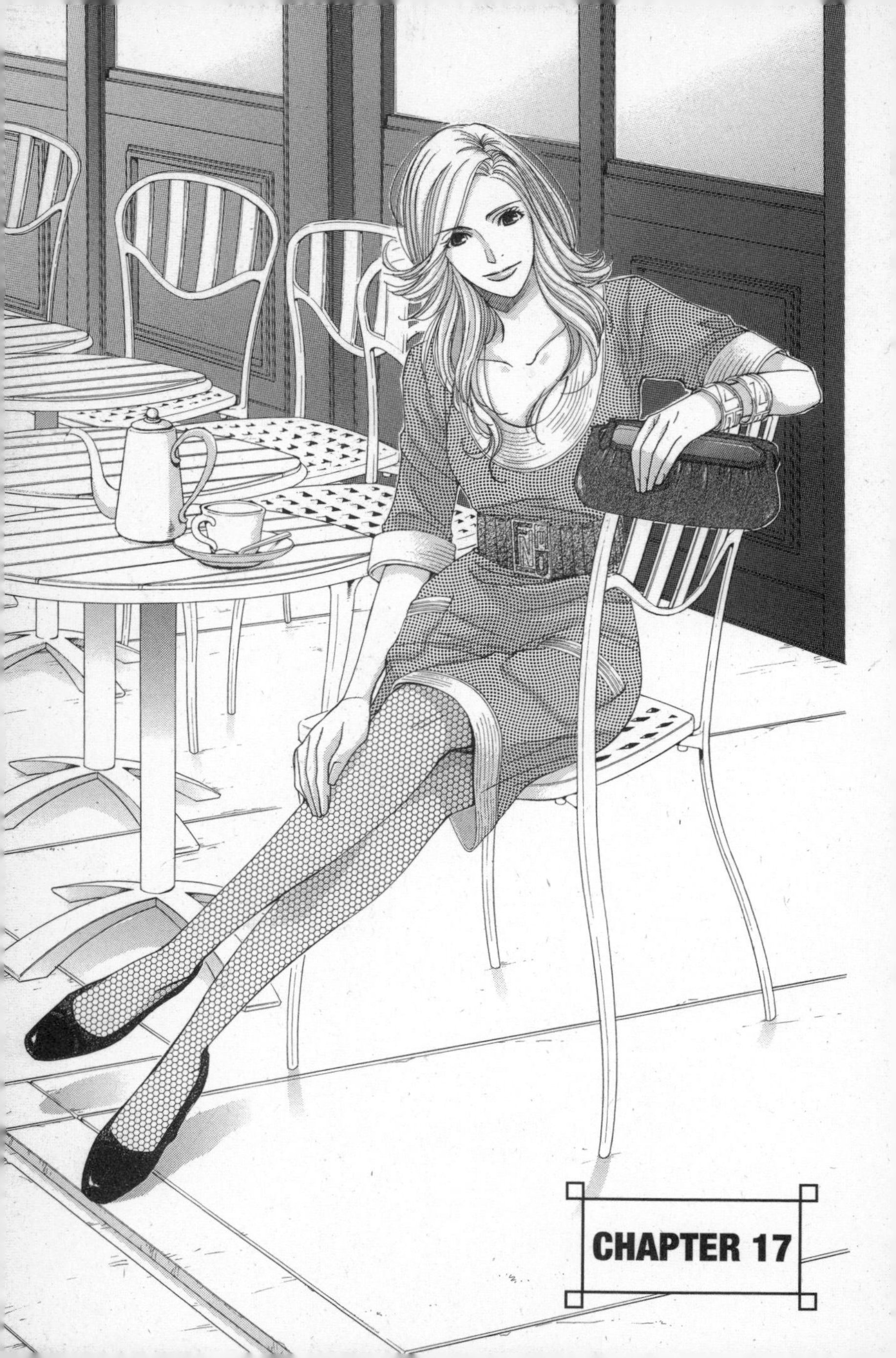
CHAPTER 17

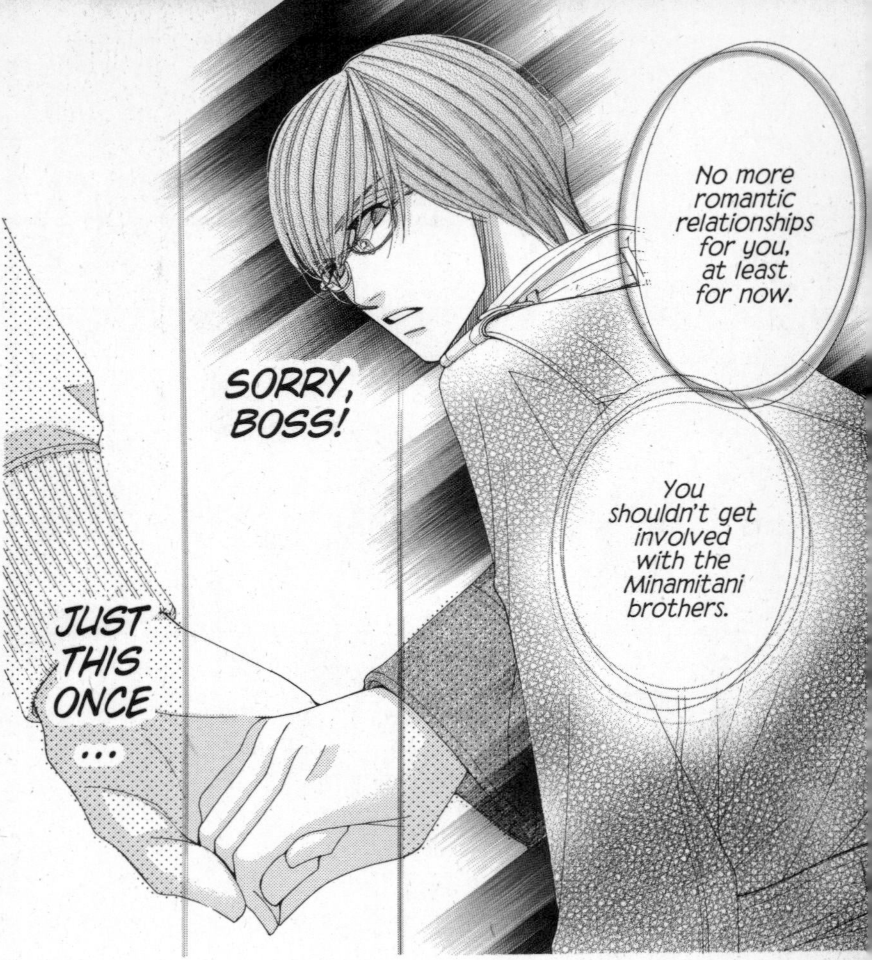
No more romantic relationships for you, at least for now.
You shouldn't get involved with the Minamitani brothers.
SORRY, BOSS!
JUST THIS ONCE ...

Honey Hunt

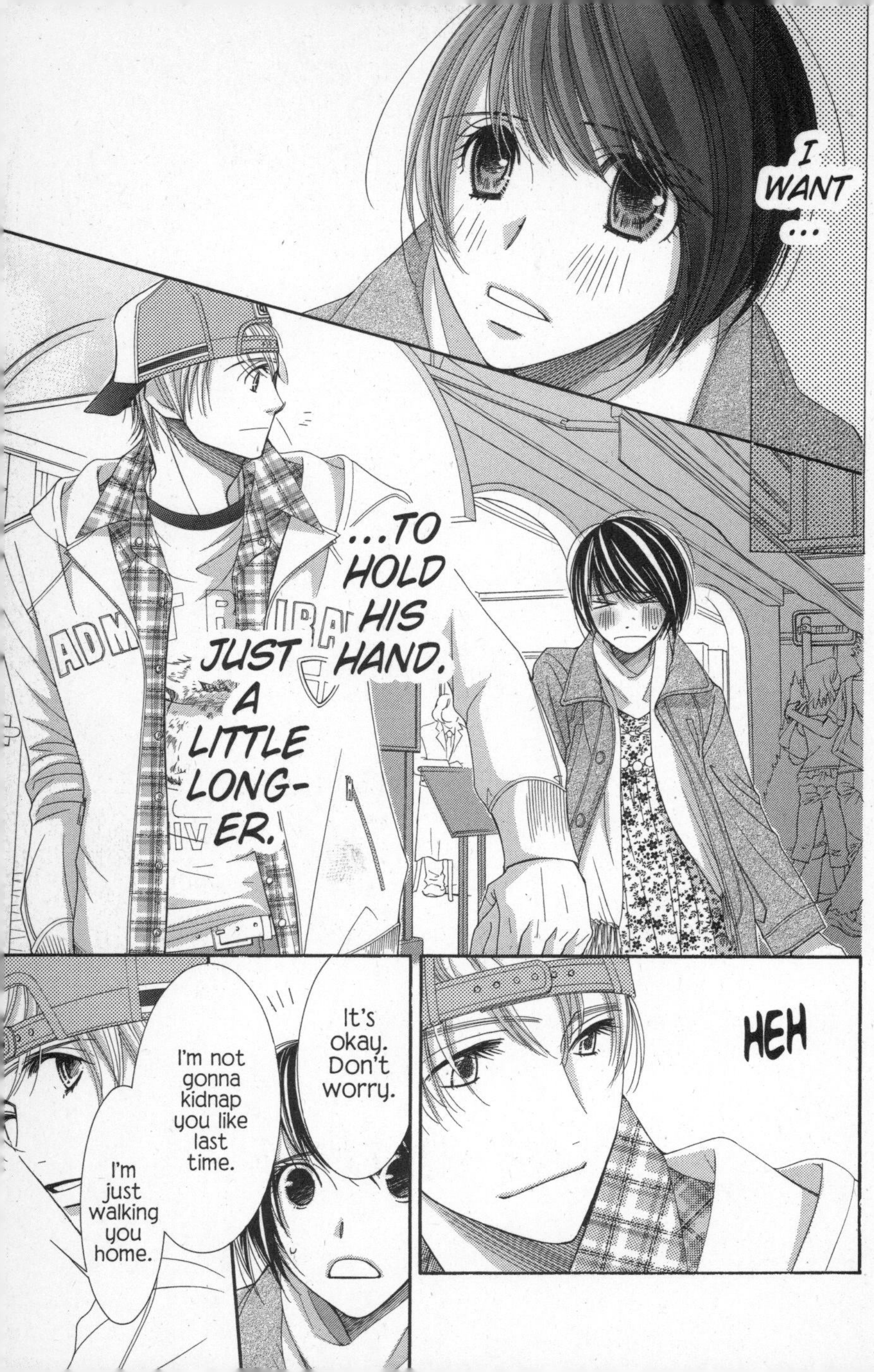
I WANT...
...TO HOLD HIS HAND.
JUST A LITTLE LONG-ER.
HEH
It's okay. Don't worry.
I'm not gonna kidnap you like last time.
I'm just walking you home.

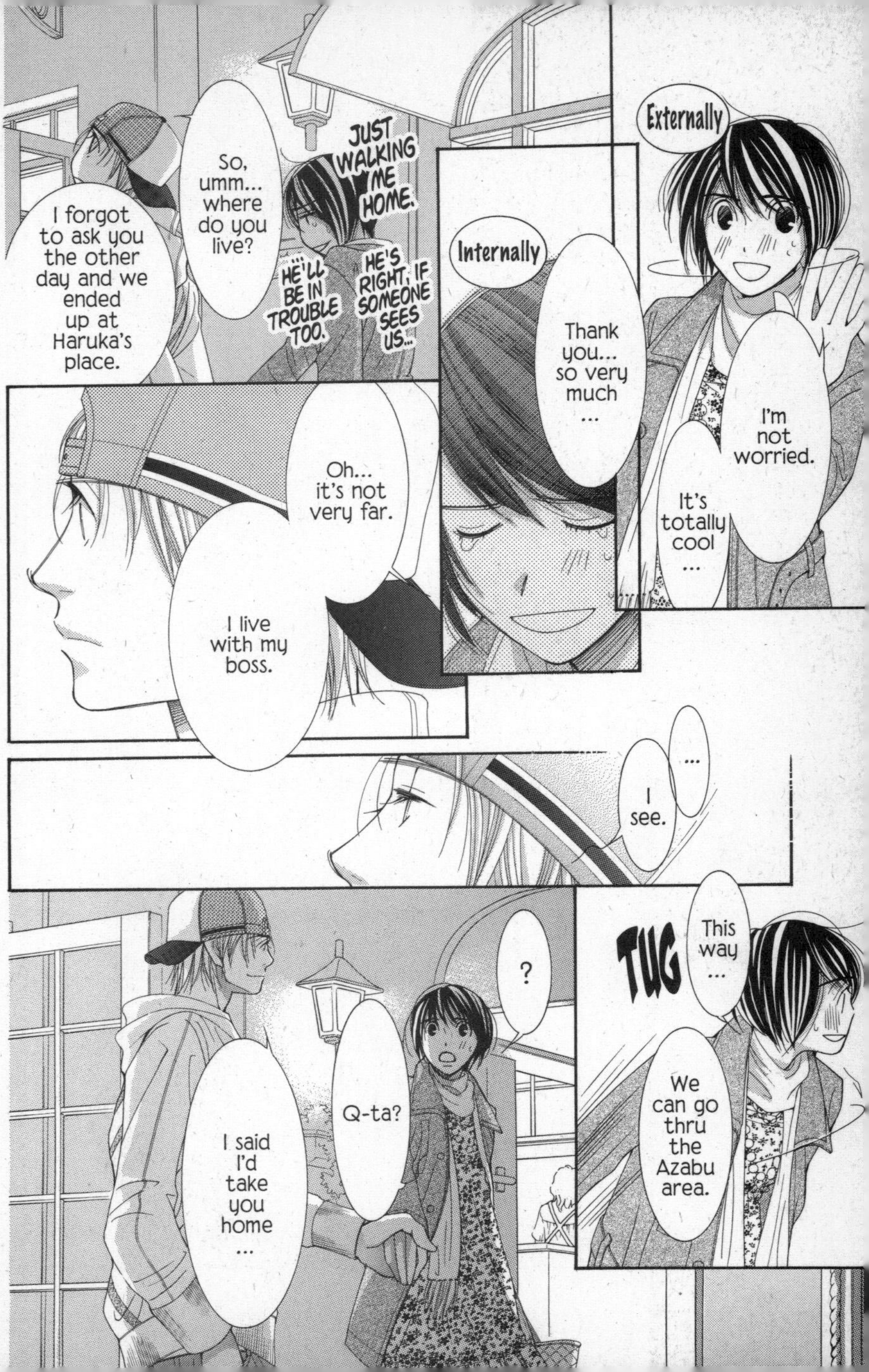
Externally
I'm not worried.
It's totally cool ...
Internally
Thank you... so very much ...
So, umm... where do you live?
I forgot to ask you the other day and we ended up at Haruka's place.
JUST WALKING ME HOME.
HE'S RIGHT, IF SOMEONE SEES US...
...HE'LL BE IN TROUBLE TOO.
Oh... it's not very far.
I live with my boss.
...
I see.
TUG
This way ...
We can go thru the Azabu area.
?
Q-ta?
I said I'd take you home ...

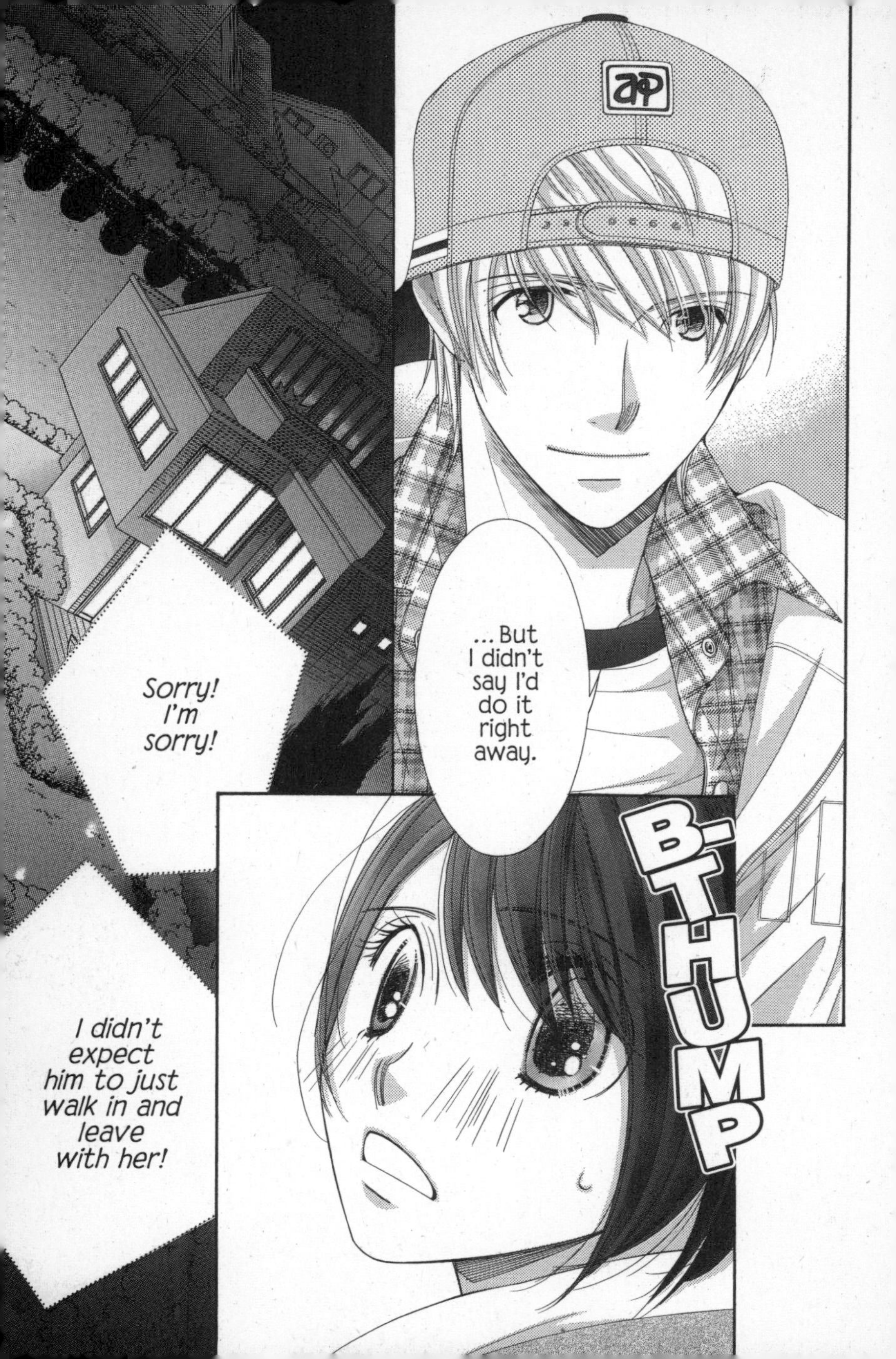
...But I didn't say I'd do it right away.
B-THUMP
Sorry! I'm sorry!
I didn't expect him to just walk in and leave with her!

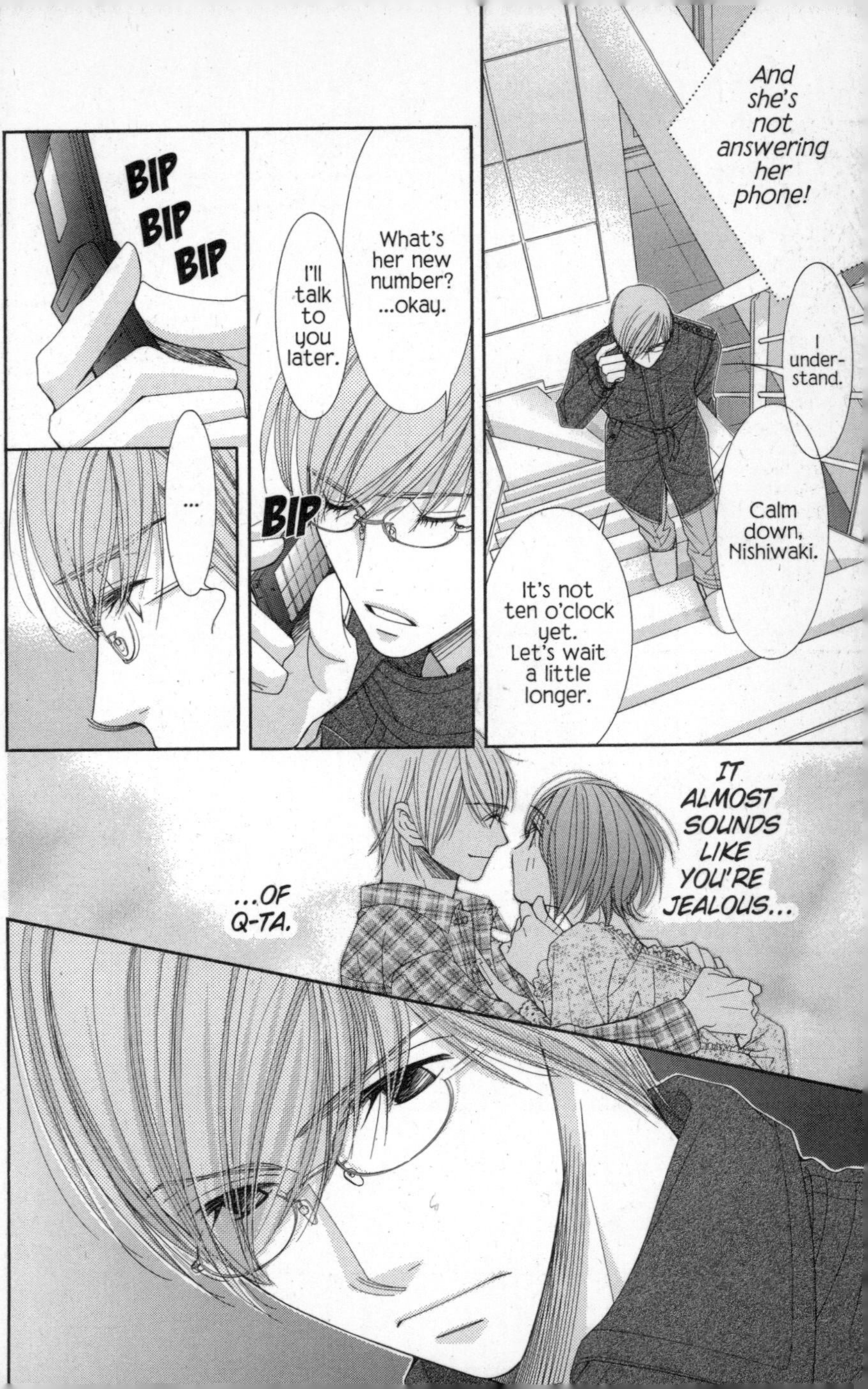

And she's not answering her phone!
I understand.
Calm down, Nishiwaki.
It's not ten o'clock yet. Let's wait a little longer.
What's her new number? ...okay.
I'll talk to you later.
BIP
BIP BIP BIP
...
IT ALMOST SOUNDS LIKE YOU'RE JEALOUS...
...OF Q-TA.

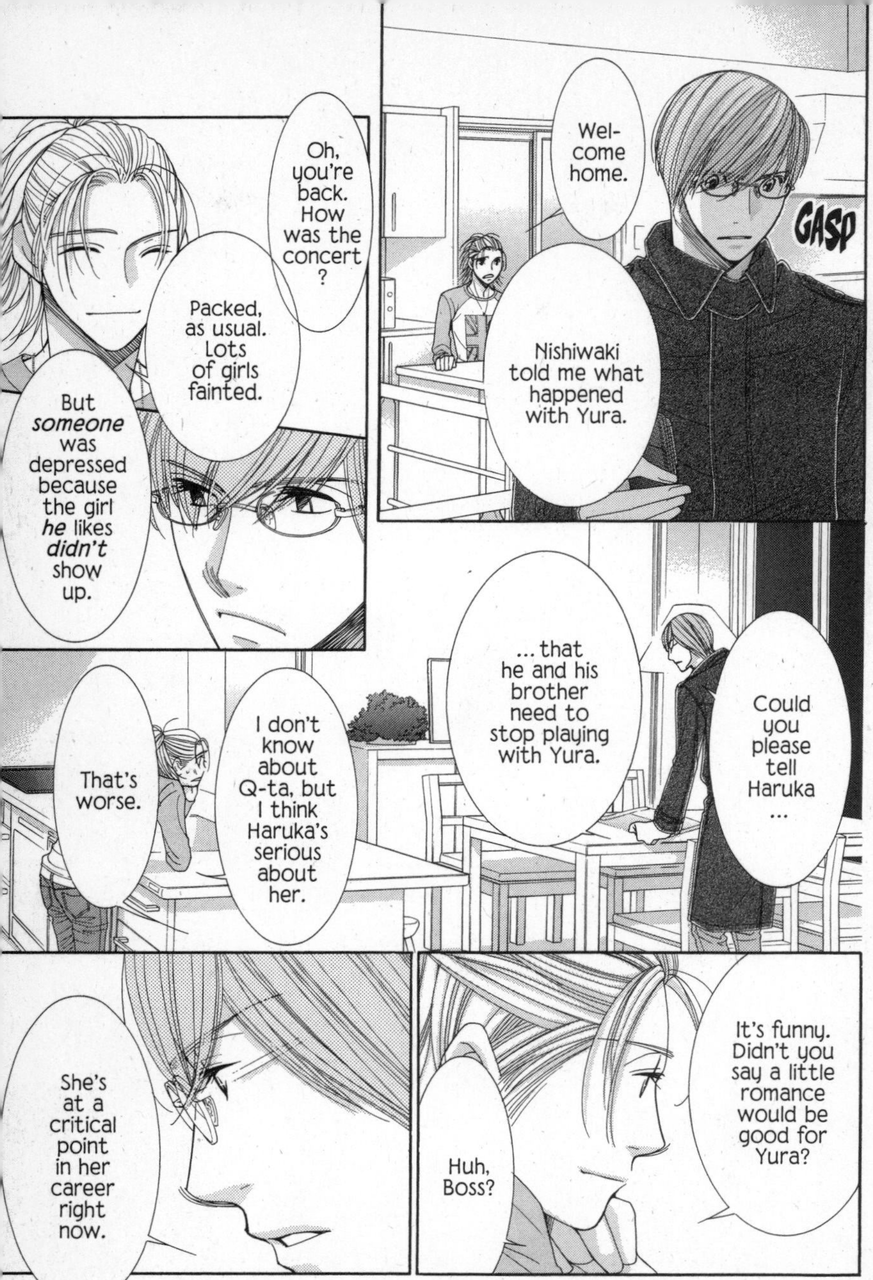
Wel-come home.
GASP
Nishiwaki told me what happened with Yura.
Oh, you're back. How was the concert?
Packed, as usual. Lots of girls fainted.
But *someone* was depressed because the girl *he* likes *didn't* show up.
Could you please tell Haruka...
...that he and his brother need to stop playing with Yura.
I don't know about Q-ta, but I think Haruka's serious about her.
That's worse.
It's funny. Didn't you say a little romance would be good for Yura?
Huh, Boss?
She's at a critical point in her career right now.

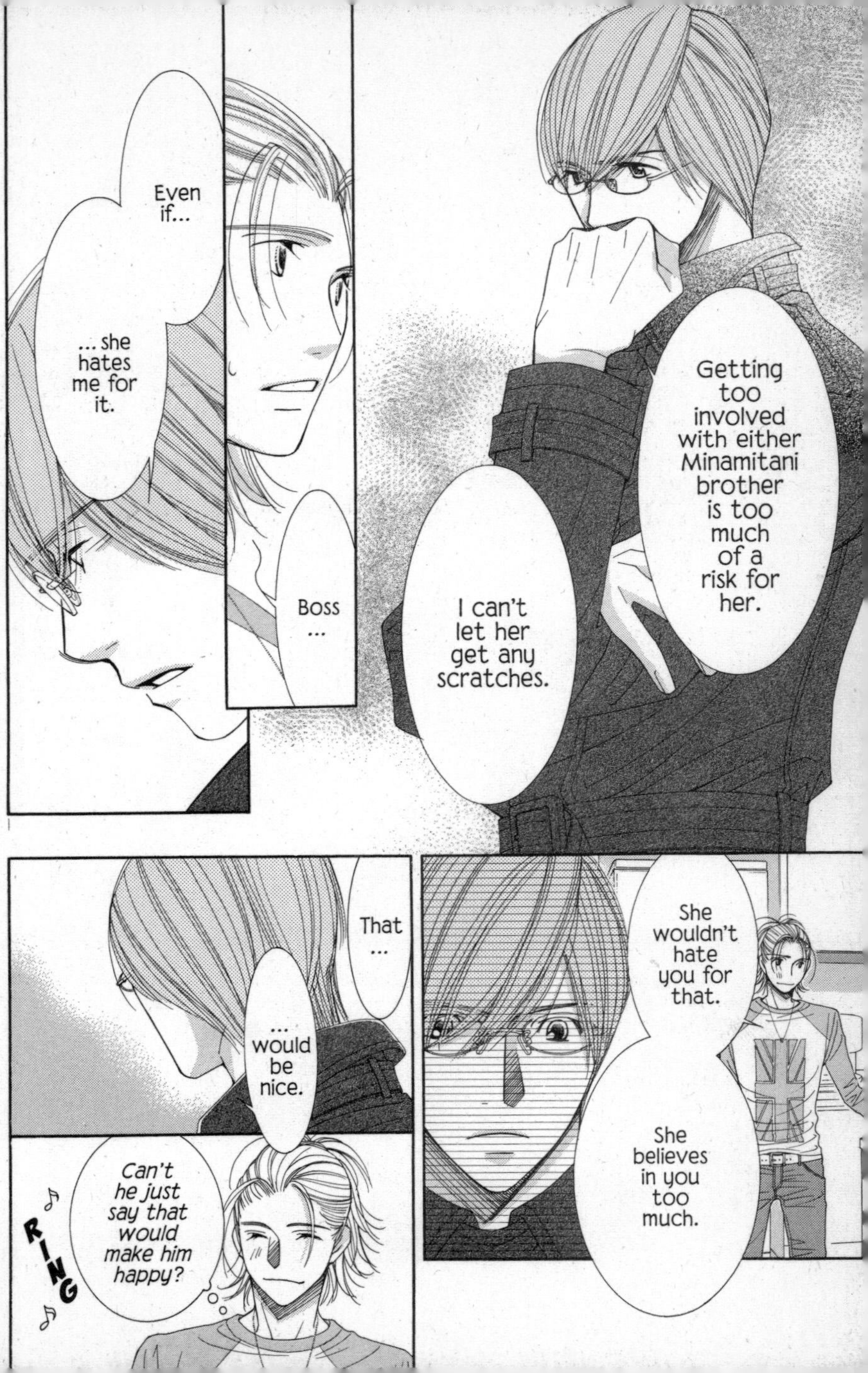
Getting too involved with either Minamitani brother is too much of a risk for her.
I can't let her get any scratches.
Even if...
... she hates me for it.
Boss ...
She wouldn't hate you for that.
She believes in you too much.
That ...
... would be nice.
Can't he just say that would make him happy?
RING

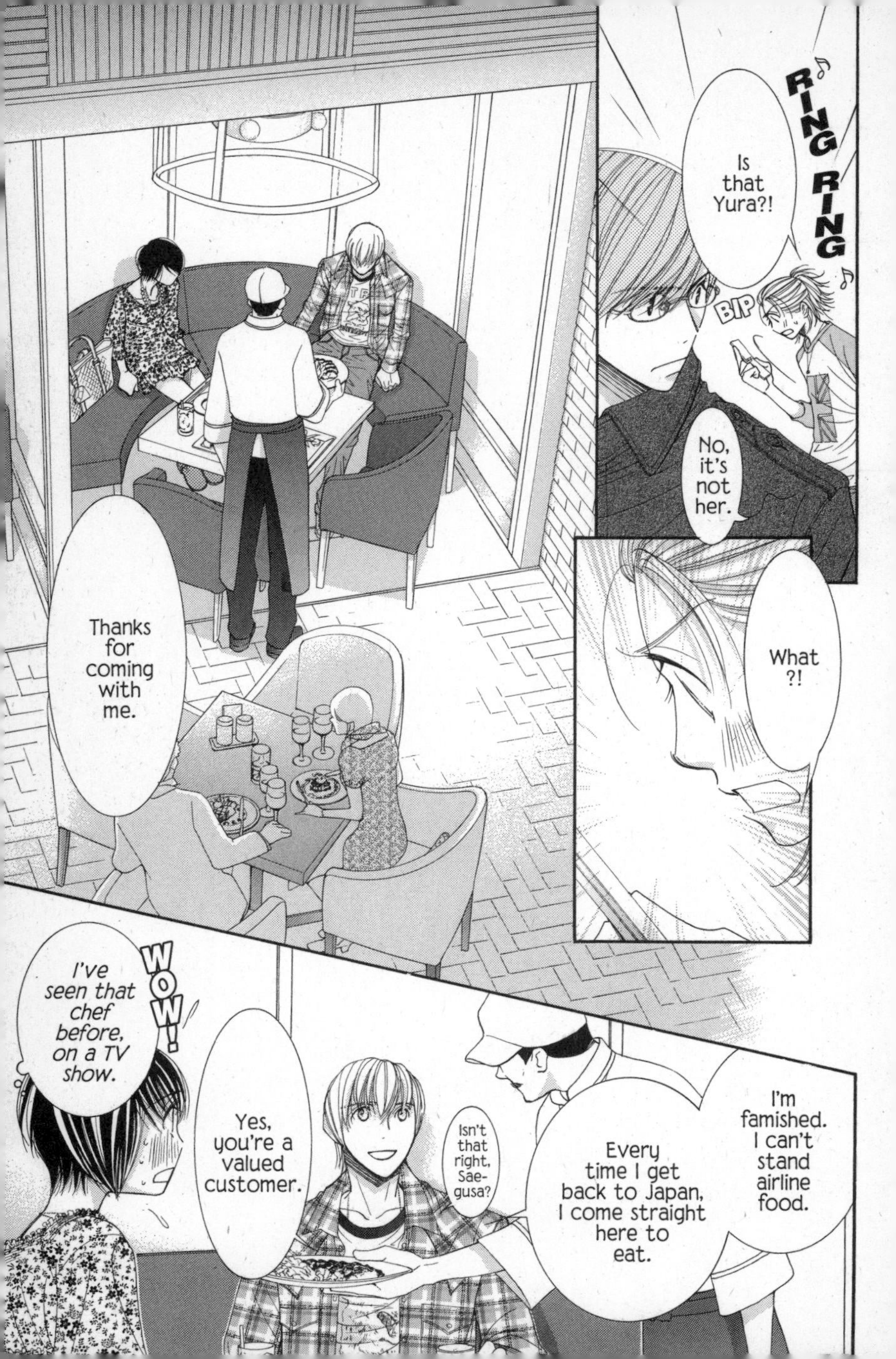
RING RING
Is that Yura?!
BIP
No, it's not her.
What?!
Thanks for coming with me.
I'm famished. I can't stand airline food.
Every time I get back to Japan, I come straight here to eat.
Isn't that right, Saegusa?
Yes, you're a valued customer.
WOW!
I've seen that chef before, on a TV show.

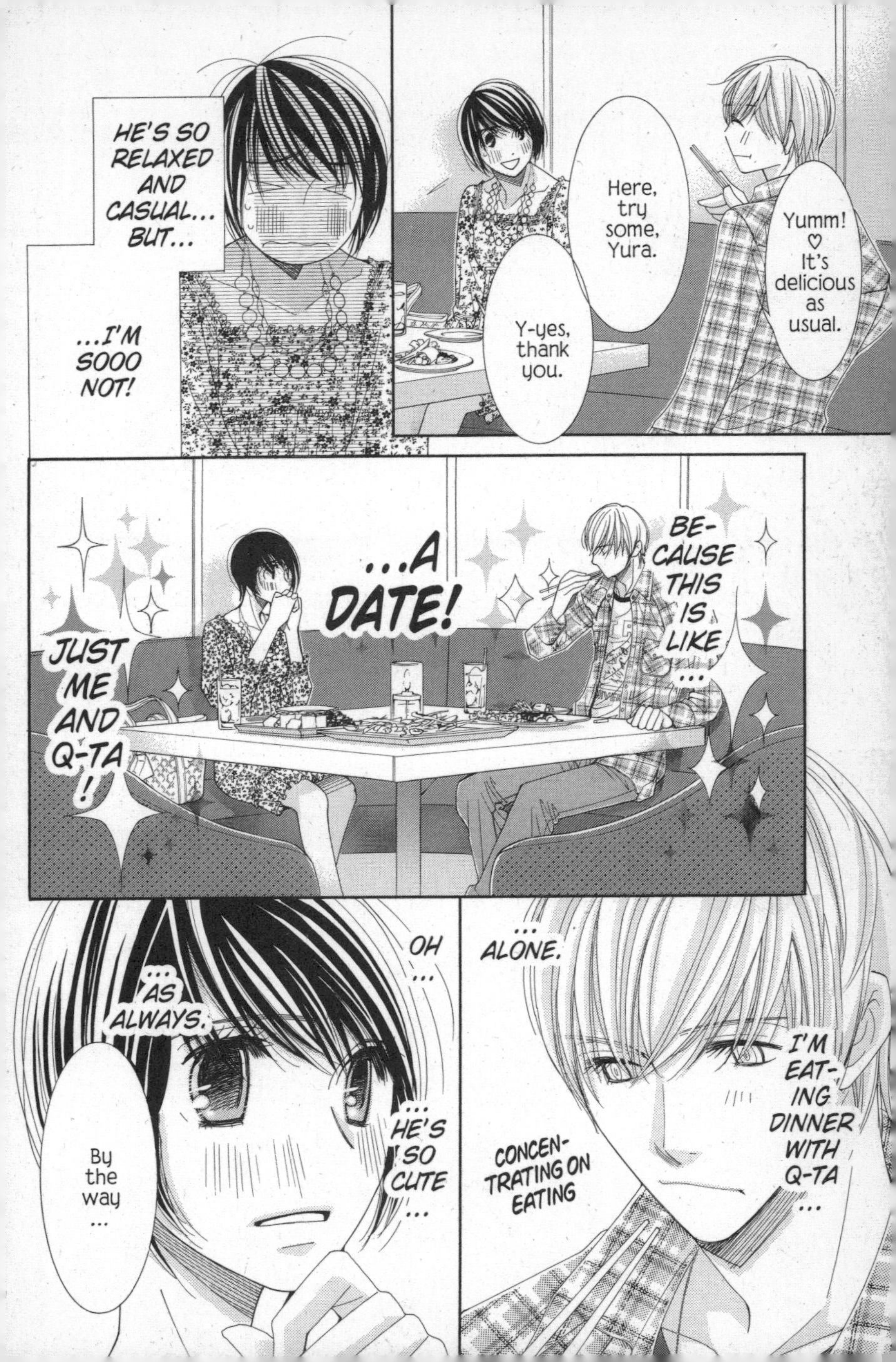

Yumm! ♡ It's delicious as usual.
Here, try some, Yura.
Y-yes, thank you.
HE'S SO RELAXED AND CASUAL... BUT...
...I'M SOOO NOT!
BE-CAUSE THIS IS LIKE...
...A DATE!
JUST ME AND Q-TA!
I'M EAT-ING DINNER WITH Q-TA...
...ALONE.
CONCEN-TRATING ON EATING
OH...
...AS ALWAYS.
...HE'S SO CUTE...
By the way...

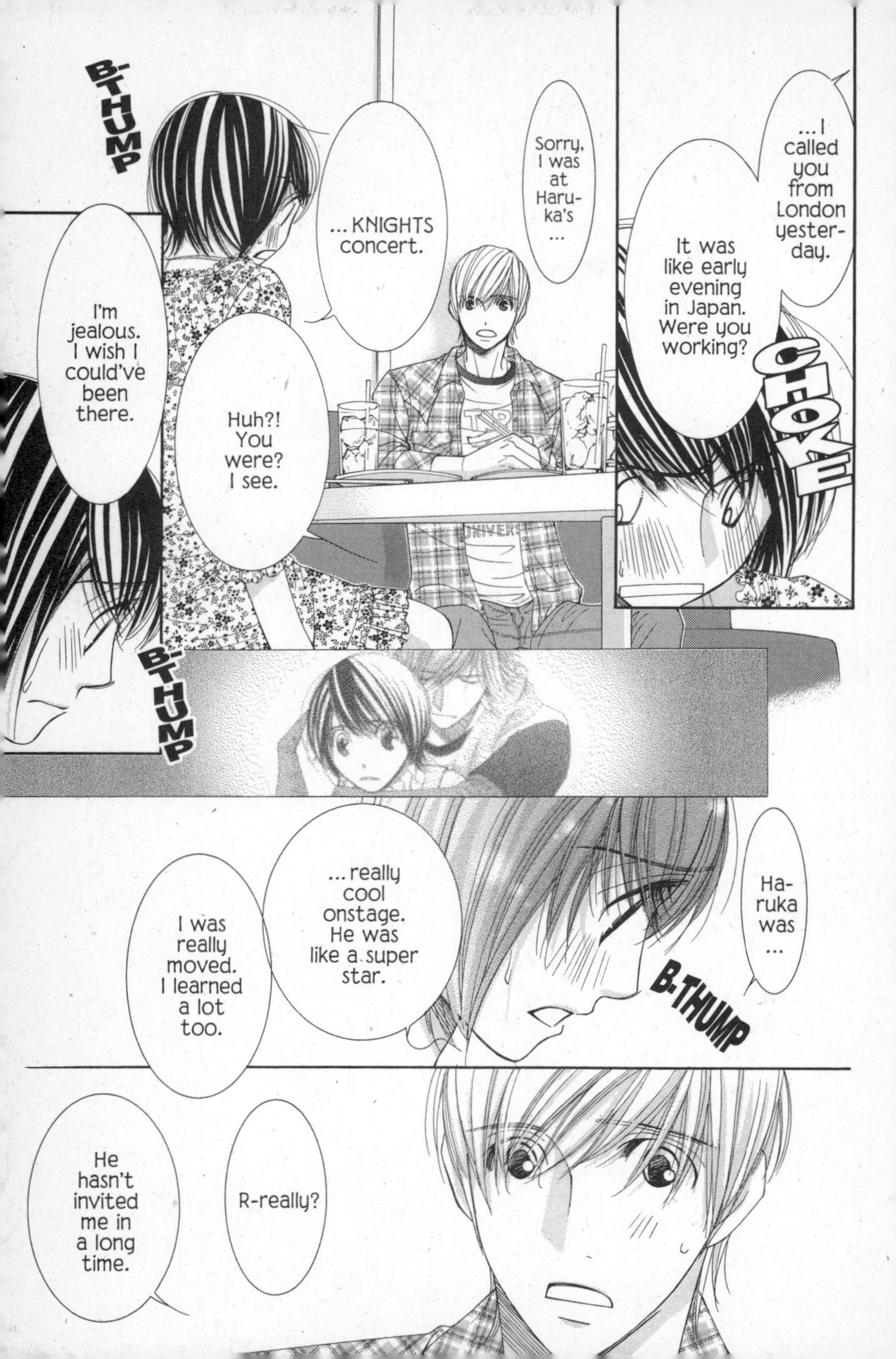

...I called you from London yester-day.
It was like early evening in Japan. Were you working?
CHOKE
Sorry, I was at Haru-ka's ...
...KNIGHTS concert.
B-THUMP
Huh?! You were? I see.
I'm jealous. I wish I could've been there.
B-THUMP
Ha-ruka was ...
B-THUMP
...really cool onstage. He was like a super star.
I was really moved. I learned a lot too.
R-really?
He hasn't invited me in a long time.

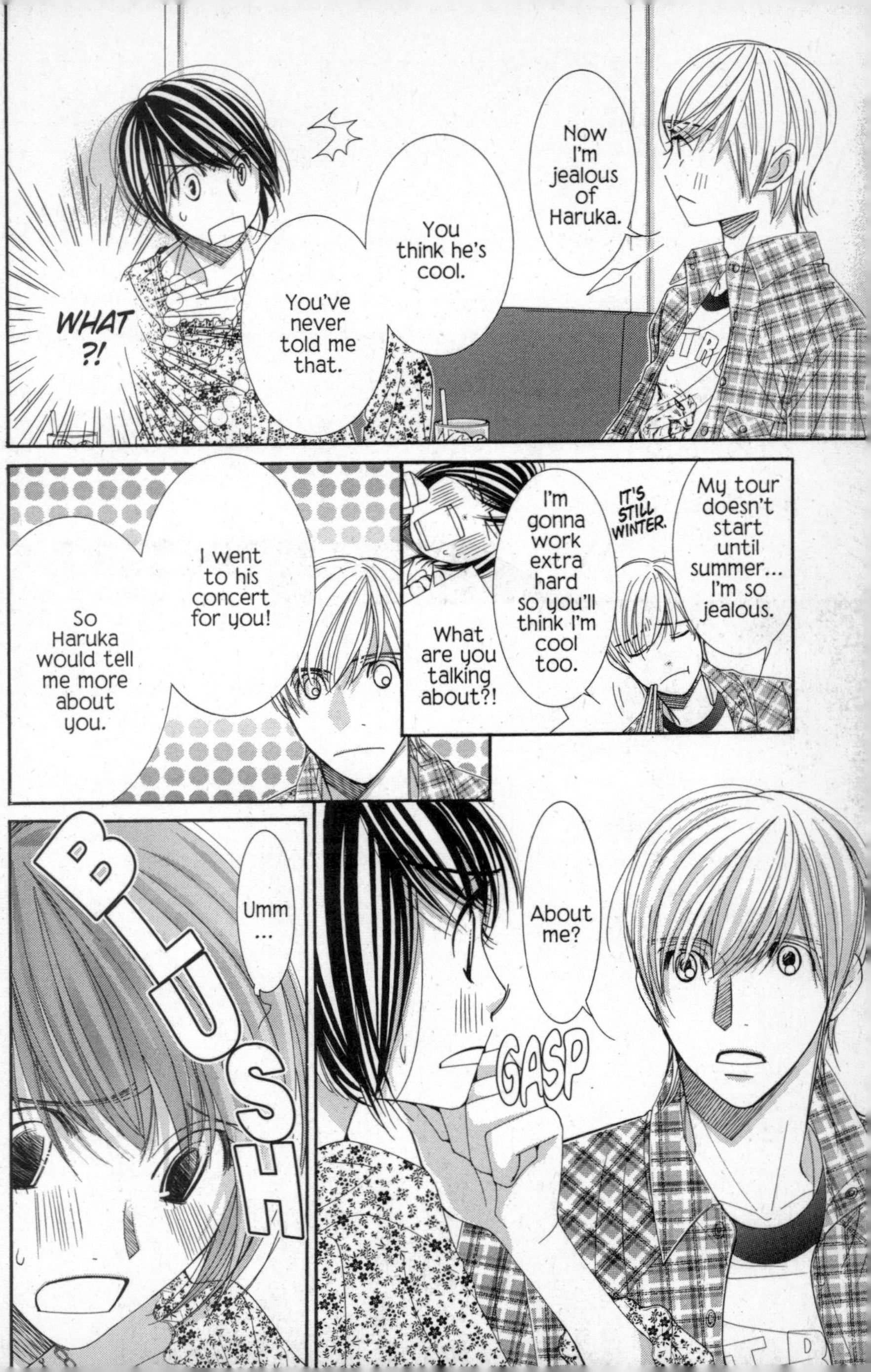
Now I'm jealous of Haruka.
You think he's cool.
You've never told me that.
WHAT ?!
My tour doesn't start until summer... I'm so jealous.
IT'S STILL WINTER.
I'm gonna work extra hard so you'll think I'm cool too.
What are you talking about?!
I went to his concert for you!
So Haruka would tell me more about you.
About me?
GASP
Umm ...
BLUSH

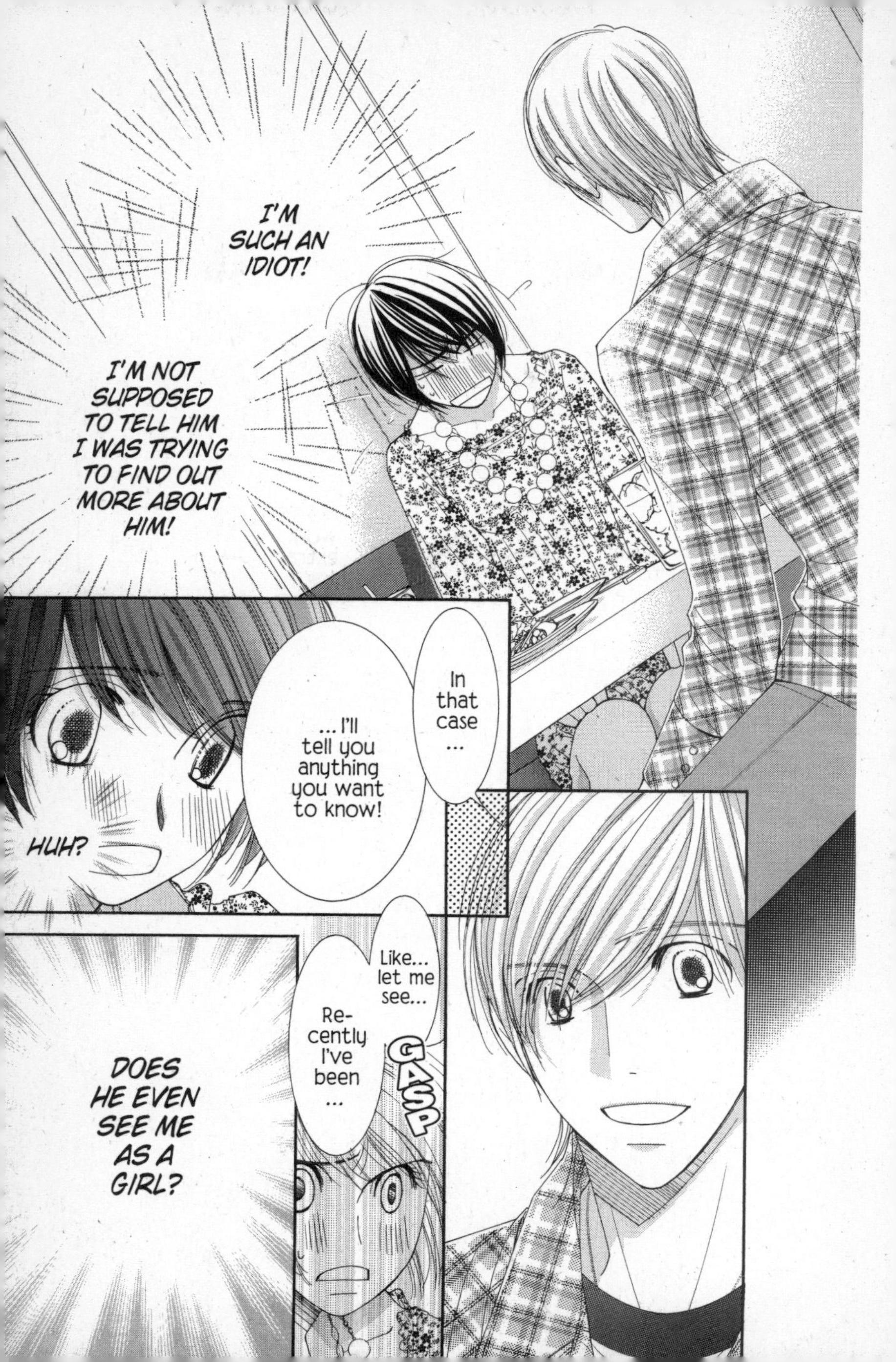
I'M SUCH AN IDIOT!
I'M NOT SUPPOSED TO TELL HIM I WAS TRYING TO FIND OUT MORE ABOUT HIM!
In that case ...
... I'll tell you anything you want to know!
Like... let me see...
Re-cently I've been ...
HUH?
GASP
DOES HE EVEN SEE ME AS A GIRL?

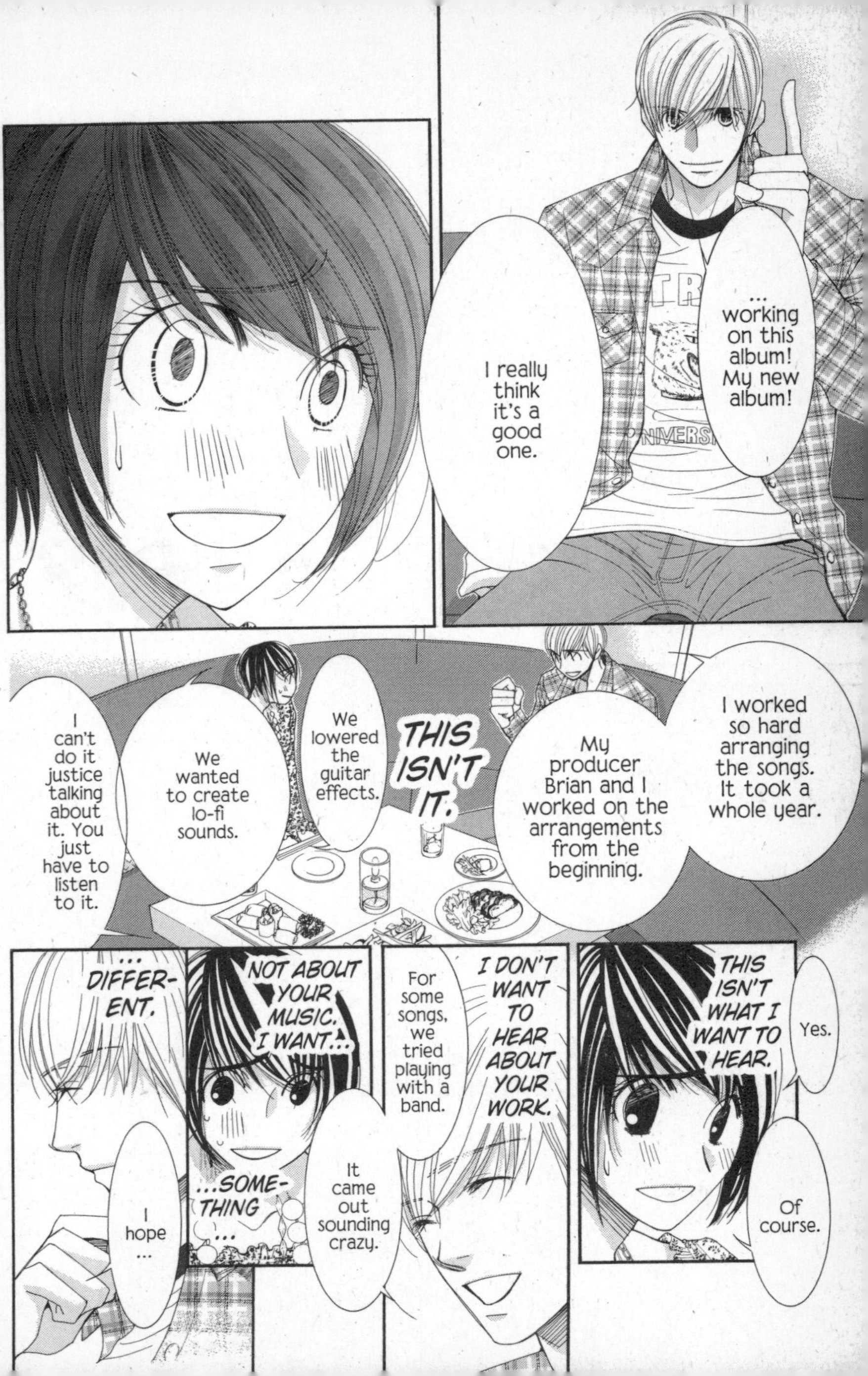

... working on this album! My new album!
I really think it's a good one.
I worked so hard arranging the songs. It took a whole year.
My producer Brian and I worked on the arrangements from the beginning.
THIS ISN'T IT.
We lowered the guitar effects.
We wanted to create lo-fi sounds.
I can't do it justice talking about it. You just have to listen to it.
Yes.
THIS ISN'T WHAT I WANT TO HEAR.
Of course.
I DON'T WANT TO HEAR ABOUT YOUR WORK.
For some songs, we tried playing with a band.
It came out sounding crazy.
NOT ABOUT YOUR MUSIC. I WANT...
...SOME-THING...
...DIFFER-ENT.
I hope...

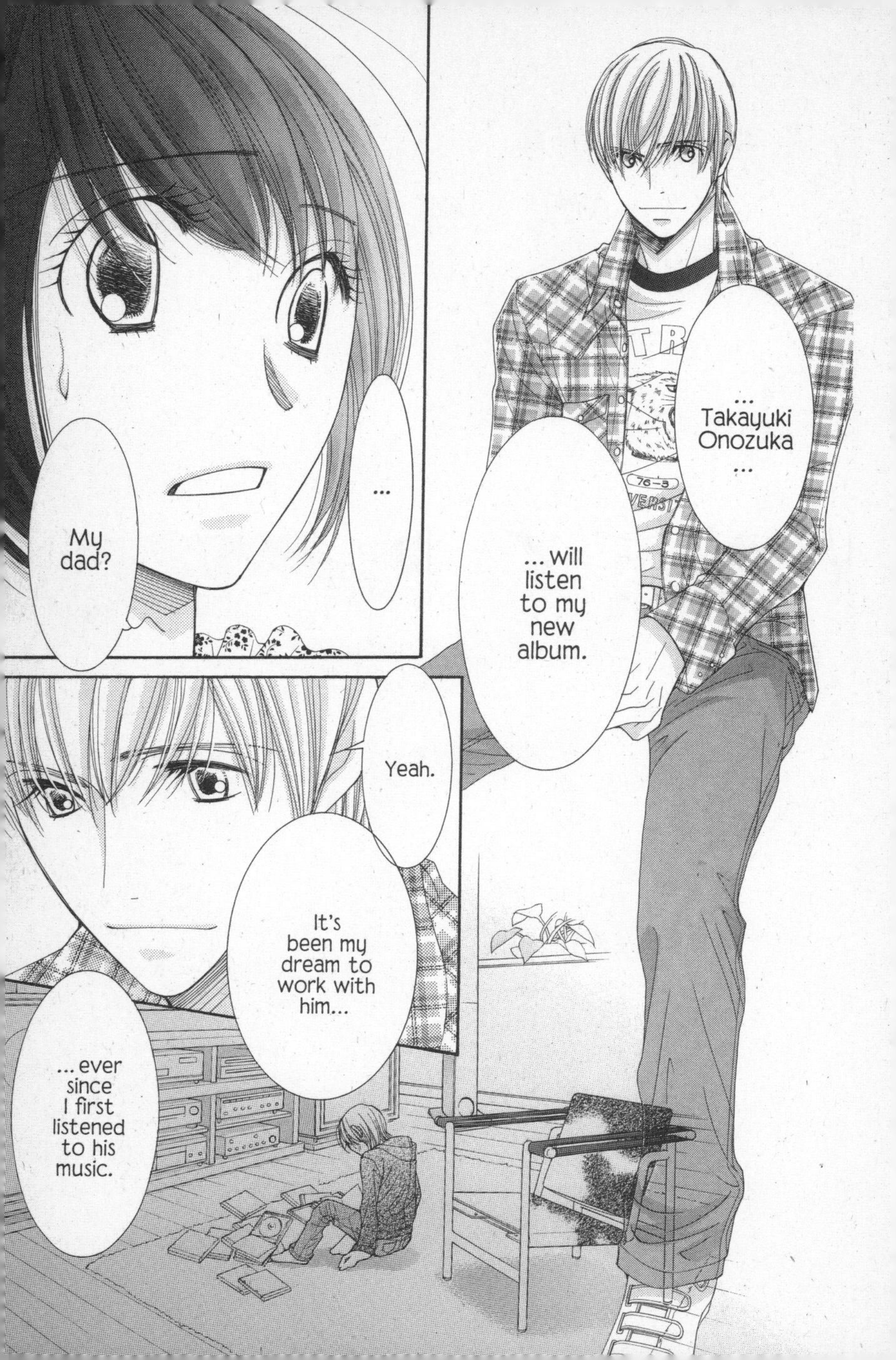

... Takayuki Onozuka ...
... will listen to my new album.
...
My dad?
Yeah.
It's been my dream to work with him...
... ever since I first listened to his music.

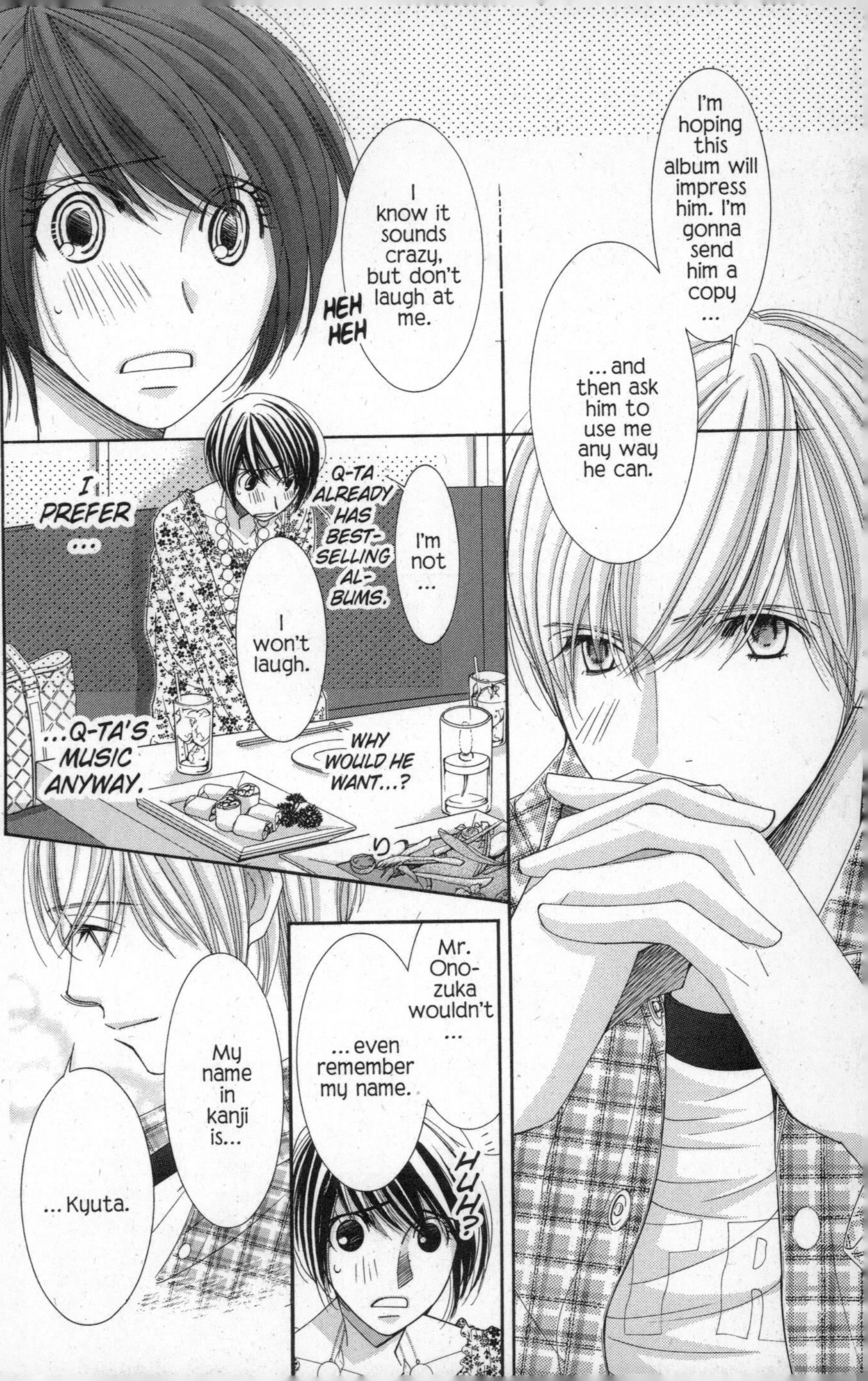
I'm hoping this album will impress him. I'm gonna send him a copy...
...and then ask him to use me any way he can.
I know it sounds crazy, but don't laugh at me.
HEH HEH
I'm not...
Q-TA ALREADY HAS BEST-SELLING AL-BUMS.
I won't laugh.
I PREFER...
...Q-TA'S MUSIC ANYWAY.
WHY WOULD HE WANT...?
Mr. Ono-zuka wouldn't...
...even remember my name.
HUH?
My name in kanji is...
...Kyuta.

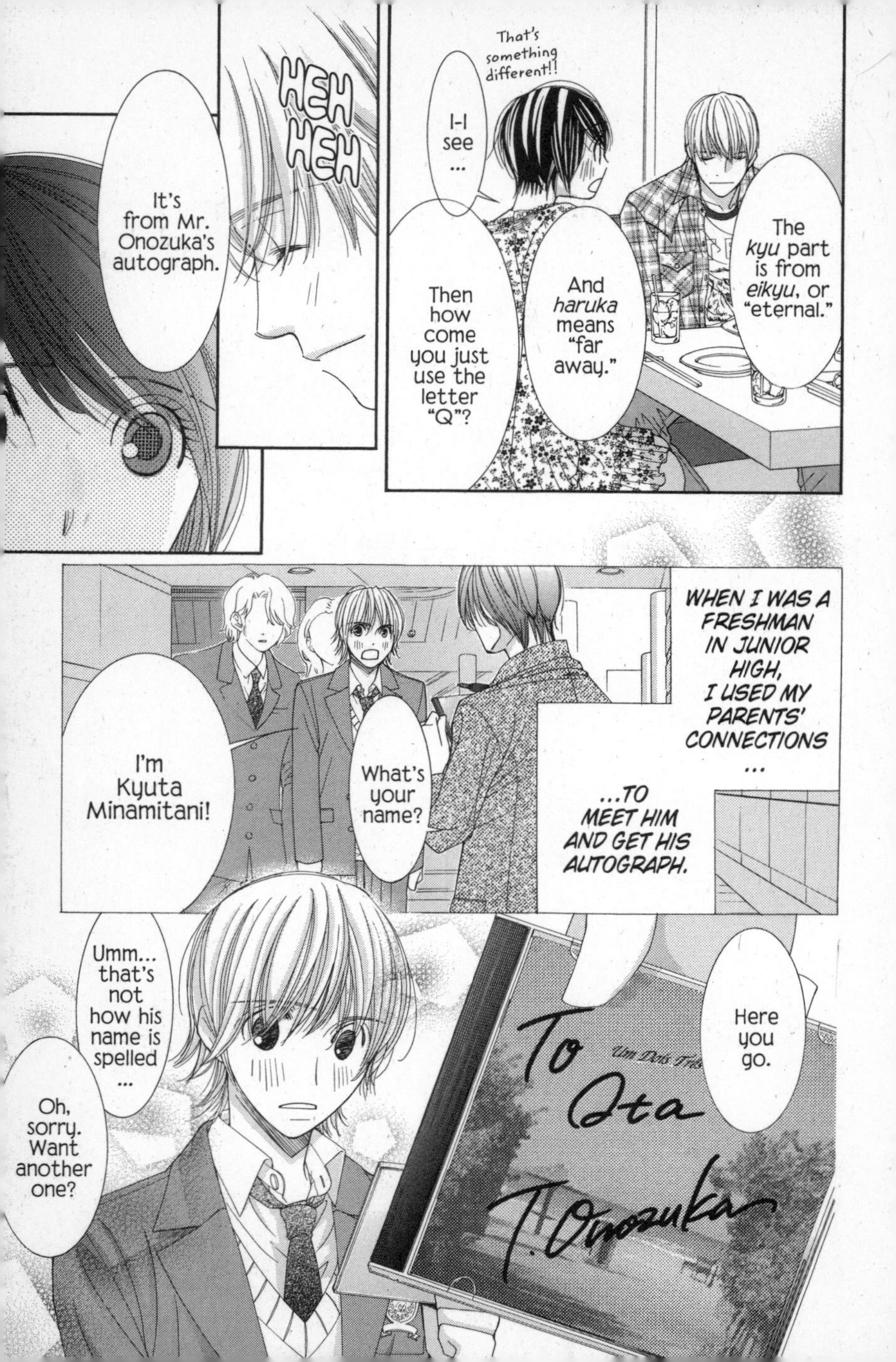

The *kyu* part is from *eikyu*, or "eternal."
And *haruka* means "far away."
That's something different!!
I-I see...
Then how come you just use the letter "Q"?
HEH HEH
It's from Mr. Onozuka's autograph.
WHEN I WAS A FRESHMAN IN JUNIOR HIGH, I USED MY PARENTS' CONNECTIONS...
...TO MEET HIM AND GET HIS AUTOGRAPH.
What's your name?
I'm Kyuta Minamitani!
Here you go.
To Qta
T. Onozuka
Umm... that's not how his name is spelled...
Oh, sorry. Want another one?

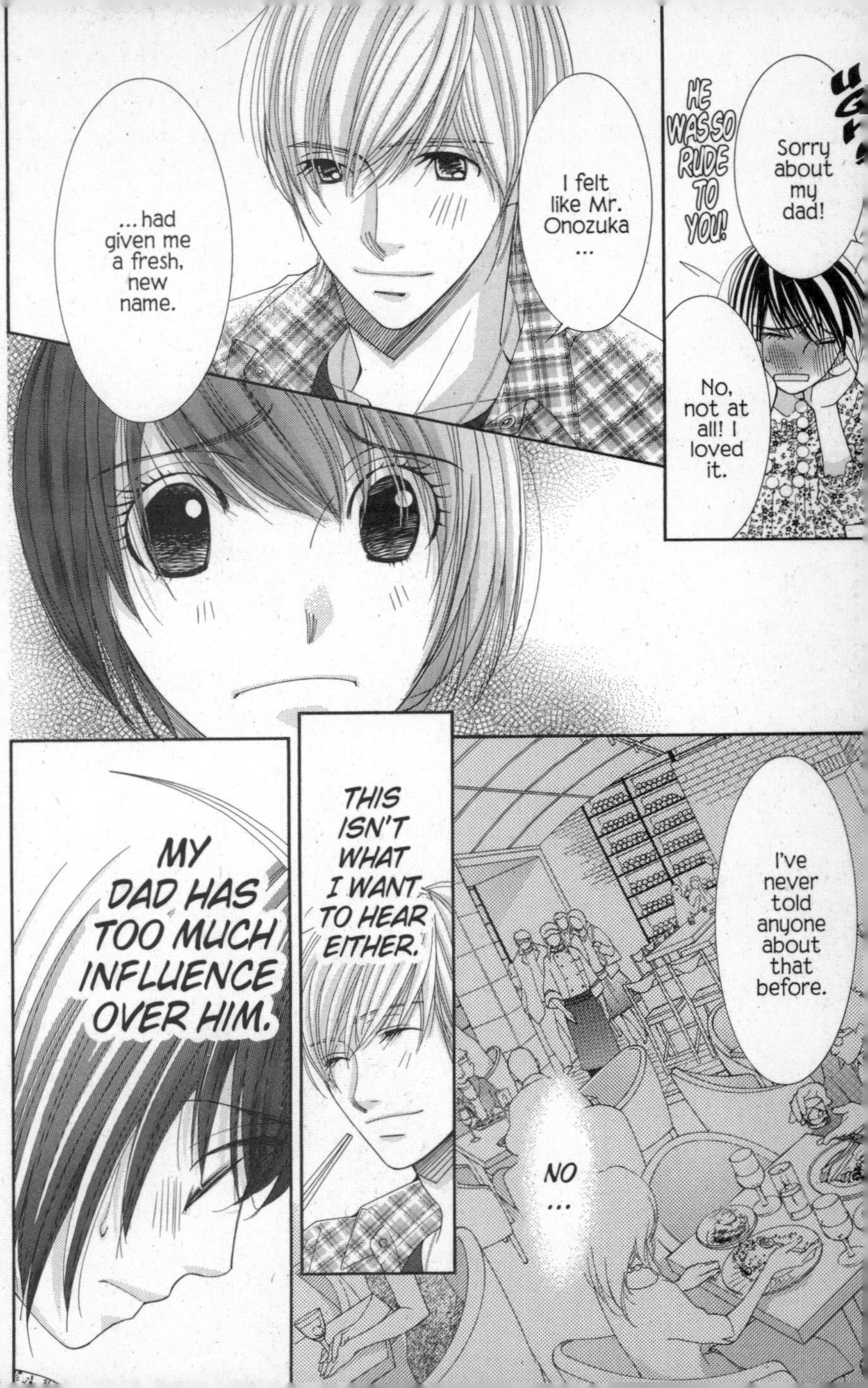

UGH
Sorry about my dad!
HE WAS SO RUDE TO YOU!
No, not at all! I loved it.
I felt like Mr. Onozuka ...
... had given me a fresh, new name.
I've never told anyone about that before.
NO ...
THIS ISN'T WHAT I WANT TO HEAR EITHER.
MY DAD HAS TOO MUCH INFLUENCE OVER HIM.

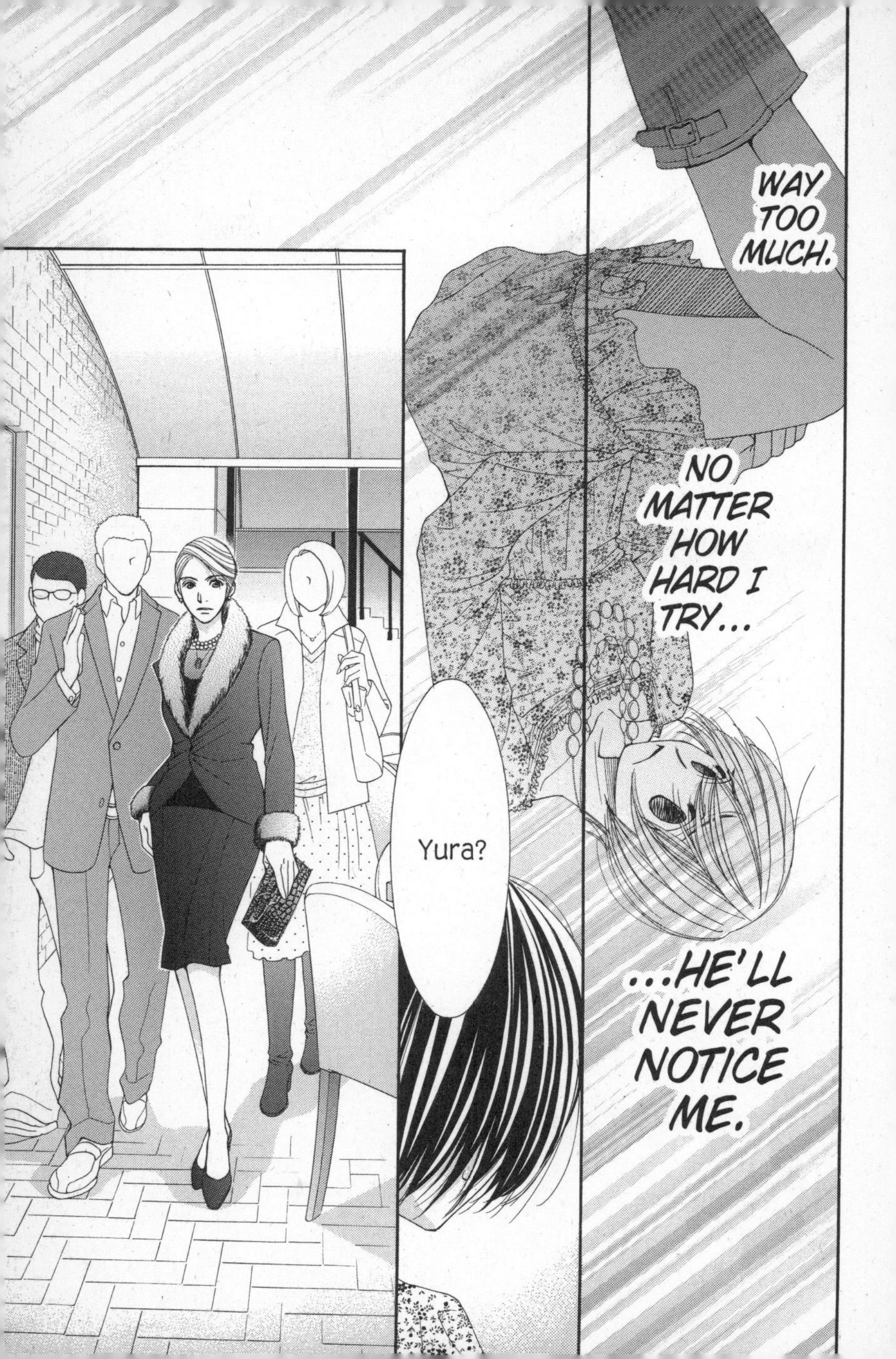
WAY TOO MUCH.
NO MATTER HOW HARD I TRY...
...HE'LL NEVER NOTICE ME.
Yura?

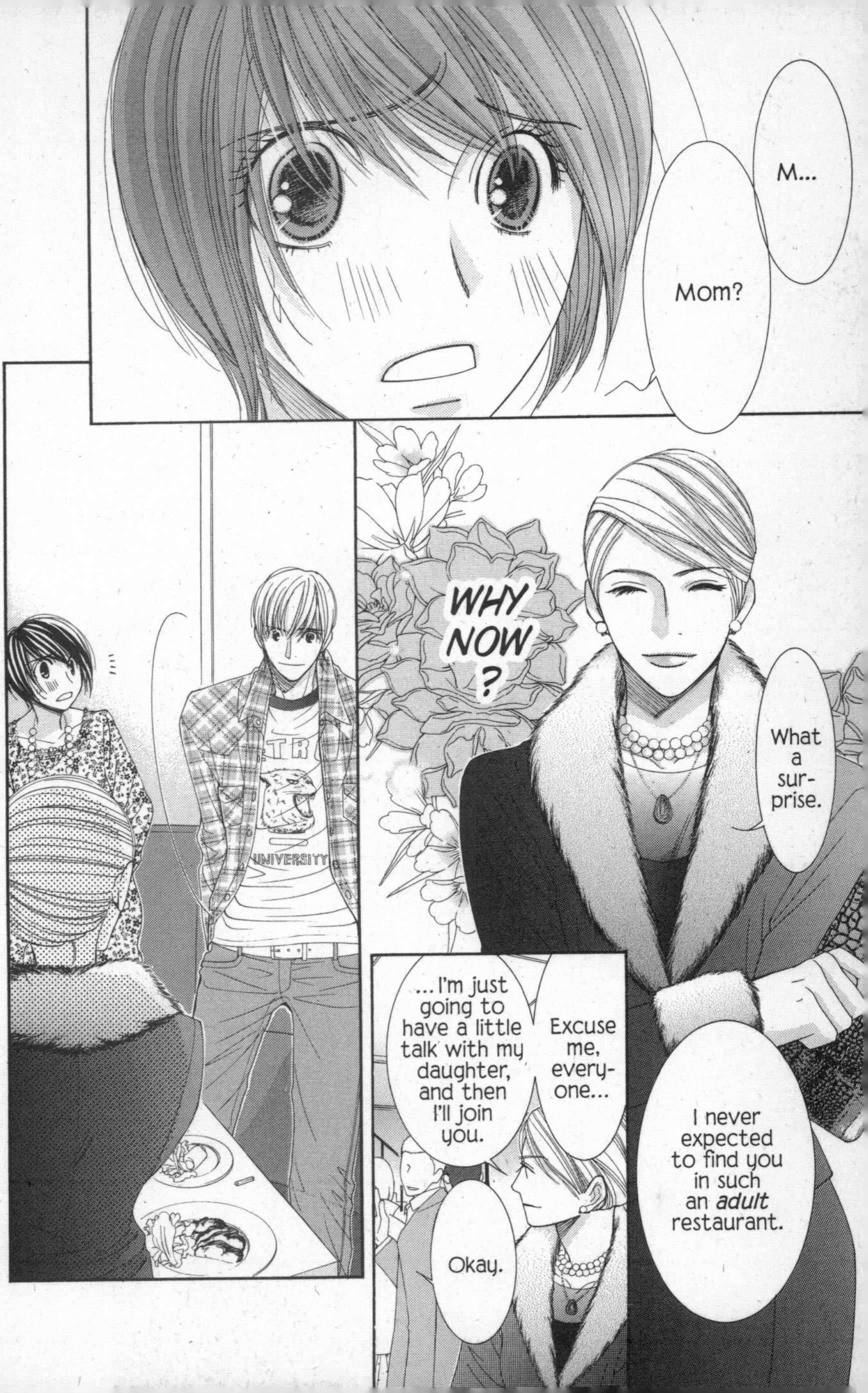
M...
Mom?
What a surprise.
WHY NOW?
I never expected to find you in such an *adult* restaurant.
Excuse me, everyone...
...I'm just going to have a little talk with my daughter, and then I'll join you.
Okay.

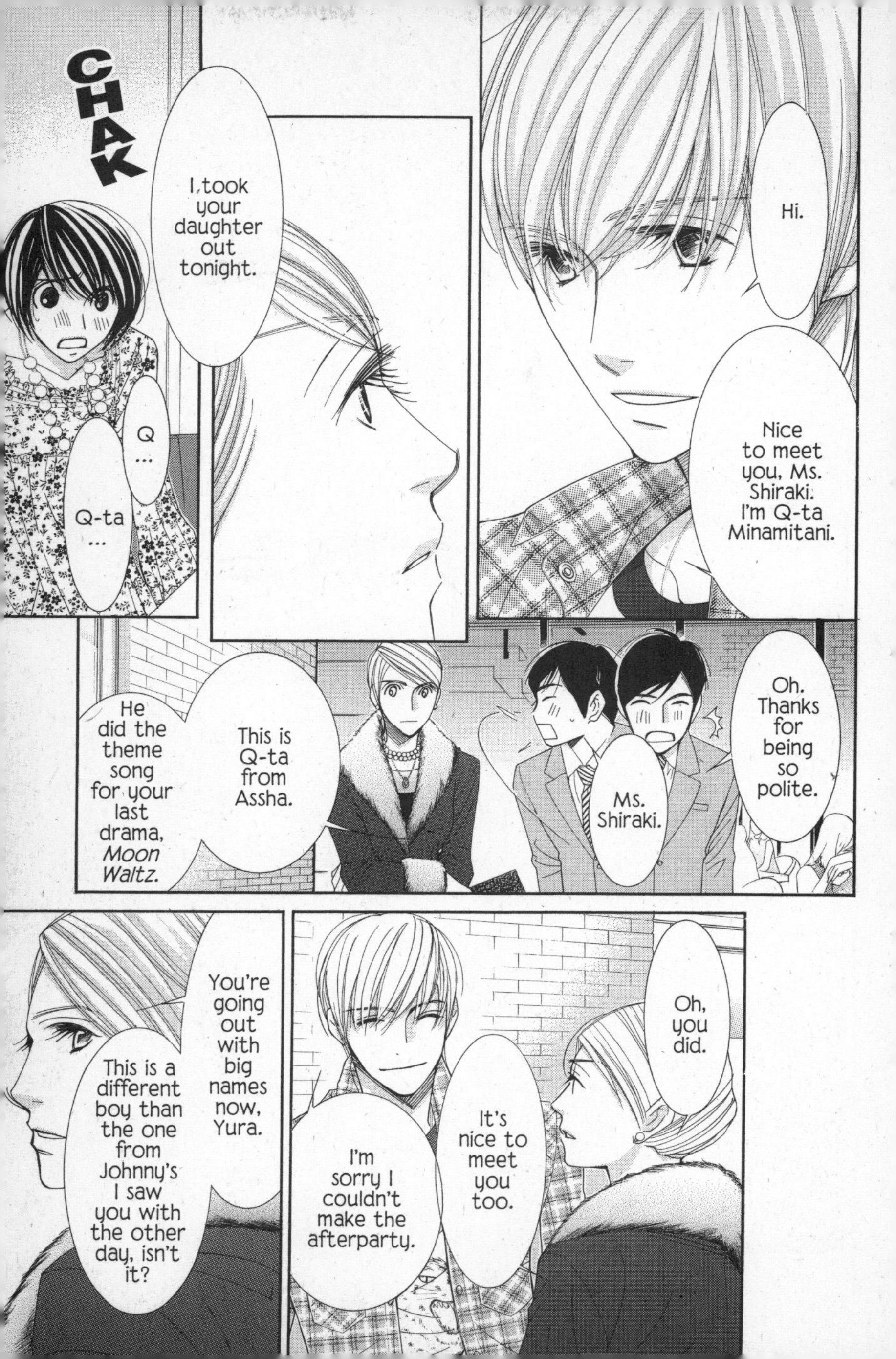
Hi.
Nice to meet you, Ms. Shiraki. I'm Q-ta Minamitani.
I took your daughter out tonight.
CHAK
Q ...
Q-ta ...
Oh. Thanks for being so polite.
Ms. Shiraki.
This is Q-ta from Assha.
He did the theme song for your last drama, *Moon Waltz*.
Oh, you did.
It's nice to meet you too.
I'm sorry I couldn't make the afterparty.
You're going out with big names now, Yura.
This is a different boy than the one from Johnny's I saw you with the other day, isn't it?

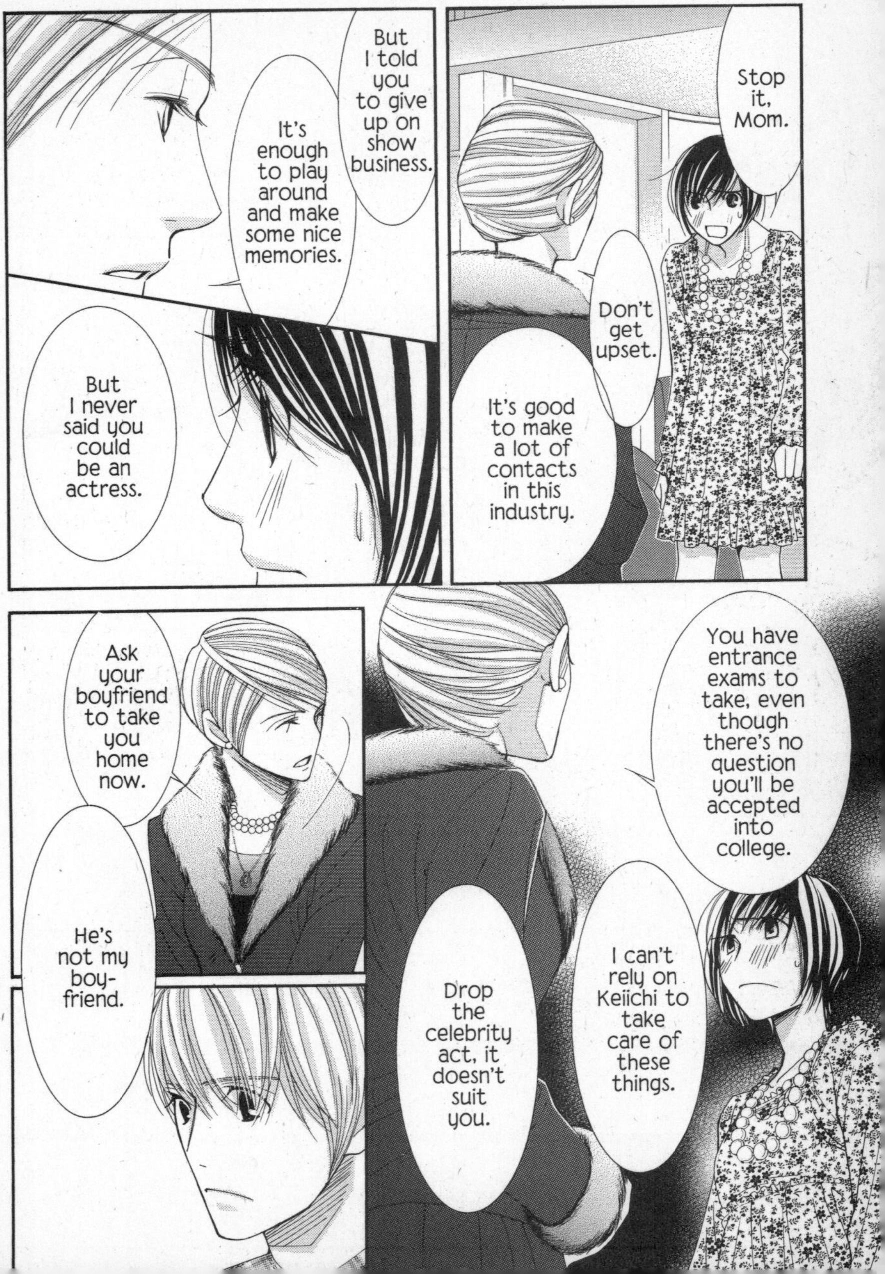
Stop it, Mom.
Don't get upset.
It's good to make a lot of contacts in this industry.
But I told you to give up on show business.
It's enough to play around and make some nice memories.
But I never said you could be an actress.
You have entrance exams to take, even though there's no question you'll be accepted into college.
I can't rely on Keiichi to take care of these things.
Drop the celebrity act, it doesn't suit you.
Ask your boyfriend to take you home now.
He's not my boy-friend.

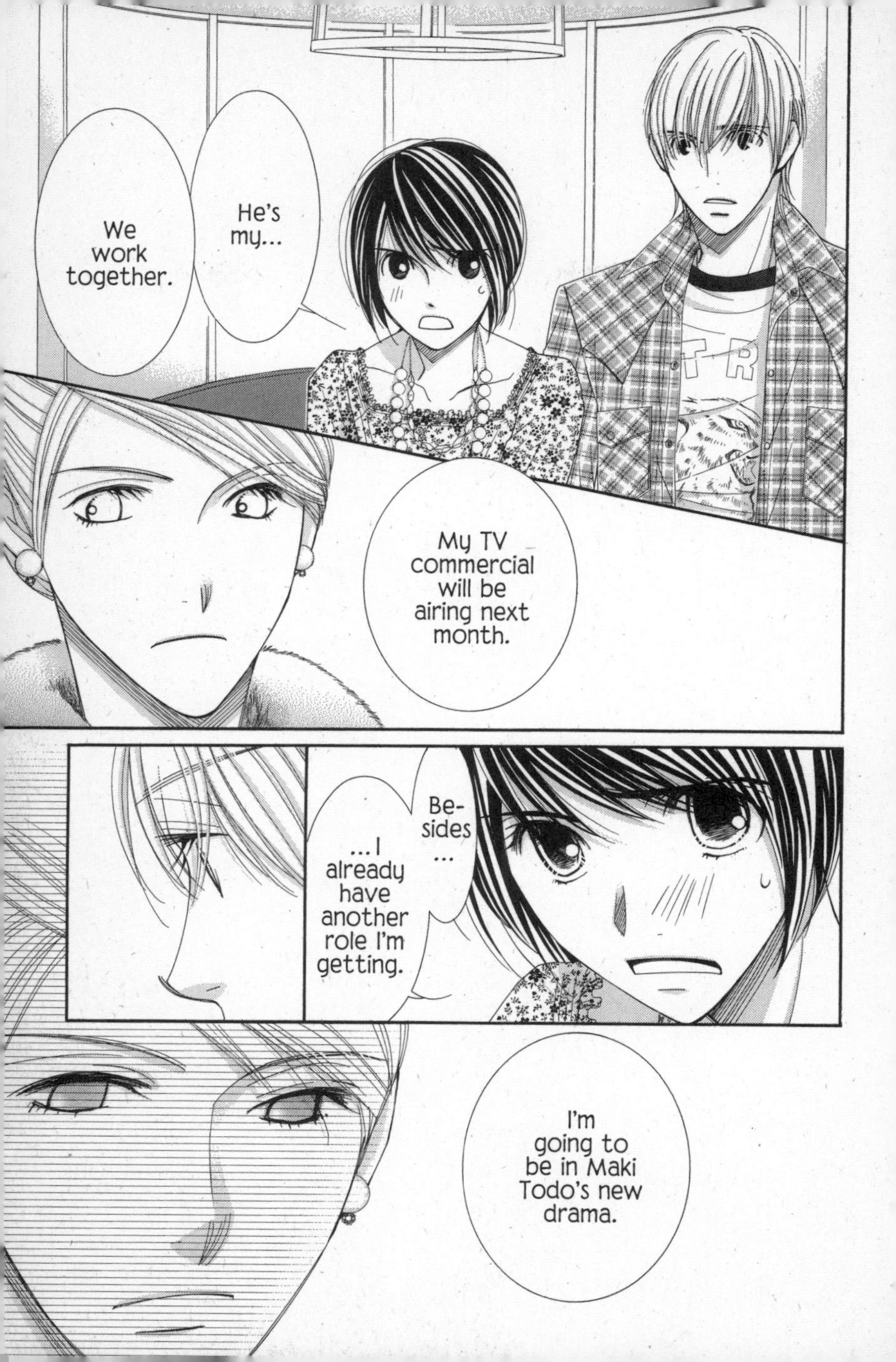
He's my...
We work together.
My TV commercial will be airing next month.
Be-sides...
...I already have another role I'm getting.
I'm going to be in Maki Todo's new drama.

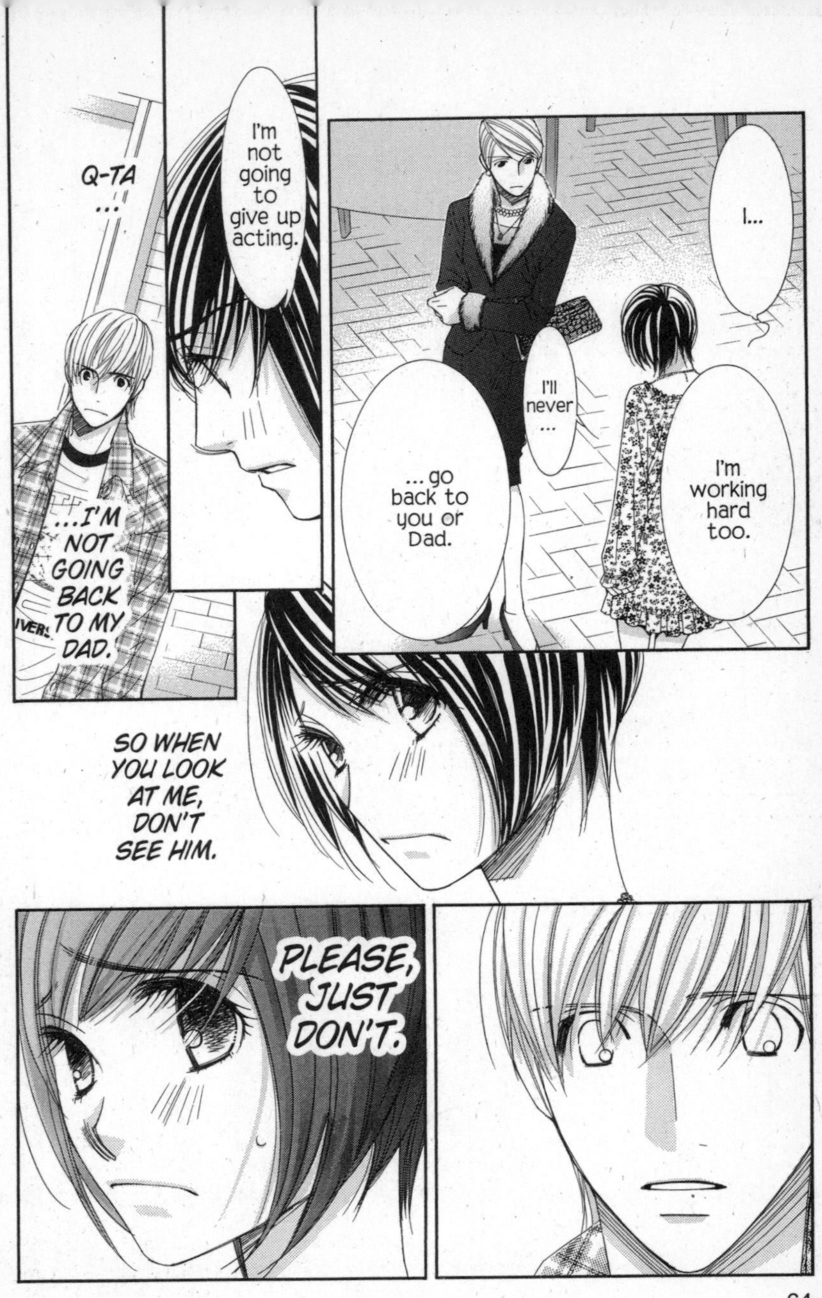
I...
I'm working hard too.
I'll never...
...go back to you or Dad.
I'm not going to give up acting.
Q-TA...
...I'M NOT GOING BACK TO MY DAD.
SO WHEN YOU LOOK AT ME, DON'T SEE HIM.
PLEASE, JUST DON'T.

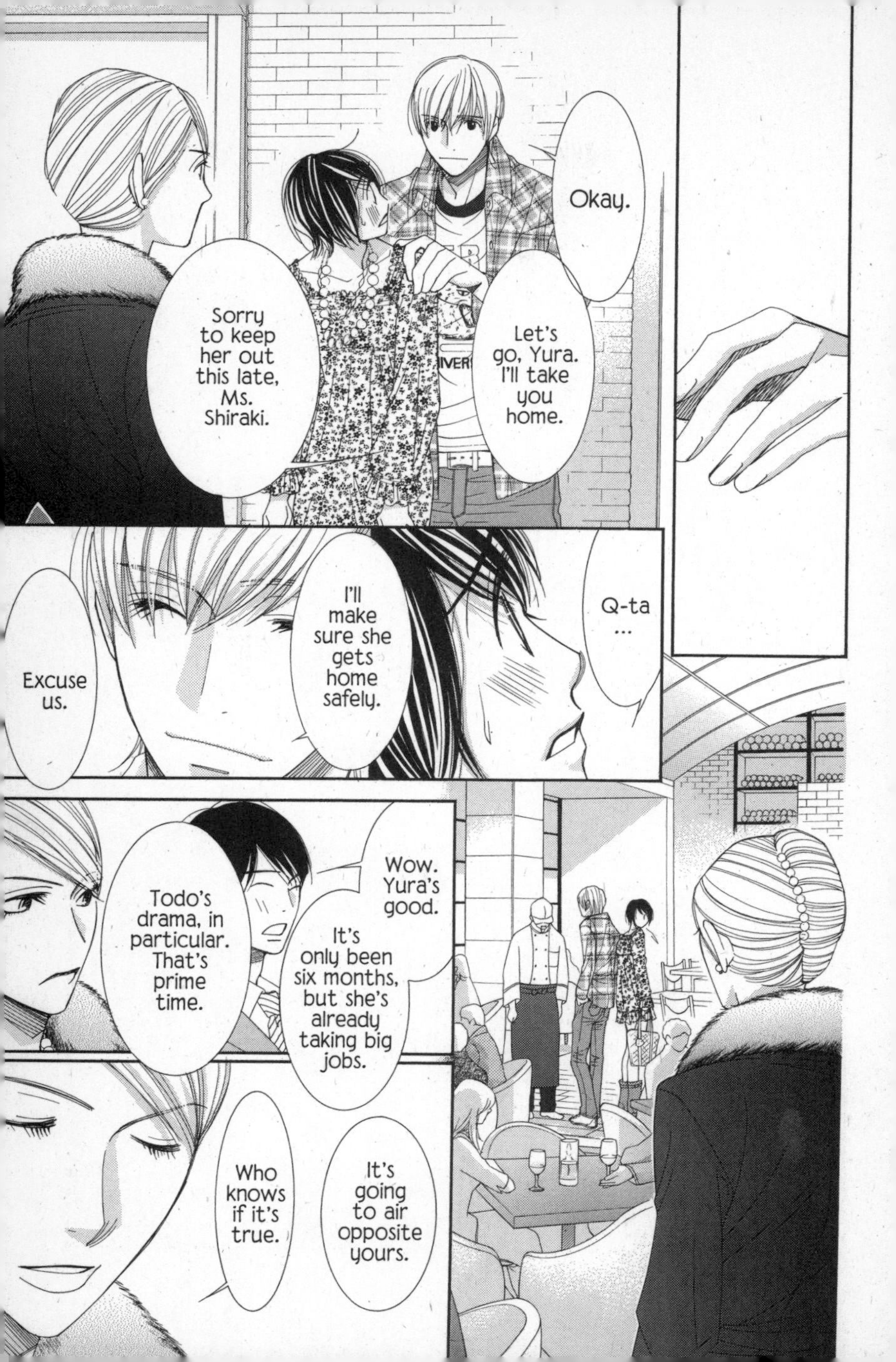
Okay.
Let's go, Yura. I'll take you home.
Sorry to keep her out this late, Ms. Shiraki.
Q-ta ...
I'll make sure she gets home safely.
Excuse us.
Wow. Yura's good.
It's only been six months, but she's already taking big jobs.
Todo's drama, in particular. That's prime time.
It's going to air opposite yours.
Who knows if it's true.

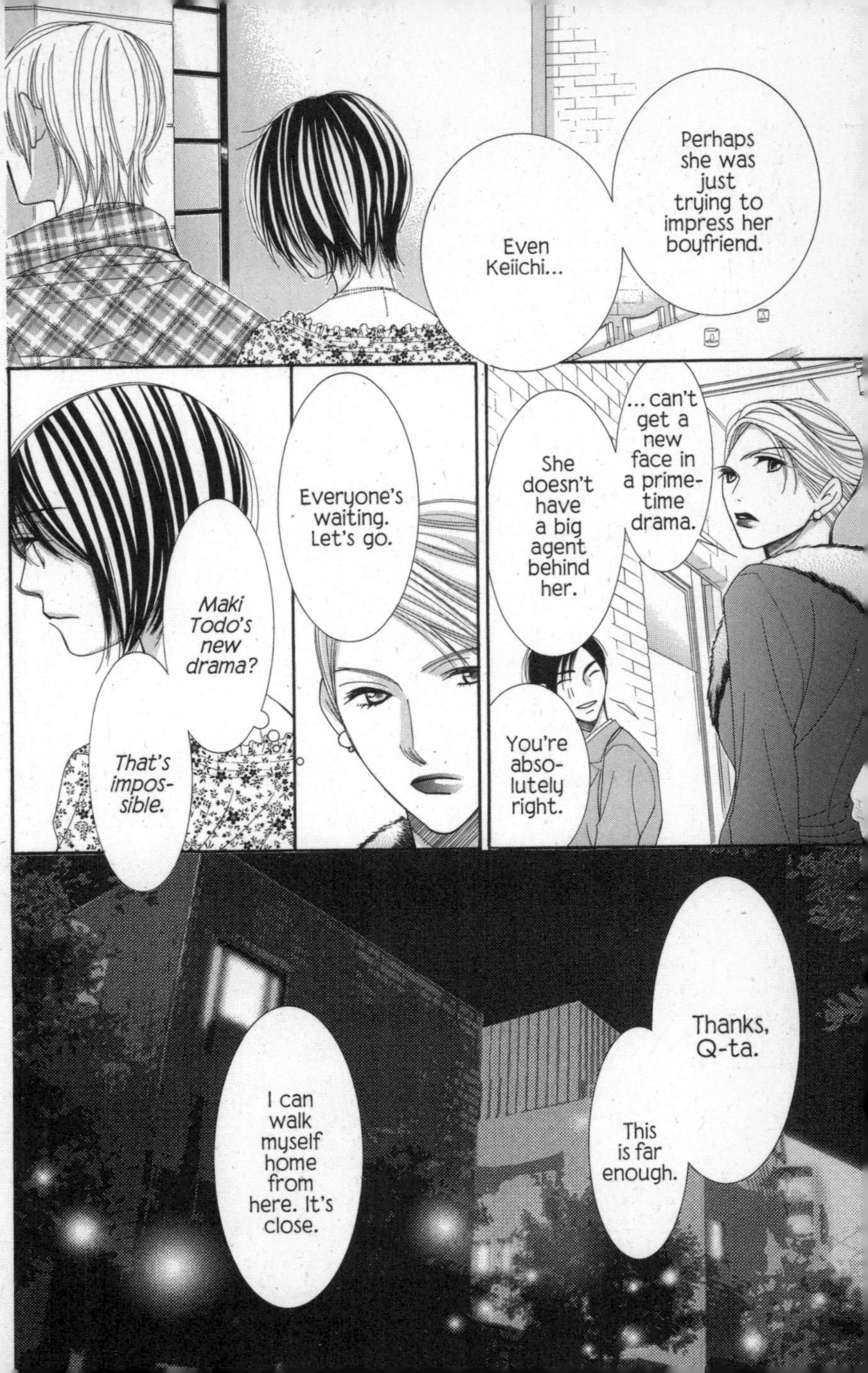
Perhaps she was just trying to impress her boyfriend.
Even Keiichi...
...can't get a new face in a prime-time drama.
She doesn't have a big agent behind her.
You're absolutely right.
Everyone's waiting. Let's go.
Maki Todo's new drama?
That's impossible.
Thanks, Q-ta.
This is far enough.
I can walk myself home from here. It's close.

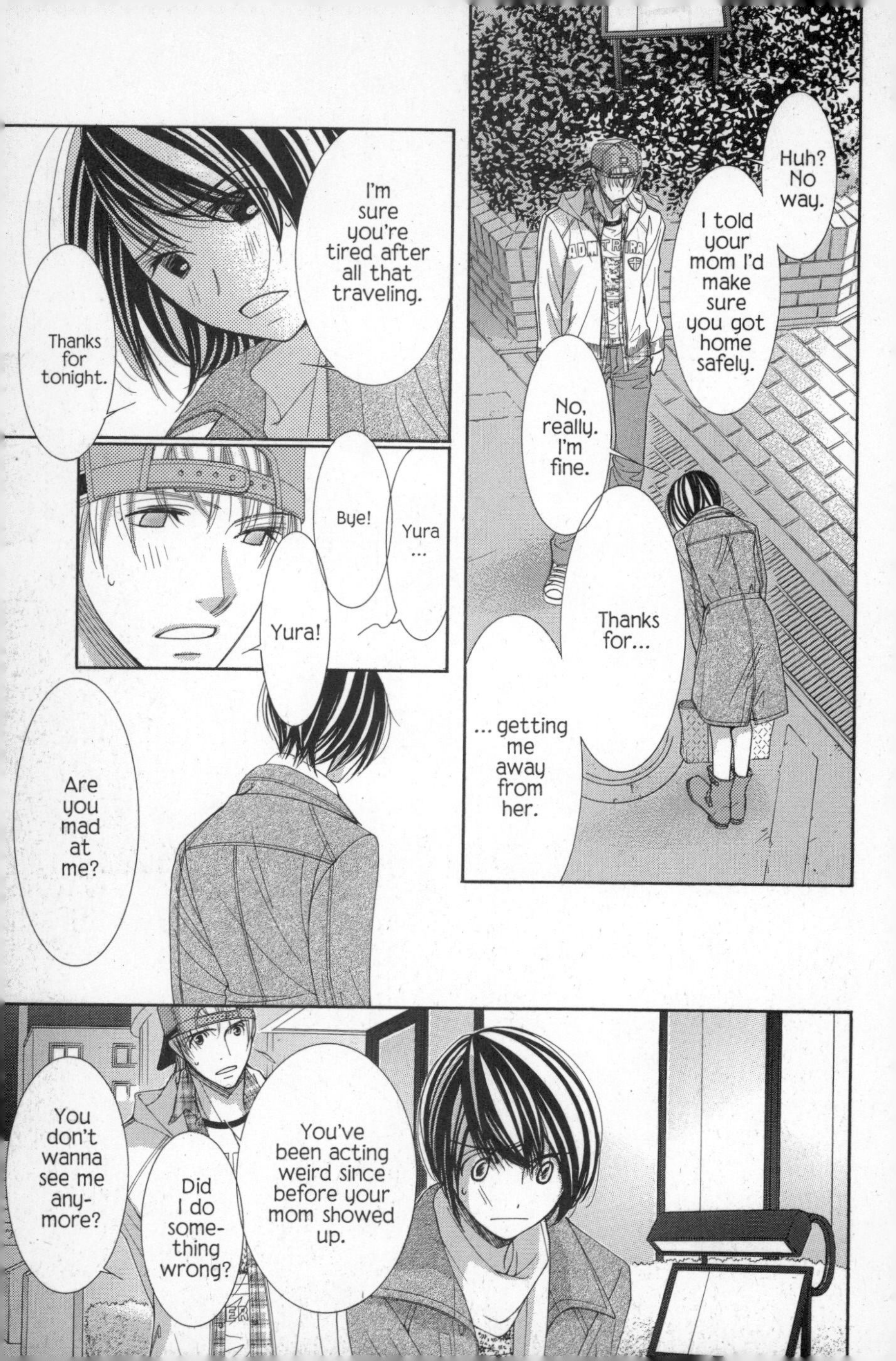
Huh? No way.
I told your mom I'd make sure you got home safely.
No, really. I'm fine.
Thanks for...
... getting me away from her.
I'm sure you're tired after all that traveling.
Thanks for tonight.
Yura ...
Bye!
Yura!
Are you mad at me?
You've been acting weird since before your mom showed up.
Did I do some-thing wrong?
You don't wanna see me any-more?

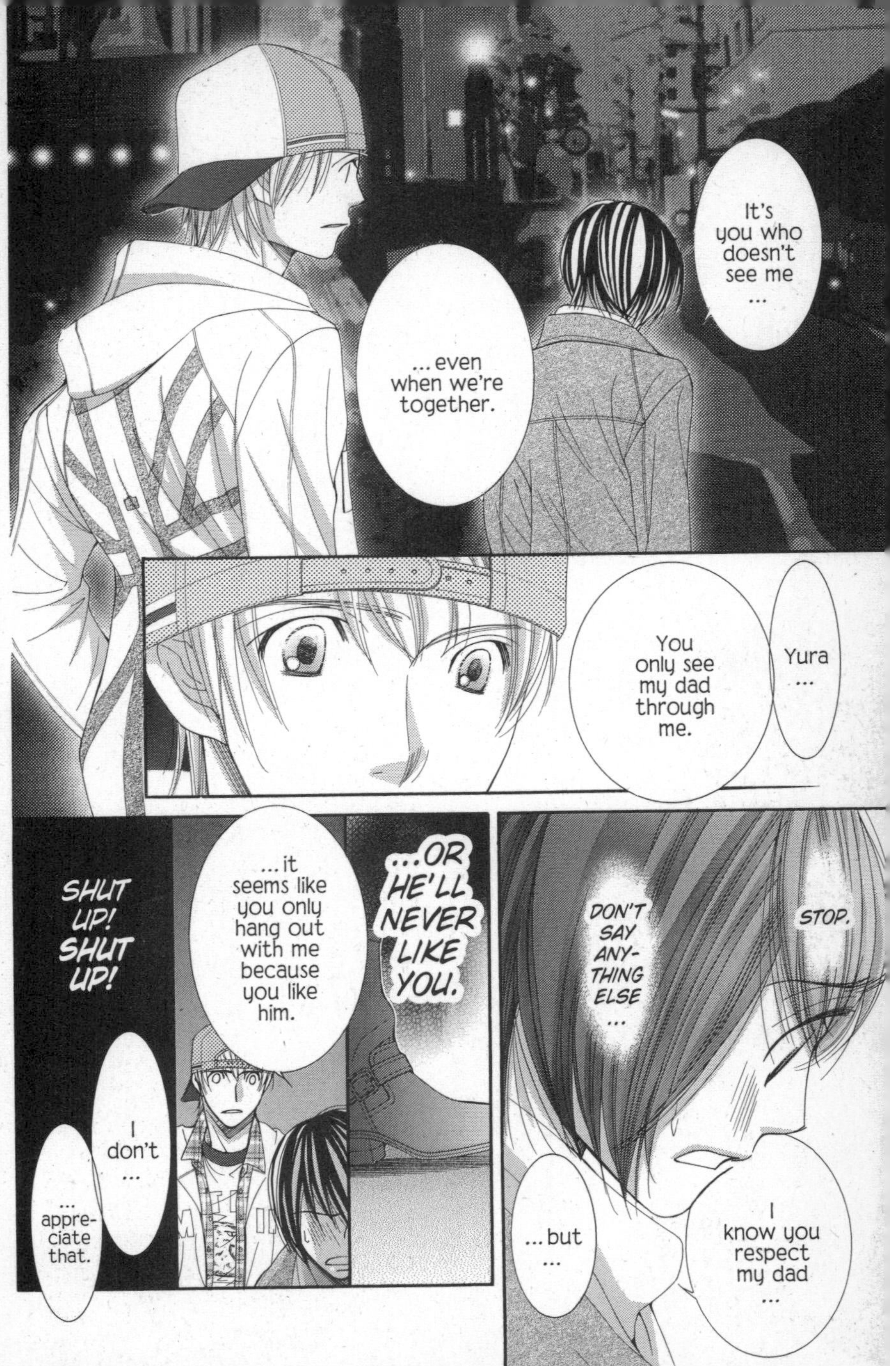
It's you who doesn't see me ...
... even when we're together.
Yura ...
You only see my dad through me.
STOP.
DON'T SAY ANY-THING ELSE ...
I know you respect my dad ...
... but ...
...OR HE'LL NEVER LIKE YOU.
... it seems like you only hang out with me because you like him.
SHUT UP! SHUT UP!
I don't ...
... appre-ciate that.

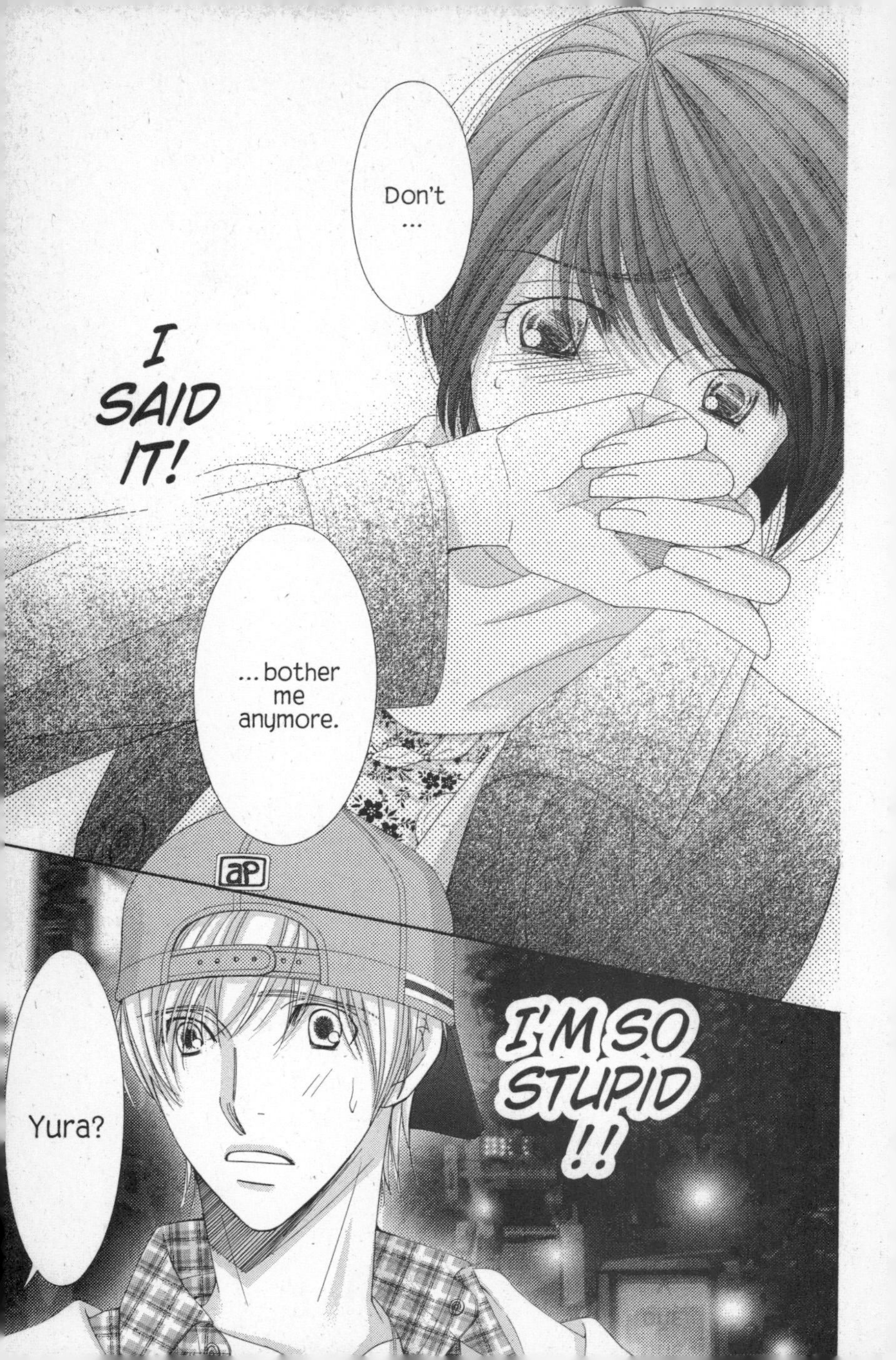

Don't ...
I SAID IT!
...bother me anymore.
I'M SO STUPID !!
Yura?

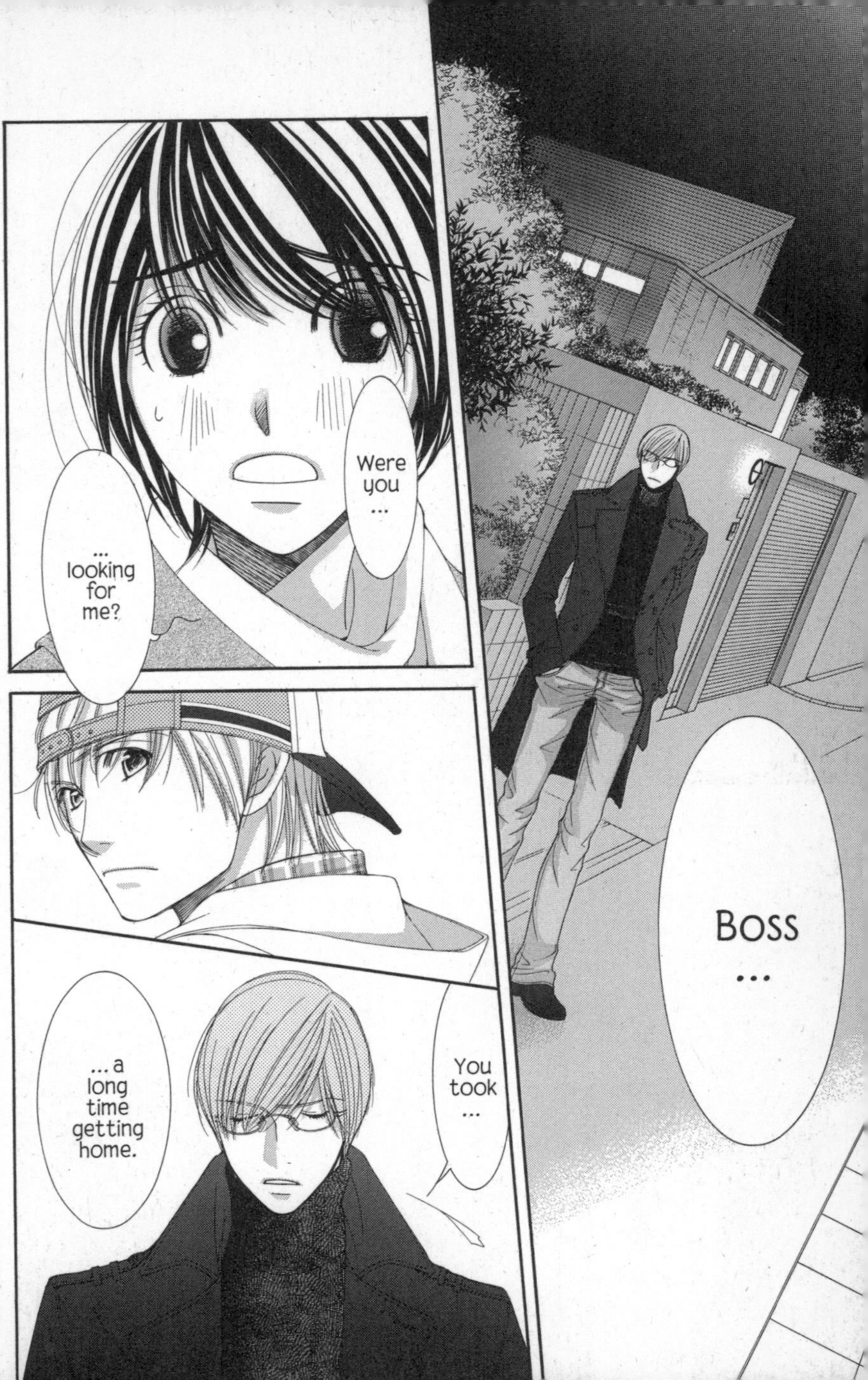
Boss ...
Were you ...
... looking for me?
You took ...
... a long time getting home.

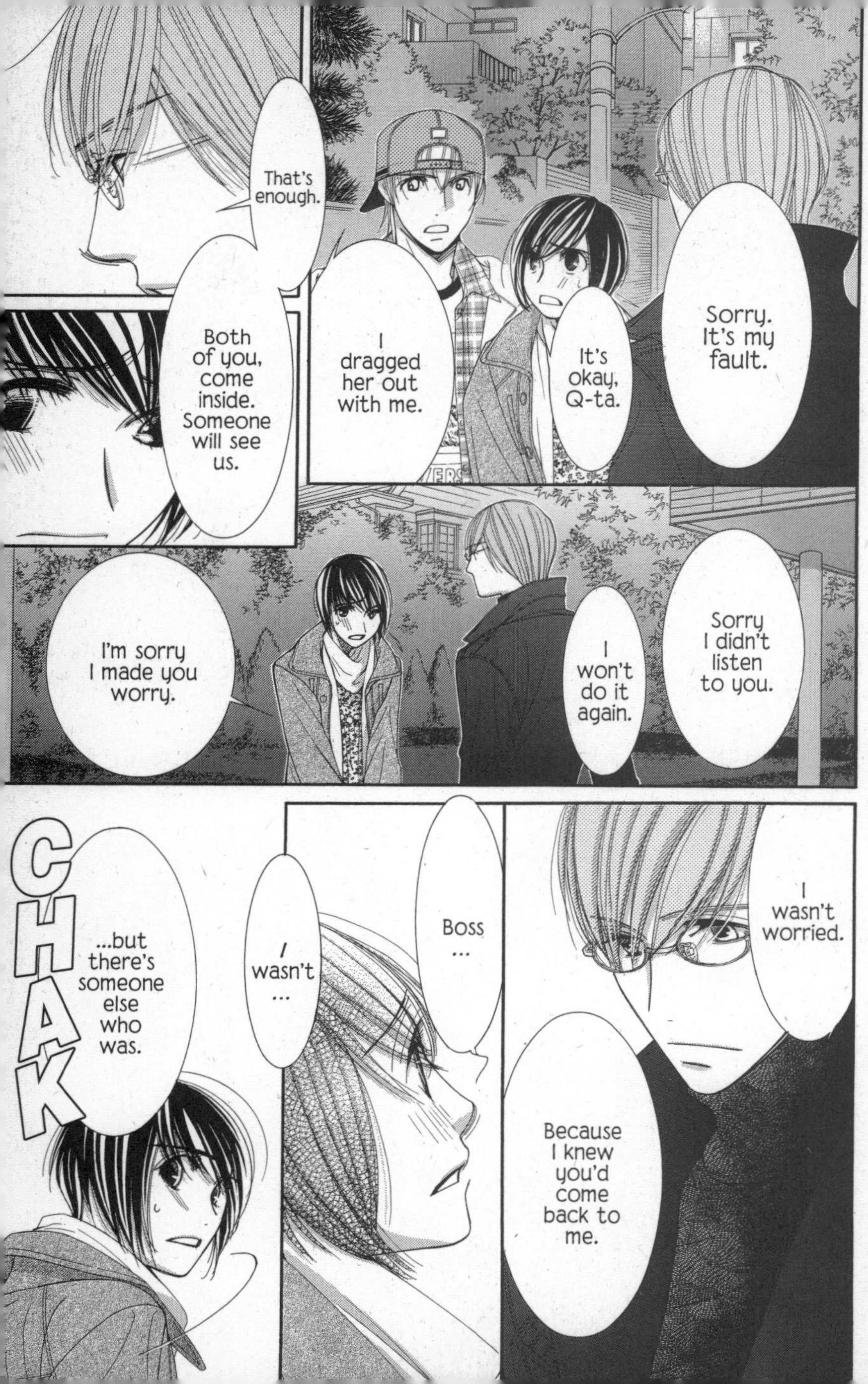
Sorry. It's my fault.
It's okay, Q-ta.
I dragged her out with me.
That's enough.
Both of you, come inside. Someone will see us.
Sorry I didn't listen to you.
I won't do it again.
I'm sorry I made you worry.
I wasn't worried.
Because I knew you'd come back to me.
Boss...
I wasn't...
...but there's someone else who was.
CHAK

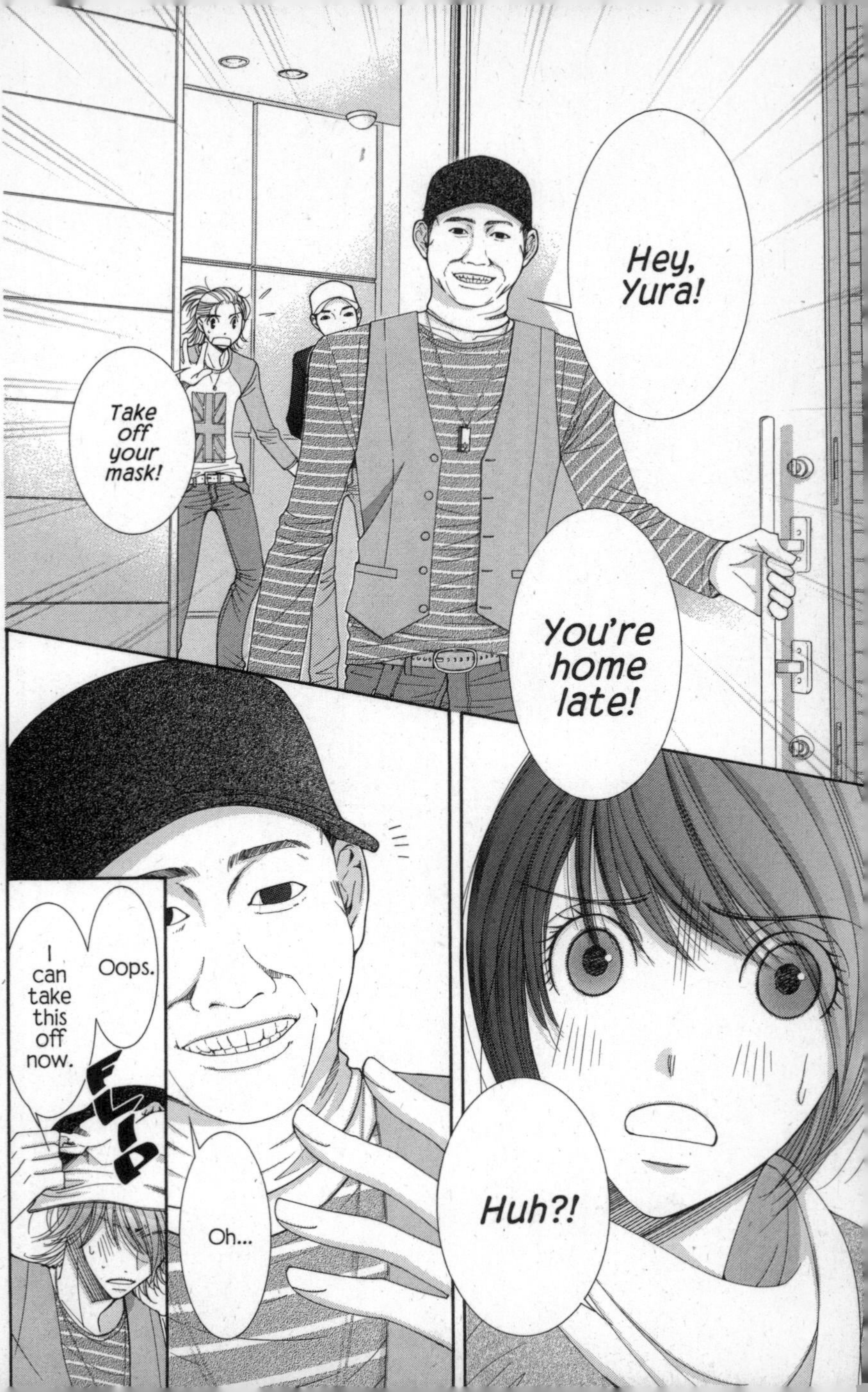
Hey, Yura!
You're home late!
Take off your mask!
Huh?!
Oh...
Oops.
I can take this off now.
FLIP

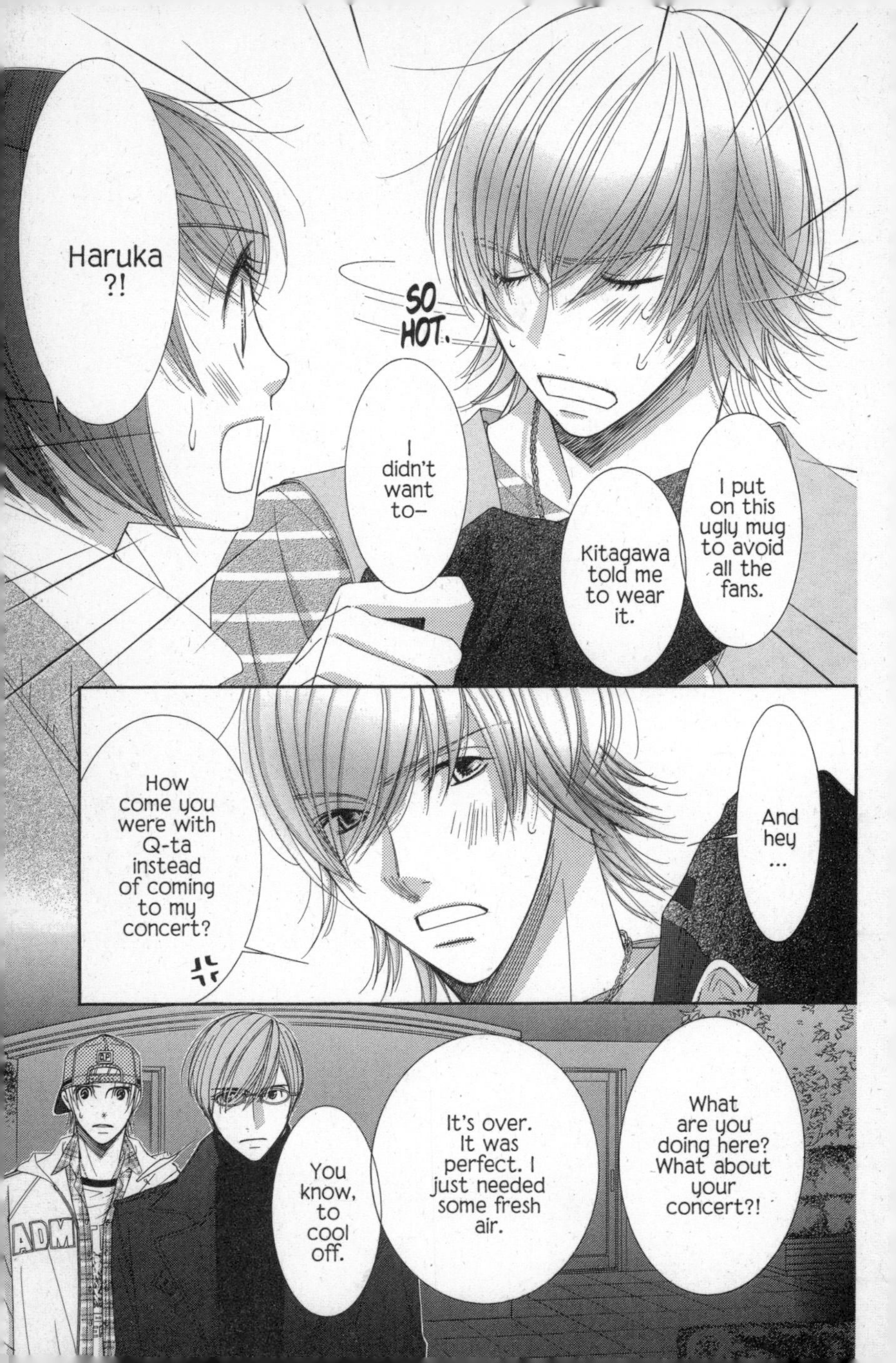
Haruka ?!
SO HOT.
I put on this ugly mug to avoid all the fans.
Kitagawa told me to wear it.
I didn't want to–
And hey ...
How come you were with Q-ta instead of coming to my concert?
What are you doing here? What about your concert?!
It's over. It was perfect. I just needed some fresh air.
You know, to cool off.

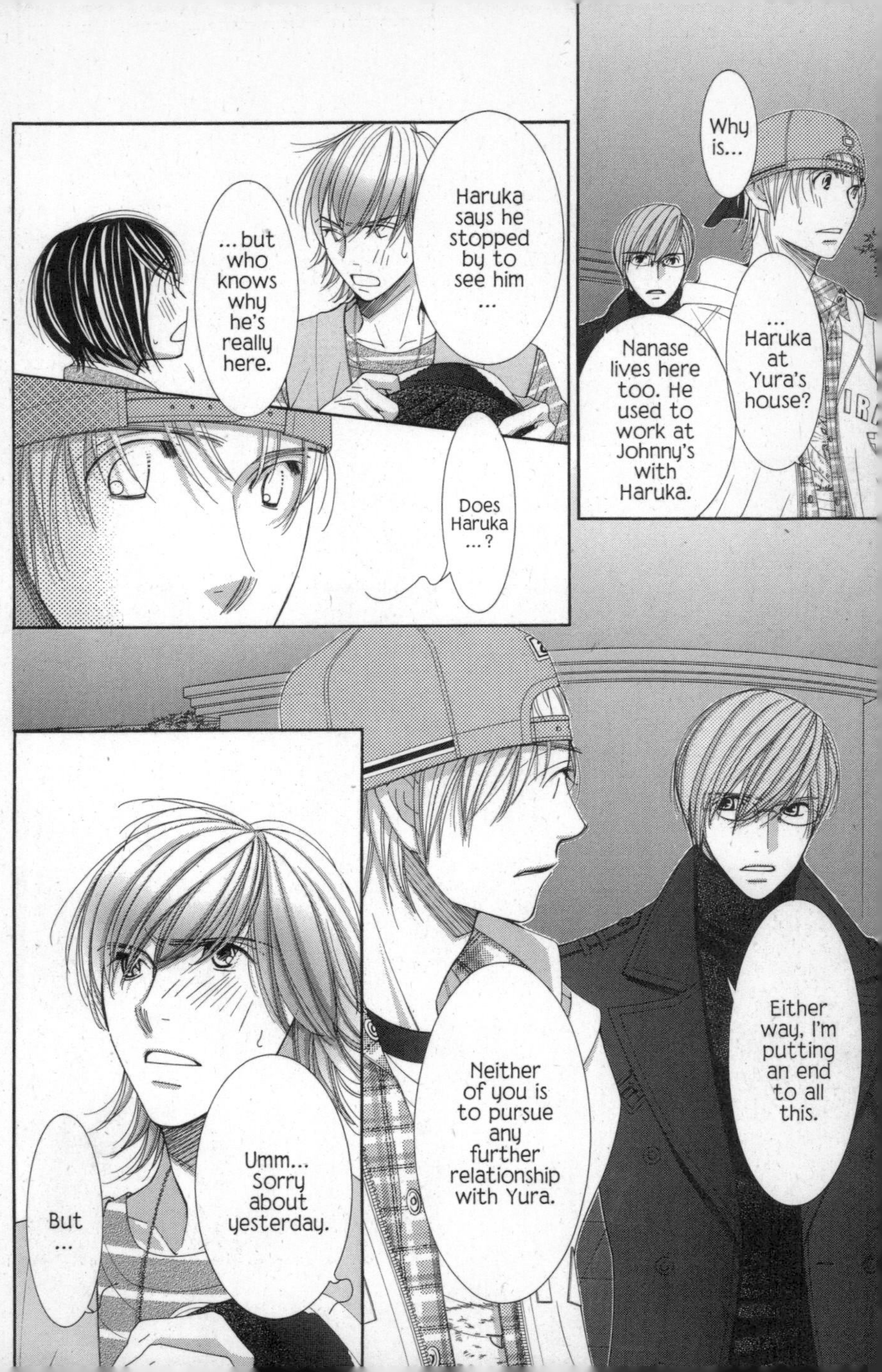
Why is...
... Haruka at Yura's house?
Nanase lives here too. He used to work at Johnny's with Haruka.
Haruka says he stopped by to see him ...
... but who knows why he's really here.
Does Haruka ...?
Either way, I'm putting an end to all this.
Neither of you is to pursue any further relationship with Yura.
Umm... Sorry about yesterday.
But ...

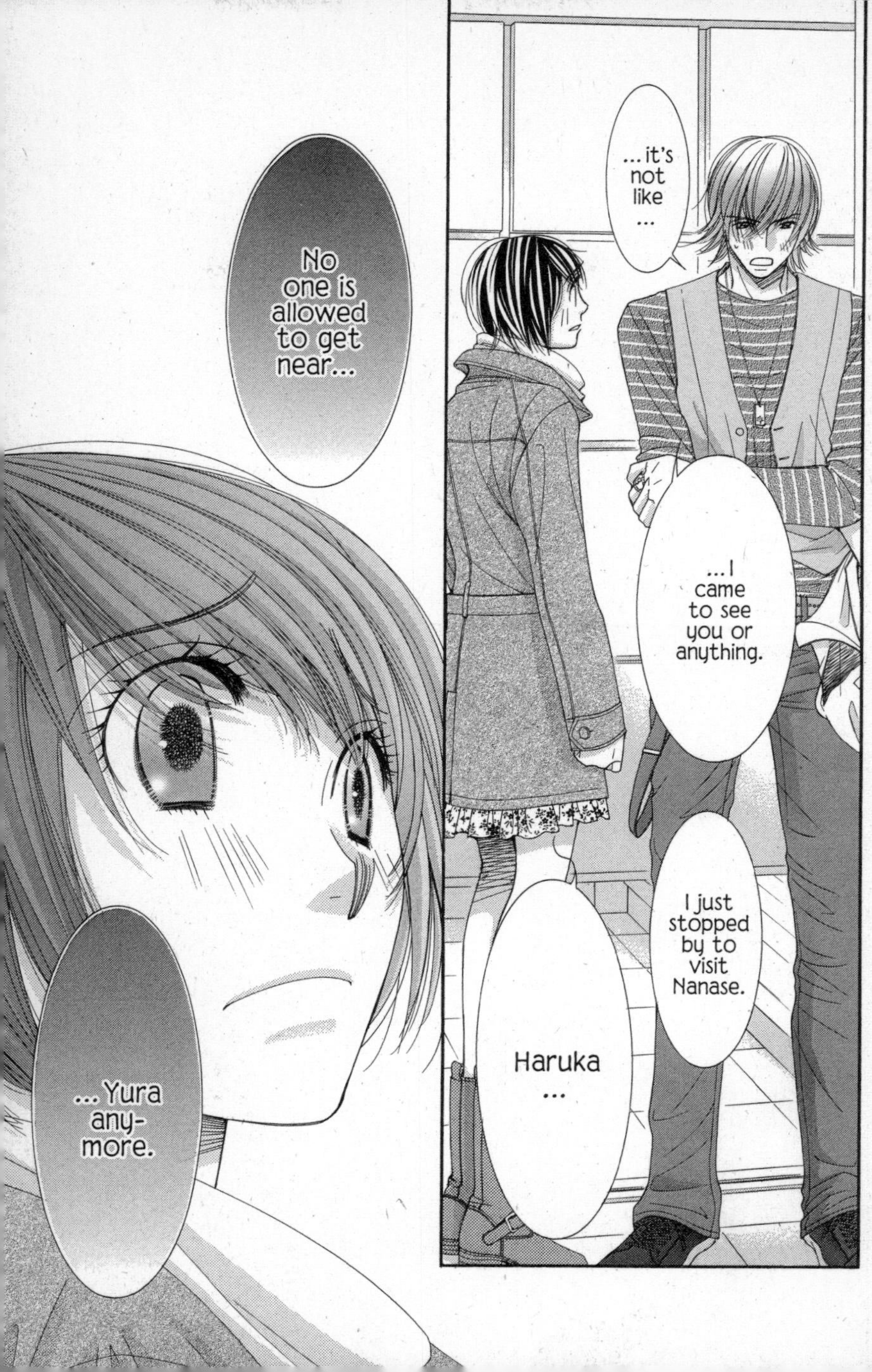
...it's not like ...
...I came to see you or anything.
I just stopped by to visit Nanase.
Haruka ...
No one is allowed to get near...
...Yura anymore.

Yukari Shiraki
(age: secret) Blood type A

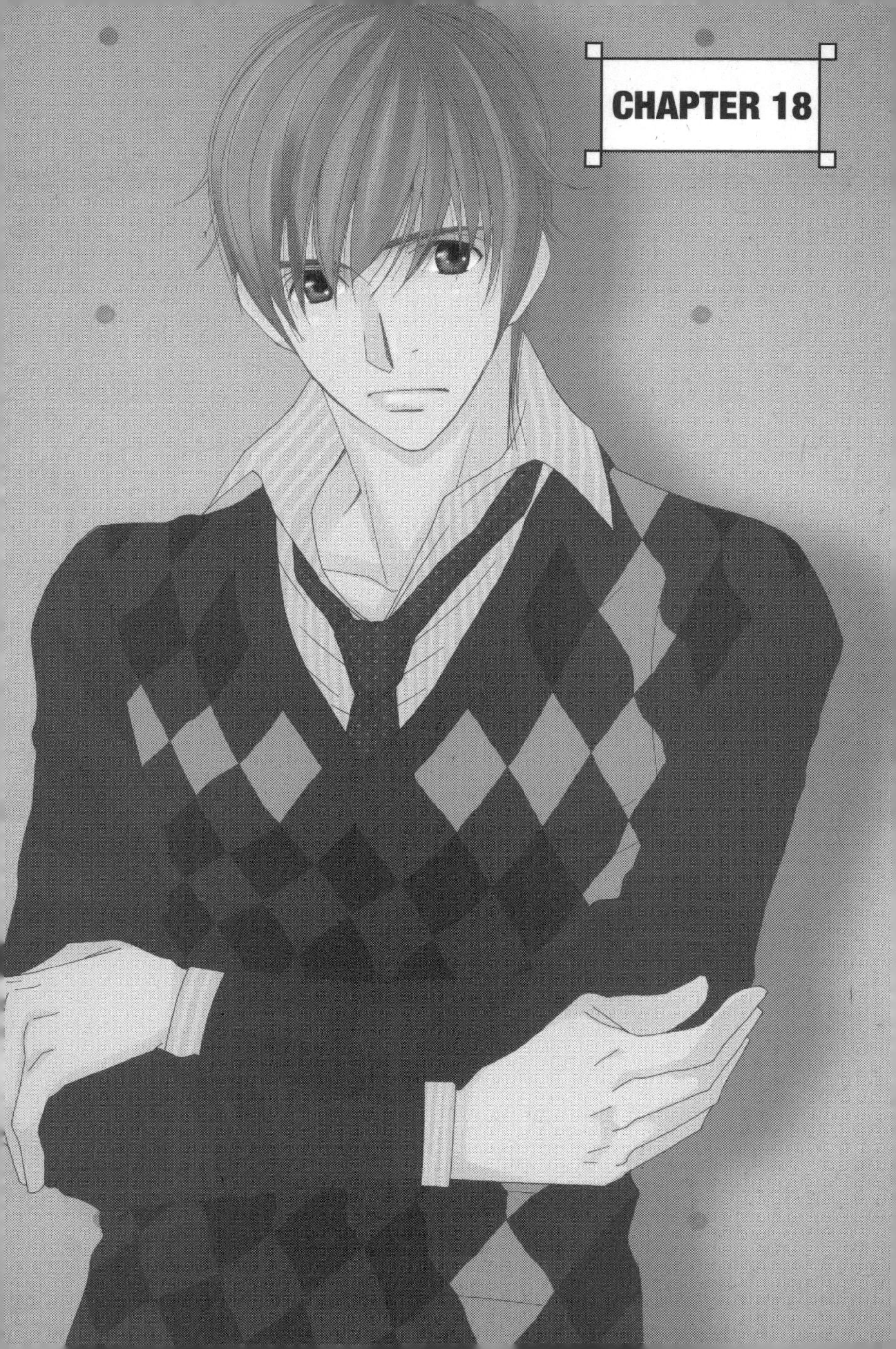
CHAPTER 18

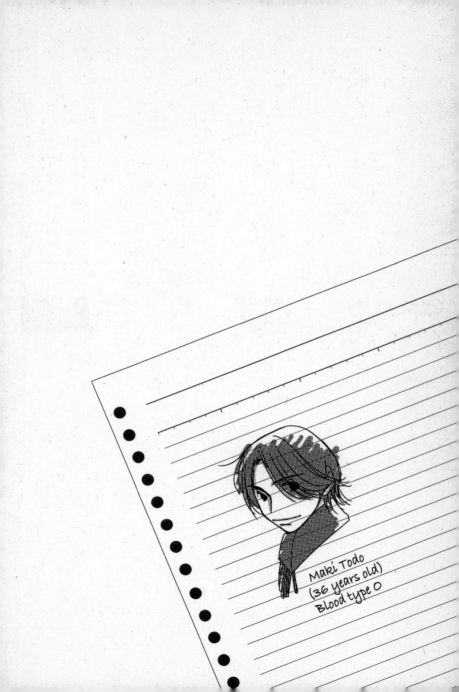

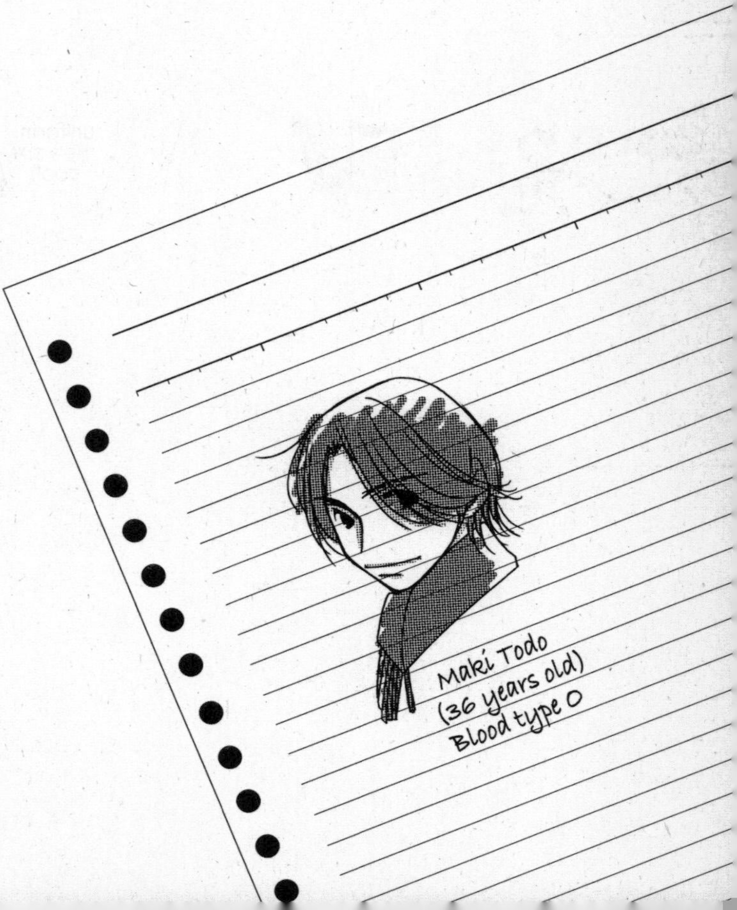
Maki Todo
(36 years old)
Blood type O

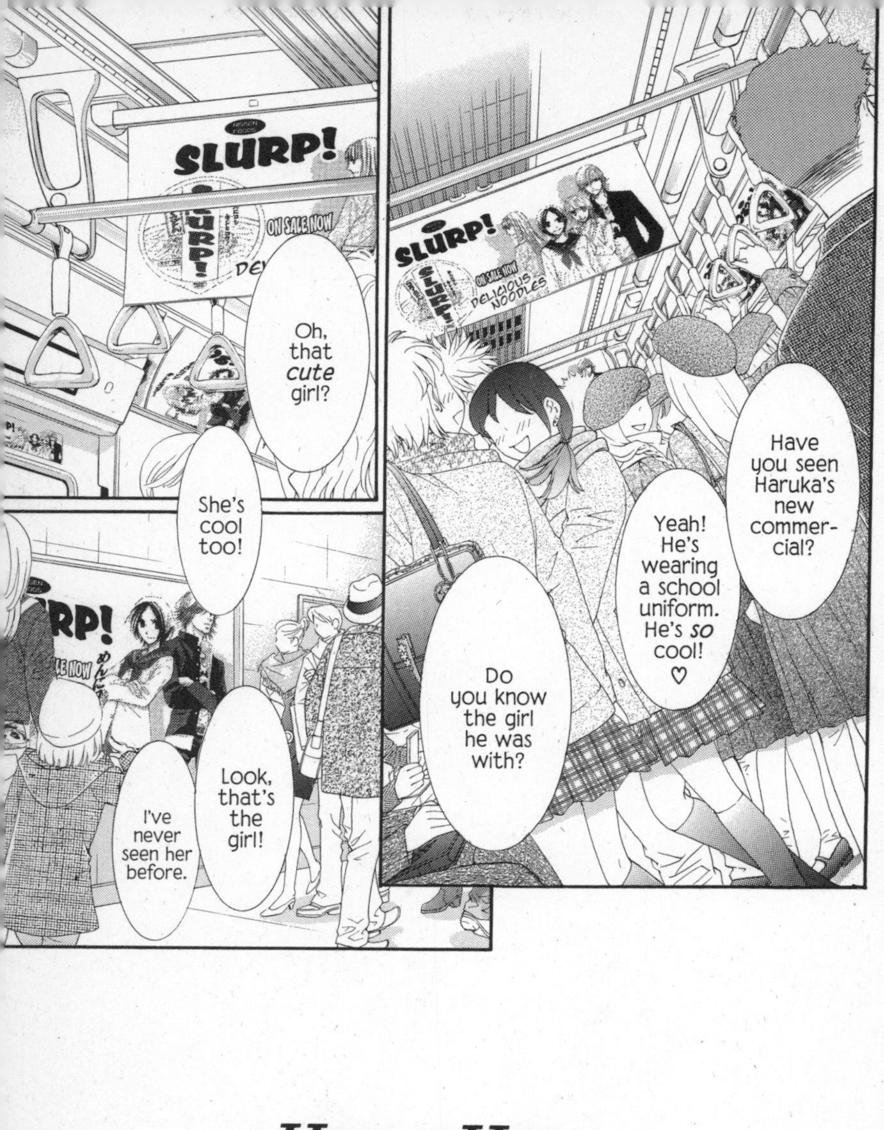
Have you seen Haruka's new commercial?
Yeah! He's wearing a school uniform. He's *so* cool! ♡
Do you know the girl he was with?
SLURP!
ON SALE NOW
DELICIOUS NOODLES
Oh, that *cute* girl?
She's cool too!
SLURP!
ON SALE NOW
Look, that's the girl!
I've never seen her before.

Honey Hunt

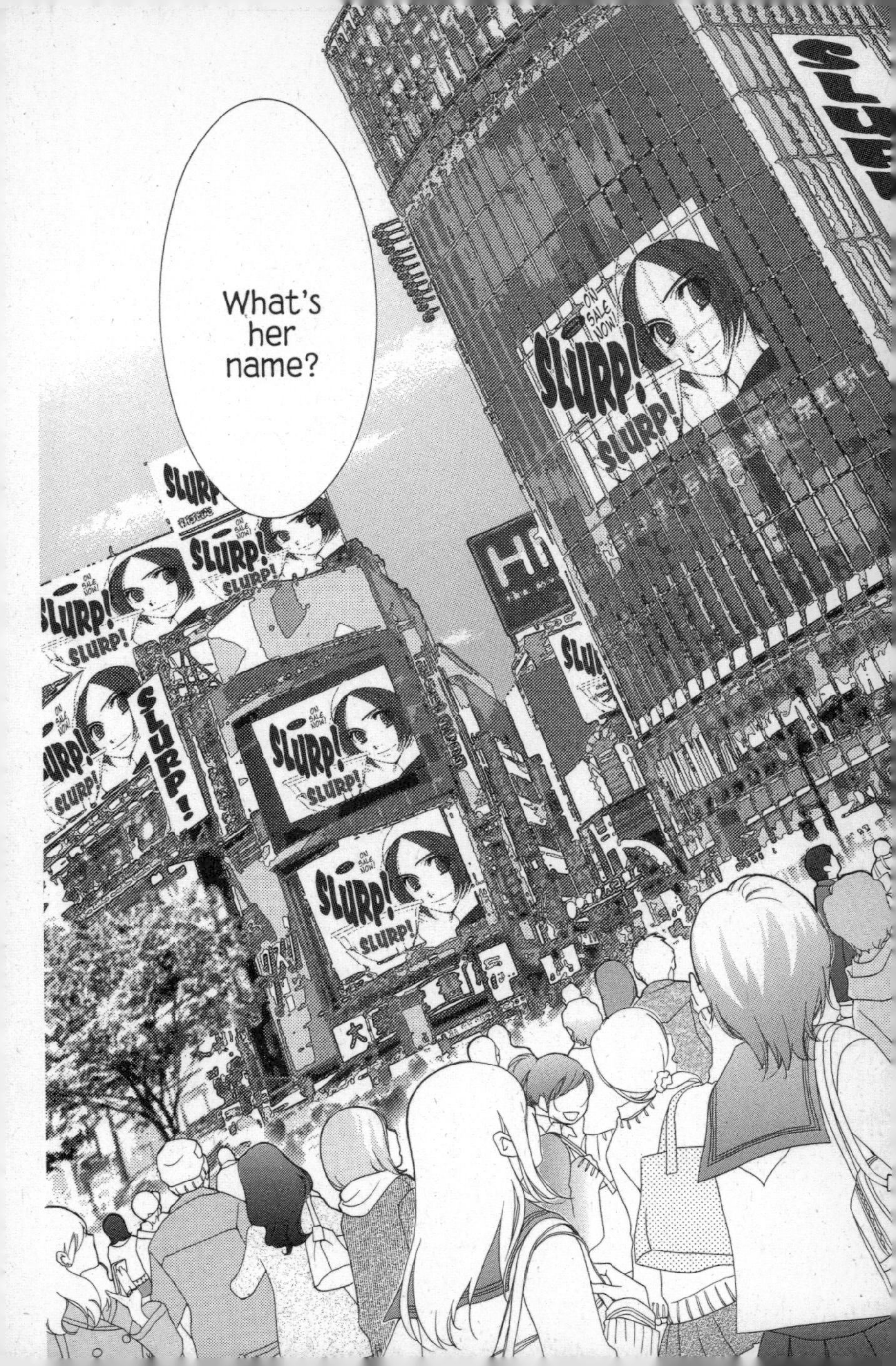
What's her name?
ON SALE NOW!
SLURP! SLURP!
SLURP! SLURP!
ON SALE NOW!
SLURP! SLURP!
ON SALE NOW!
SLURP! SLURP!

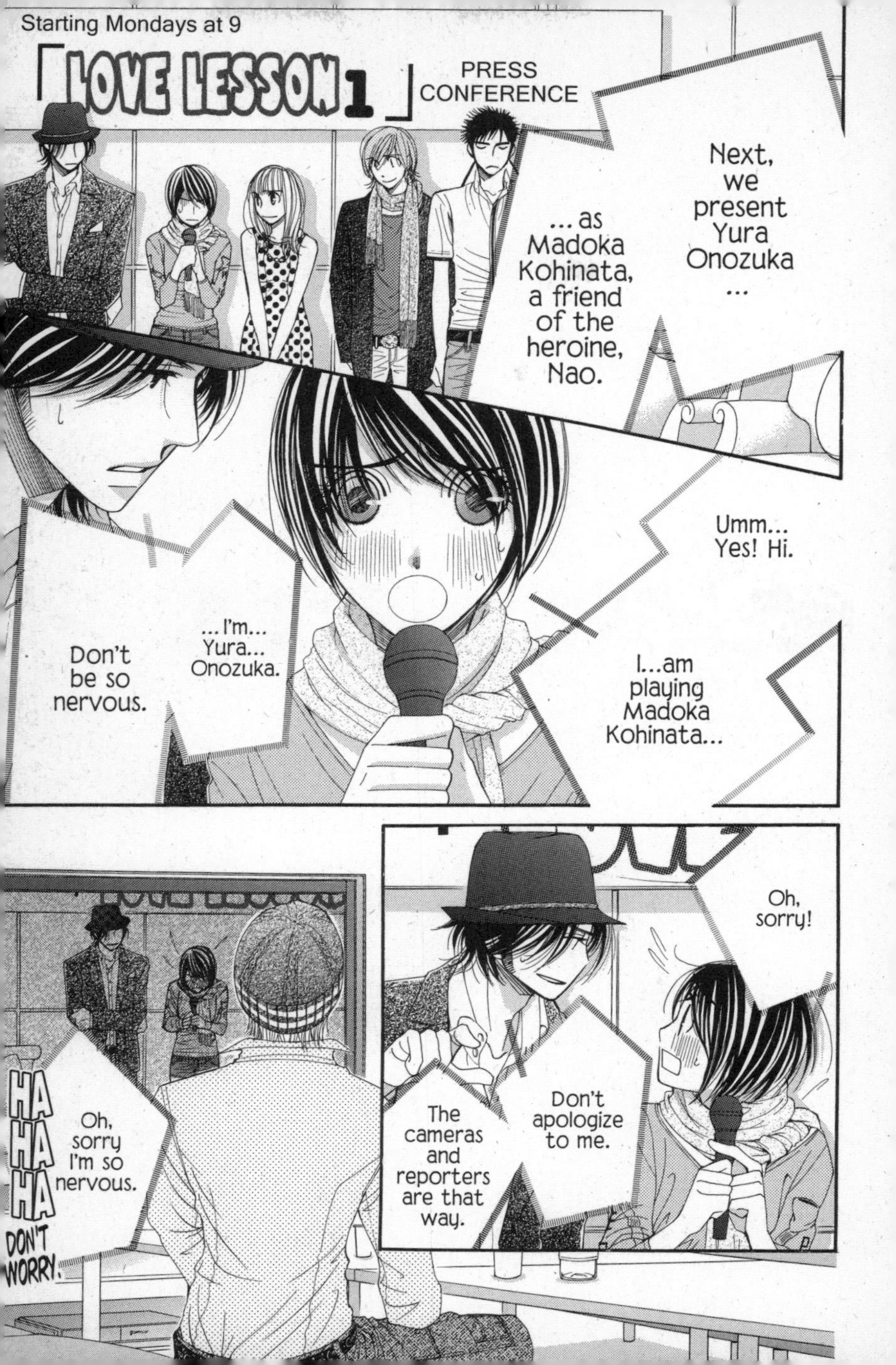
Next, we present Yura Onozuka...
...as Madoka Kohinata, a friend of the heroine, Nao.
Starting Mondays at 9
「LOVE LESSON 1」
PRESS CONFERENCE
Umm... Yes! Hi.
I...am playing Madoka Kohinata...
...I'm... Yura... Onozuka.
Don't be so nervous.
Oh, sorry!
Don't apologize to me.
The cameras and reporters are that way.
Oh, sorry I'm so nervous.
HA HA HA
DON'T WORRY.

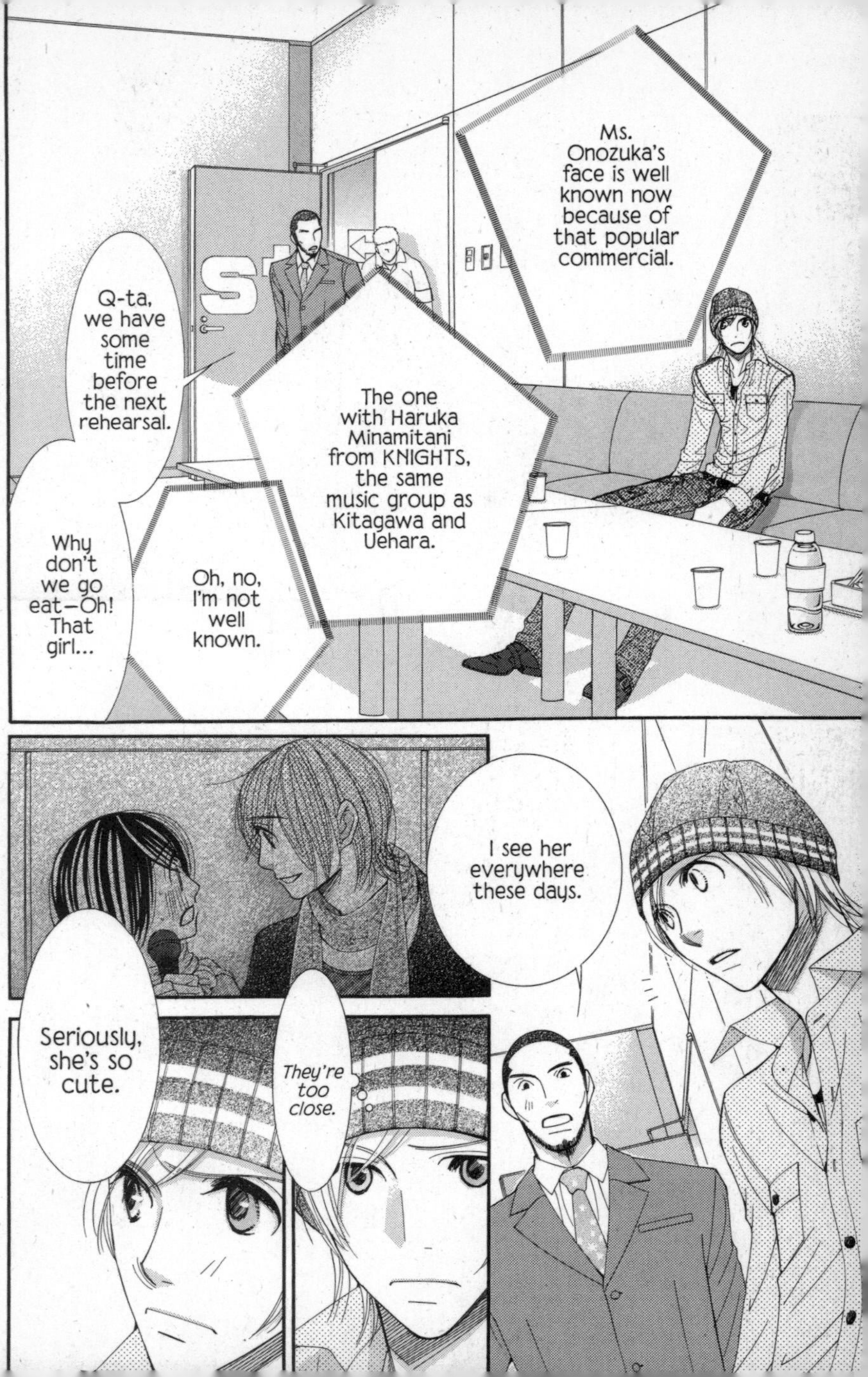

Ms. Onozuka's face is well known now because of that popular commercial.
The one with Haruka Minamitani from KNIGHTS, the same music group as Kitagawa and Uehara.
Oh, no, I'm not well known.
Q-ta, we have some time before the next rehearsal.
Why don't we go eat—Oh! That girl...
I see her everywhere these days.
They're too close.
Seriously, she's so cute.

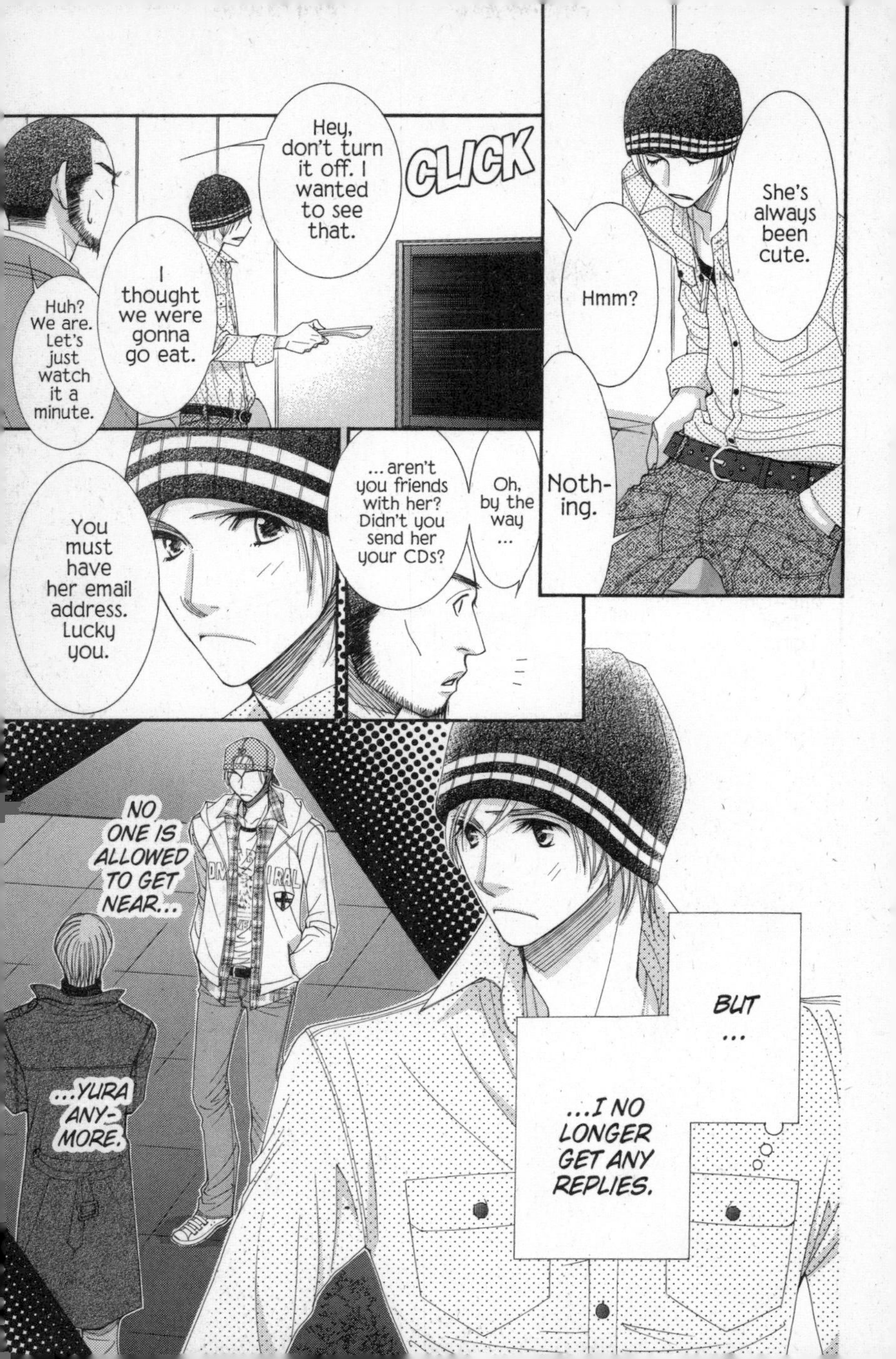
She's always been cute.
Hmm?
Nothing.
CLICK
Hey, don't turn it off. I wanted to see that.
I thought we were gonna go eat.
Huh? We are. Let's just watch it a minute.
Oh, by the way ...
...aren't you friends with her? Didn't you send her your CDs?
You must have her email address. Lucky you.
BUT ...
...I NO LONGER GET ANY REPLIES.
NO ONE IS ALLOWED TO GET NEAR...
...YURA ANY-MORE.

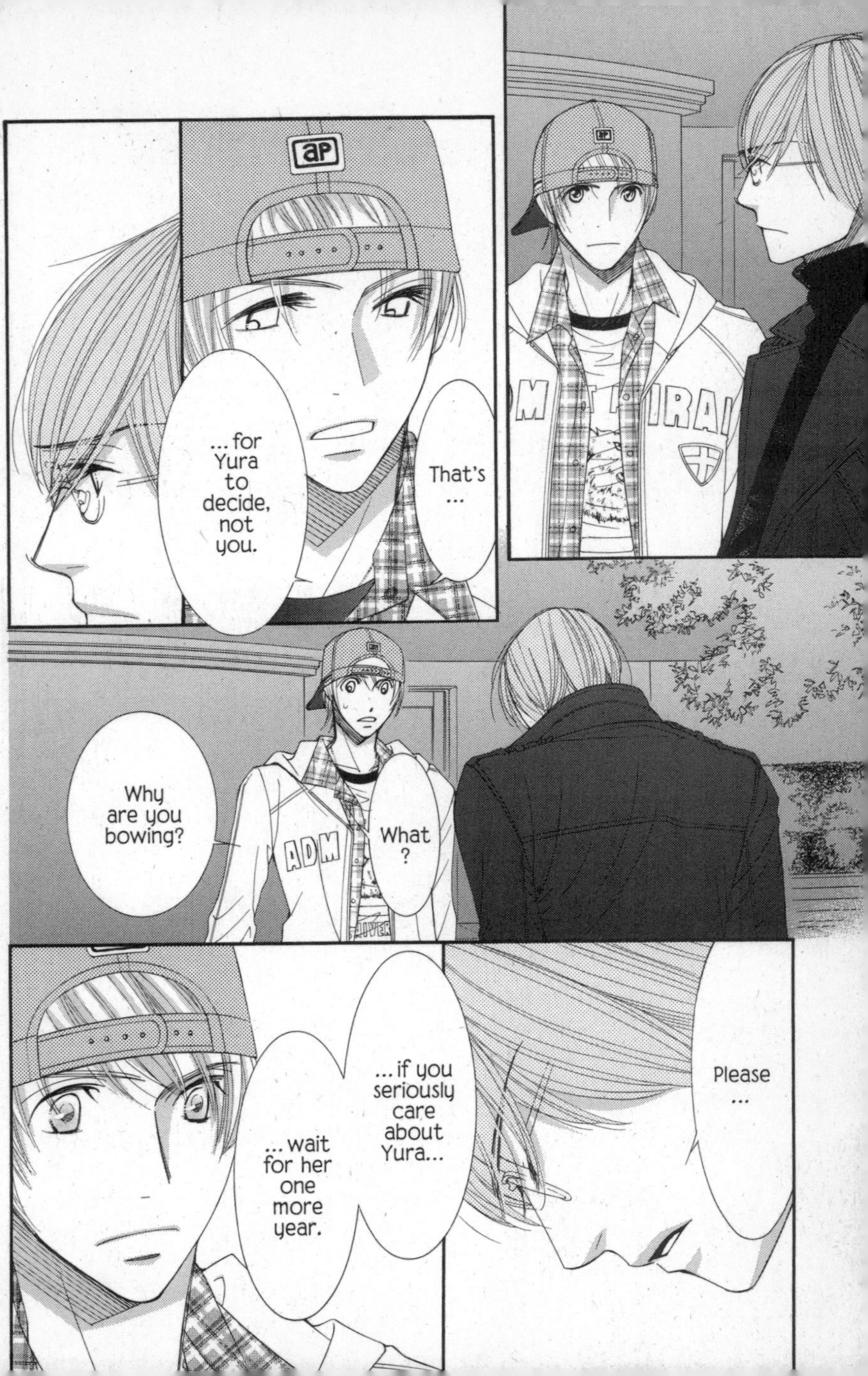
That's ...
... for Yura to decide, not you.
What?
Why are you bowing?
Please ...
... if you seriously care about Yura...
... wait for her one more year.

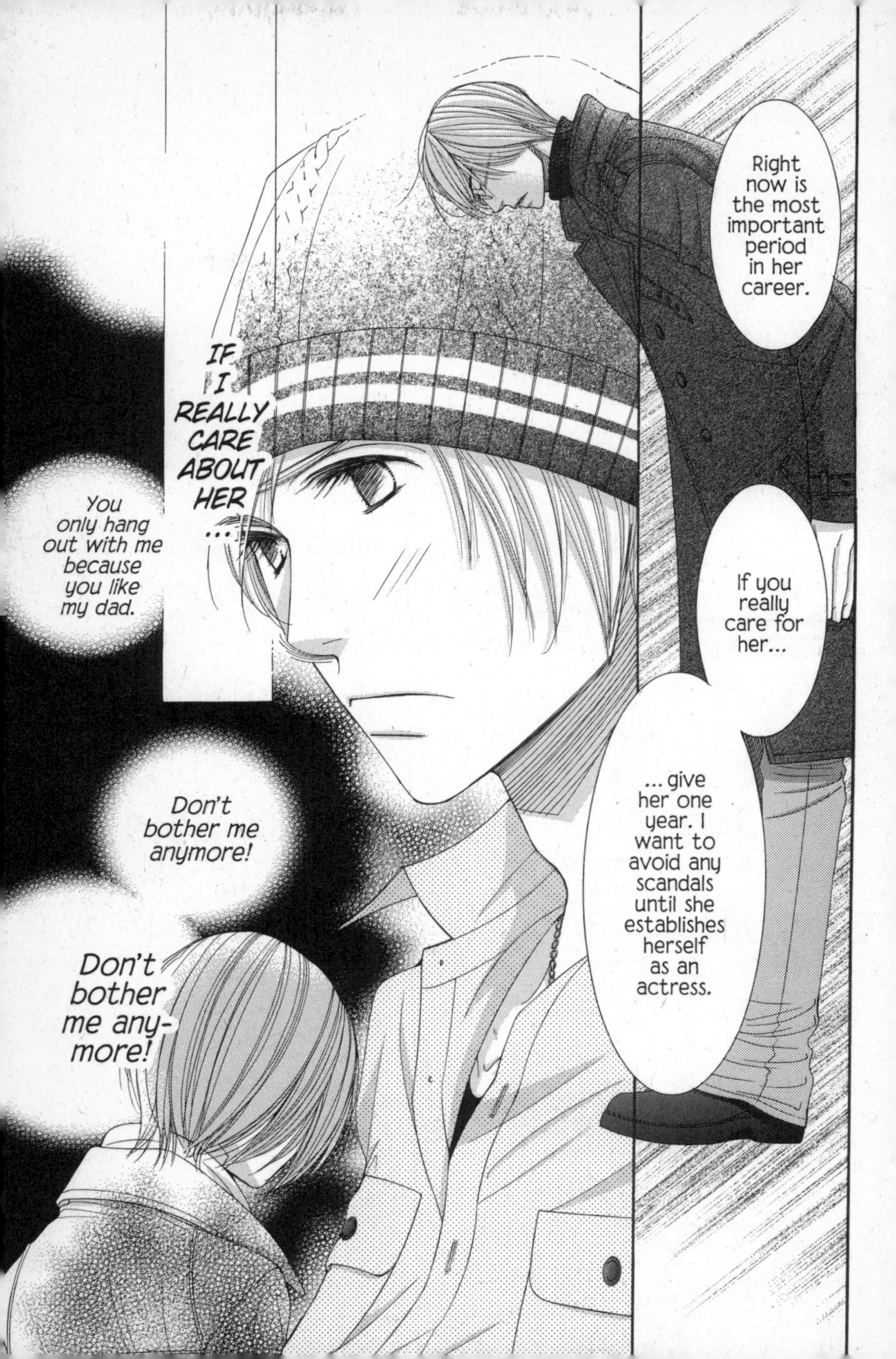
Right now is the most important period in her career.
If you really care for her...
... give her one year. I want to avoid any scandals until she establishes herself as an actress.
IF I REALLY CARE ABOUT HER ...
You only hang out with me because you like my dad.
Don't bother me anymore!
Don't bother me any-more!

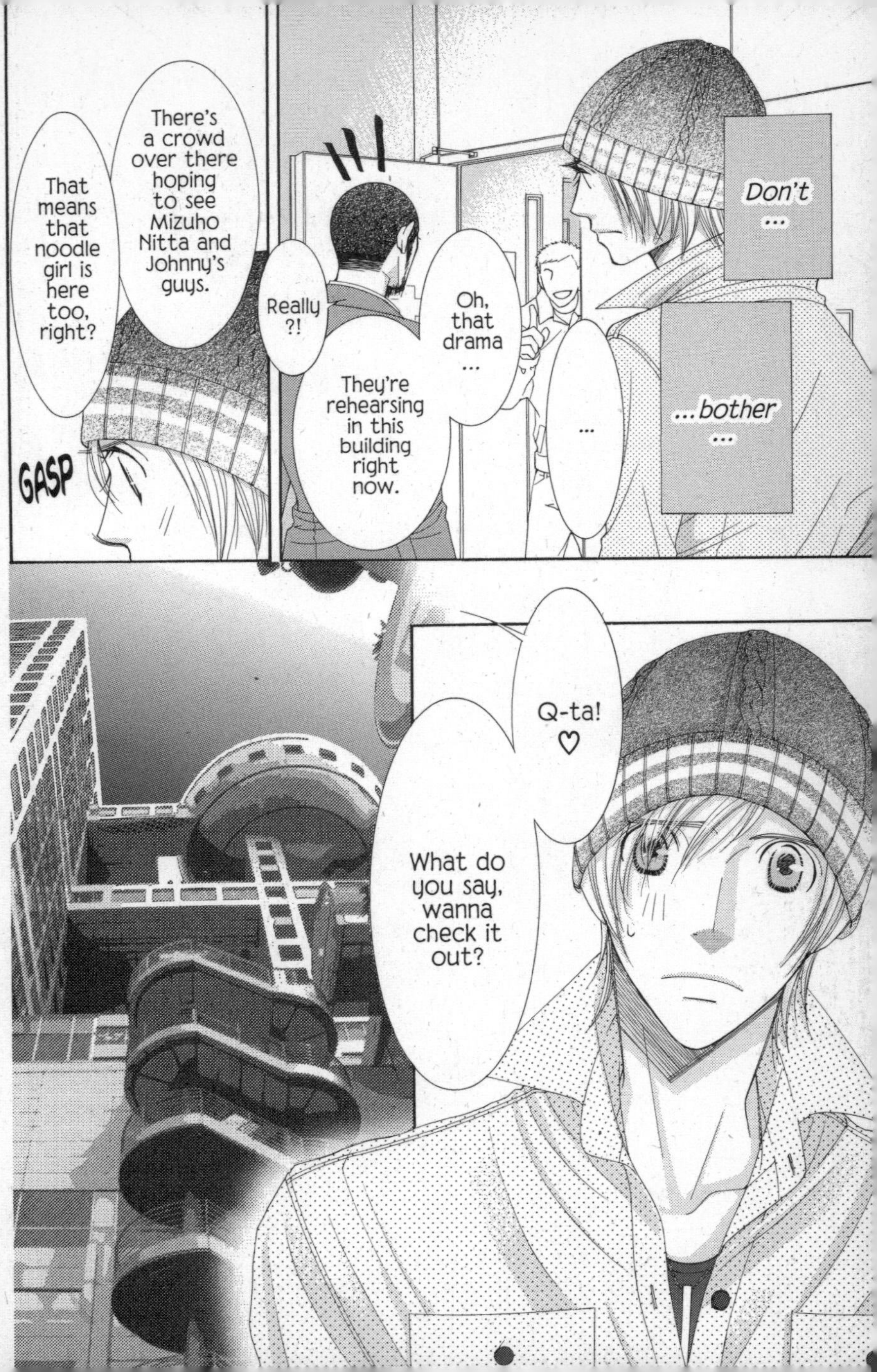
Don't ...
...bother ...
Oh, that drama ...
They're rehearsing in this building right now.
Really ?!
...
There's a crowd over there hoping to see Mizuho Nitta and Johnny's guys.
That means that noodle girl is here too, right?
GASP
Q-ta! ♡
What do you say, wanna check it out?

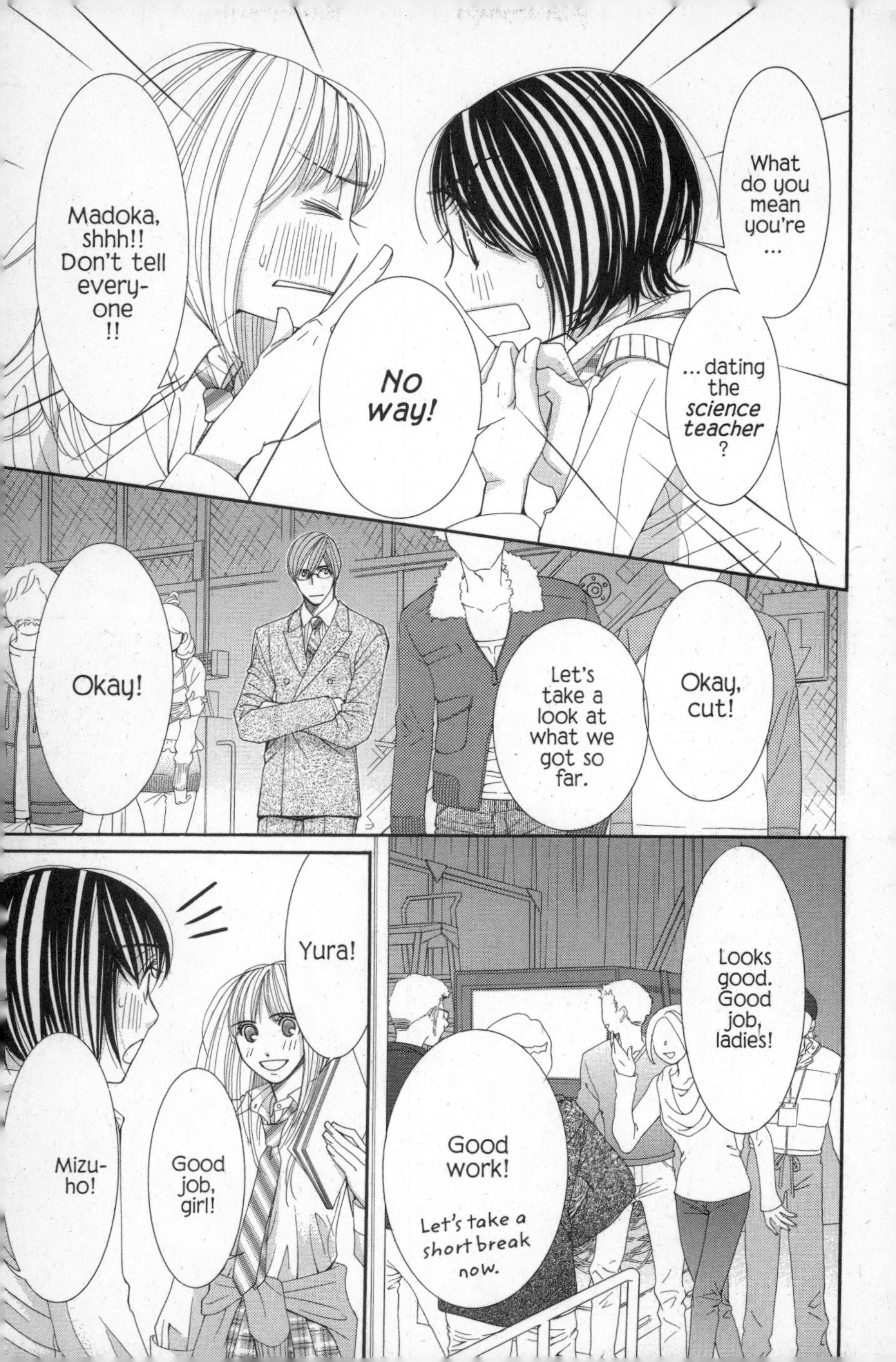
What do you mean you're ...
... dating the *science teacher* ?
No way!
Madoka, shhh!! Don't tell every-one !!
Okay, cut!
Let's take a look at what we got so far.
Okay!
Looks good. Good job, ladies!
Good work!
Let's take a short break now.
Yura!
Good job, girl!
Mizu-ho!

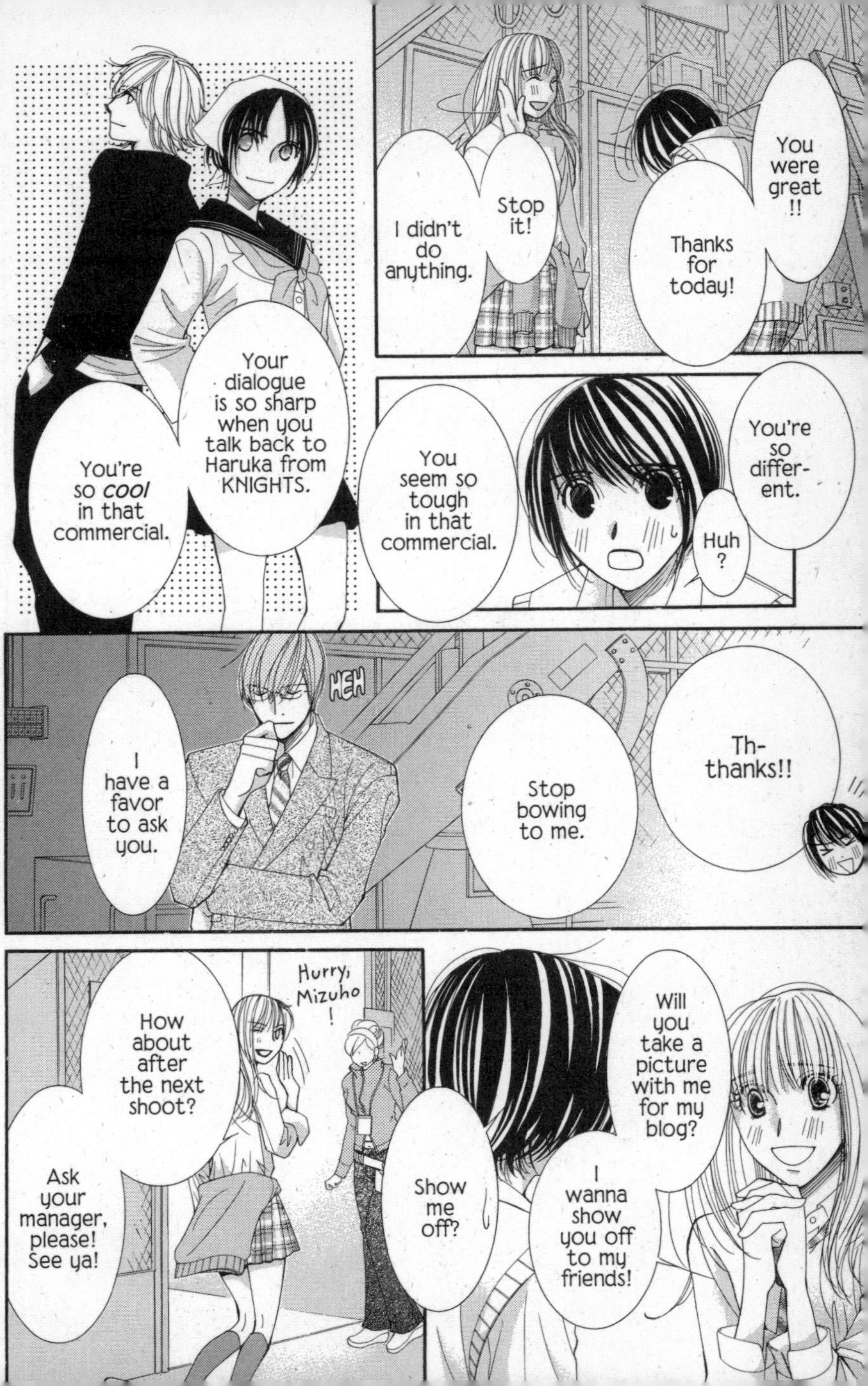
You were great!!
Thanks for today!
Stop it!
I didn't do anything.
You're so different.
Huh?
You seem so tough in that commercial.
Your dialogue is so sharp when you talk back to Haruka from KNIGHTS.
You're so *cool* in that commercial.
Th-thanks!!
Stop bowing to me.
HEH
I have a favor to ask you.
Will you take a picture with me for my blog?
I wanna show you off to my friends!
Show me off?
Hurry, Mizuho!
How about after the next shoot?
Ask your manager, please! See ya!

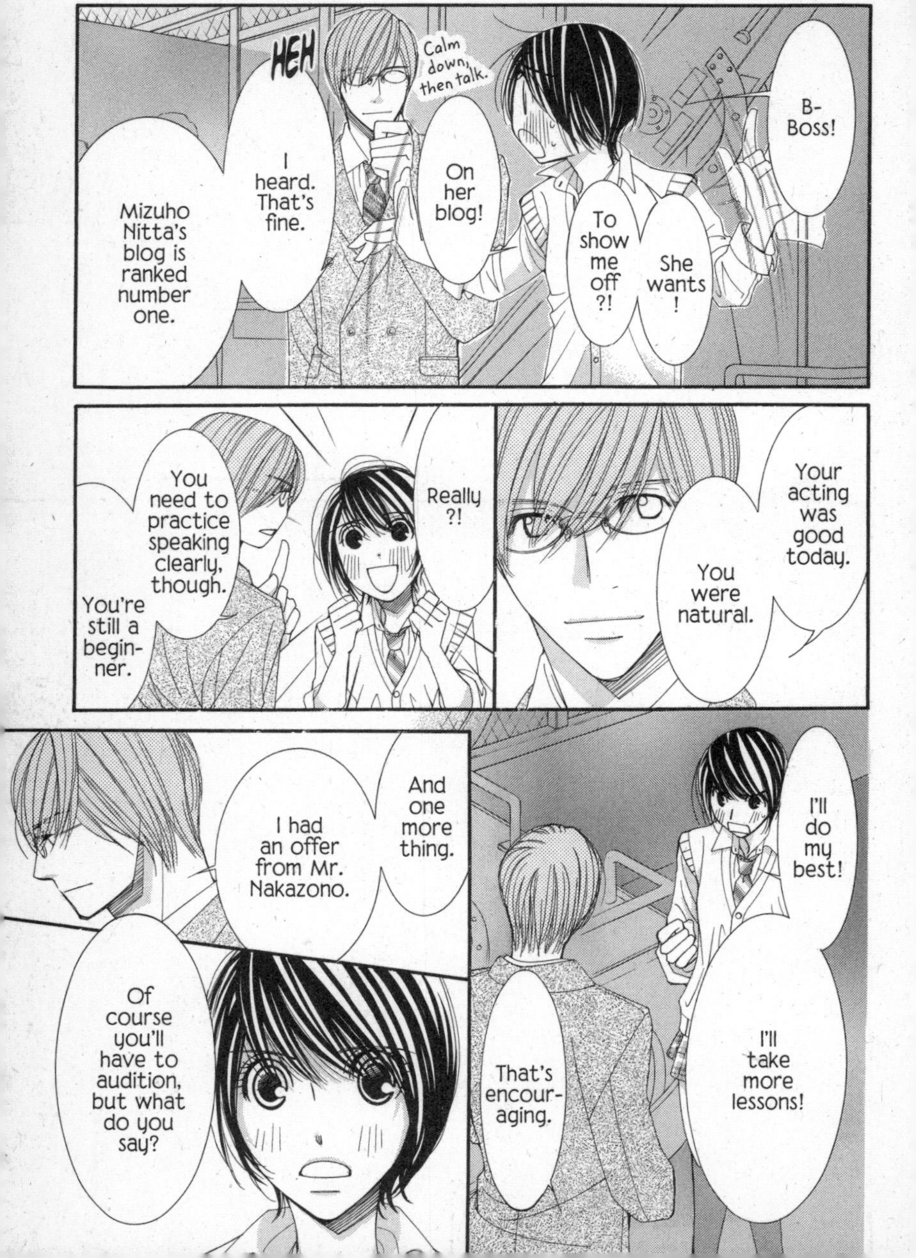
B-Boss!
She wants!
To show me off?!
On her blog!
Calm down, then talk.
HEH
I heard. That's fine.
Mizuho Nitta's blog is ranked number one.
Your acting was good today.
You were natural.
Really?!
You need to practice speaking clearly, though.
You're still a beginner.
I'll do my best!
I'll take more lessons!
That's encouraging.
And one more thing.
I had an offer from Mr. Nakazono.
Of course you'll have to audition, but what do you say?

Of course.
If there's a chance I can get it ...
...I'll try anything.
I NEED TO KEEP MYSELF BUSY ...
...SO I WON'T START THINK-ING...
...ABOUT OTHER THINGS.
Don't bother me anymore!
I SAID SUCH TERRIBLE THINGS.
I WAS JEALOUS OF MY DAD.
I MUST'VE SOUNDED SO ARROGANT.
I'M SURE HE HATES ME NOW.
I'm going to the backroom to get my phone.
I want to take a picture with her too.
The phone ...

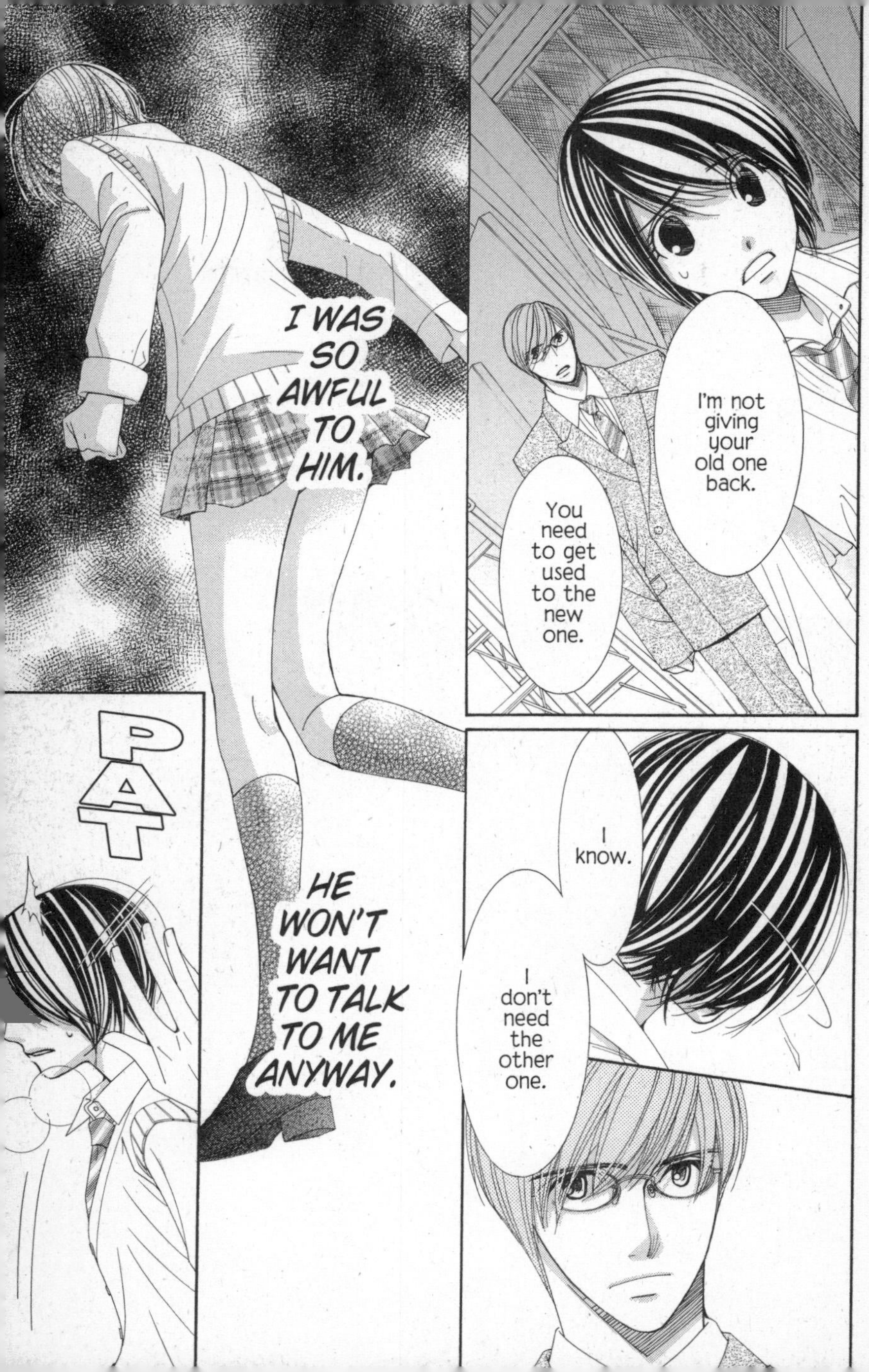
I'm not giving your old one back.
You need to get used to the new one.
I know.
I don't need the other one.
I WAS SO AWFUL TO HIM.
HE WON'T WANT TO TALK TO ME ANYWAY.
PAT

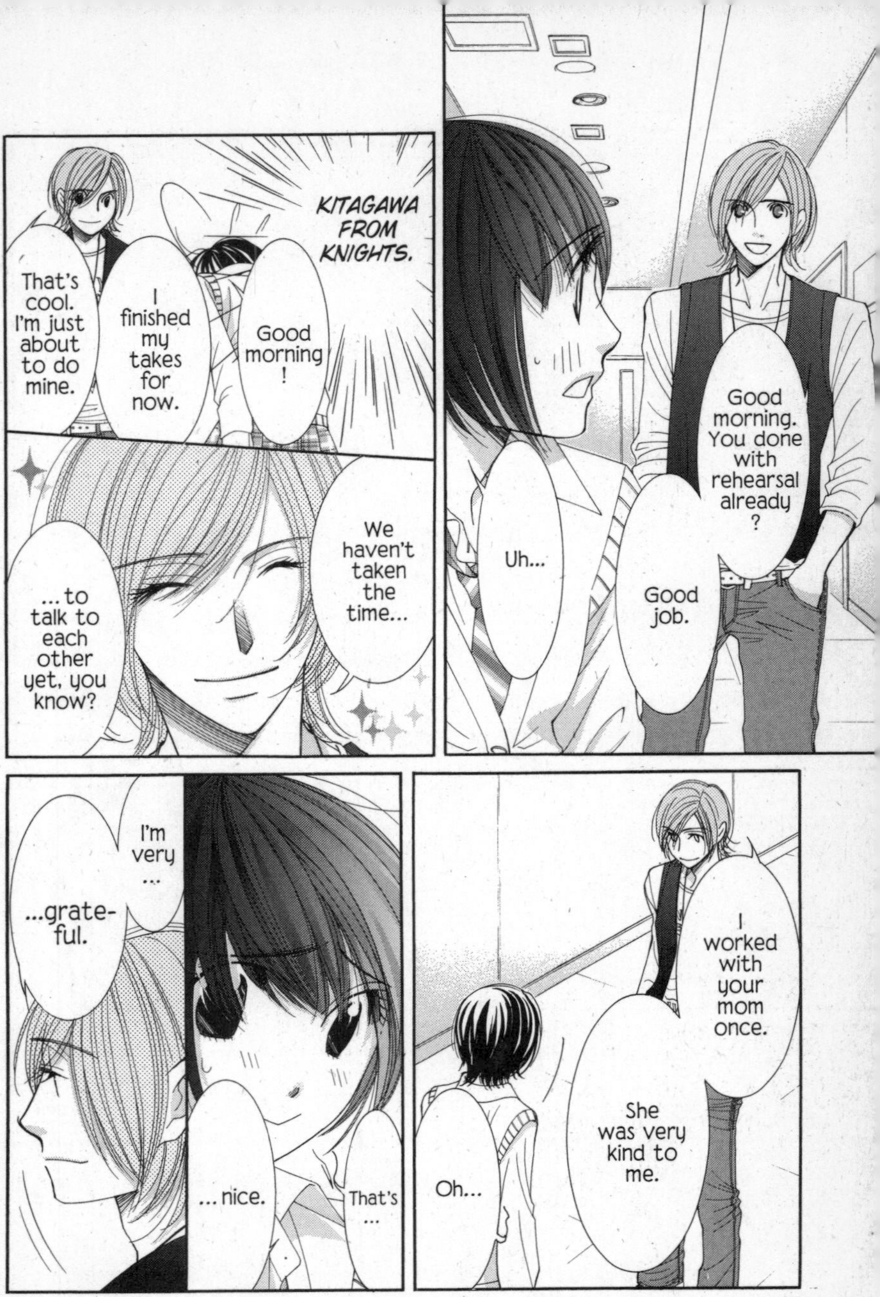
Good morning. You done with rehearsal already?
Good job.
Uh...
KITAGAWA FROM KNIGHTS.
Good morning!
I finished my takes for now.
That's cool. I'm just about to do mine.
We haven't taken the time...
...to talk to each other yet, you know?
I worked with your mom once.
She was very kind to me.
Oh...
That's...
...nice.
I'm very...
...grateful.

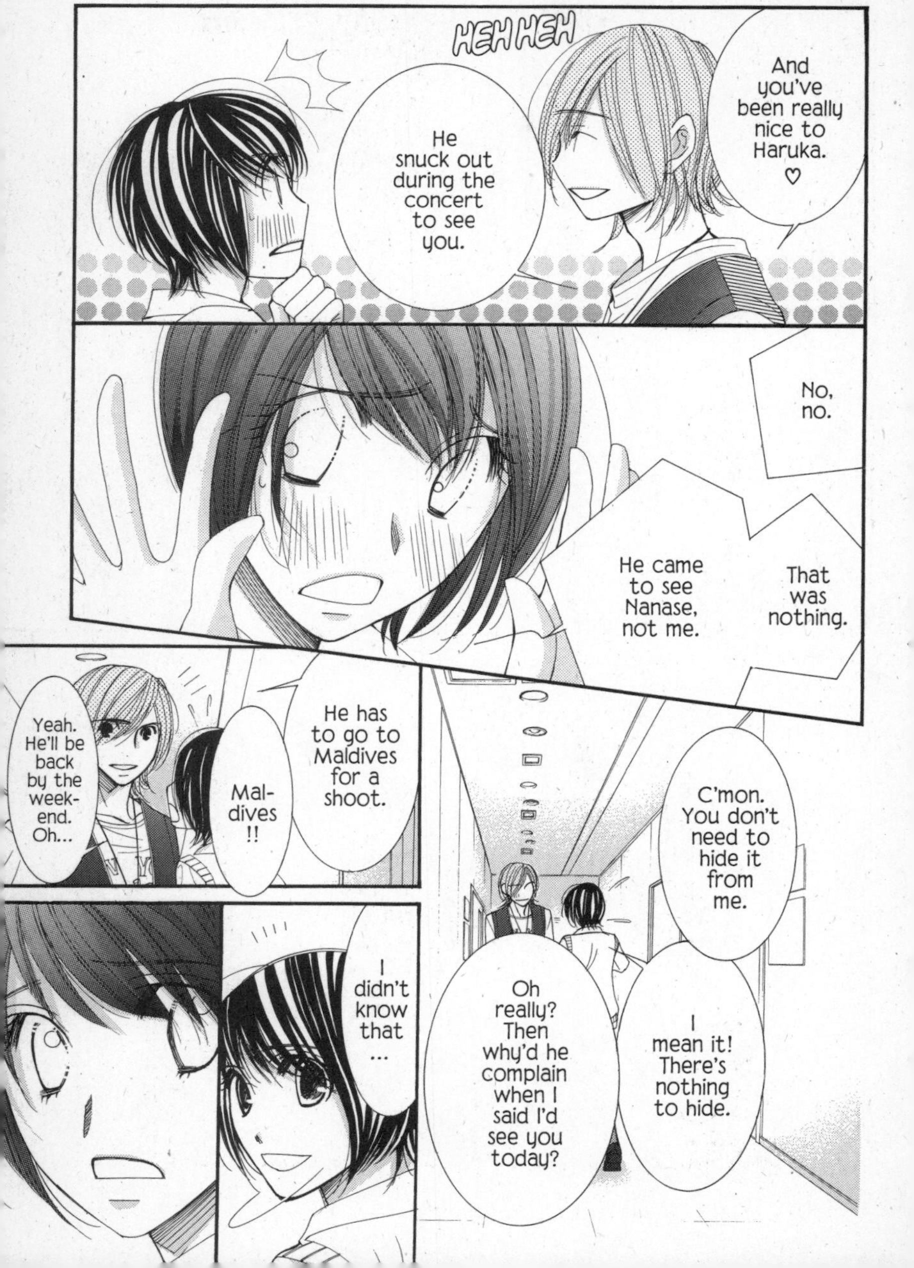

And you've been really nice to Haruka. ♡
HEH HEH
He snuck out during the concert to see you.
No, no.
That was nothing.
He came to see Nanase, not me.
C'mon. You don't need to hide it from me.
I mean it! There's nothing to hide.
Oh really? Then why'd he complain when I said I'd see you today?
He has to go to Maldives for a shoot.
Mal-dives!!
Yeah. He'll be back by the week-end. Oh...
I didn't know that ...

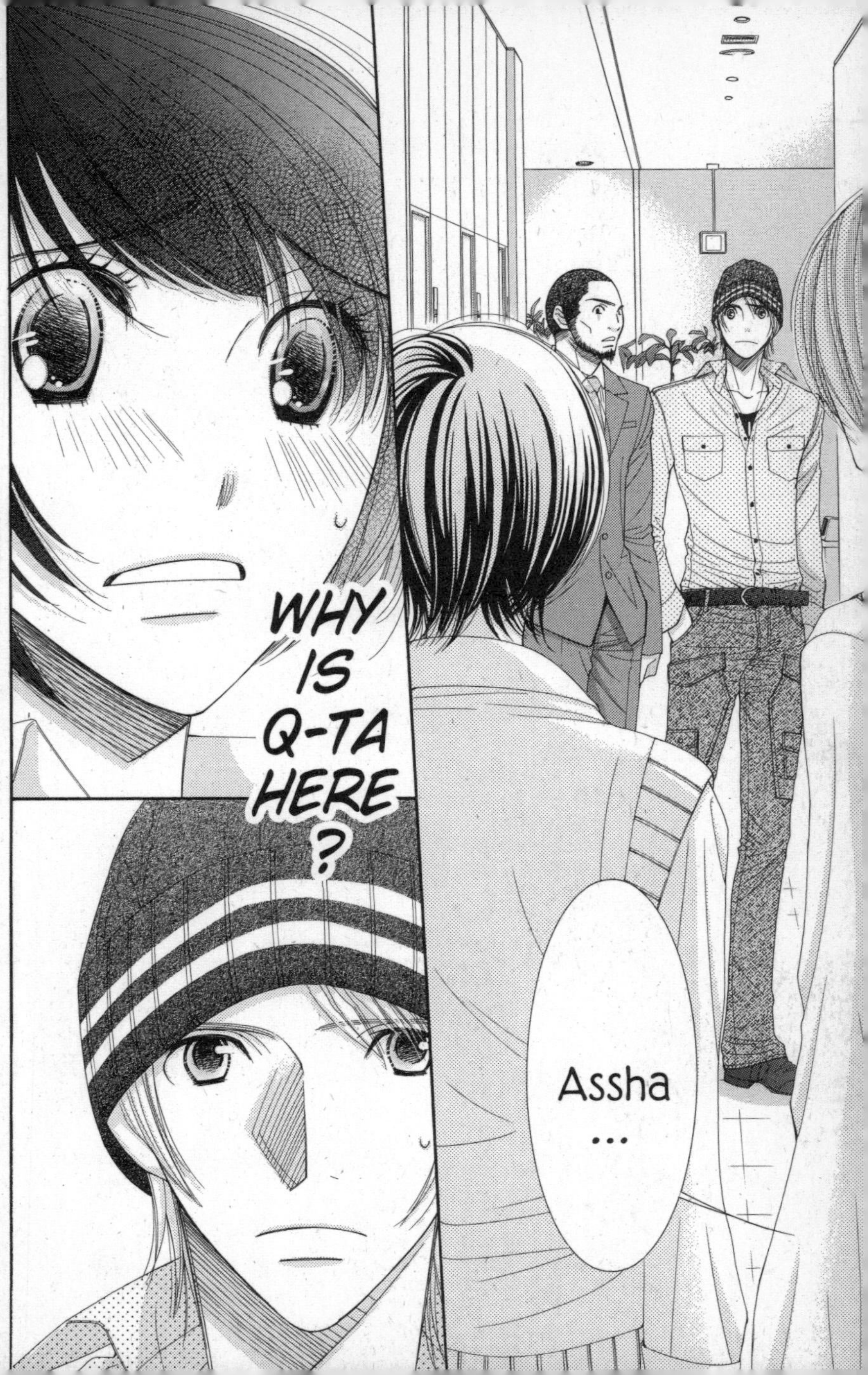
Assha ...
WHY IS Q-TA HERE?

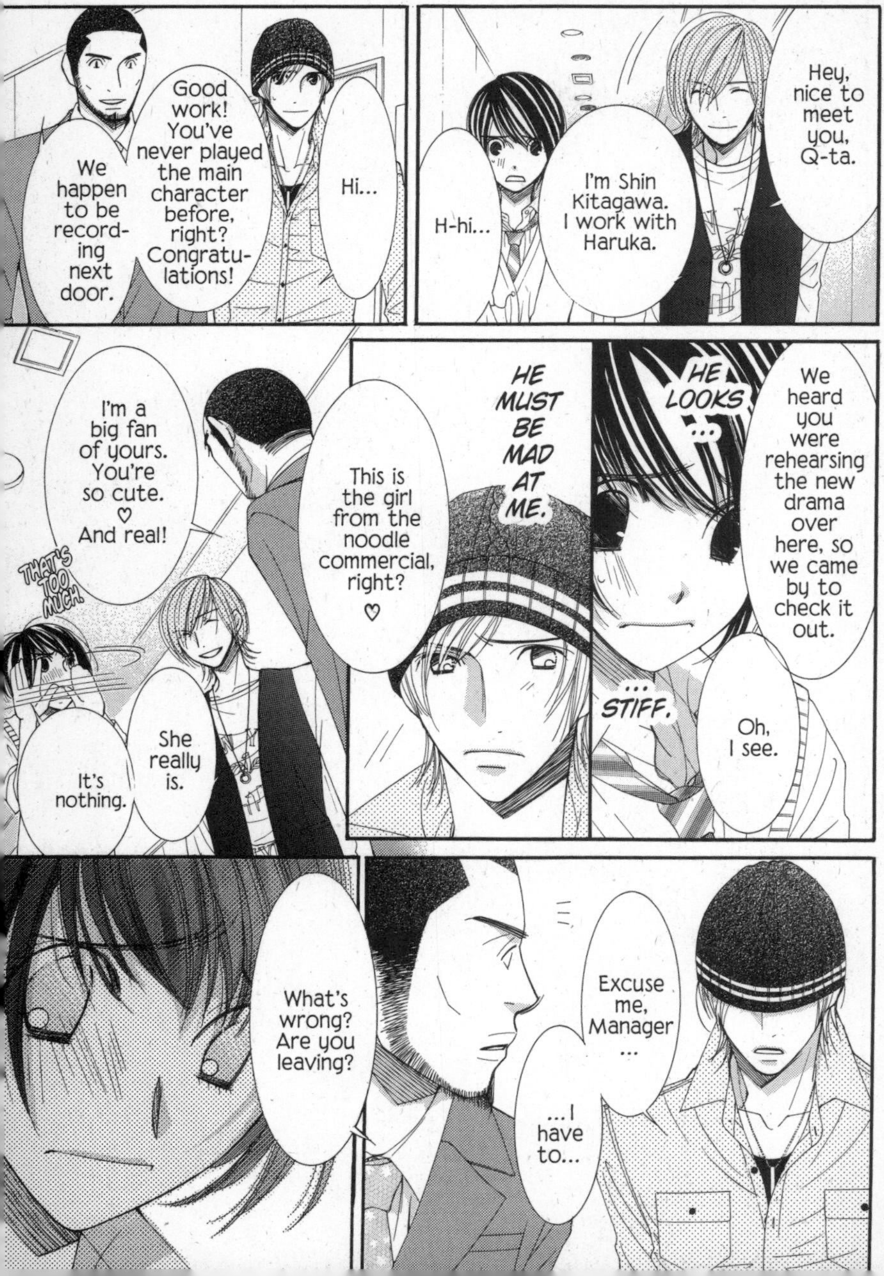
Hey, nice to meet you, Q-ta.
I'm Shin Kitagawa. I work with Haruka.
H-hi...
Hi...
Good work! You've never played the main character before, right? Congratulations!
We happen to be recording next door.
We heard you were rehearsing the new drama over here, so we came by to check it out.
HE LOOKS ...
... STIFF.
Oh, I see.
HE MUST BE MAD AT ME.
This is the girl from the noodle commercial, right? ♡
I'm a big fan of yours. You're so cute. ♡ And real!
THAT'S TOO MUCH
She really is.
It's nothing.
Excuse me, Manager ...
...I have to...
What's wrong? Are you leaving?

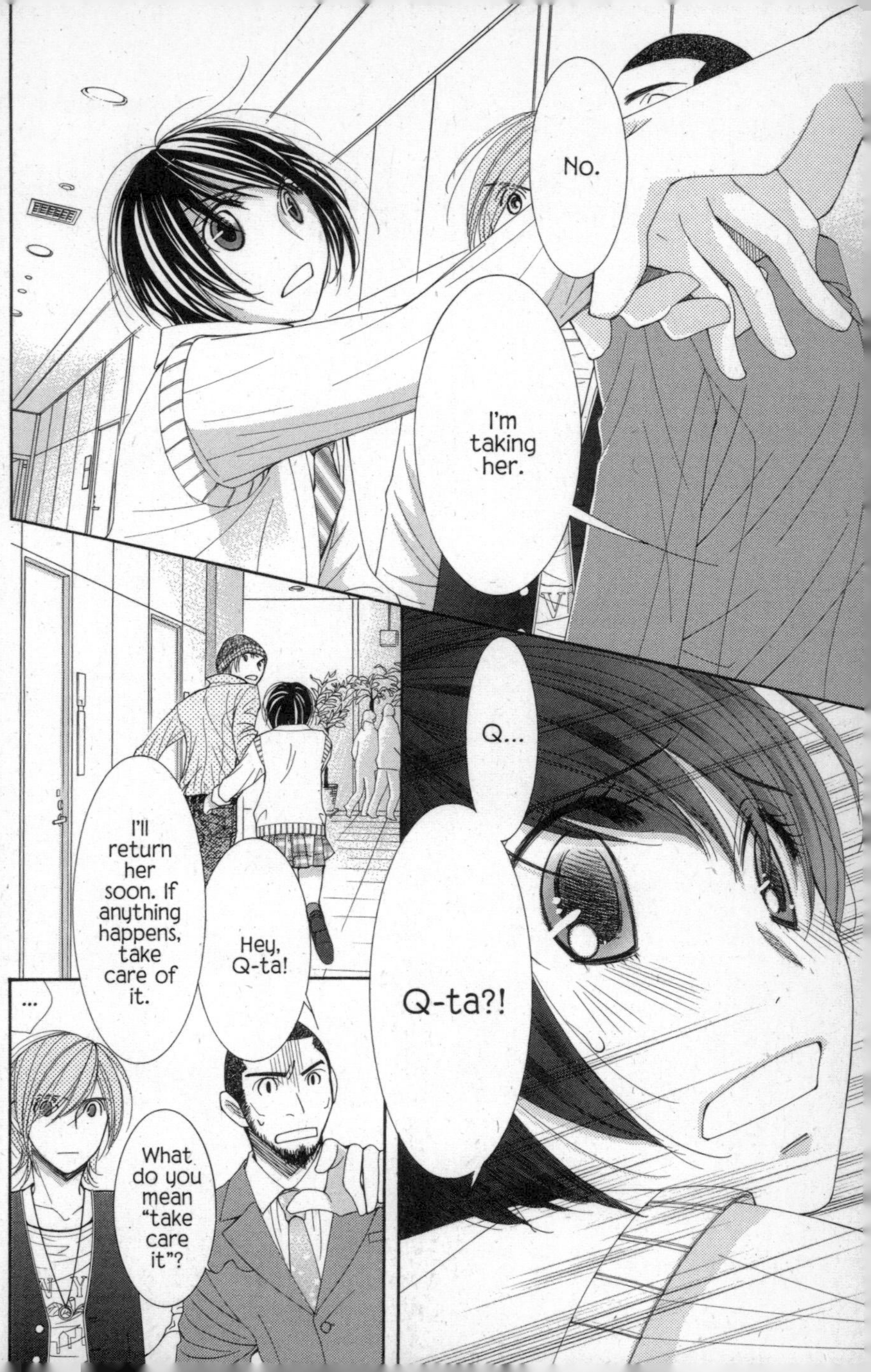
No.
I'm taking her.
Q...
Q-ta?!
Hey, Q-ta!
I'll return her soon. If anything happens, take care of it.
...
What do you mean "take care it"?

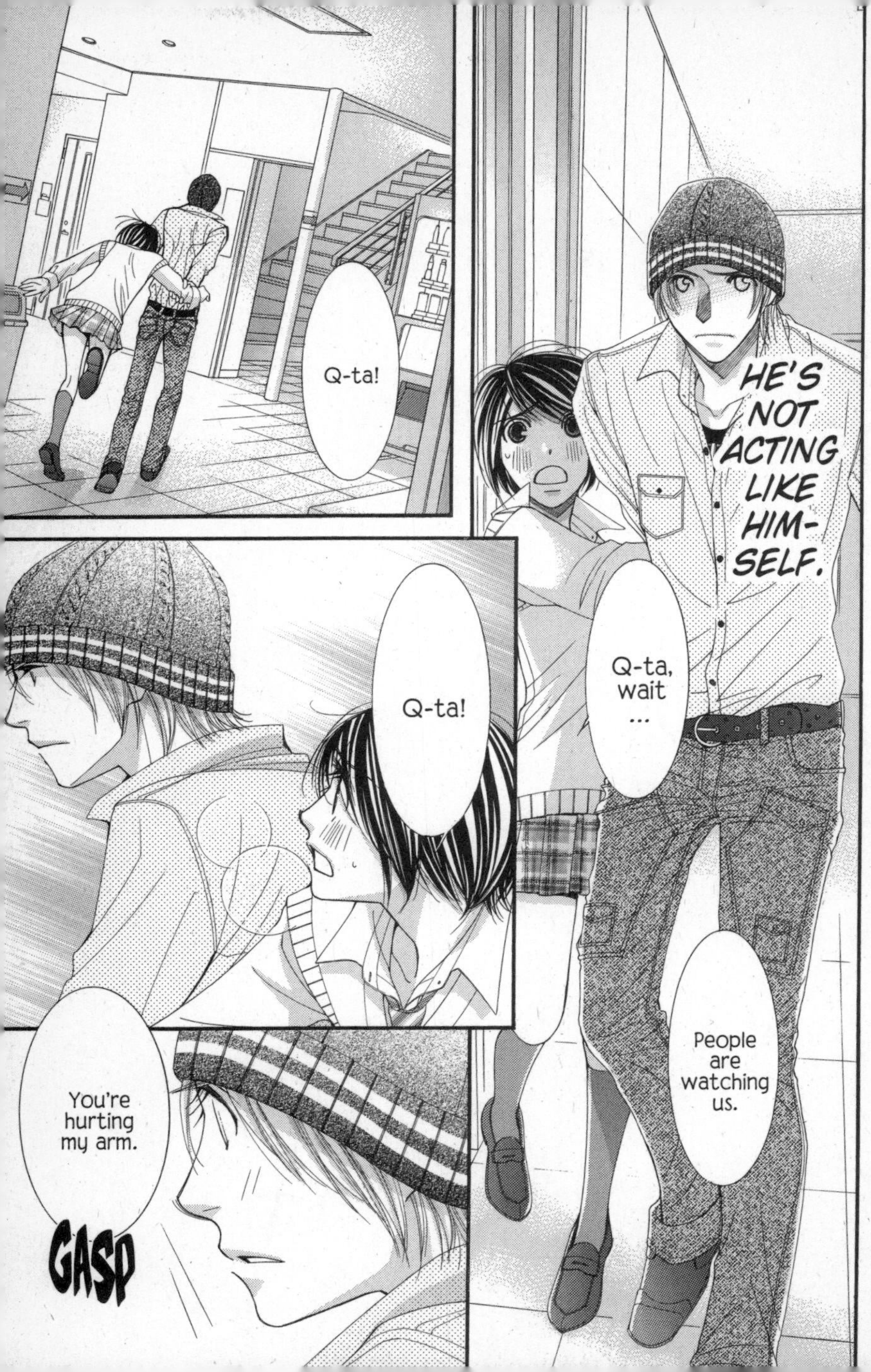
HE'S NOT ACTING LIKE HIM-SELF.
Q-ta, wait ...
People are watching us.
Q-ta!
Q-ta!
You're hurting my arm.
GASP

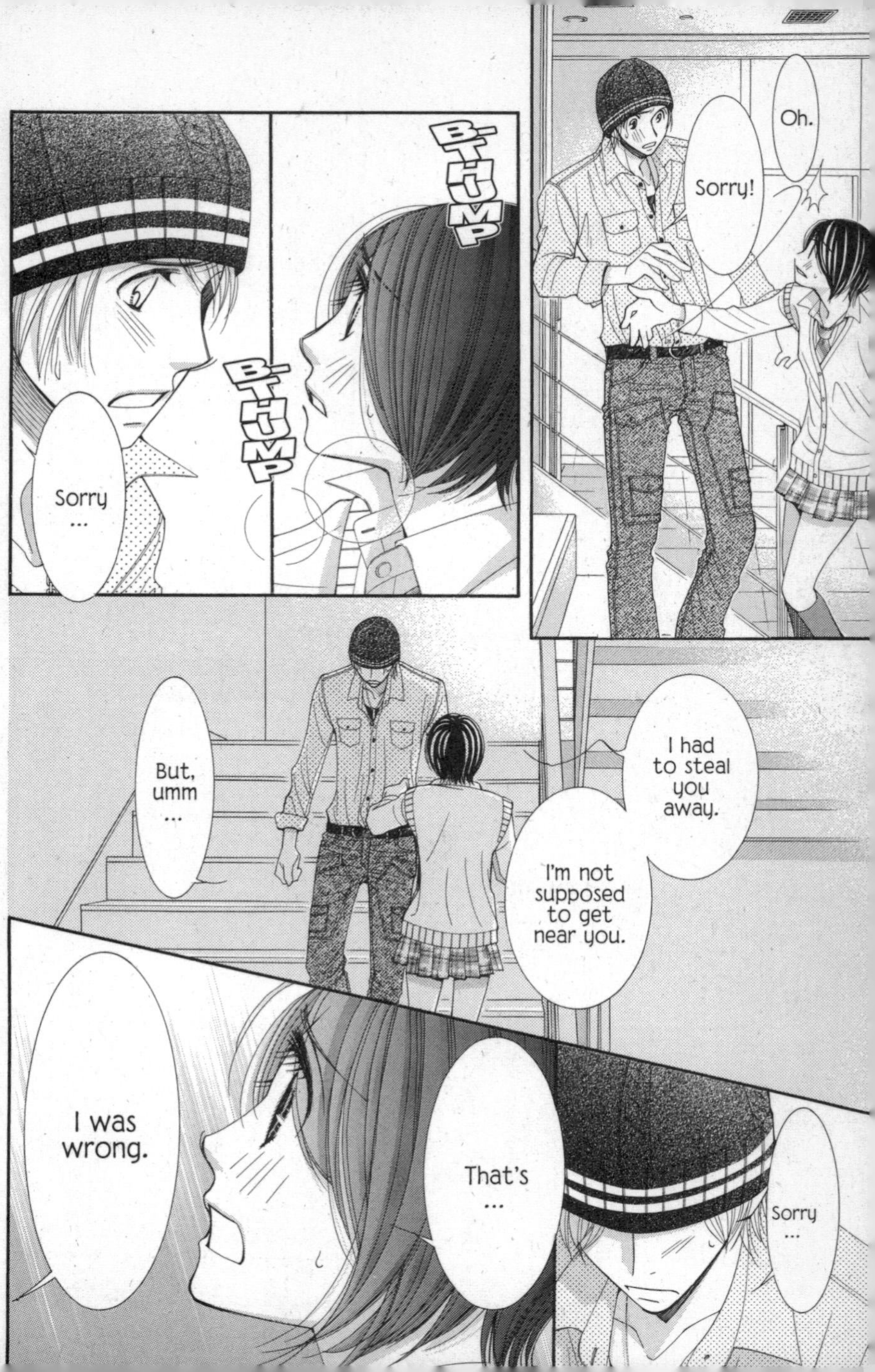

Oh.
Sorry!
B-THUMP
B-THUMP
Sorry ...
I had to steal you away.
I'm not supposed to get near you.
But, umm ...
Sorry ...
That's ...
I was wrong.

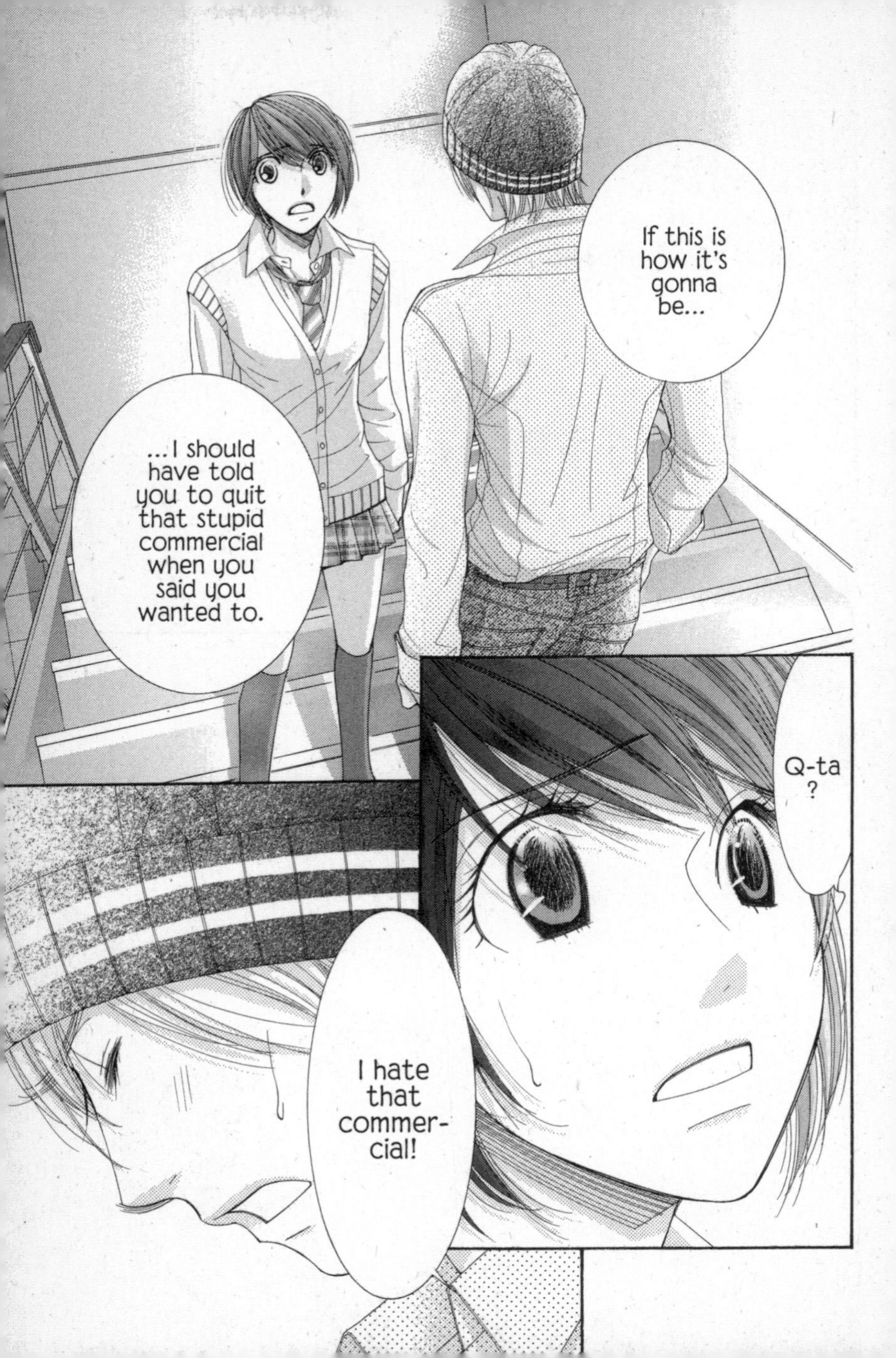
If this is how it's gonna be...
...I should have told you to quit that stupid commercial when you said you wanted to.
Q-ta?
I hate that commercial!

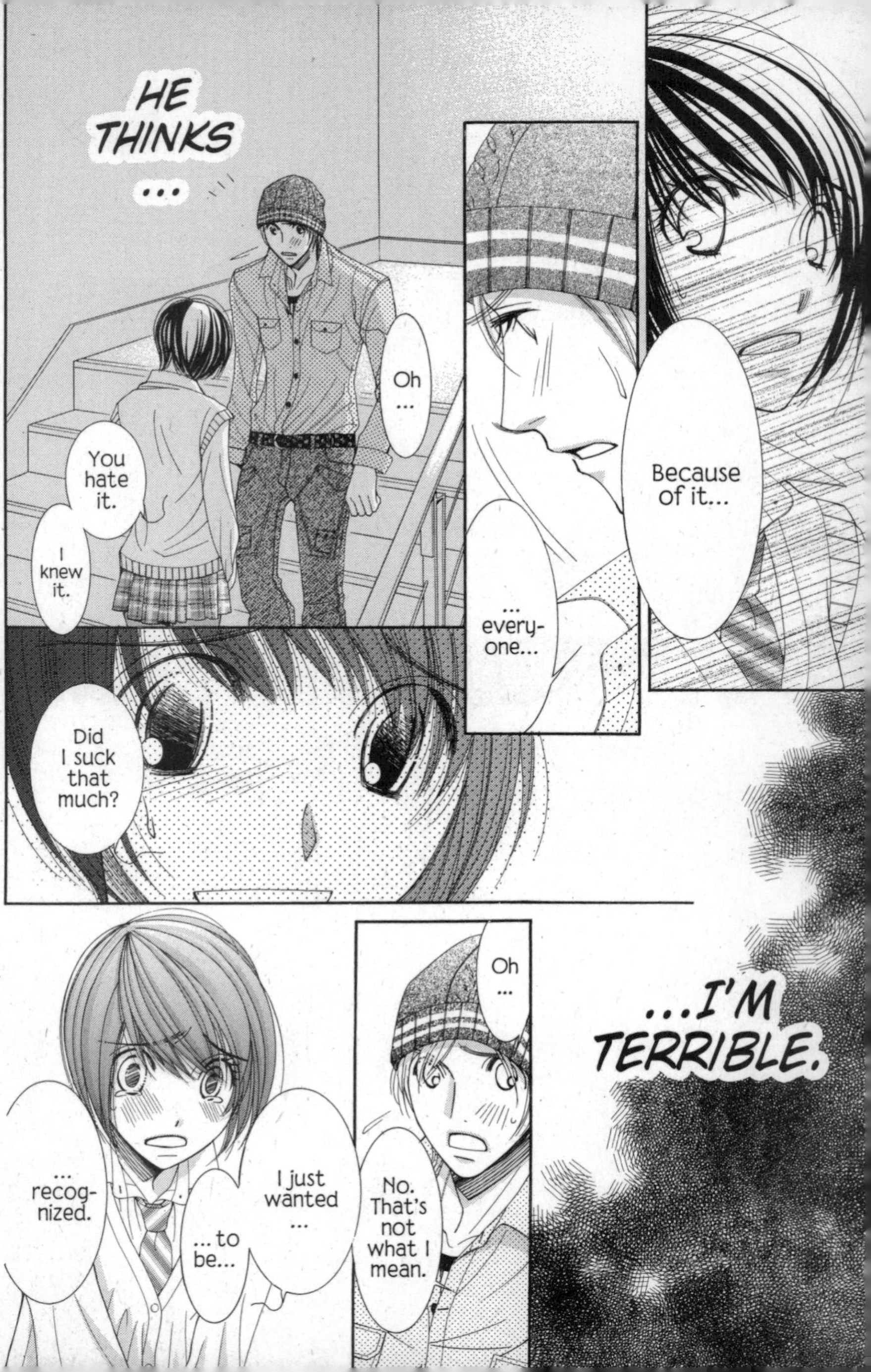
Because of it...
... every-one...
HE THINKS ...
Oh ...
You hate it.
I knew it.
Did I suck that much?
...I'M TERRIBLE.
Oh ...
No. That's not what I mean.
I just wanted ...
...to be...
... recog-nized.

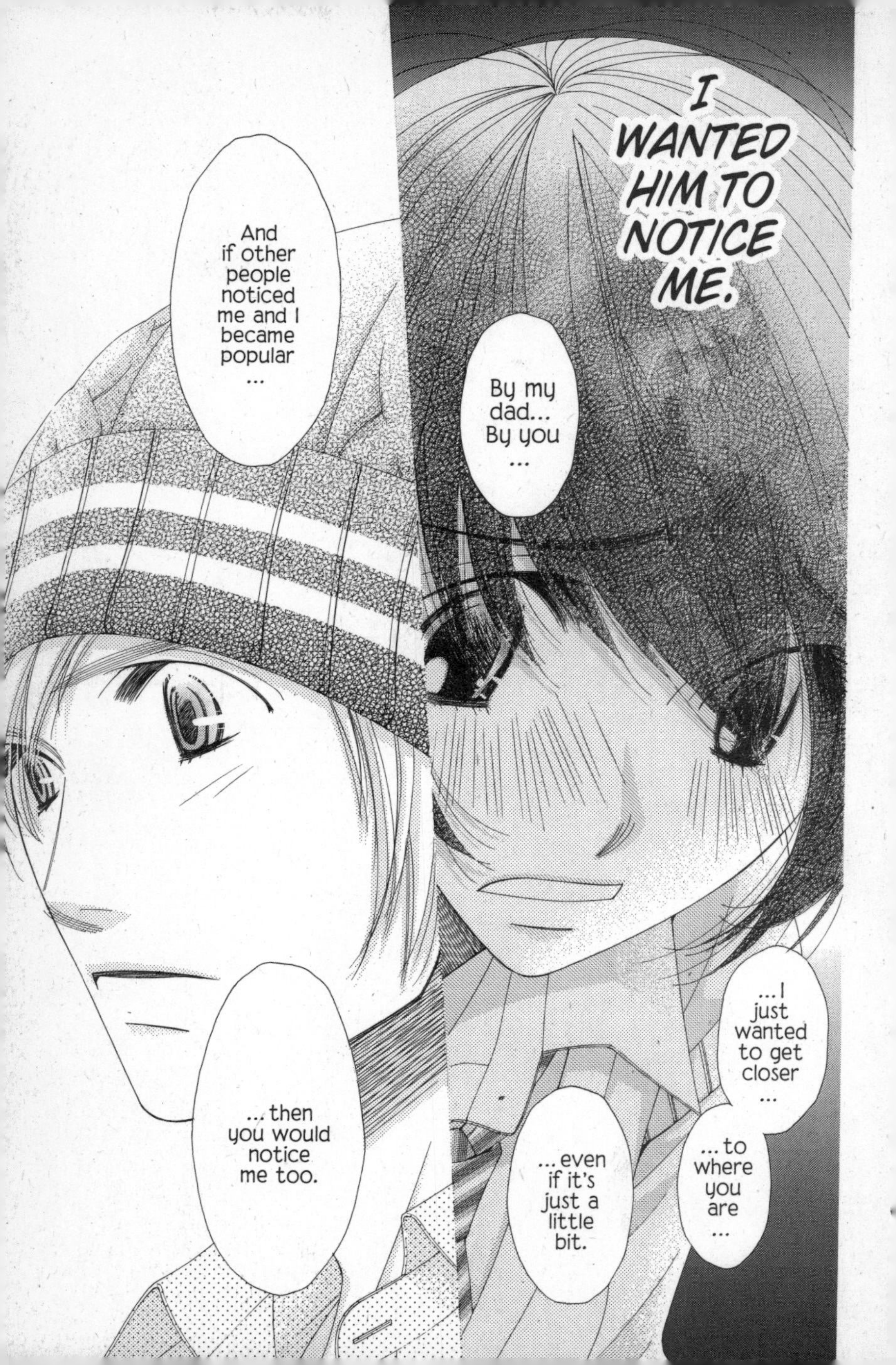
I WANTED HIM TO NOTICE ME.
By my dad... By you ...
...I just wanted to get closer ...
...to where you are ...
...even if it's just a little bit.
And if other people noticed me and I became popular ...
...then you would notice me too.

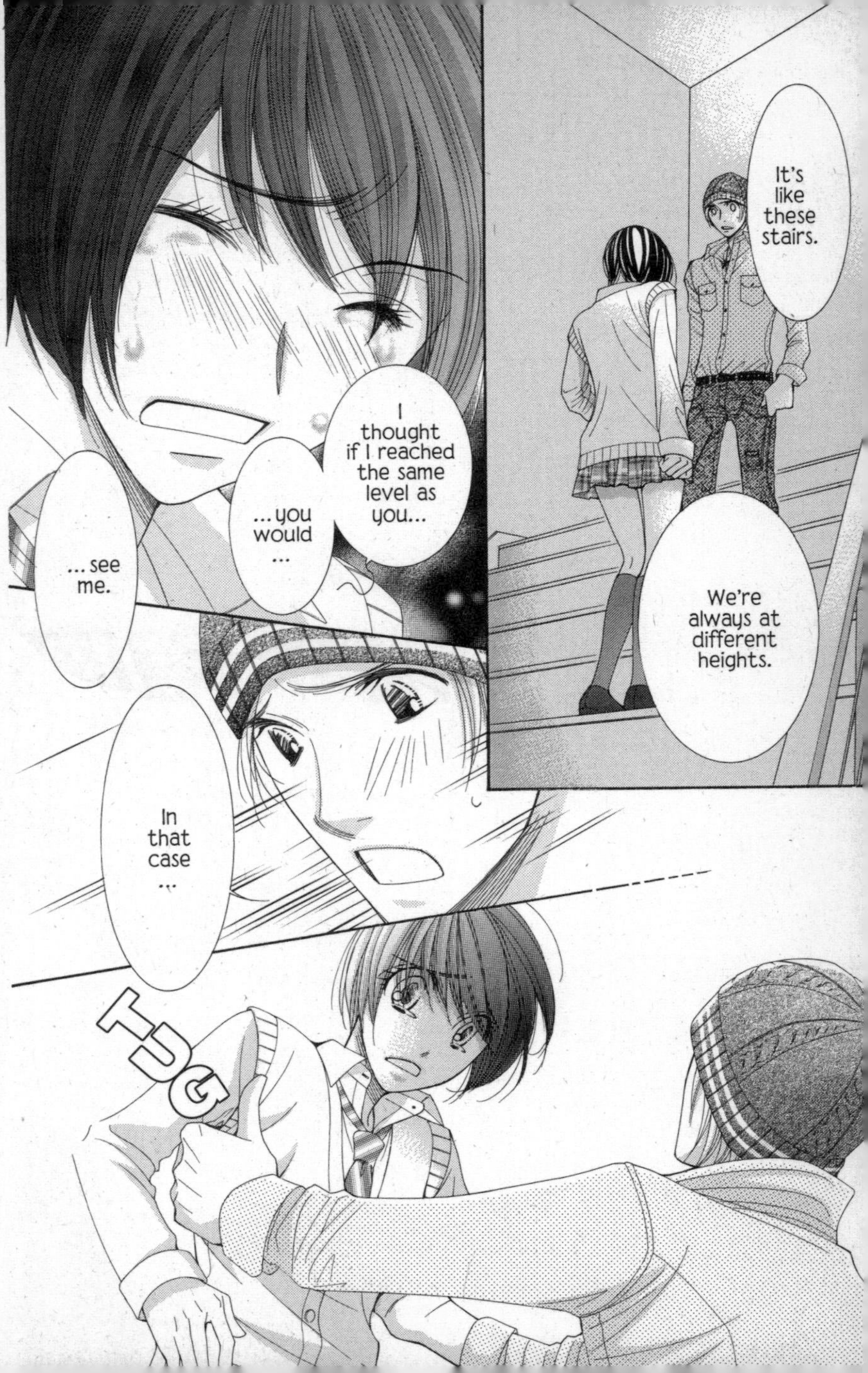
It's like these stairs.
We're always at different heights.
I thought if I reached the same level as you...
...you would ...
...see me.
In that case ...
TUG

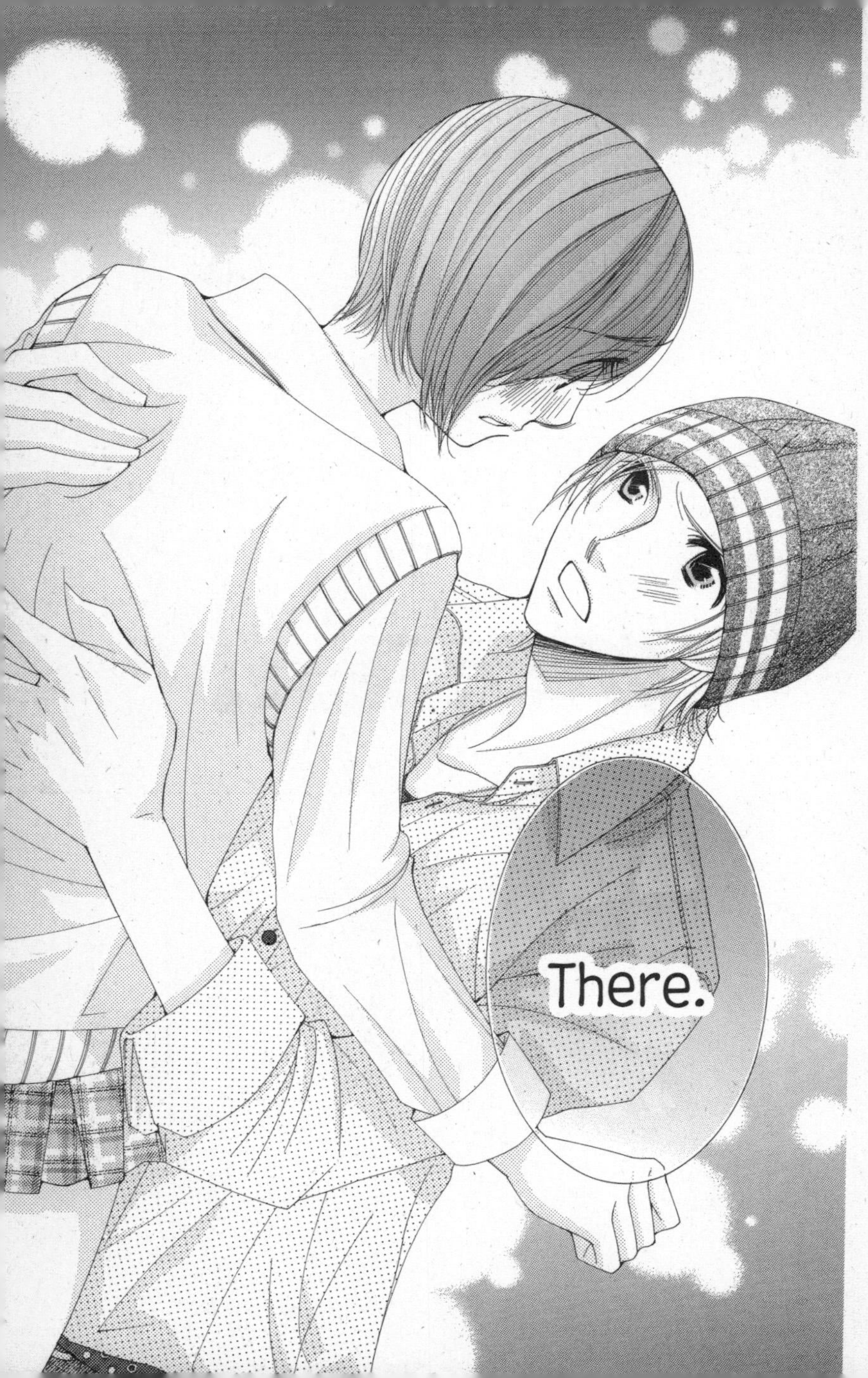
There.

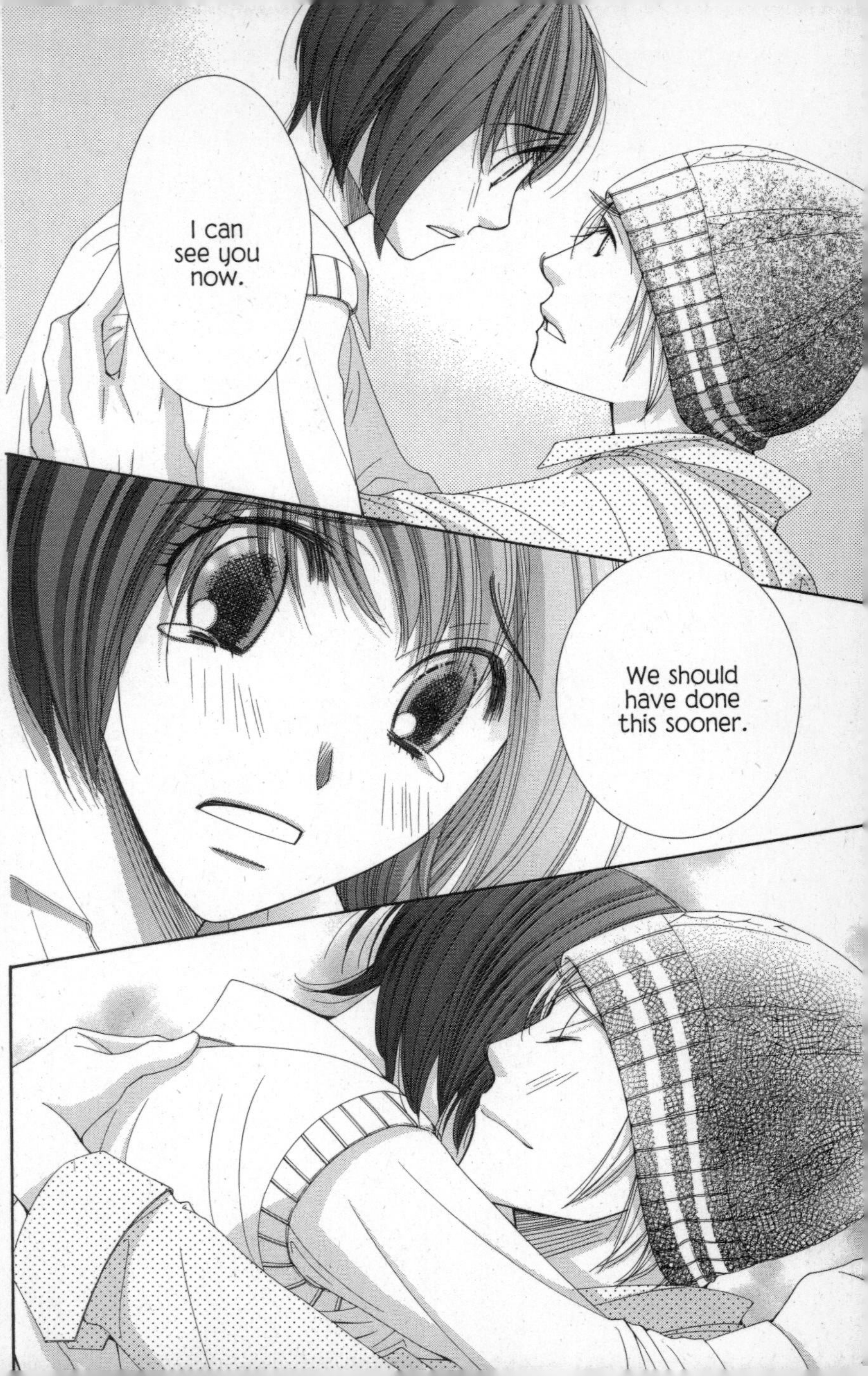
I can see you now.
We should have done this sooner.

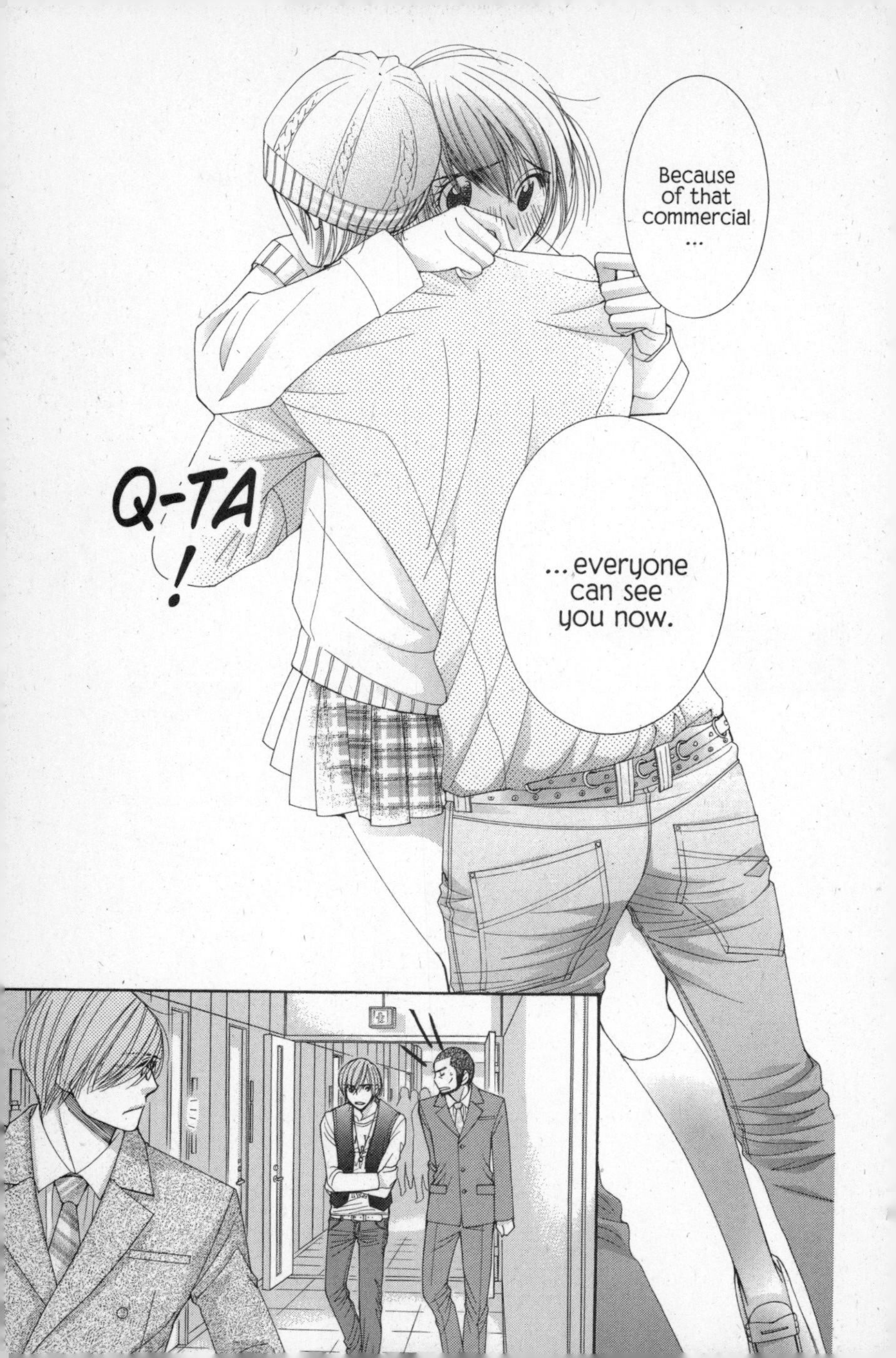
Because of that commercial ...
Q-TA!
... everyone can see you now.

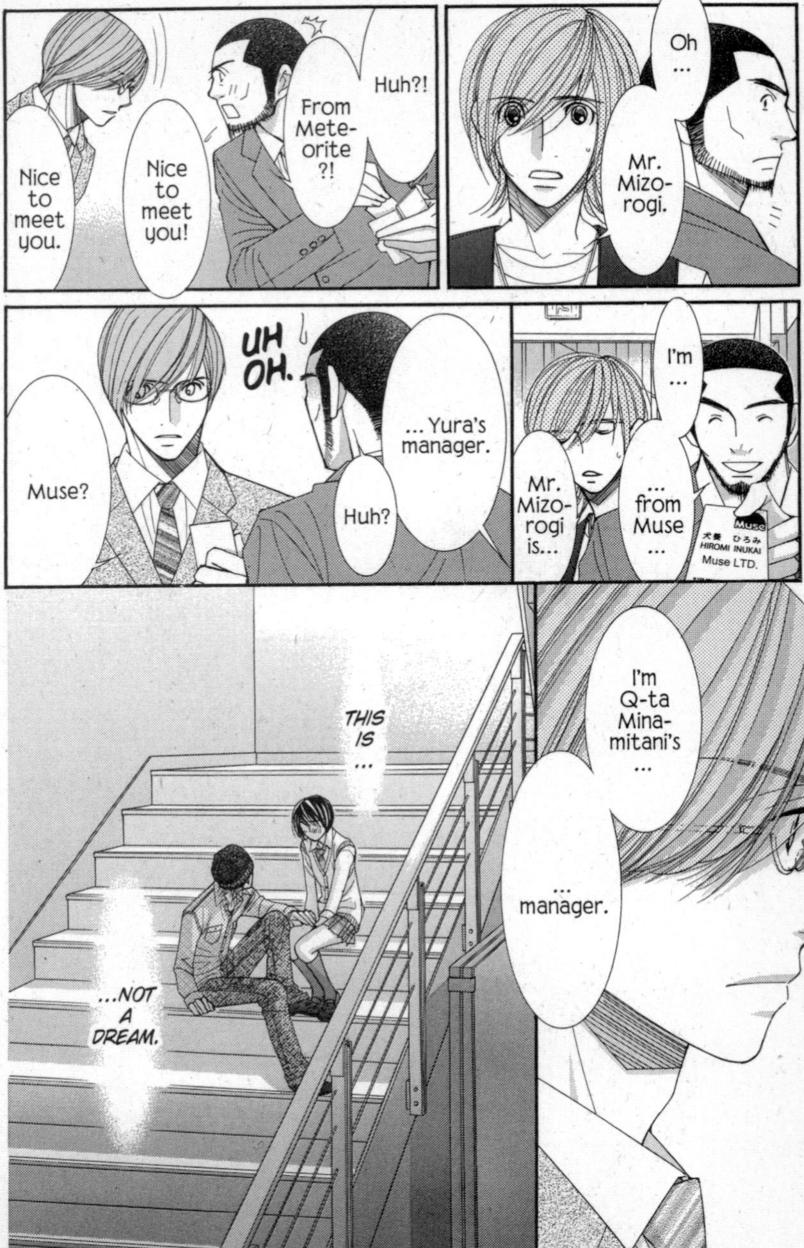
Oh ...
Mr. Mizorogi.
Huh?!
From Meteorite ?!
Nice to meet you!
Nice to meet you.
I'm ...
... from Muse ...
Mr. Mizorogi is...
Muse
犬養 ひろみ
HIROMI INUKAI
Muse LTD.
... Yura's manager.
UH OH.
Huh?
Muse?
I'm Q-ta Minamitani's ...
... manager.
THIS IS ...
...NOT A DREAM.

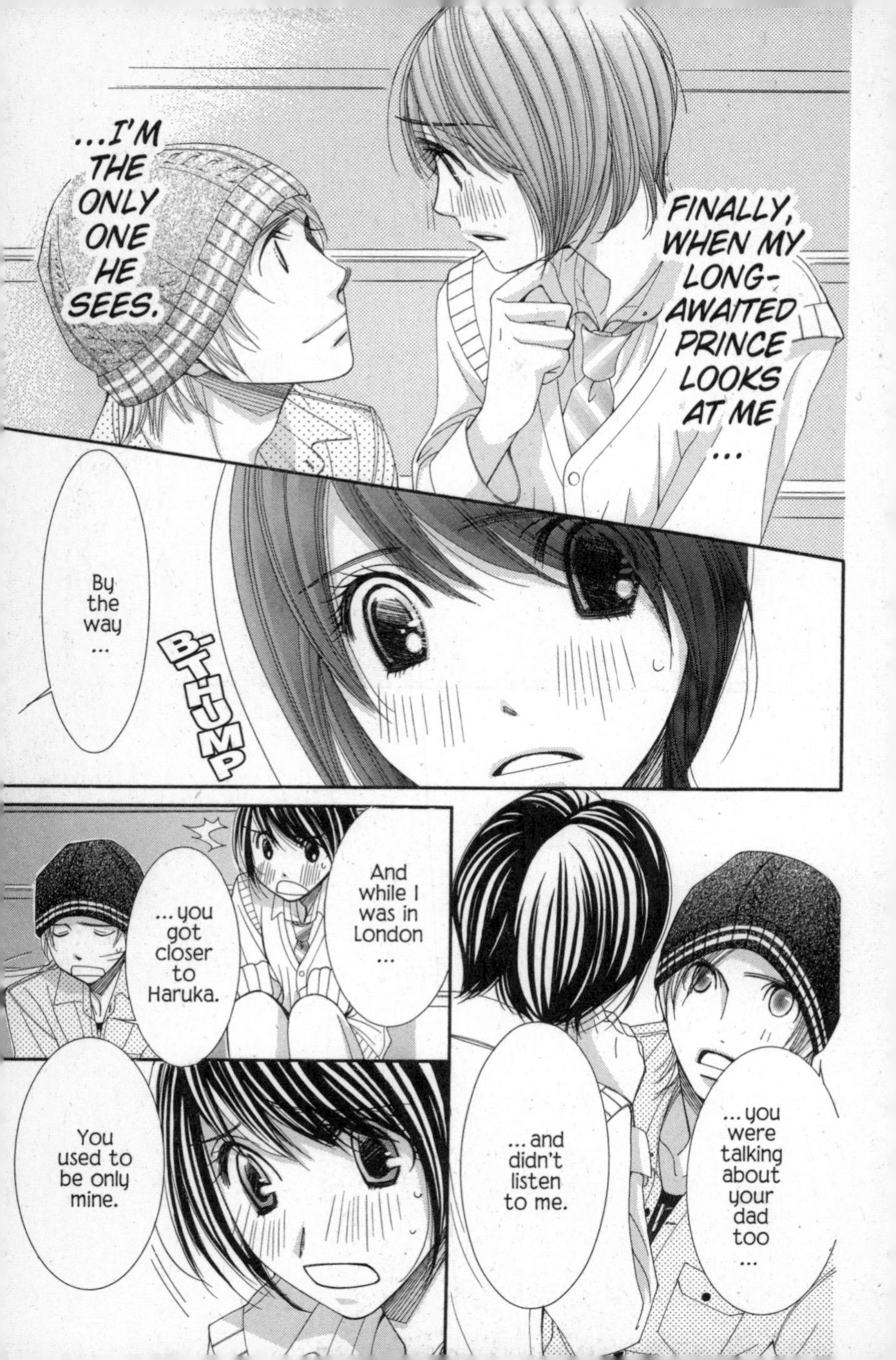
FINALLY, WHEN MY LONG-AWAITED PRINCE LOOKS AT ME...
...I'M THE ONLY ONE HE SEES.
B-THUMP
By the way...
...you were talking about your dad too...
...and didn't listen to me.
And while I was in London...
...you got closer to Haruka.
You used to be only mine.

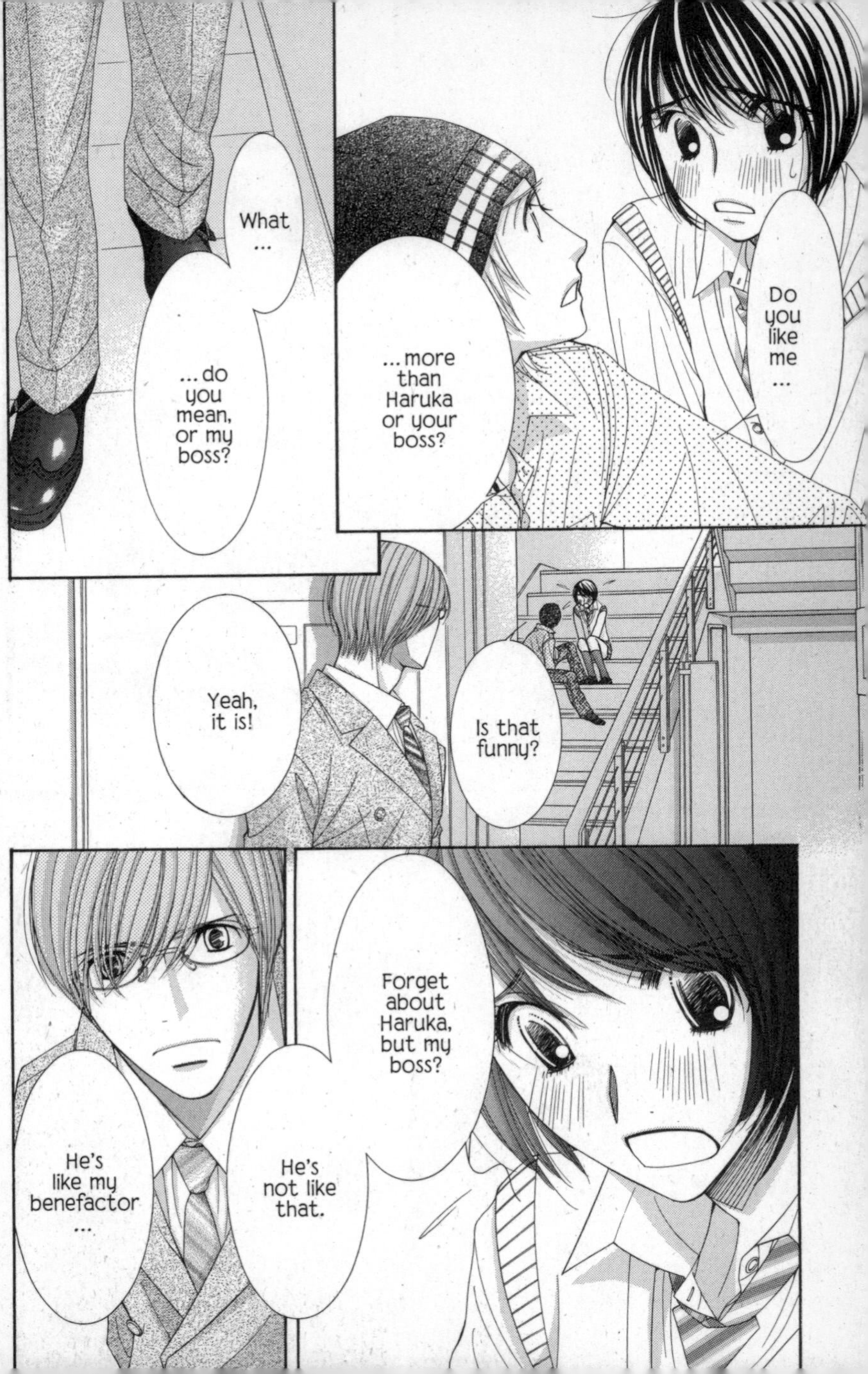
Do you like me ...
... more than Haruka or your boss?
What ...
... do you mean, or my boss?
Is that funny?
Yeah, it is!
Forget about Haruka, but my boss?
He's not like that.
He's like my benefactor ...

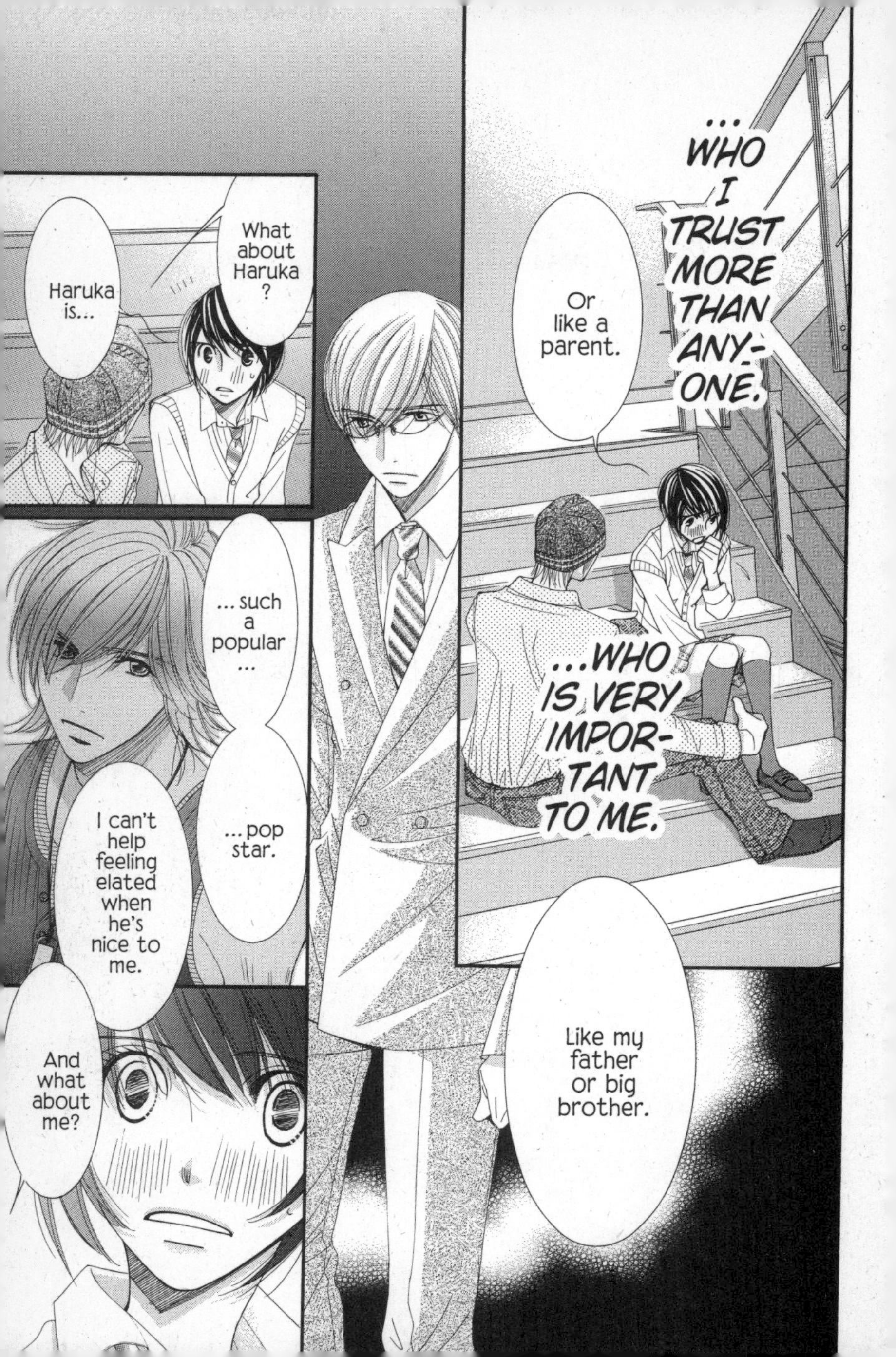
...WHO I TRUST MORE THAN ANY-ONE.
Or like a parent.
...WHO IS VERY IMPORTANT TO ME.
Like my father or big brother.
What about Haruka?
Haruka is...
...such a popular...
...pop star.
I can't help feeling elated when he's nice to me.
And what about me?

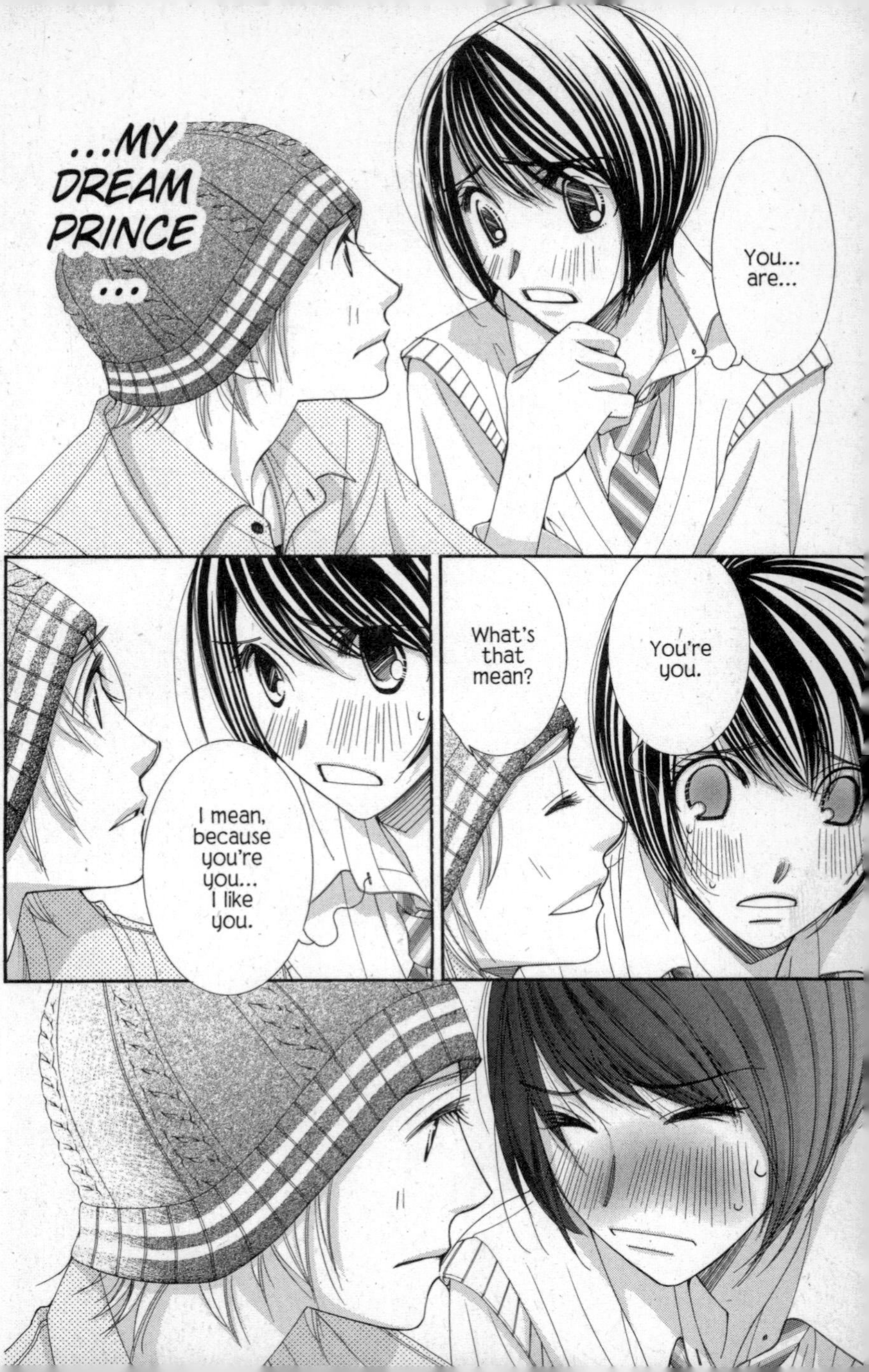
You... are...
...MY DREAM PRINCE ...
You're you.
What's that mean?
I mean, because you're you... I like you.

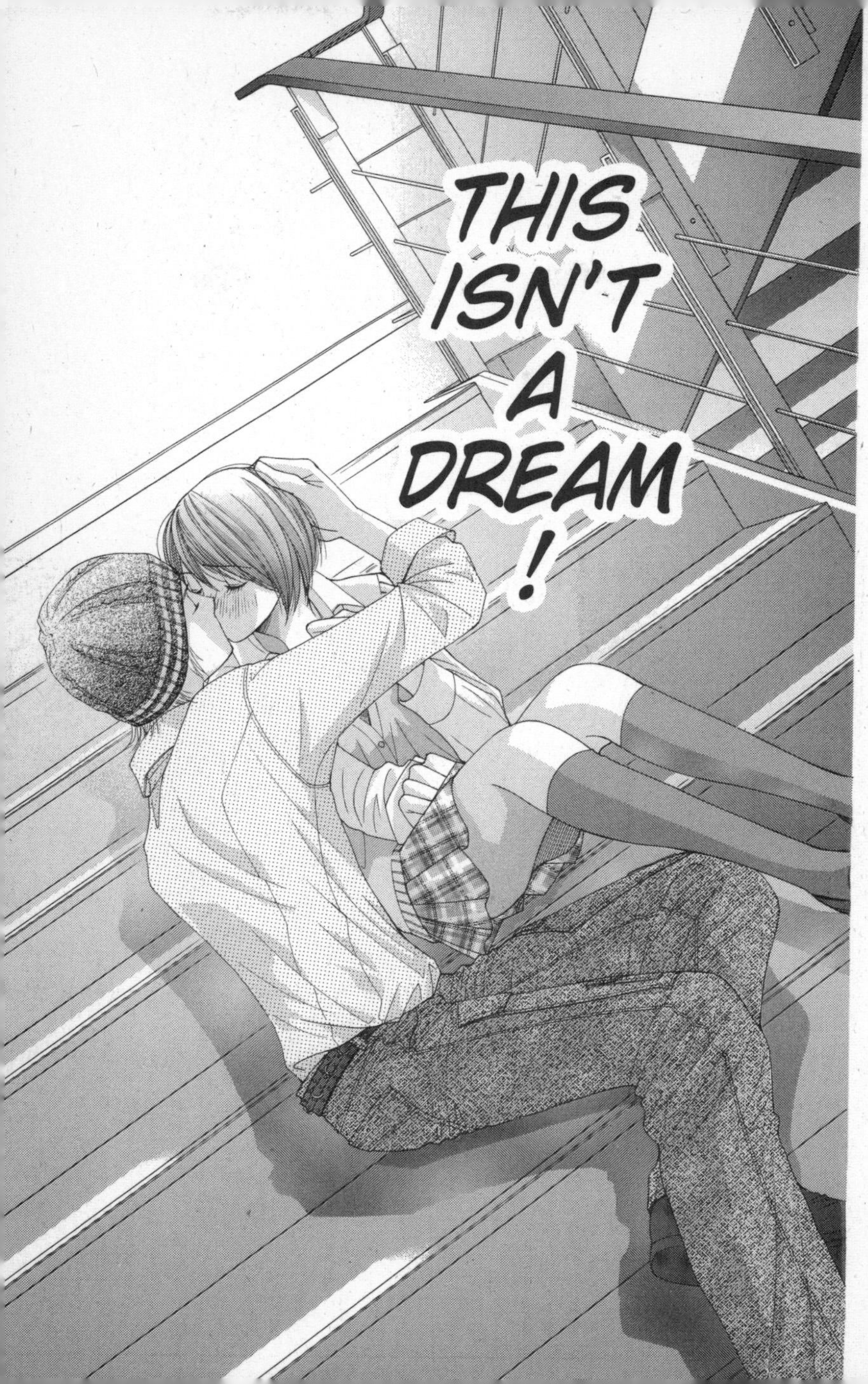
THIS ISN'T A DREAM!

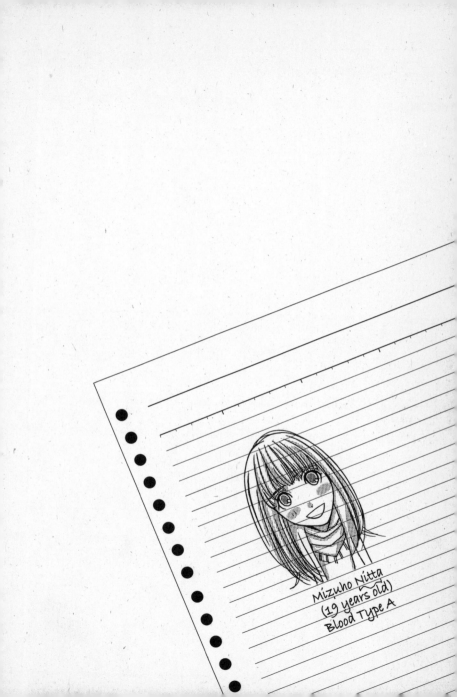

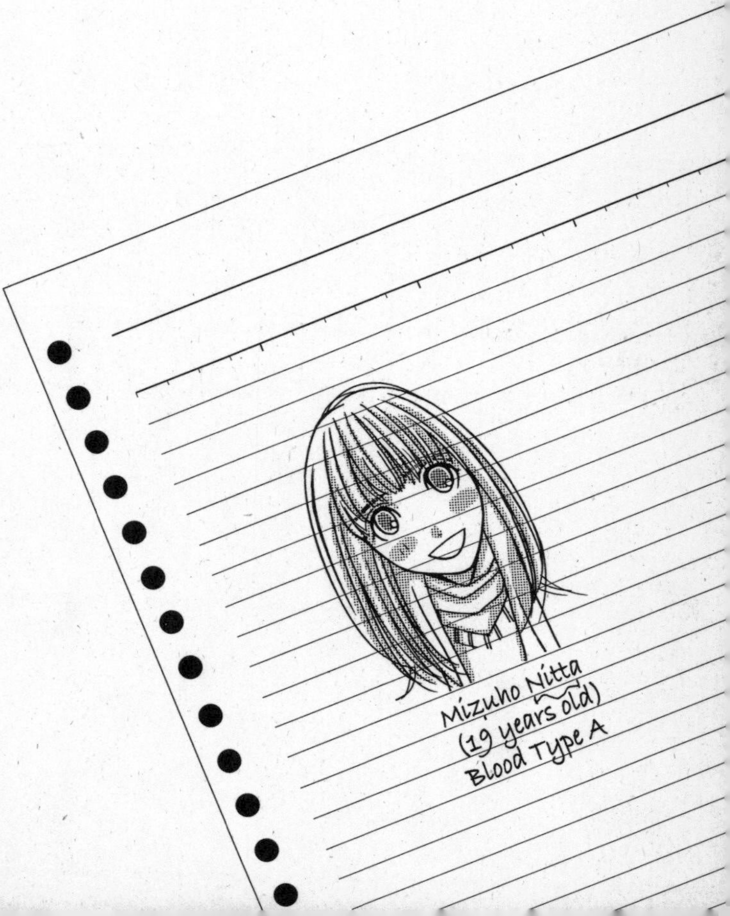
Mizuho Nitta
(19 years old)
Blood Type A

CHAPTER 19

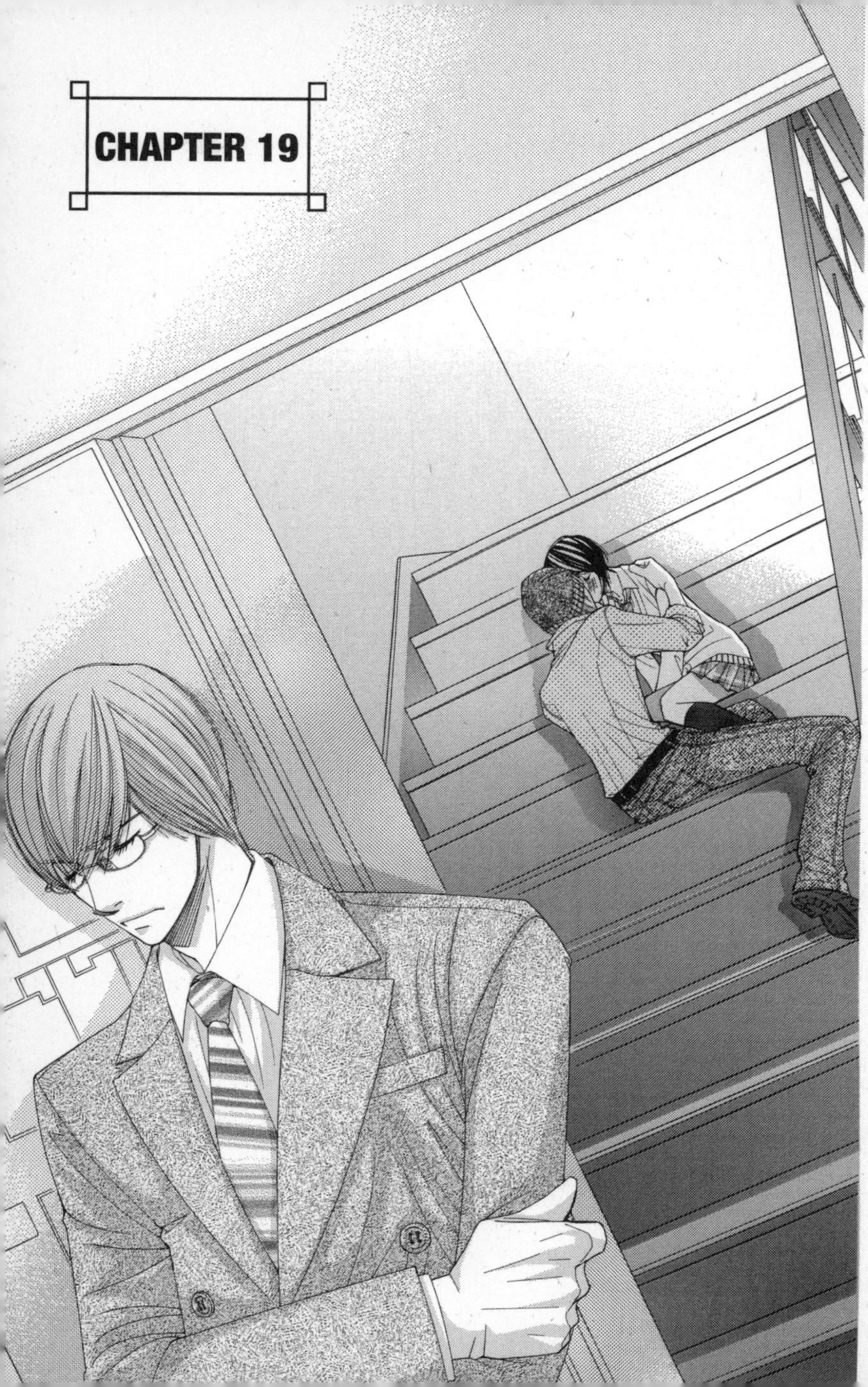

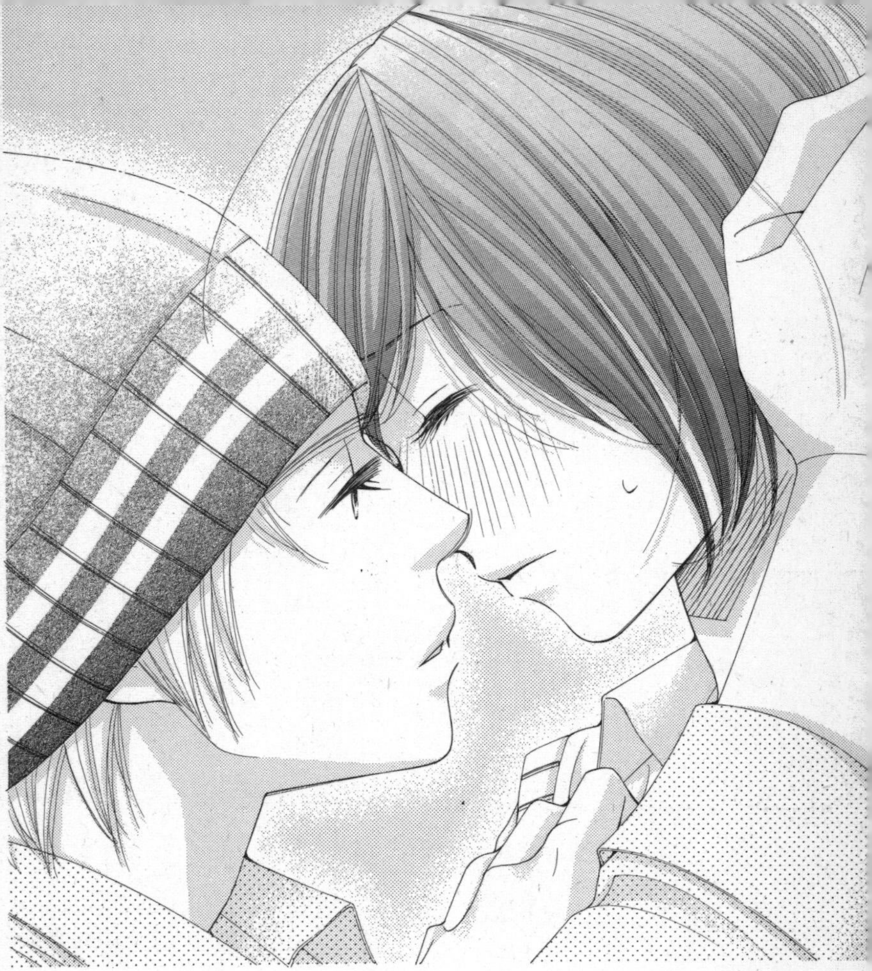

Honey Hunt

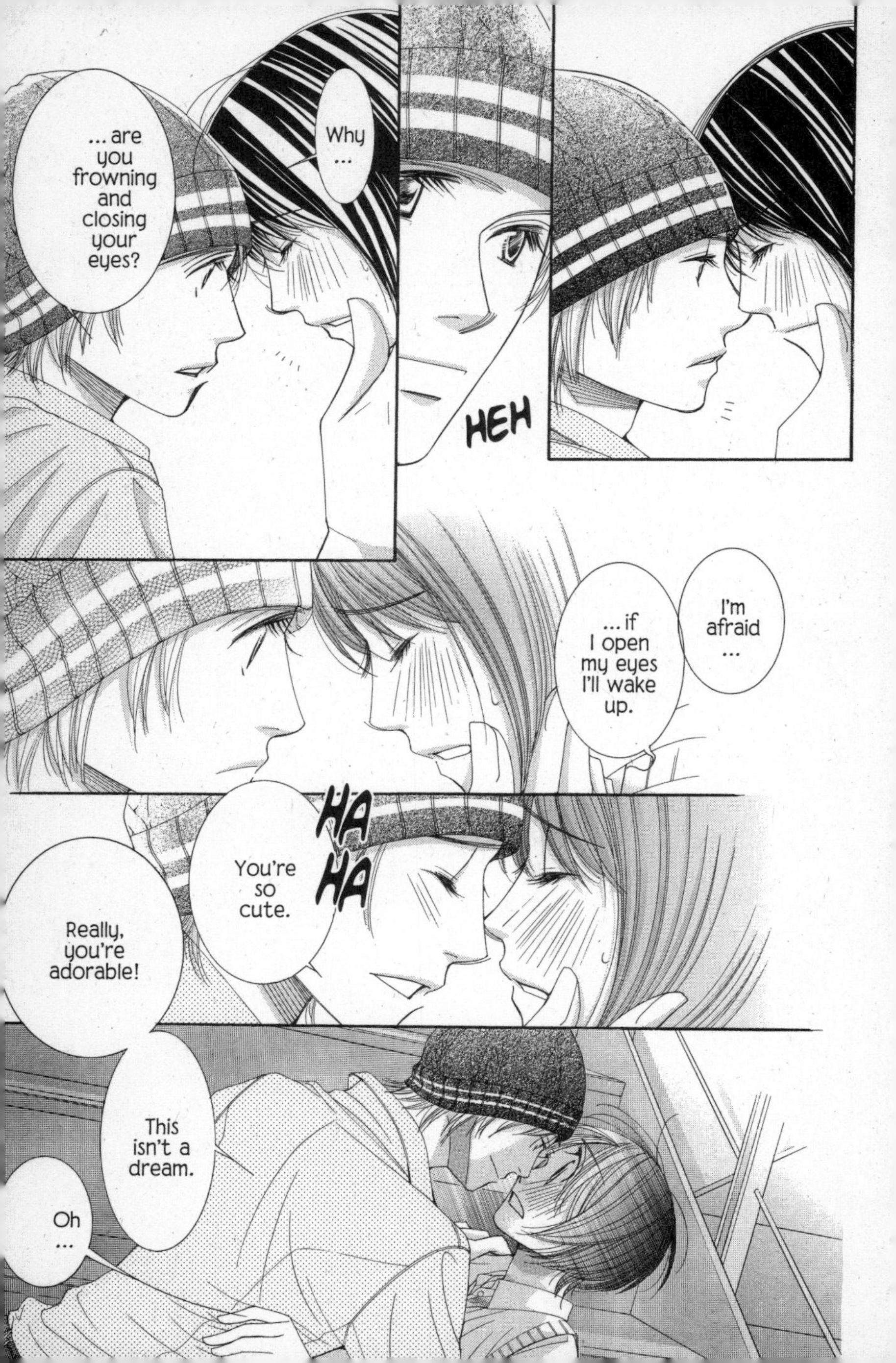
HEH
Why ...
... are you frowning and closing your eyes?
I'm afraid ...
... if I open my eyes I'll wake up.
HA HA
You're so cute.
Really, you're adorable!
This isn't a dream.
Oh ...

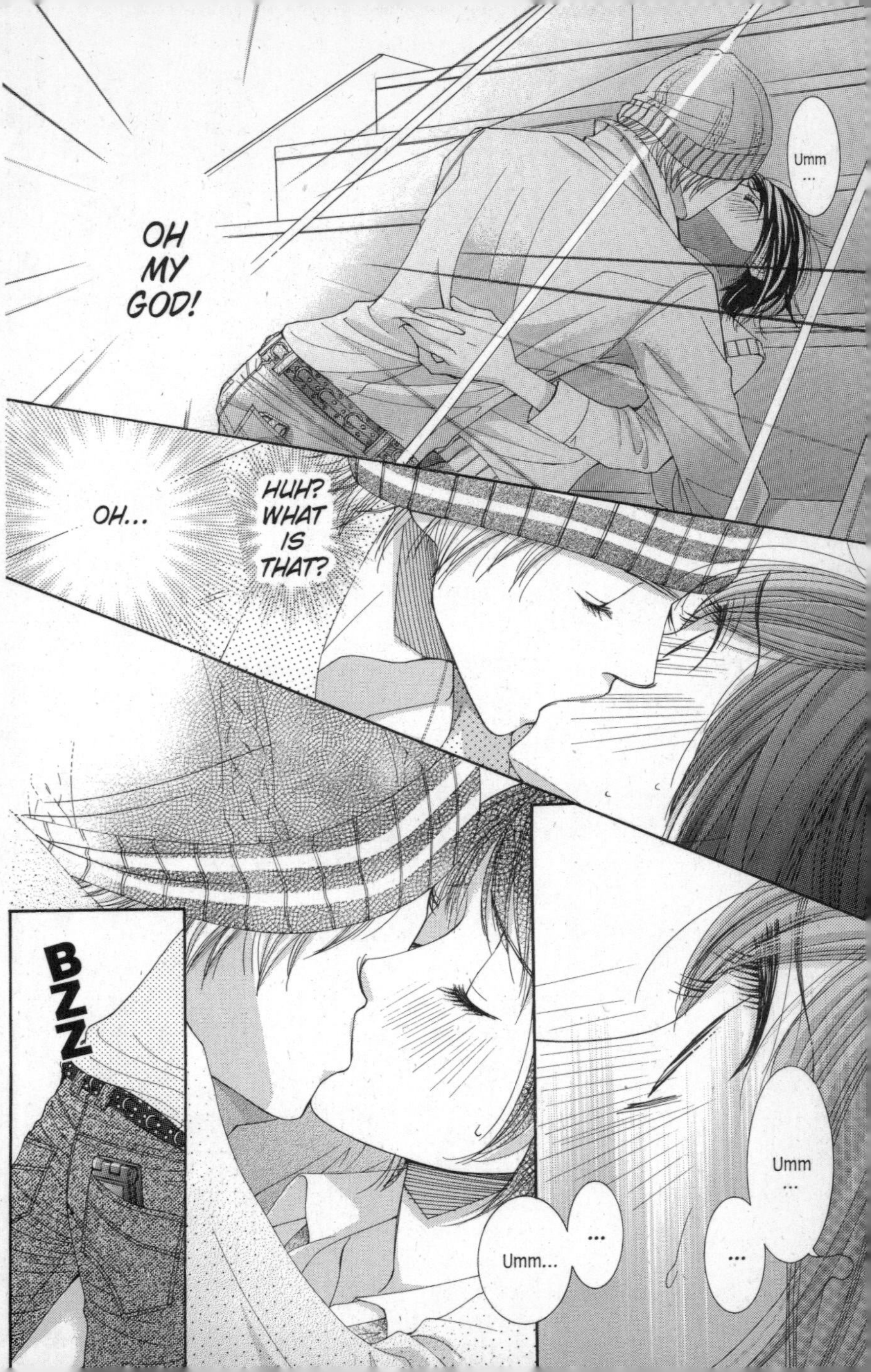
Umm ...
OH MY GOD!
HUH? WHAT IS THAT?
OH...
Umm ...
...
...
Umm...
BZZ

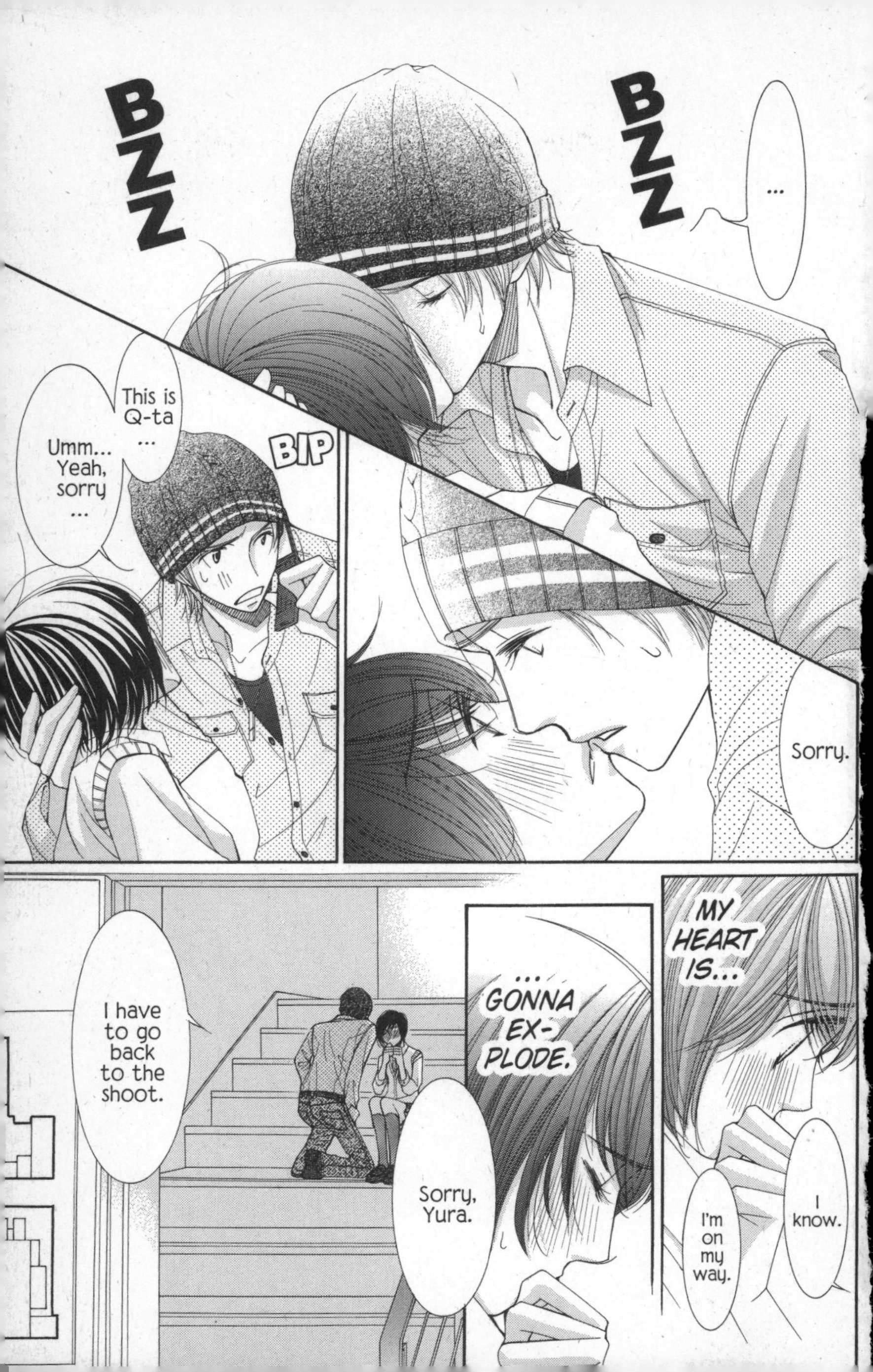
...
BZZ
BZZ
Sorry.
BIP
This is Q-ta ...
Umm... Yeah, sorry ...
MY HEART IS...
I know.
I'm on my way.
...GONNA EX-PLODE.
Sorry, Yura.
I have to go back to the shoot.

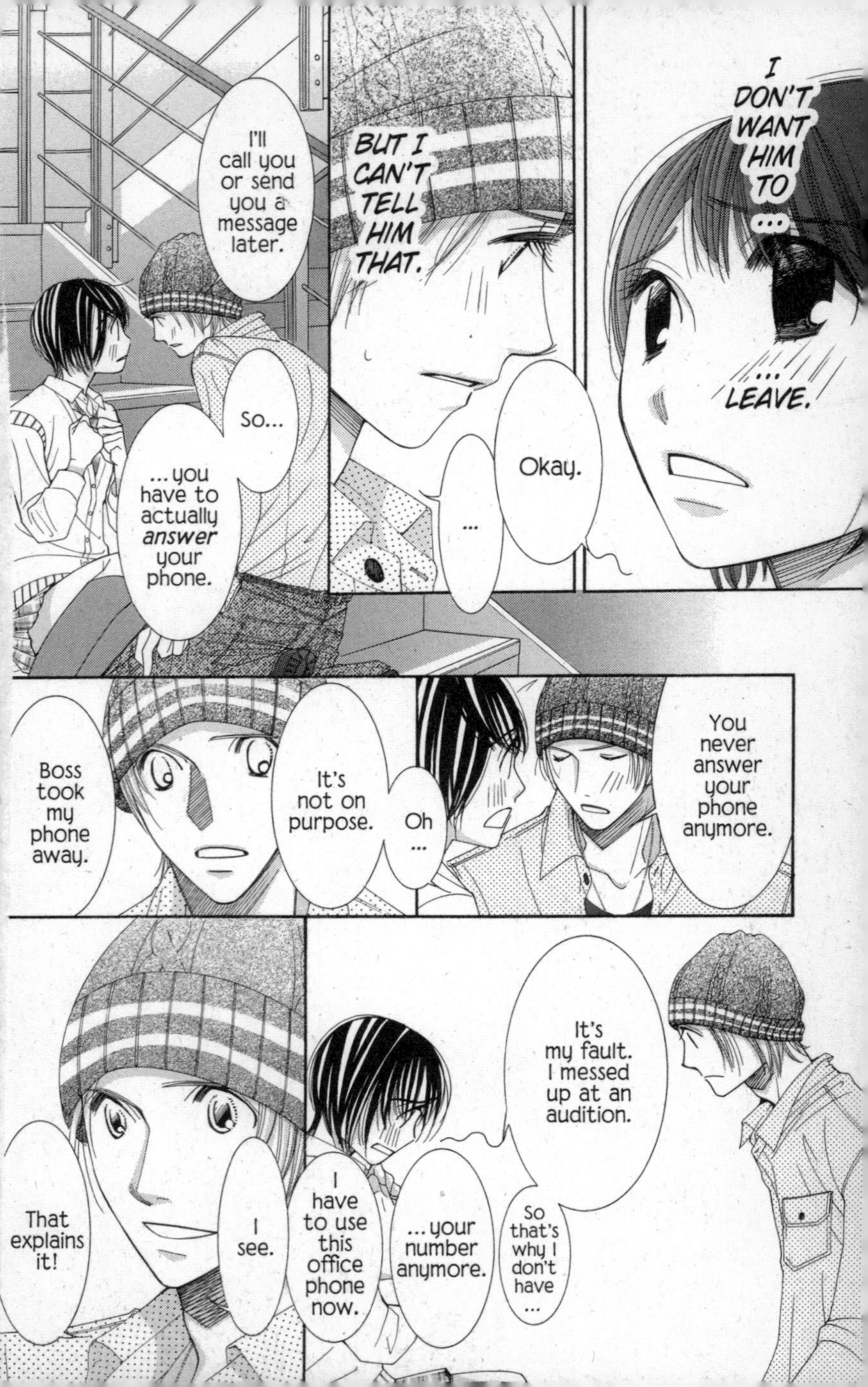
I DON'T WANT HIM TO ...
... LEAVE.
BUT I CAN'T TELL HIM THAT.
Okay.
...
I'll call you or send you a message later.
So...
... you have to actually *answer* your phone.
You never answer your phone anymore.
Oh ...
It's not on purpose.
Boss took my phone away.
It's my fault. I messed up at an audition.
So that's why I don't have ...
... your number anymore.
I have to use this office phone now.
I see.
That explains it!

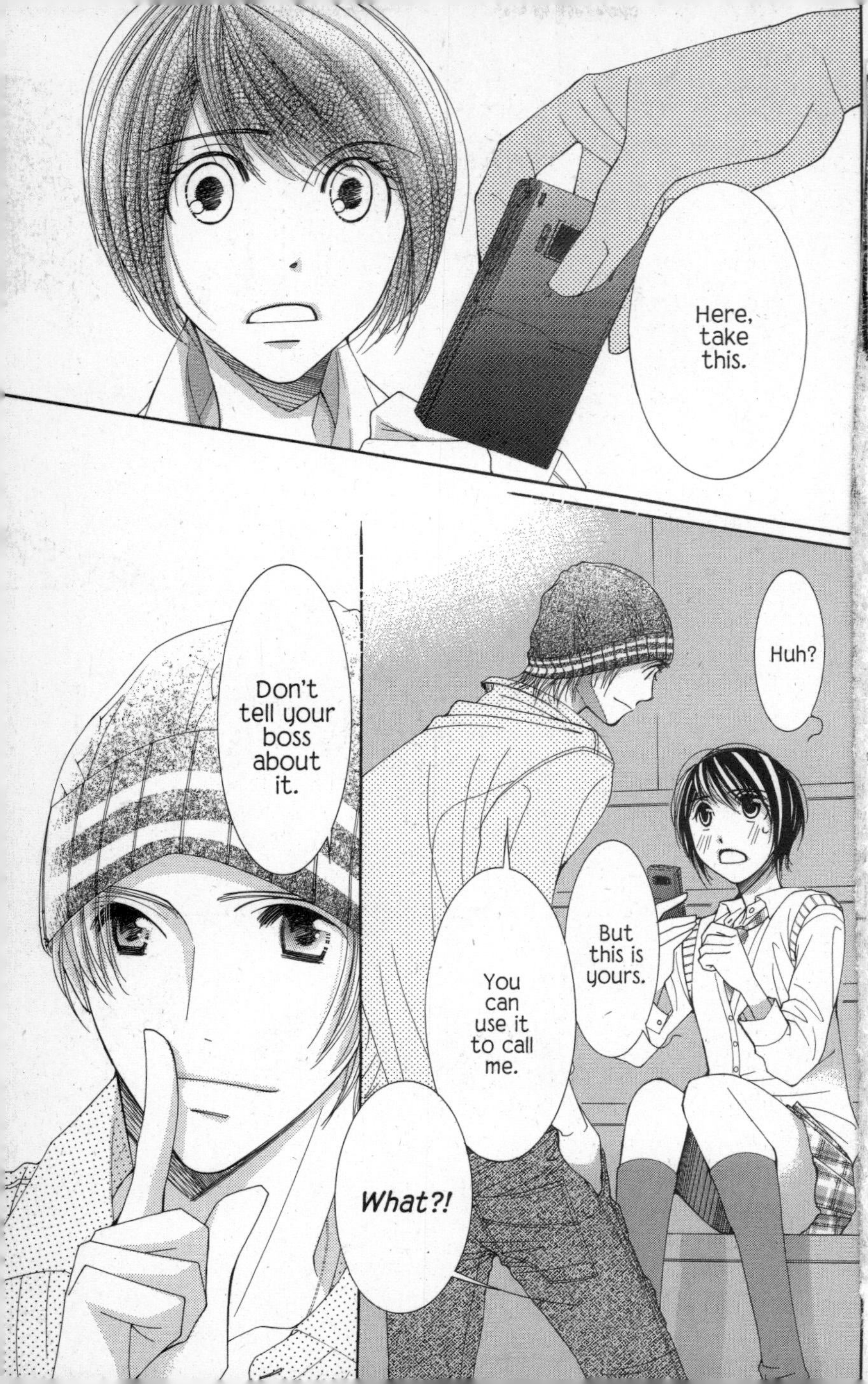
Here, take this.
Huh?
But this is yours.
You can use it to call me.
What?!
Don't tell your boss about it.

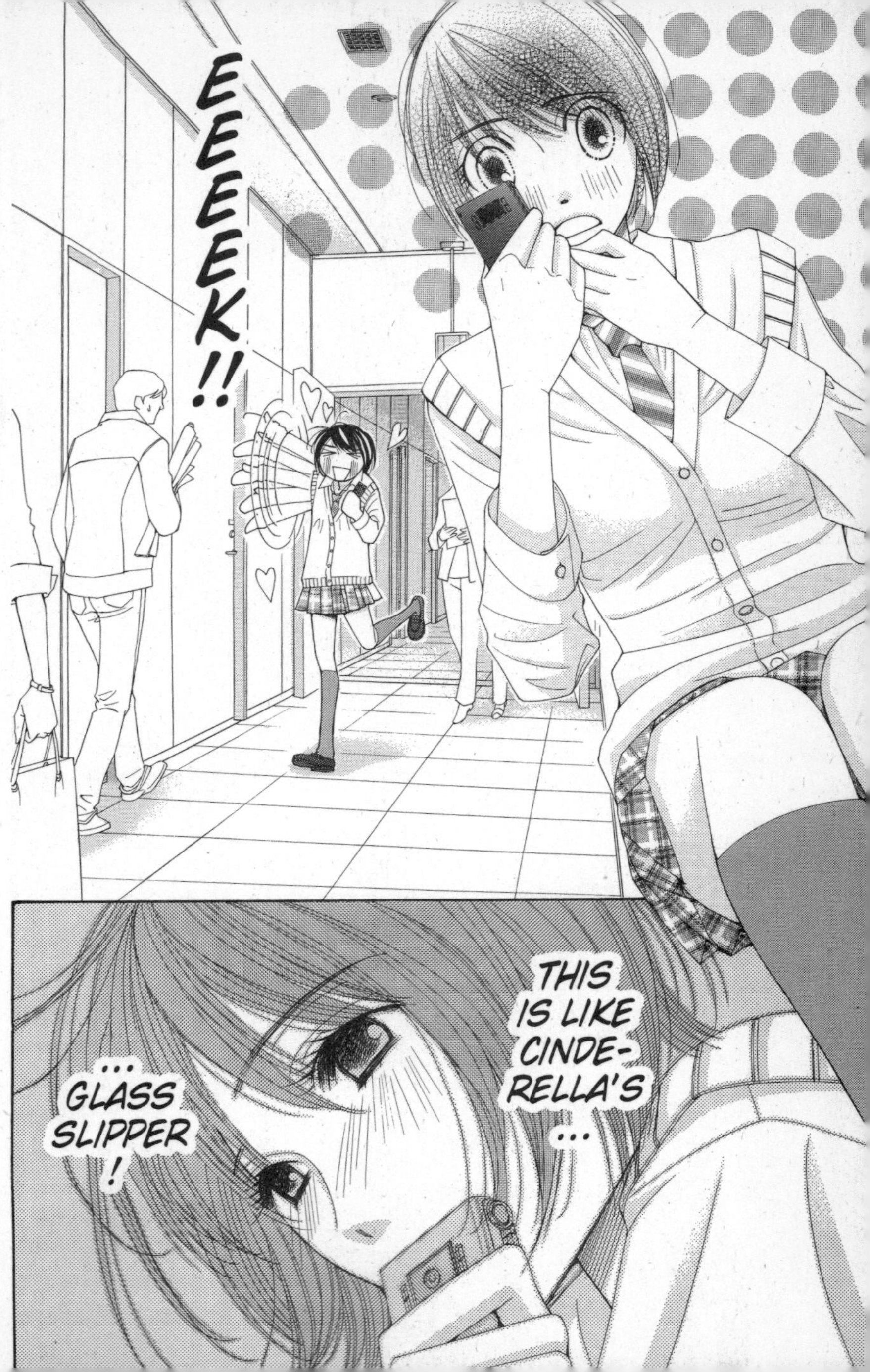
EEEEEK!!
THIS IS LIKE CINDE-RELLA'S ...
... GLASS SLIPPER!

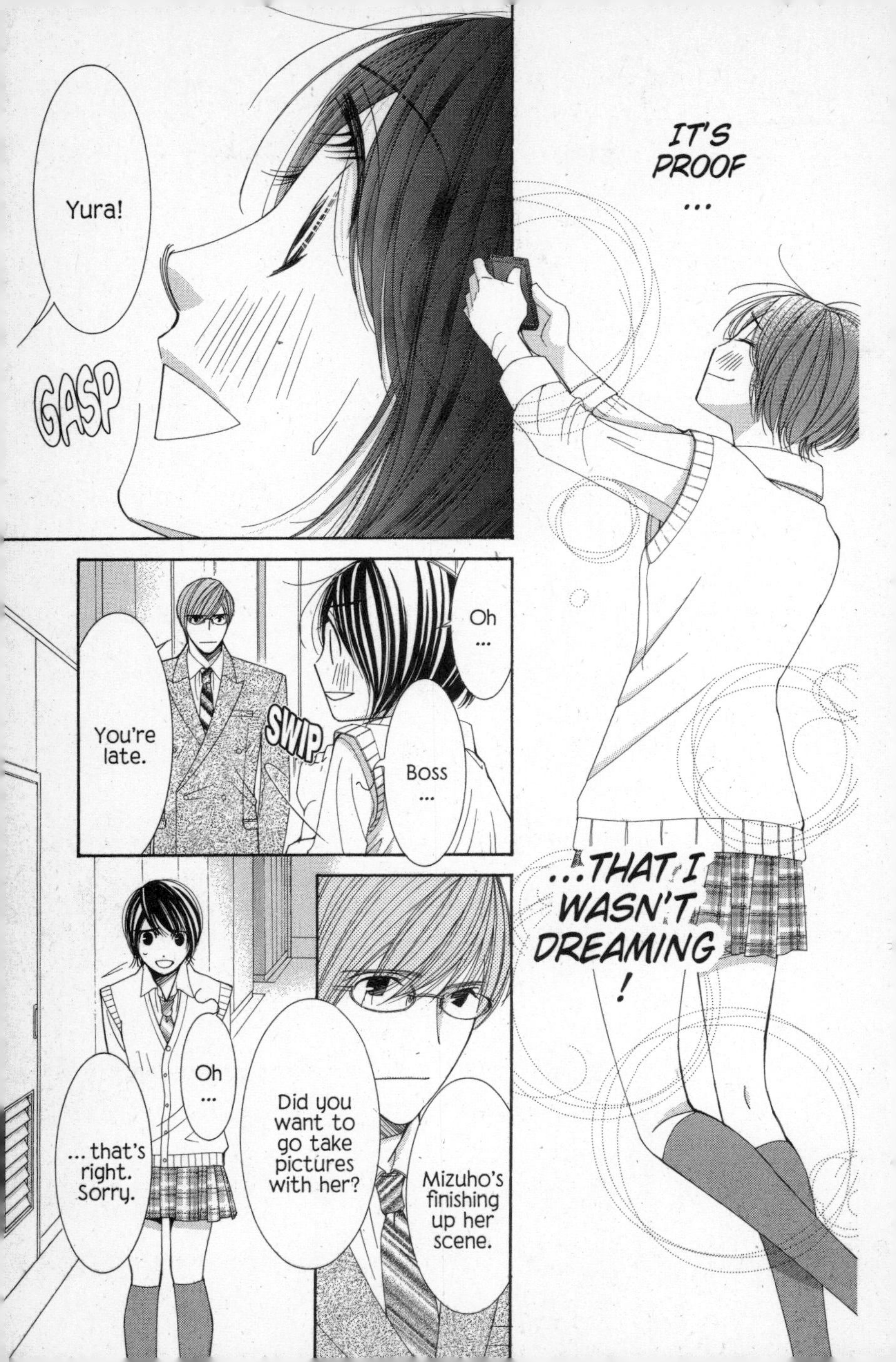

IT'S PROOF ...
...THAT I WASN'T DREAMING!
Yura!
GASP
Oh ...
Boss ...
SWIP
You're late.
Mizuho's finishing up her scene.
Did you want to go take pictures with her?
Oh ...
... that's right. Sorry.

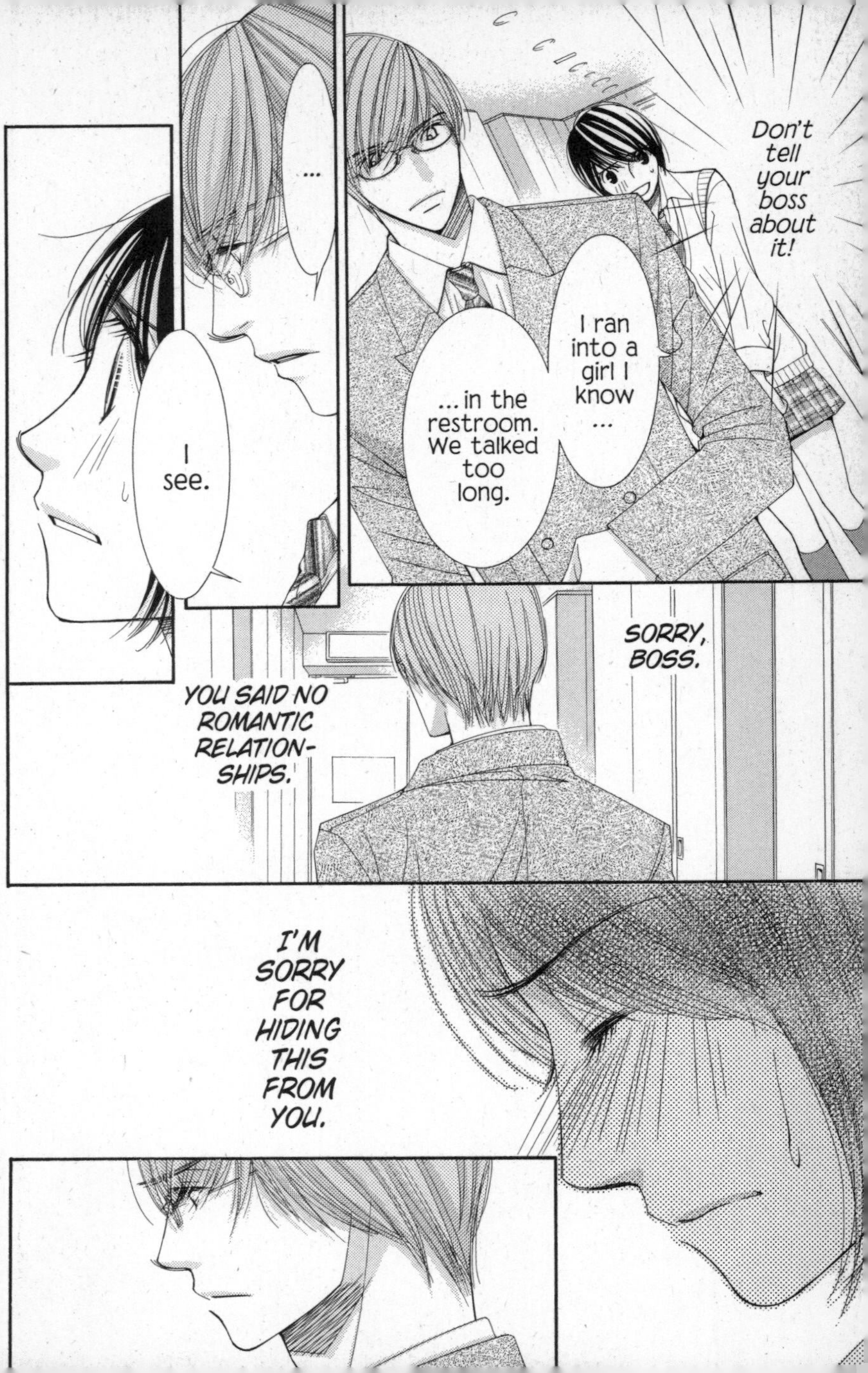
Don't tell your boss about it!
I ran into a girl I know ...
... in the restroom. We talked too long.
...
I see.
SORRY, BOSS.
YOU SAID NO ROMANTIC RELATION-SHIPS.
I'M SORRY FOR HIDING THIS FROM YOU.

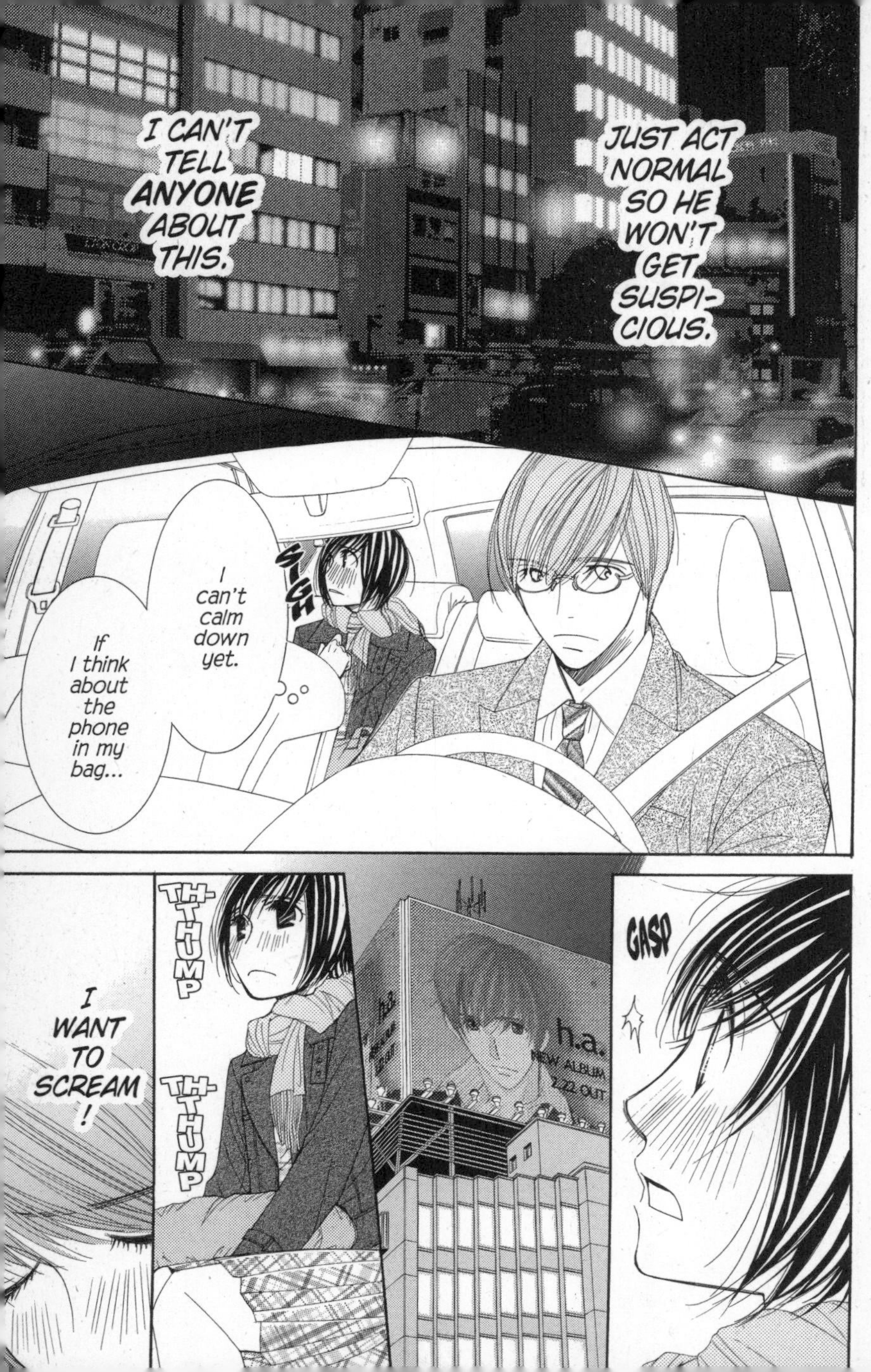
JUST ACT NORMAL SO HE WON'T GET SUSPICIOUS.
I CAN'T TELL ANYONE ABOUT THIS.
SIGH
I can't calm down yet.
If I think about the phone in my bag...
GASP
h.a. NEW ALBUM 2.22 OUT
TH-THUMP
TH-THUMP
I WANT TO SCREAM!

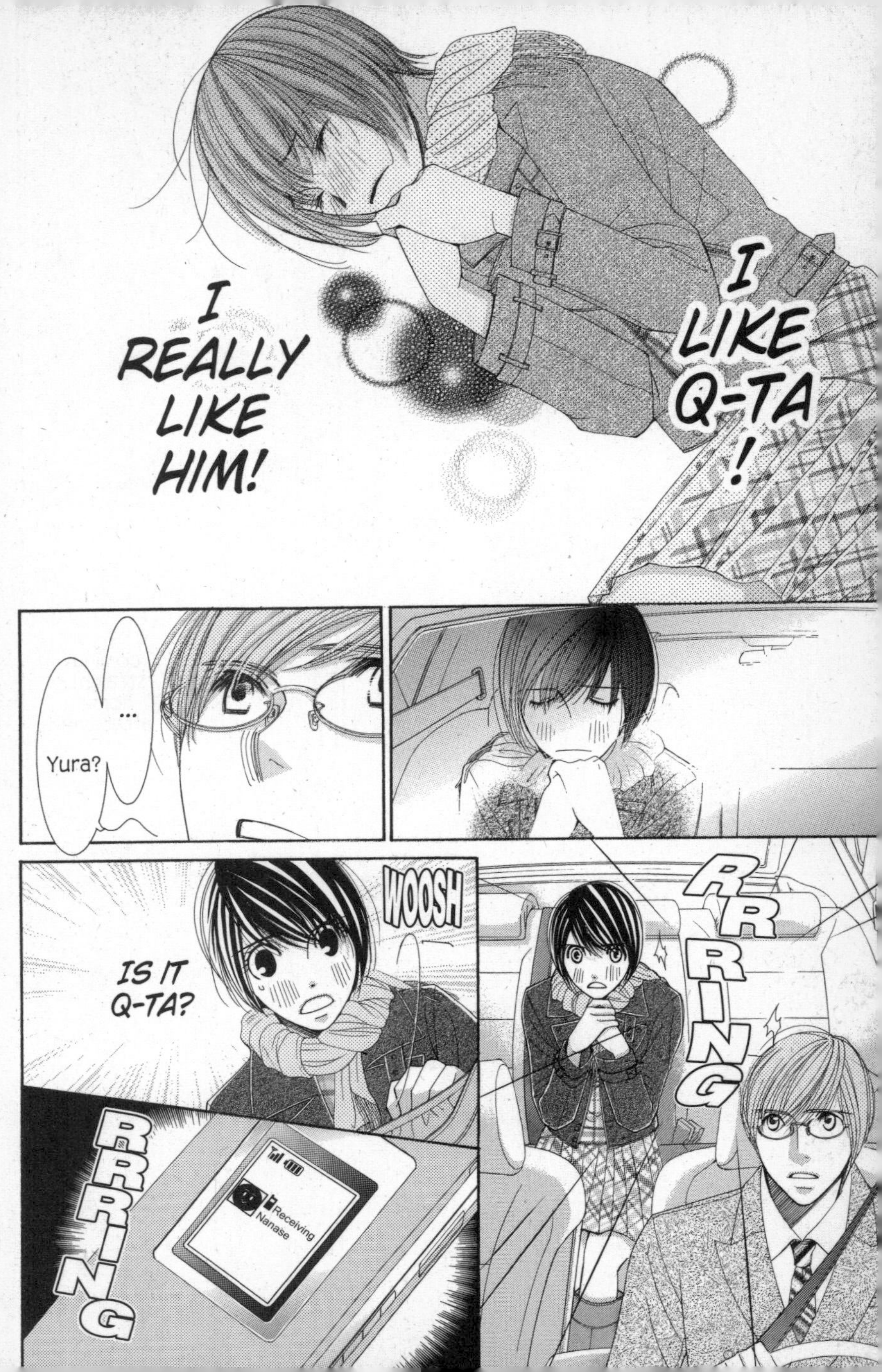
I LIKE Q-TA!
I REALLY LIKE HIM!
...
Yura?
RRRING
WOOSH
IS IT Q-TA?
Receiving
Nanase
RRRING

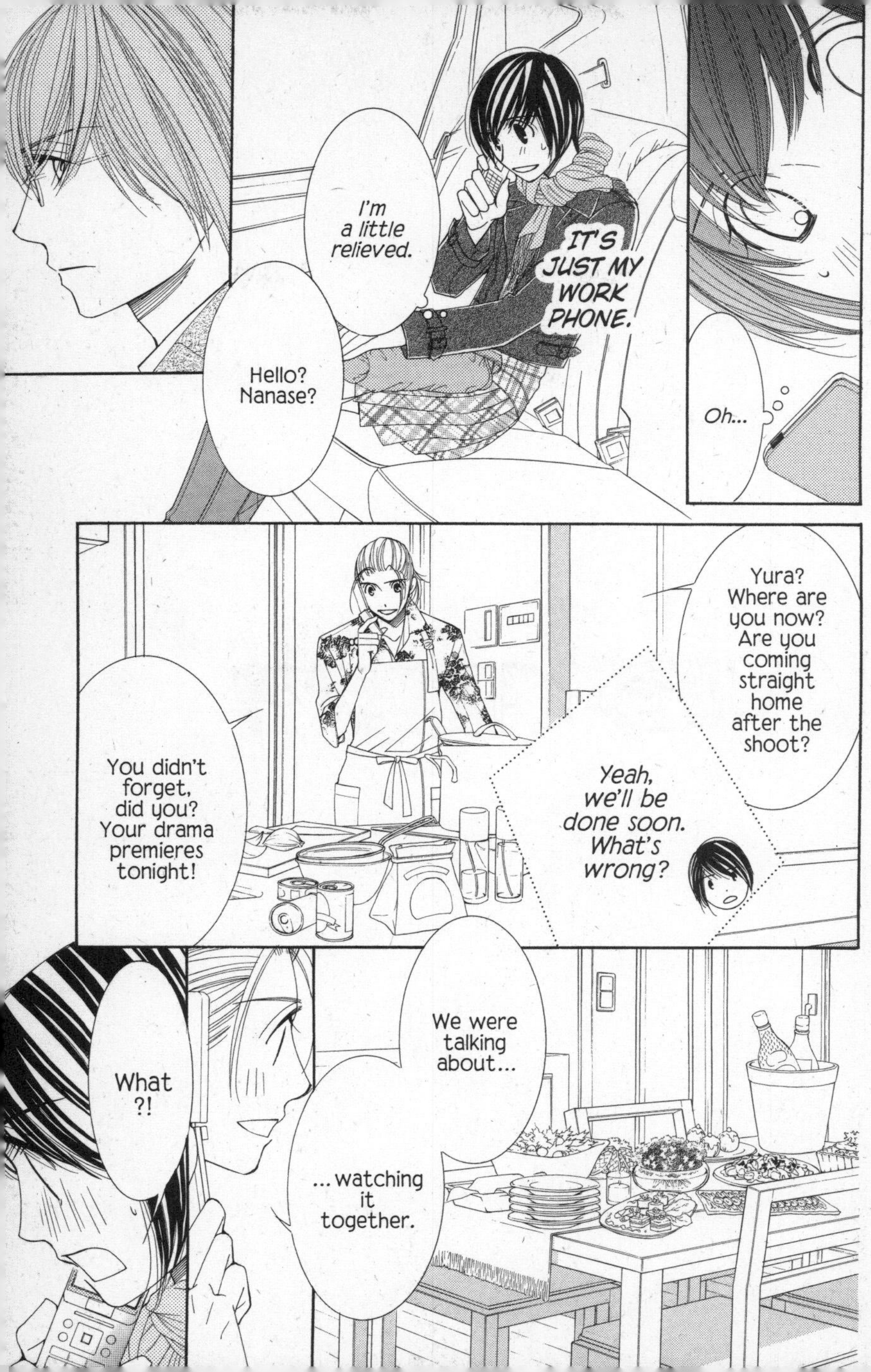
Oh...
IT'S JUST MY WORK PHONE.
I'm a little relieved.
Hello? Nanase?
Yura? Where are you now? Are you coming straight home after the shoot?
Yeah, we'll be done soon. What's wrong?
You didn't forget, did you? Your drama premieres tonight!
We were talking about...
...watching it together.
What ?!

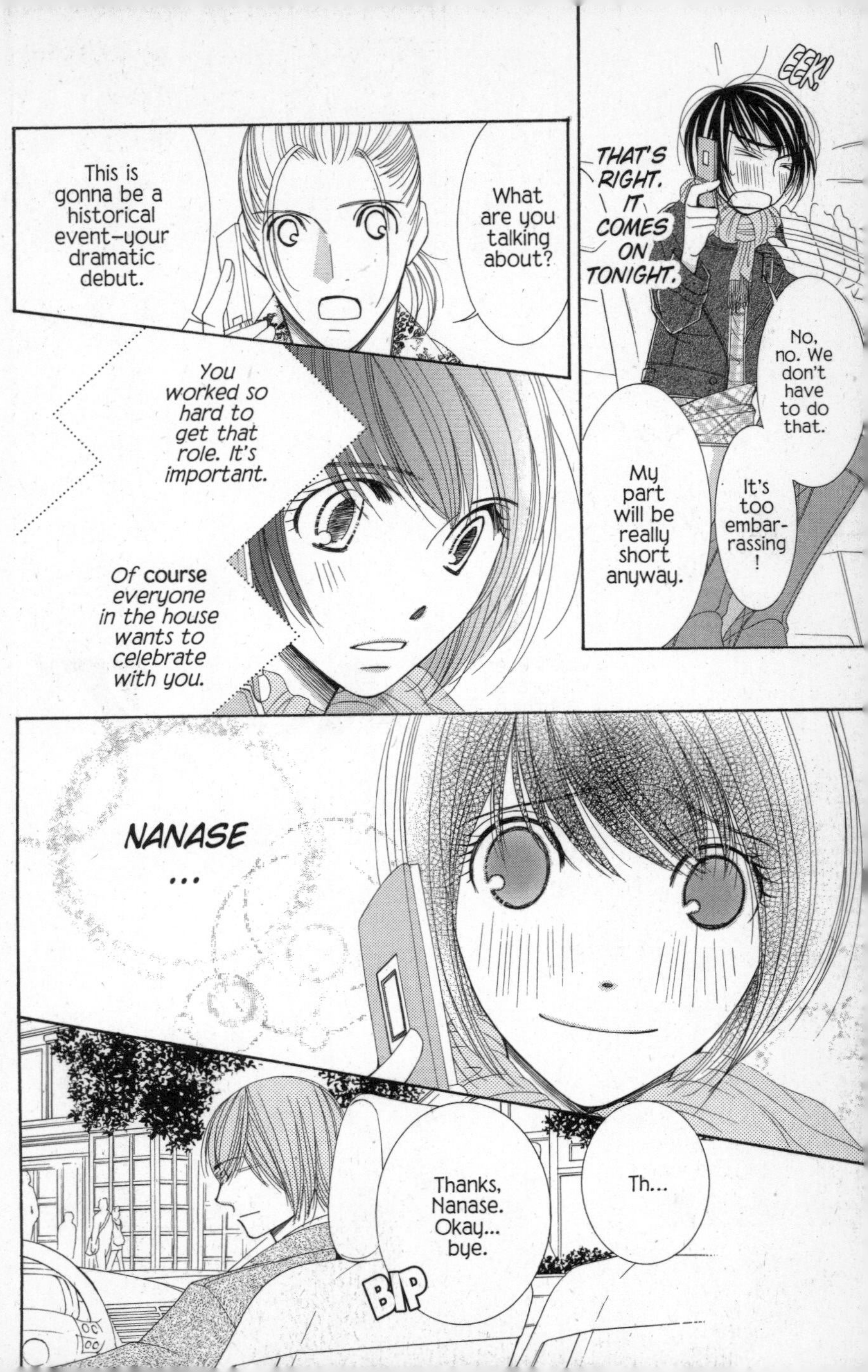

EEK!
THAT'S RIGHT. IT COMES ON TONIGHT.
No, no. We don't have to do that.
It's too embarrassing!
My part will be really short anyway.
What are you talking about?
This is gonna be a historical event—your dramatic debut.
You worked so hard to get that role. It's important.
Of course everyone in the house wants to celebrate with you.
NANASE ...
Th...
Thanks, Nanase. Okay... bye.
BIP

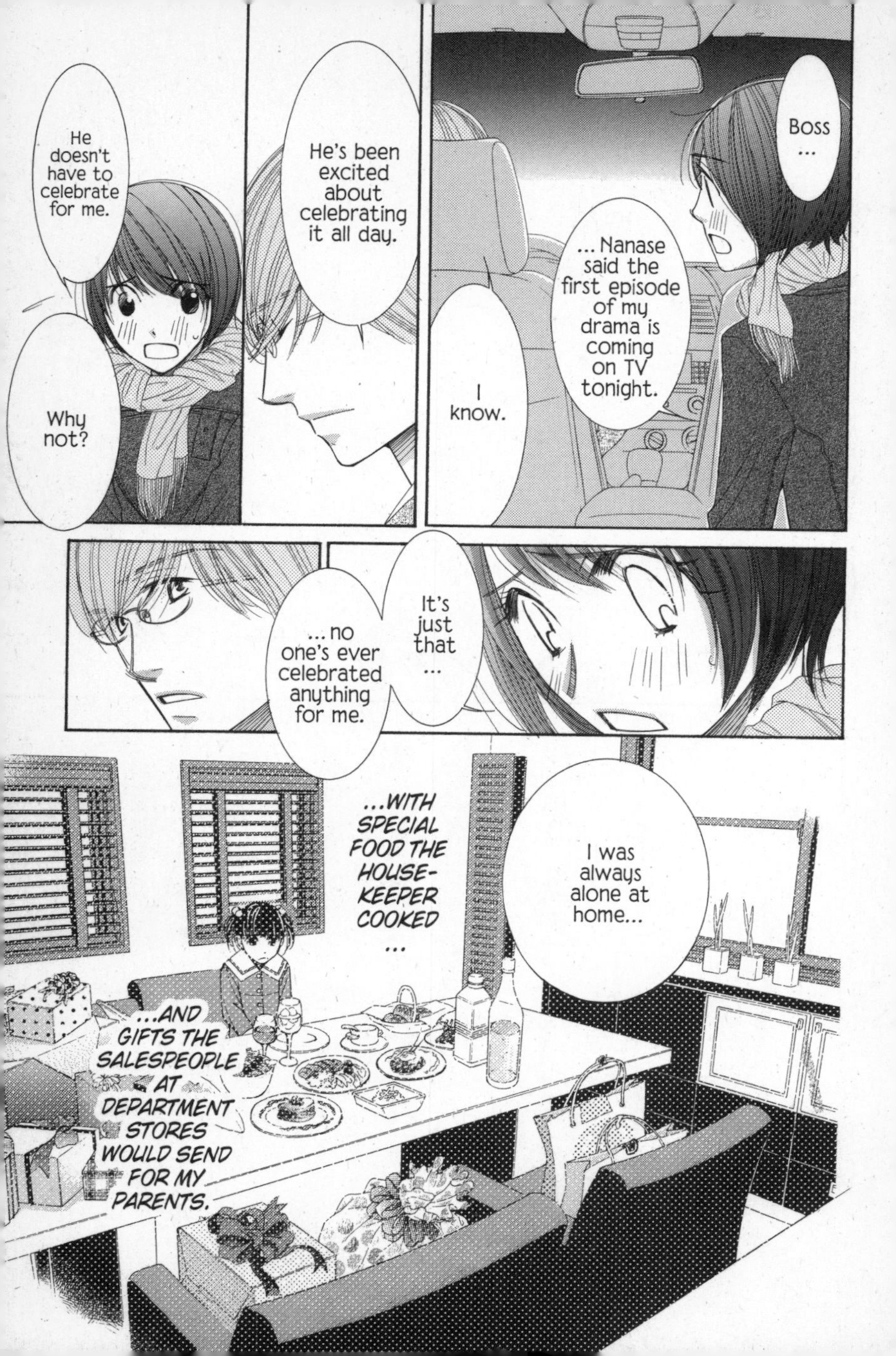
Boss ...
... Nanase said the first episode of my drama is coming on TV tonight.
I know.
He's been excited about celebrating it all day.
He doesn't have to celebrate for me.
Why not?
It's just that ...
... no one's ever celebrated anything for me.
I was always alone at home...
...WITH SPECIAL FOOD THE HOUSE-KEEPER COOKED ...
...AND GIFTS THE SALESPEOPLE AT DEPARTMENT STORES WOULD SEND FOR MY PARENTS.

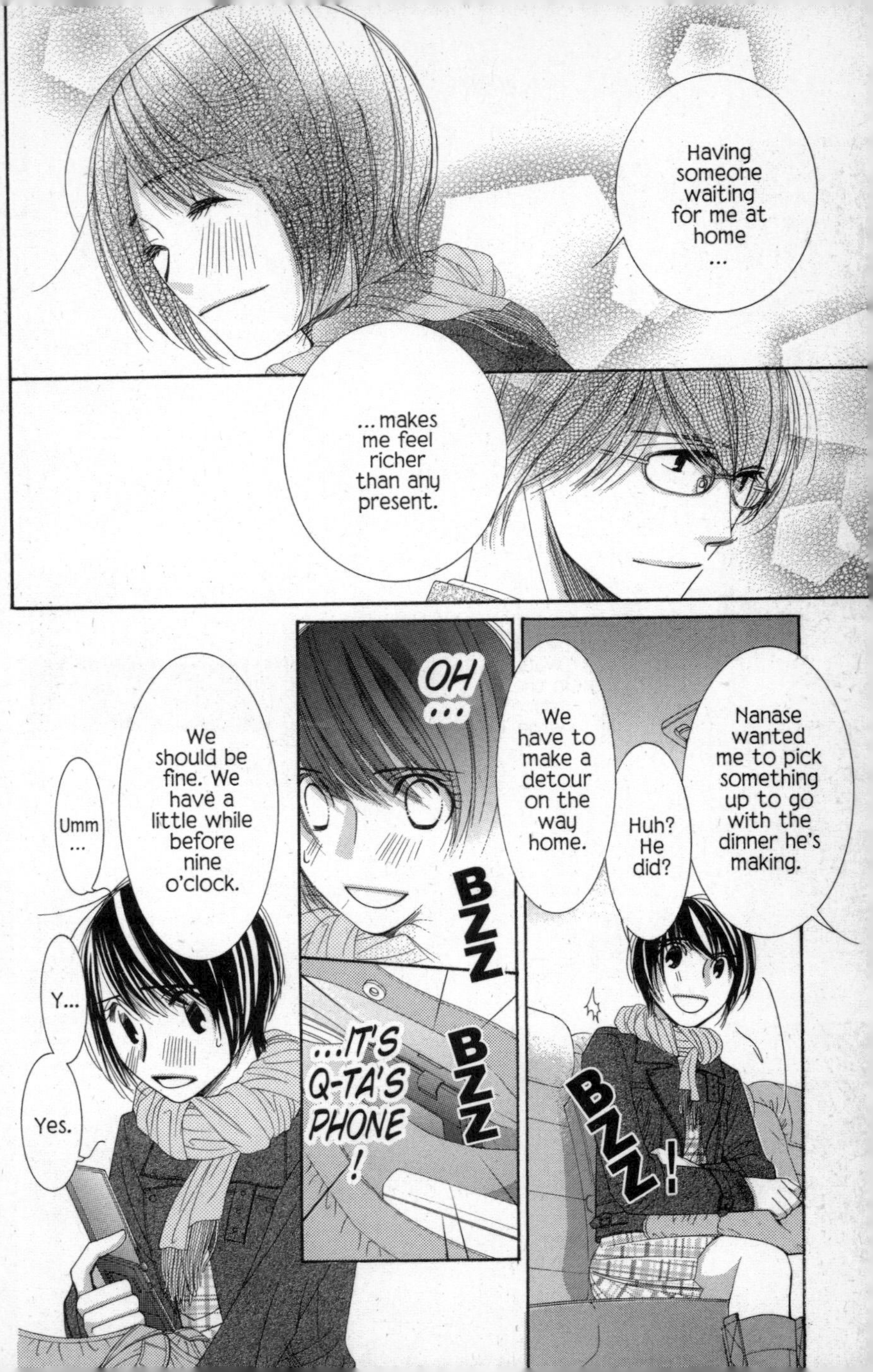

Having someone waiting for me at home ...
... makes me feel richer than any present.
Nanase wanted me to pick something up to go with the dinner he's making.
Huh? He did?
We have to make a detour on the way home.
BZZ!
OH ...
BZZ
...IT'S Q-TA'S PHONE!
BZZ
We should be fine. We have a little while before nine o'clock.
Umm ...
Y...
Yes.

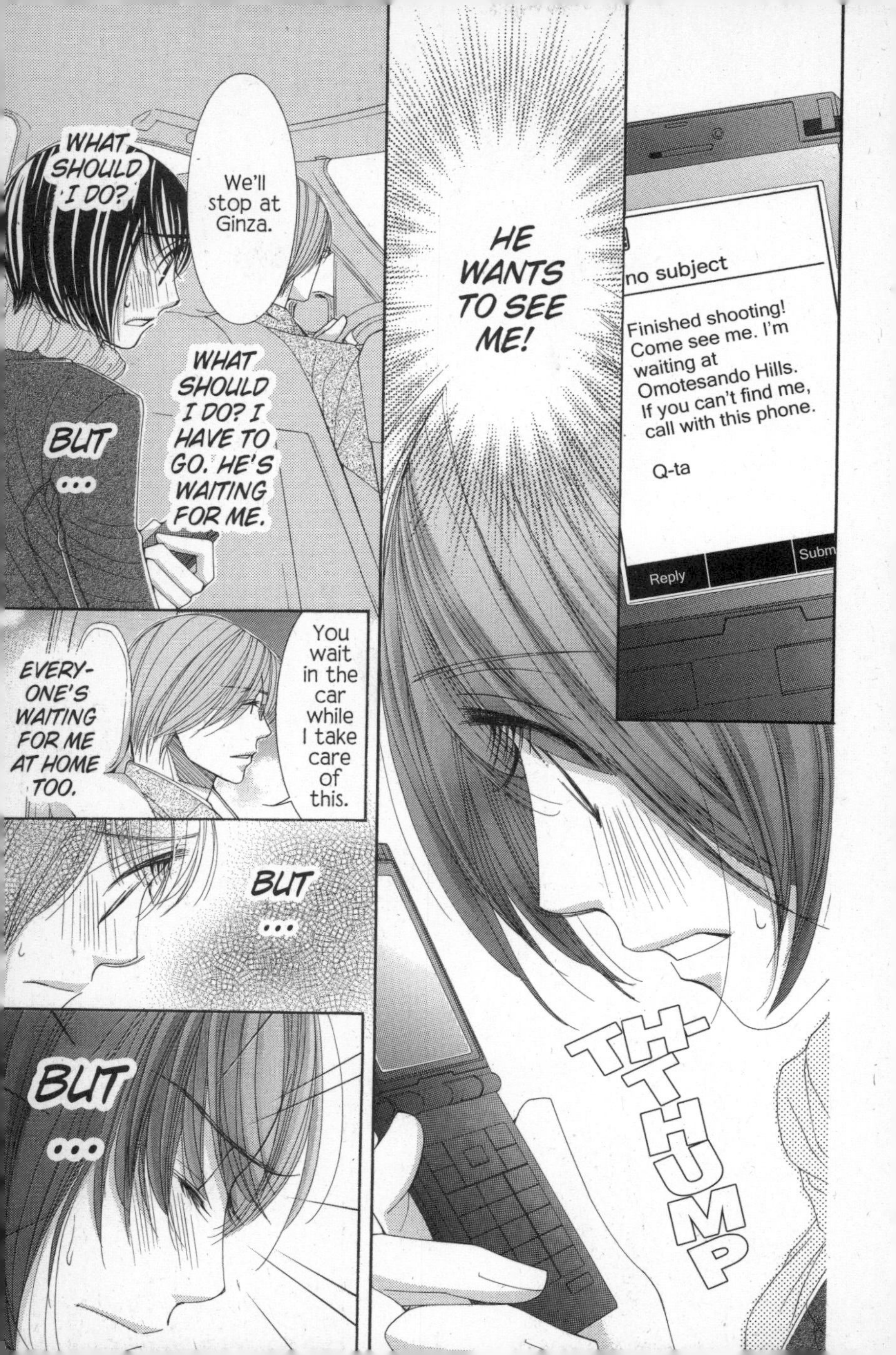
no subject
Finished shooting! Come see me. I'm waiting at Omotesando Hills. If you can't find me, call with this phone.
Q-ta
Reply
Subm
HE WANTS TO SEE ME!
TH-THUMP
We'll stop at Ginza.
WHAT SHOULD I DO?
WHAT SHOULD I DO? I HAVE TO GO. HE'S WAITING FOR ME.
BUT ...
You wait in the car while I take care of this.
EVERYONE'S WAITING FOR ME AT HOME TOO.
BUT ...
BUT ...

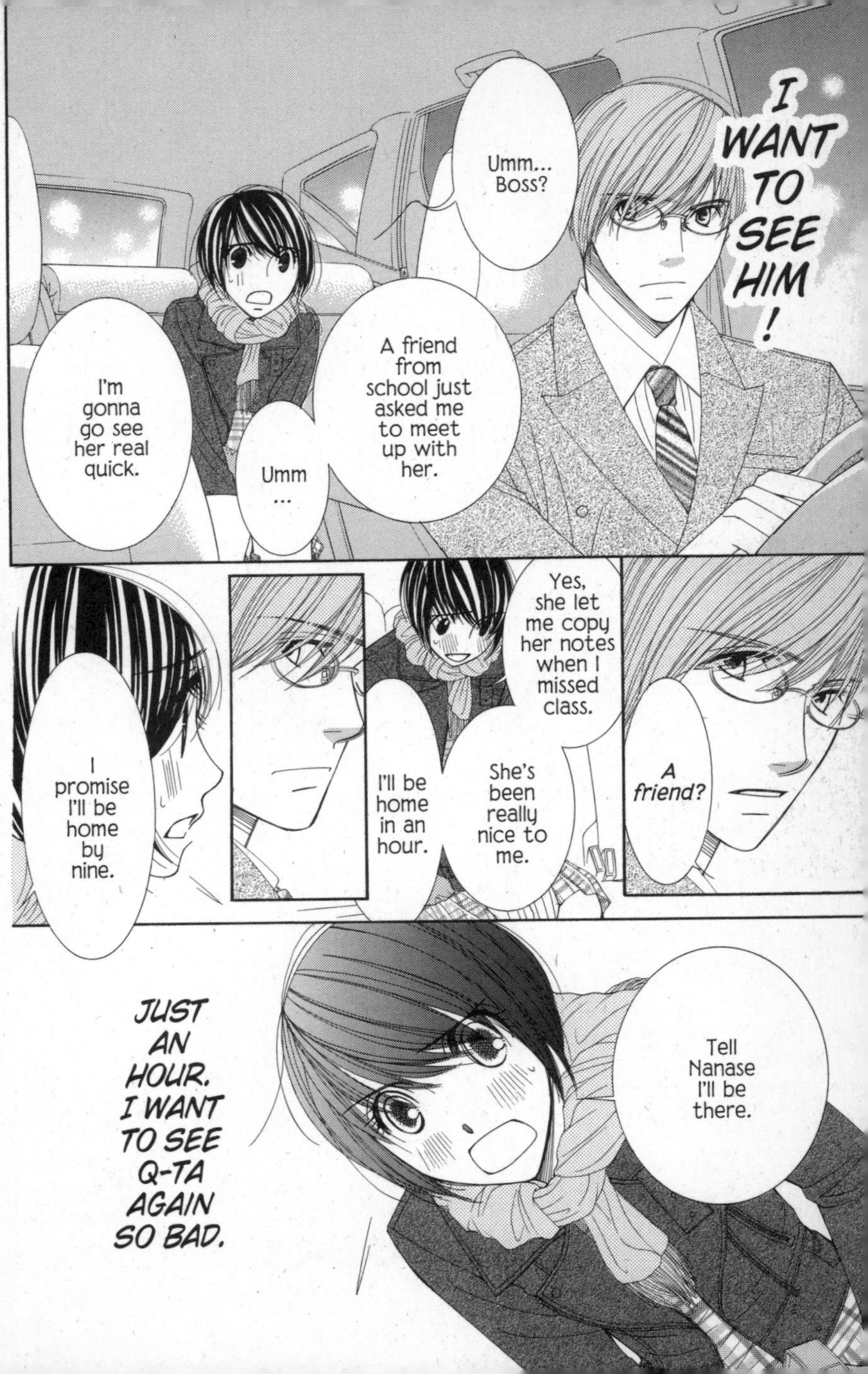
I WANT TO SEE HIM!
Umm... Boss?
A friend from school just asked me to meet up with her.
Umm...
I'm gonna go see her real quick.
A friend?
Yes, she let me copy her notes when I missed class.
She's been really nice to me.
I'll be home in an hour.
I promise I'll be home by nine.
Tell Nanase I'll be there.
JUST AN HOUR. I WANT TO SEE Q-TA AGAIN SO BAD.

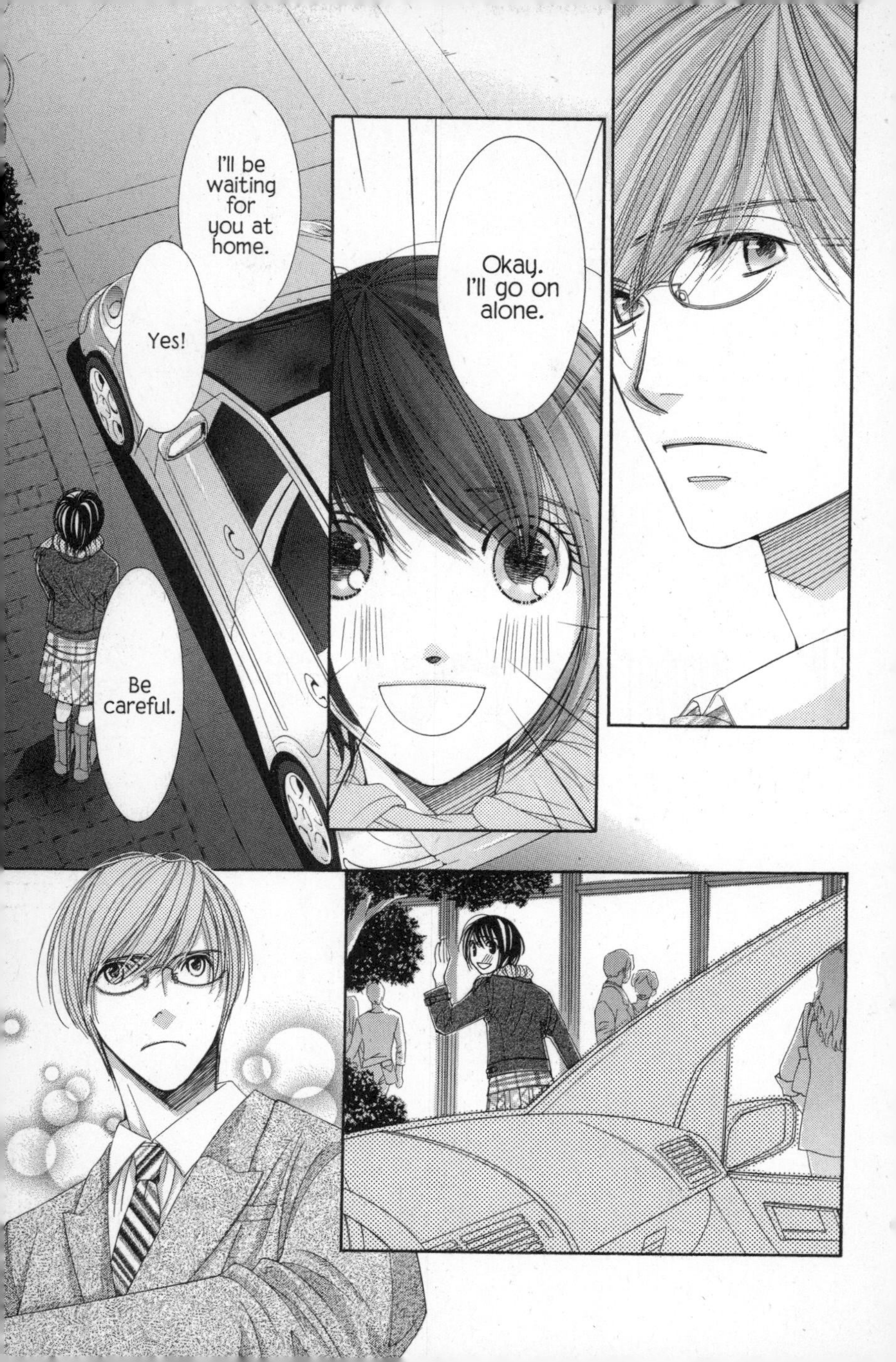
Okay. I'll go on alone.
I'll be waiting for you at home.
Yes!
Be careful.

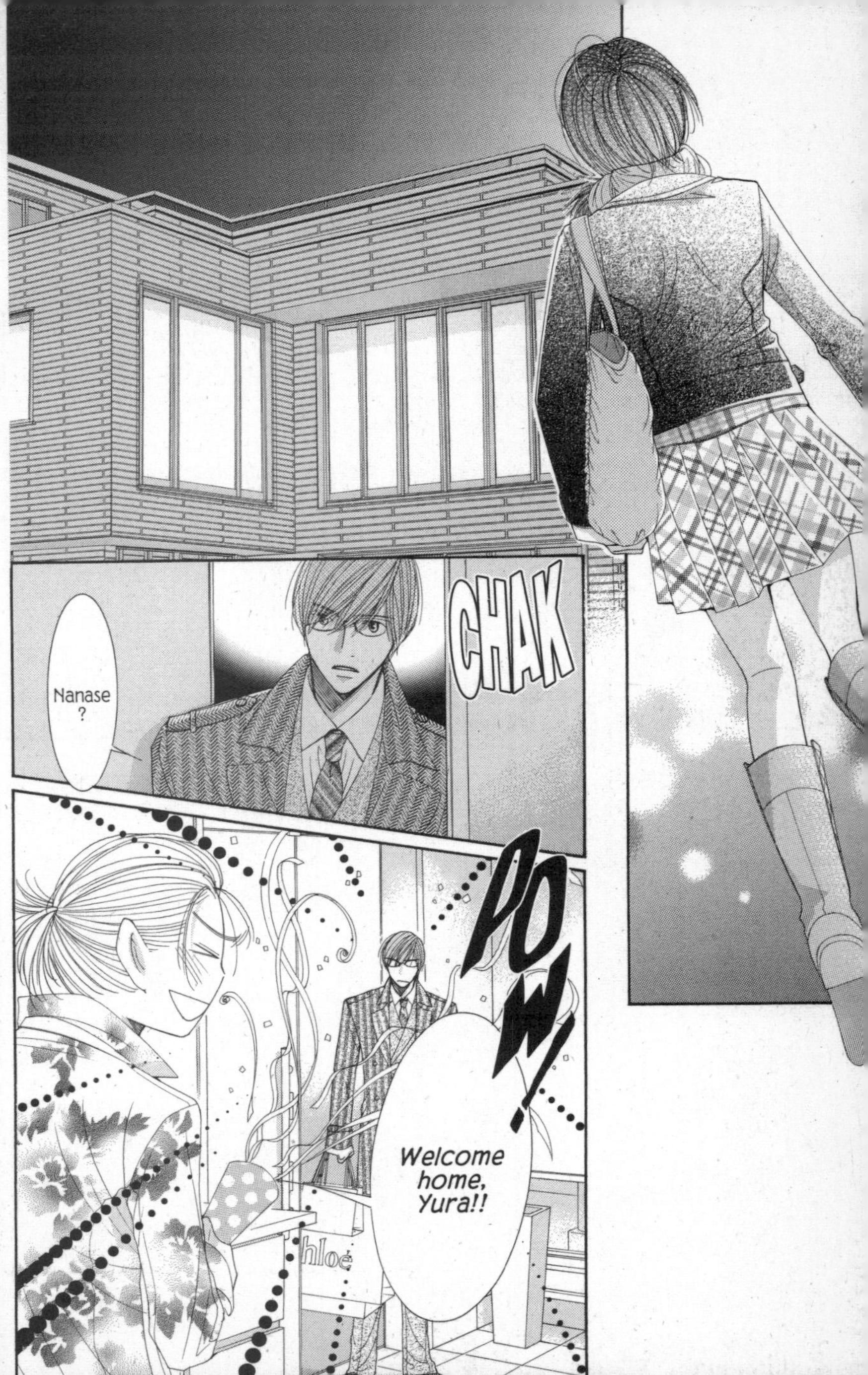
CHAK
Nanase ?
POW!
Welcome home, Yura!!

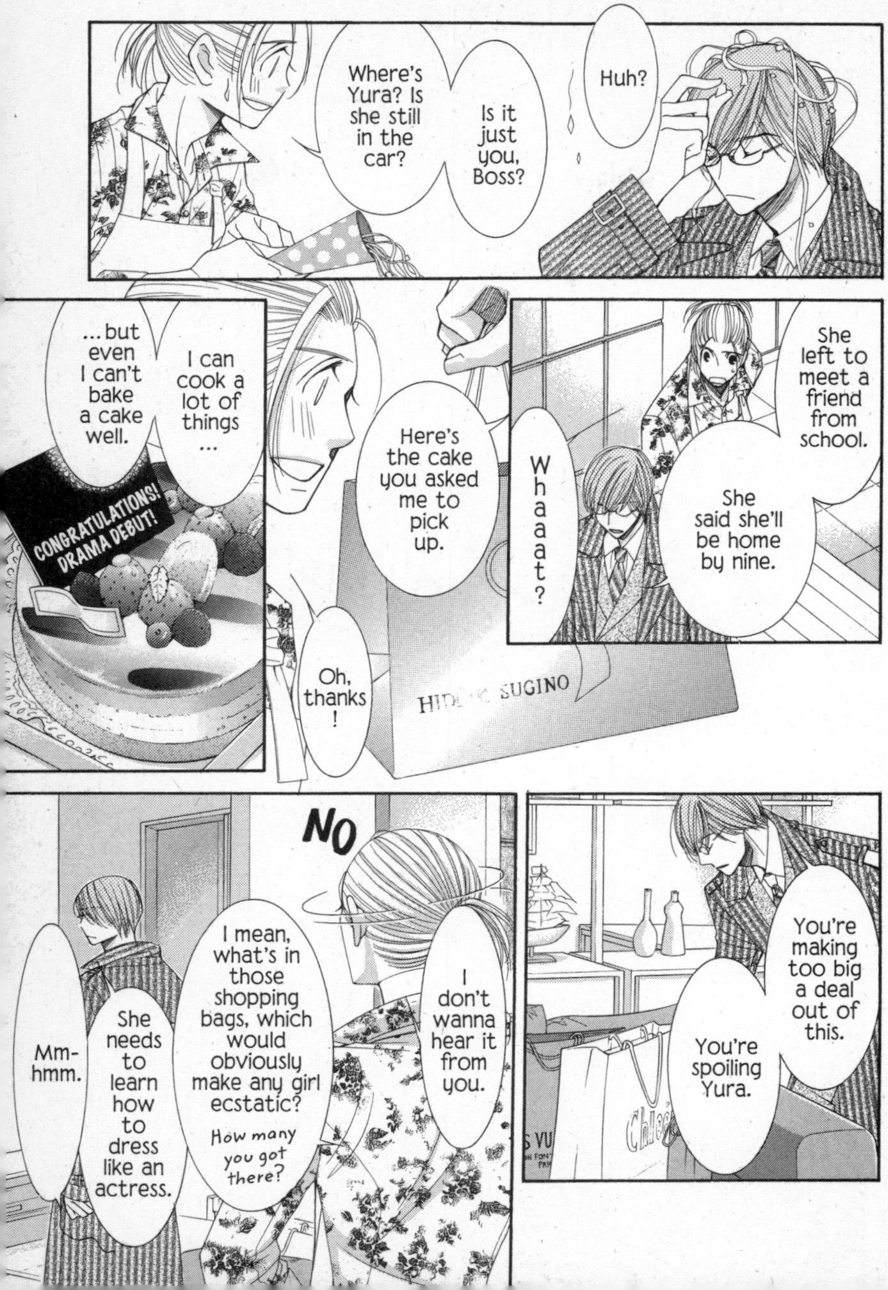

Huh?
Is it just you, Boss?
Where's Yura? Is she still in the car?
She left to meet a friend from school.
She said she'll be home by nine.
Whaaat?
Here's the cake you asked me to pick up.
Oh, thanks!
I can cook a lot of things...
...but even I can't bake a cake well.
CONGRATULATIONS! DRAMA DEBUT!
You're making too big a deal out of this.
You're spoiling Yura.
NO
I don't wanna hear it from you.
I mean, what's in those shopping bags, which would obviously make any girl ecstatic?
How many you got there?
She needs to learn how to dress like an actress.
Mm-hmm.

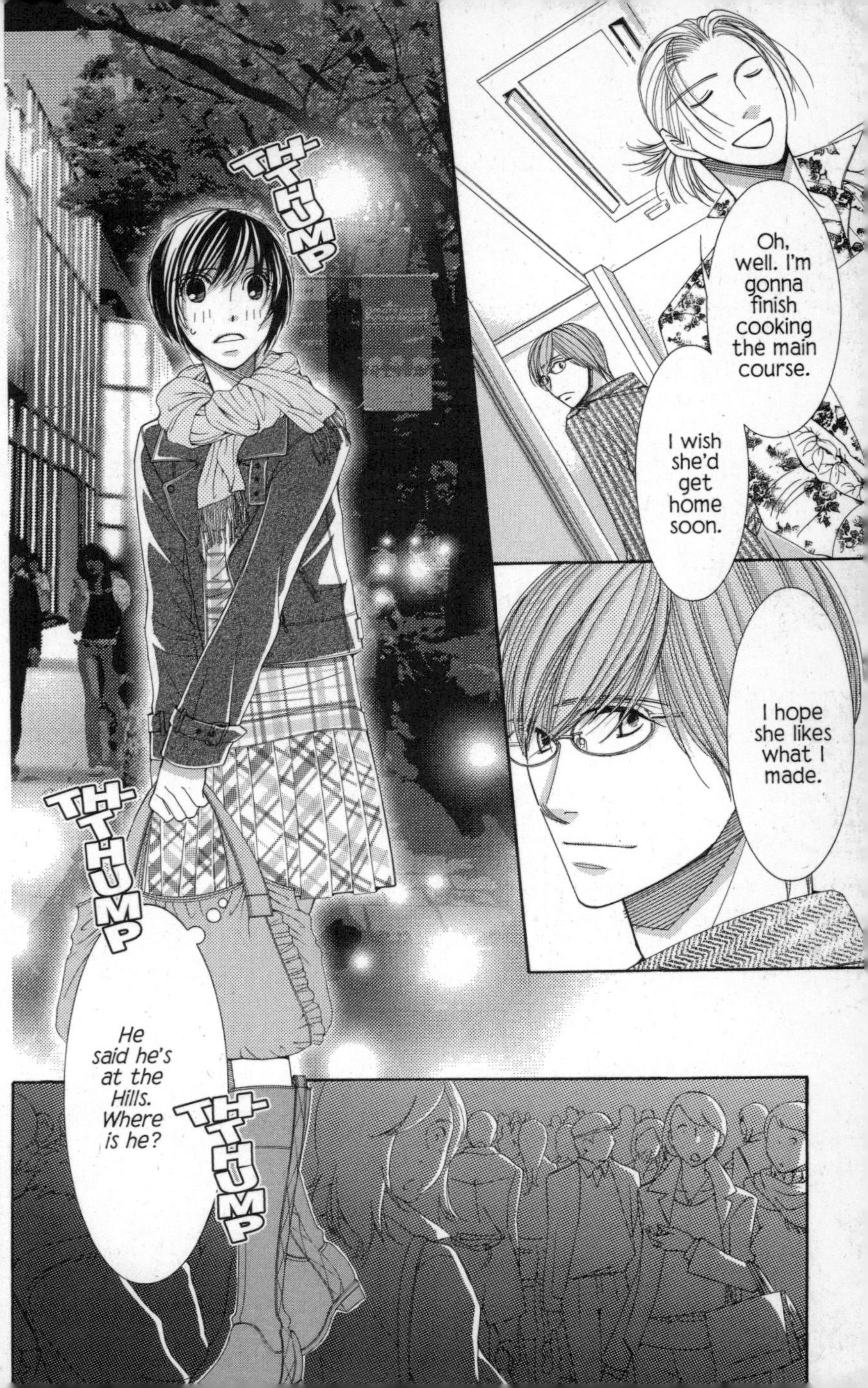
Oh, well. I'm gonna finish cooking the main course.
I wish she'd get home soon.
I hope she likes what I made.
TH-THUMP
TH-THUMP
He said he's at the Hills. Where is he?
TH-THUMP

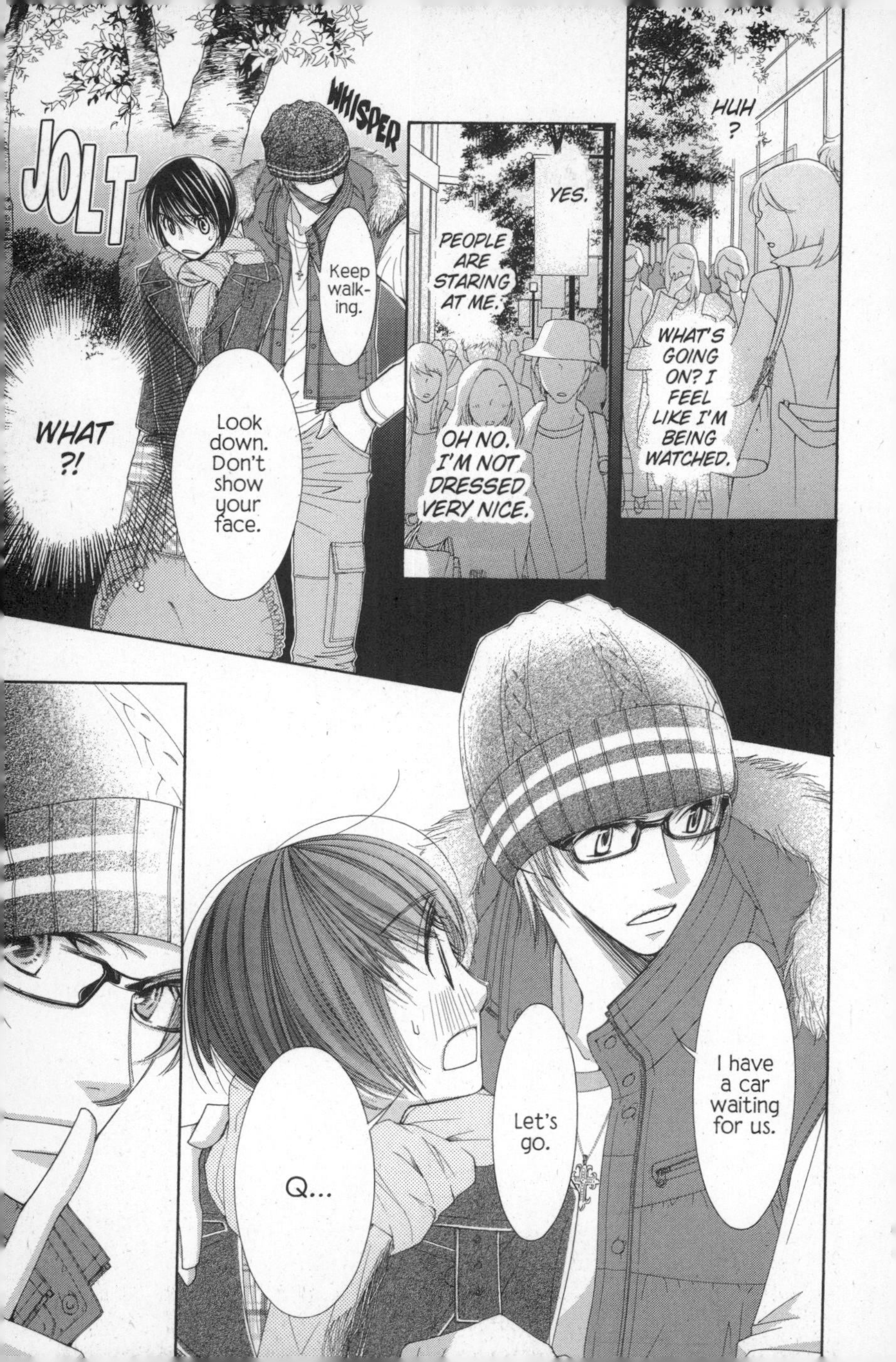
HUH ?
WHAT'S GOING ON? I FEEL LIKE I'M BEING WATCHED.
YES.
PEOPLE ARE STARING AT ME.
OH NO. I'M NOT DRESSED VERY NICE.
WHISPER
Keep walk-ing.
JOLT
Look down. Don't show your face.
WHAT ?!
I have a car waiting for us.
Let's go.
Q...

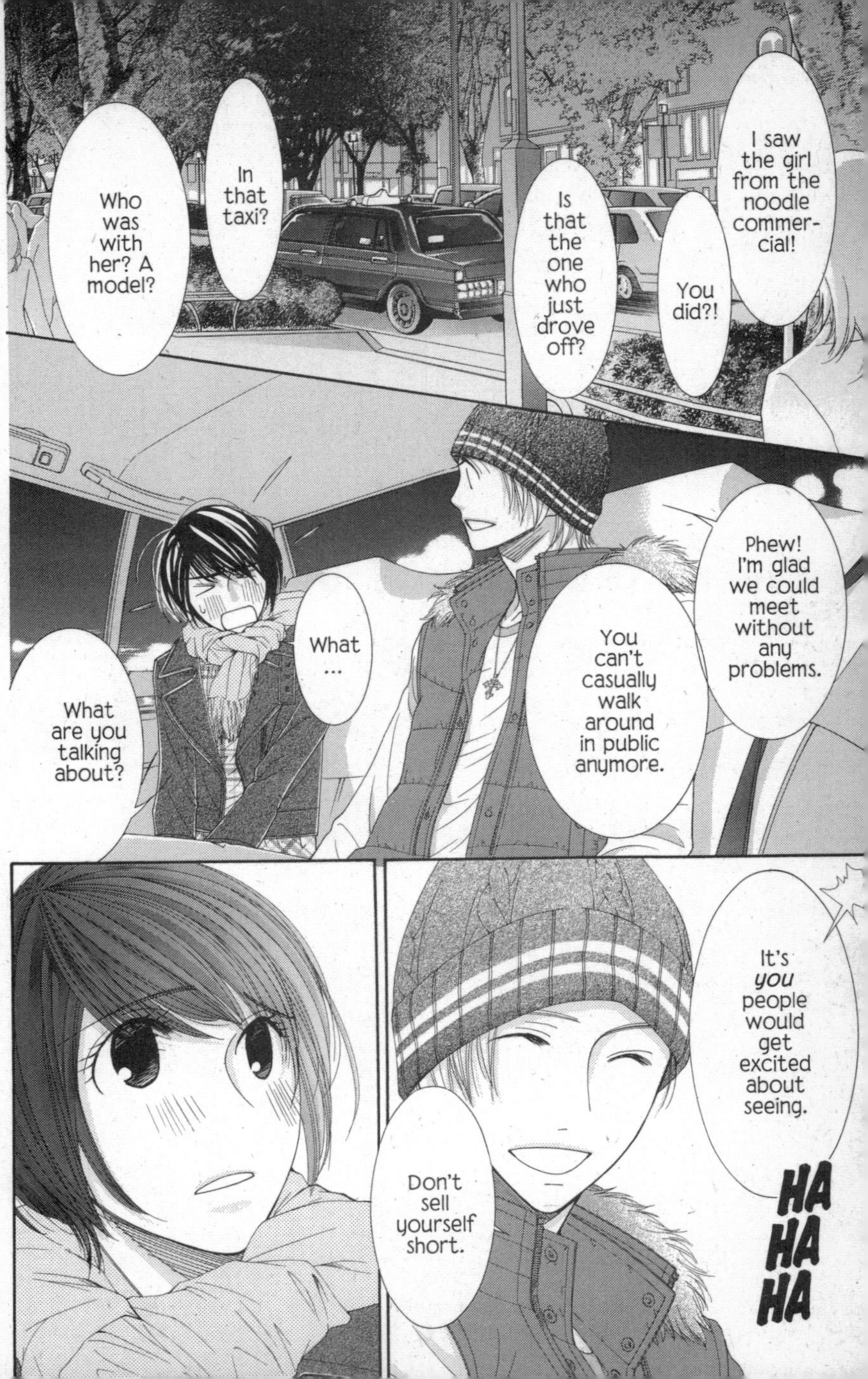
I saw the girl from the noodle commercial!
You did?!
Is that the one who just drove off?
In that taxi?
Who was with her? A model?
Phew! I'm glad we could meet without any problems.
You can't casually walk around in public anymore.
What ...
What are you talking about?
It's *you* people would get excited about seeing.
HA HA HA
Don't sell yourself short.

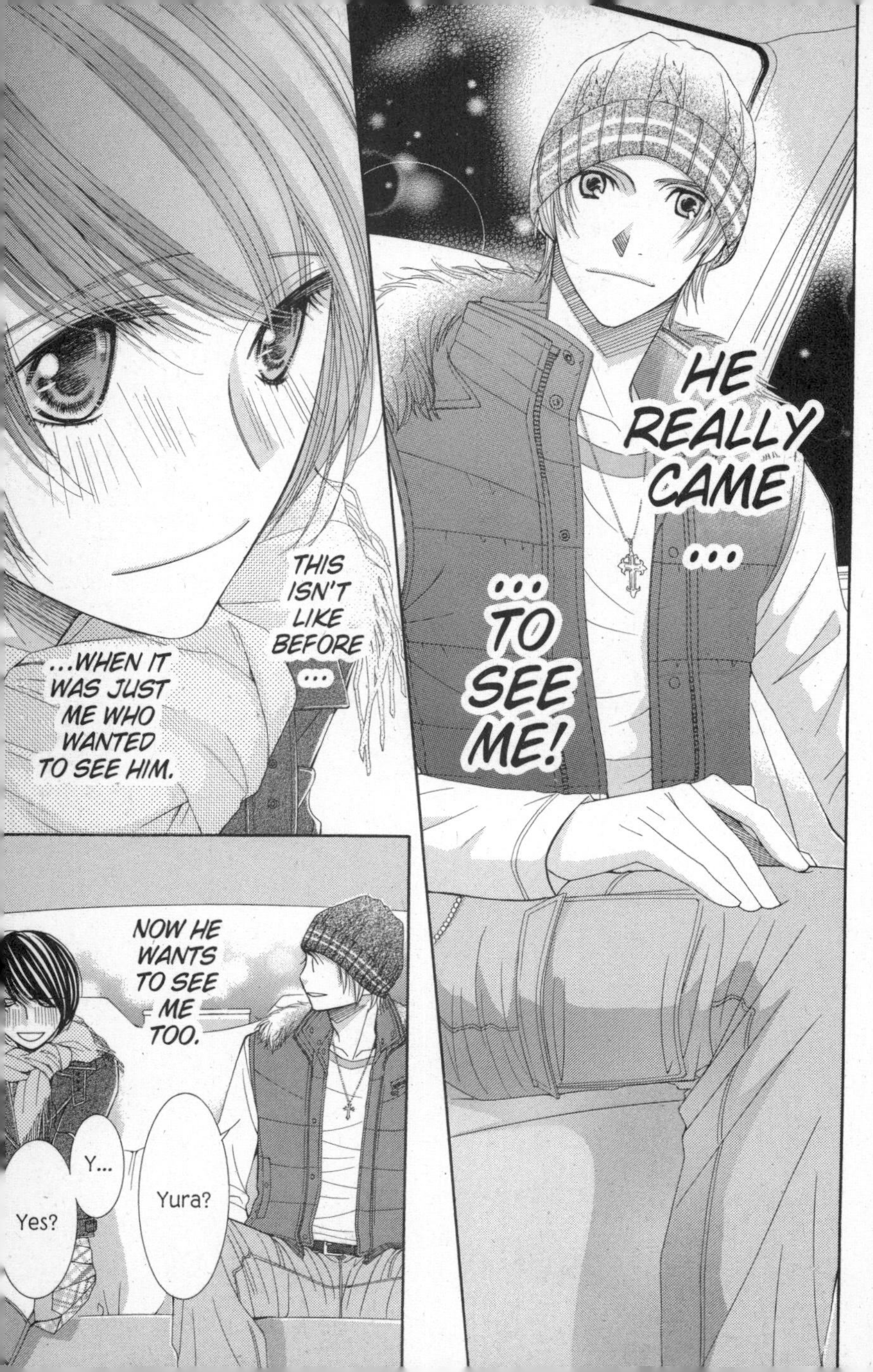
HE REALLY CAME...
...TO SEE ME!
THIS ISN'T LIKE BEFORE...
...WHEN IT WAS JUST ME WHO WANTED TO SEE HIM.
NOW HE WANTS TO SEE ME TOO.
Yura?
Y...
Yes?

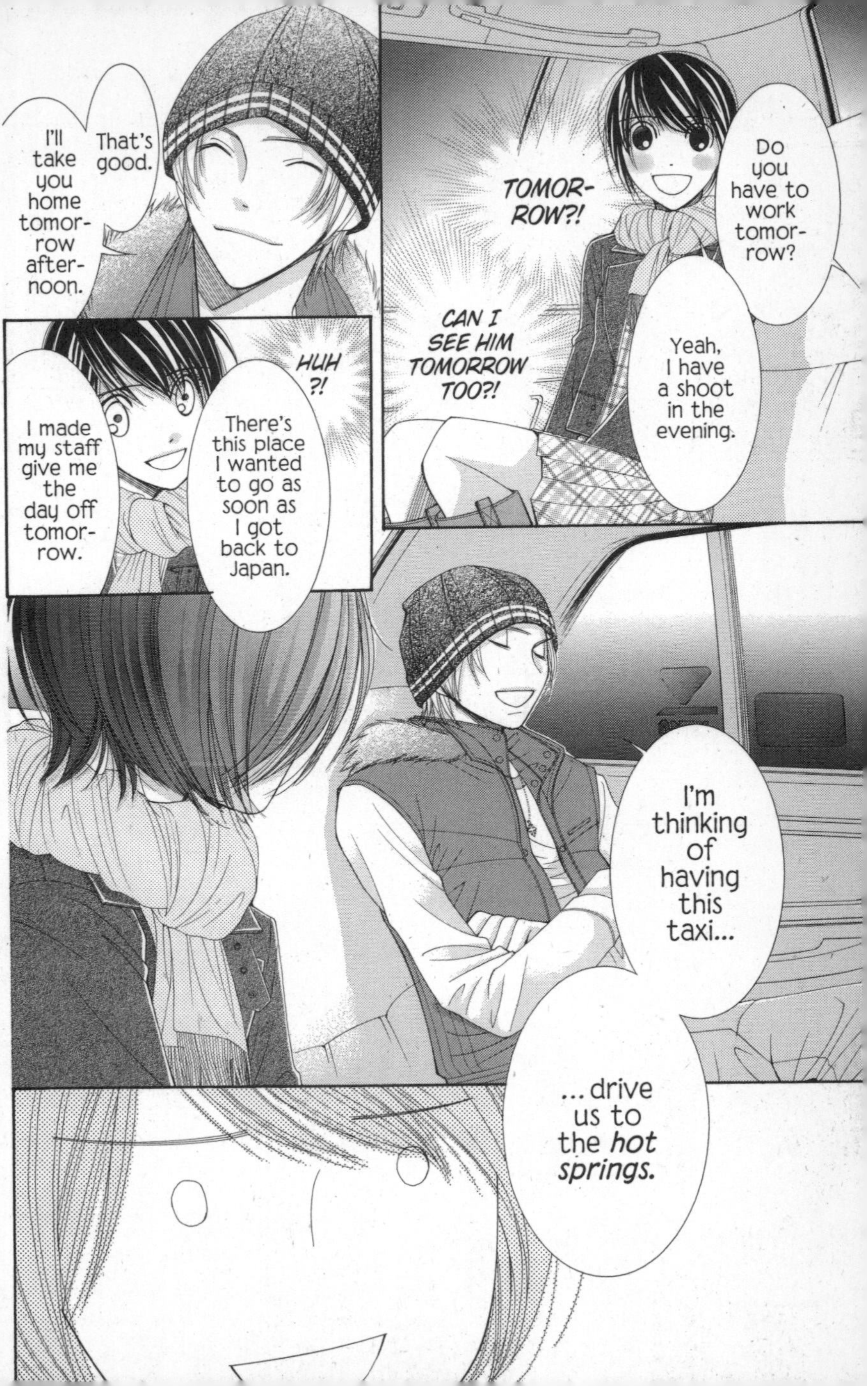
Do you have to work tomorrow?
Yeah, I have a shoot in the evening.
TOMORROW?!
CAN I SEE HIM TOMORROW TOO?!
That's good.
I'll take you home tomorrow afternoon.
HUH?!
I made my staff give me the day off tomorrow.
There's this place I wanted to go as soon as I got back to Japan.
I'm thinking of having this taxi...
...drive us to the *hot springs.*

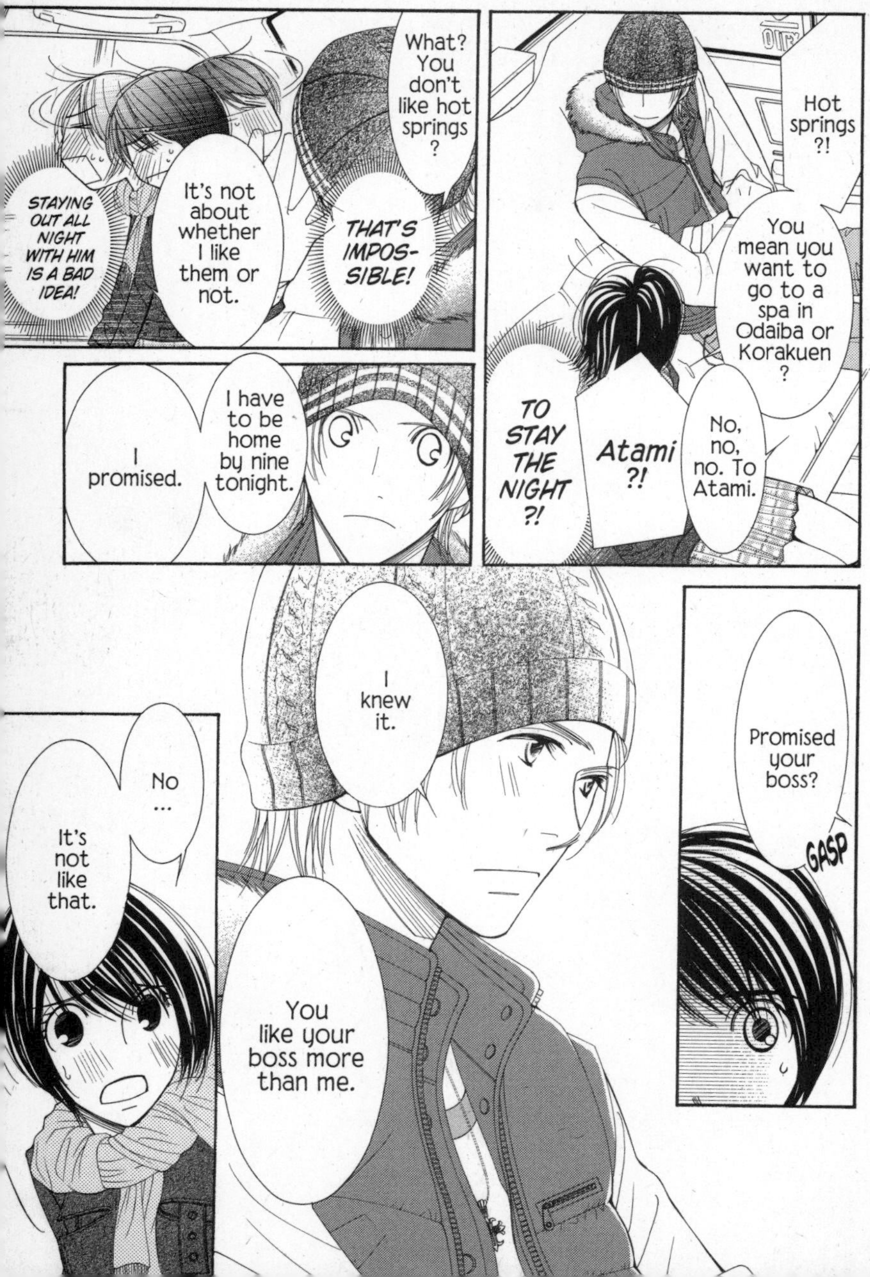

Hot springs ?!
You mean you want to go to a spa in Odaiba or Korakuen ?
No, no, no. To Atami.
Atami ?!
TO STAY THE NIGHT ?!
What? You don't like hot springs ?
THAT'S IMPOSSIBLE!
It's not about whether I like them or not.
STAYING OUT ALL NIGHT WITH HIM IS A BAD IDEA!
I have to be home by nine tonight.
I promised.
Promised your boss?
GASP
I knew it.
You like your boss more than me.
No ...
It's not like that.

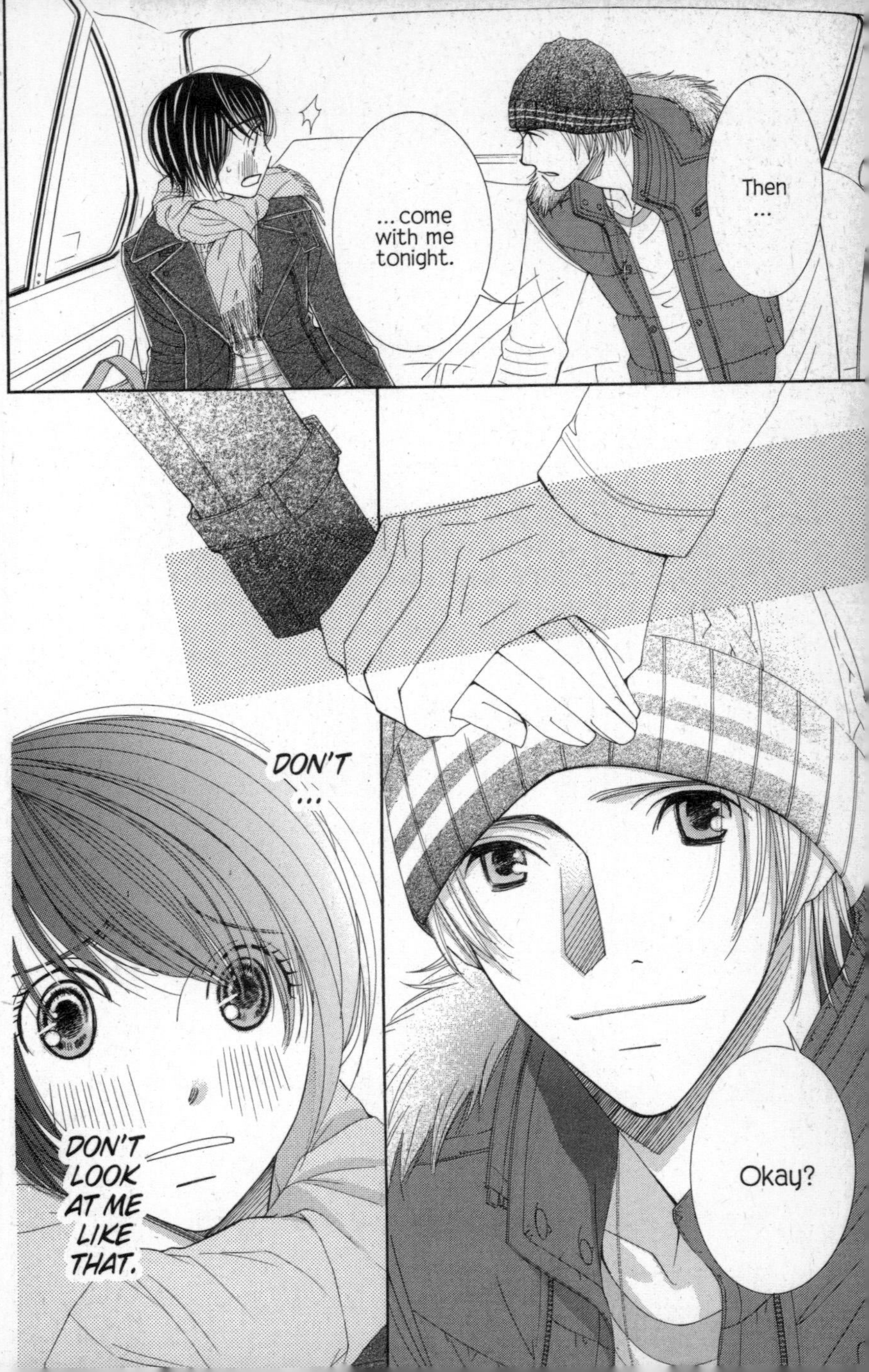
Then ...
...come with me tonight.
Okay?
DON'T ...
DON'T LOOK AT ME LIKE THAT.

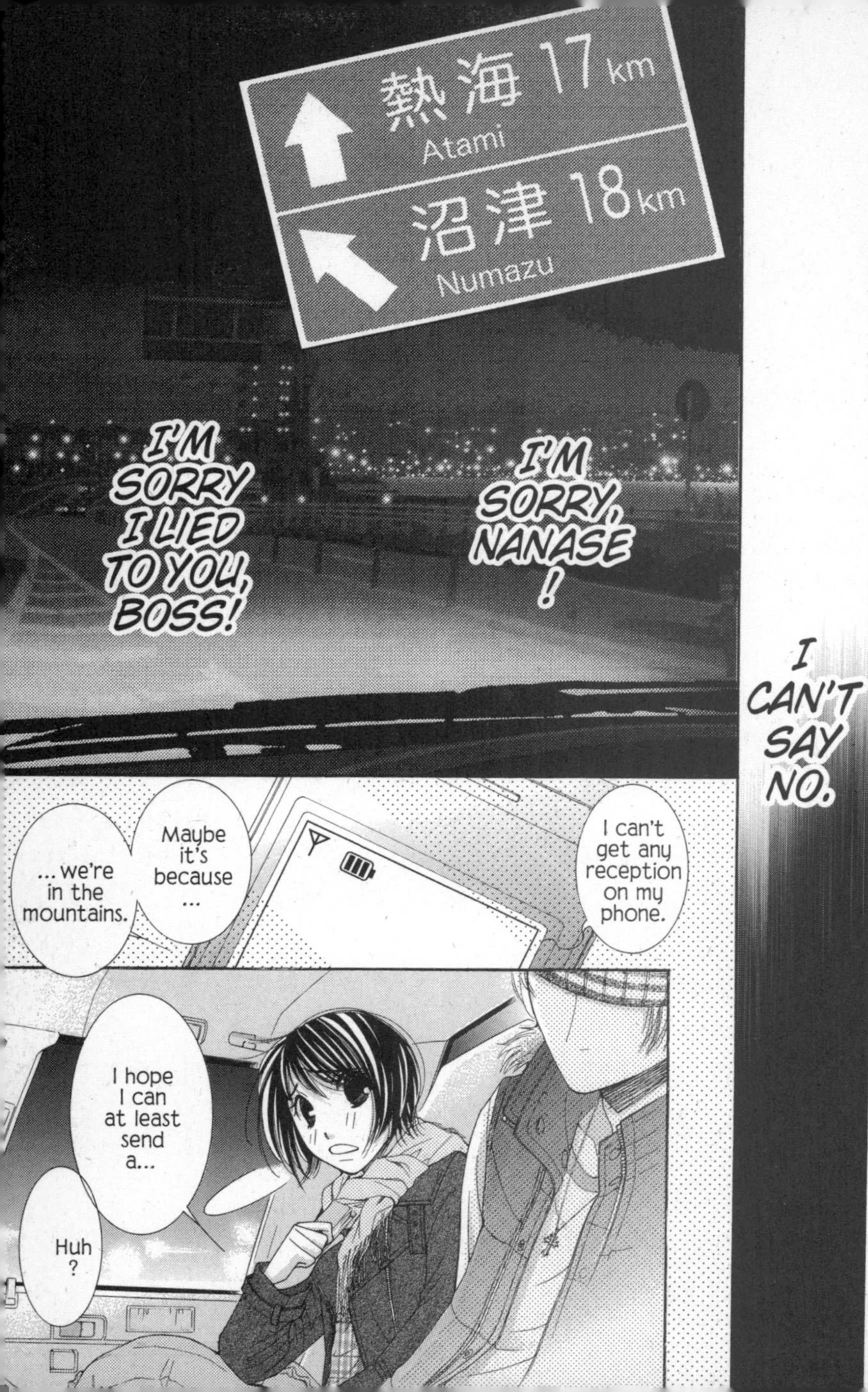
熱海 17 km
Atami
沼津 18 km
Numazu
I'M SORRY, NANASE!
I'M SORRY I LIED TO YOU, BOSS!
I CAN'T SAY NO.
I can't get any reception on my phone.
Maybe it's because...
...we're in the mountains.
I hope I can at least send a...
Huh?

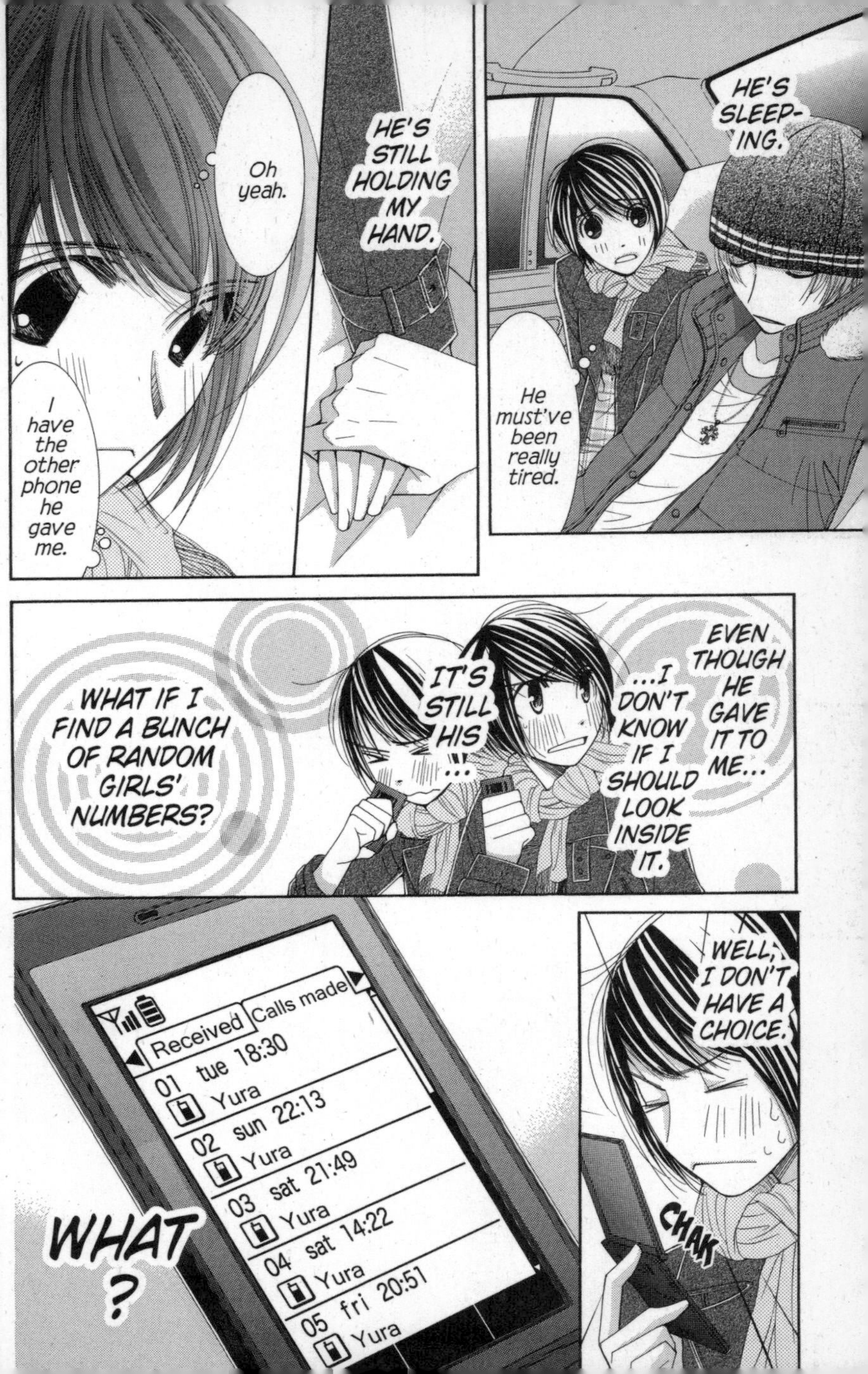
HE'S SLEEPING.
He must've been really tired.
HE'S STILL HOLDING MY HAND.
Oh yeah.
I have the other phone he gave me.
EVEN THOUGH HE GAVE IT TO ME...
...I DON'T KNOW IF I SHOULD LOOK INSIDE IT.
IT'S STILL HIS...
WHAT IF I FIND A BUNCH OF RANDOM GIRLS' NUMBERS?
WELL, I DON'T HAVE A CHOICE.
CHAK
Received
Calls made
01 tue 18:30
Yura
02 sun 22:13
Yura
03 sat 21:49
Yura
04 sat 14:22
Yura
05 fri 20:51
Yura
WHAT?

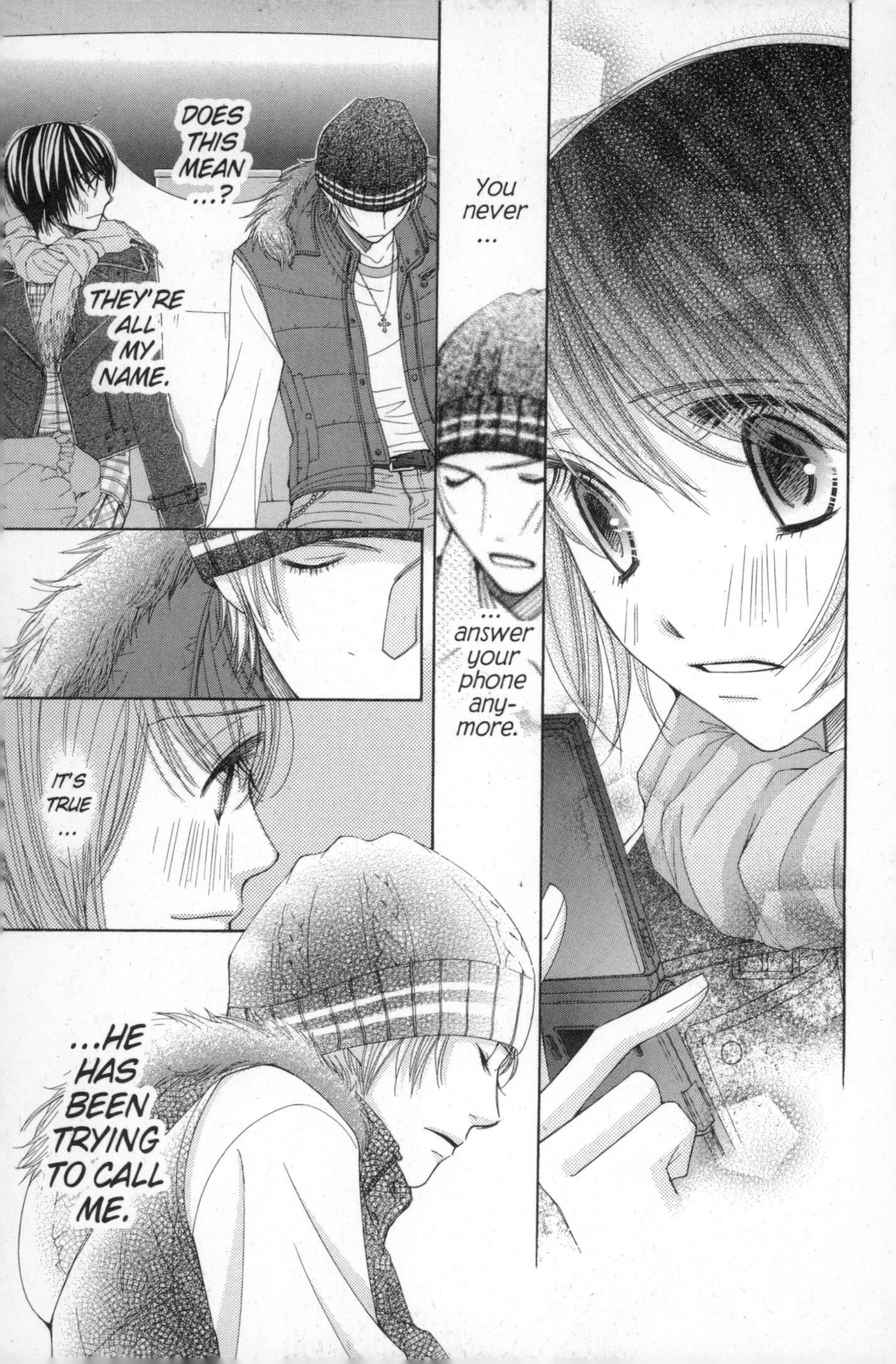
You never ...
... answer your phone any-more.
DOES THIS MEAN ...?
THEY'RE ALL MY NAME.
IT'S TRUE ...
...HE HAS BEEN TRYING TO CALL ME.

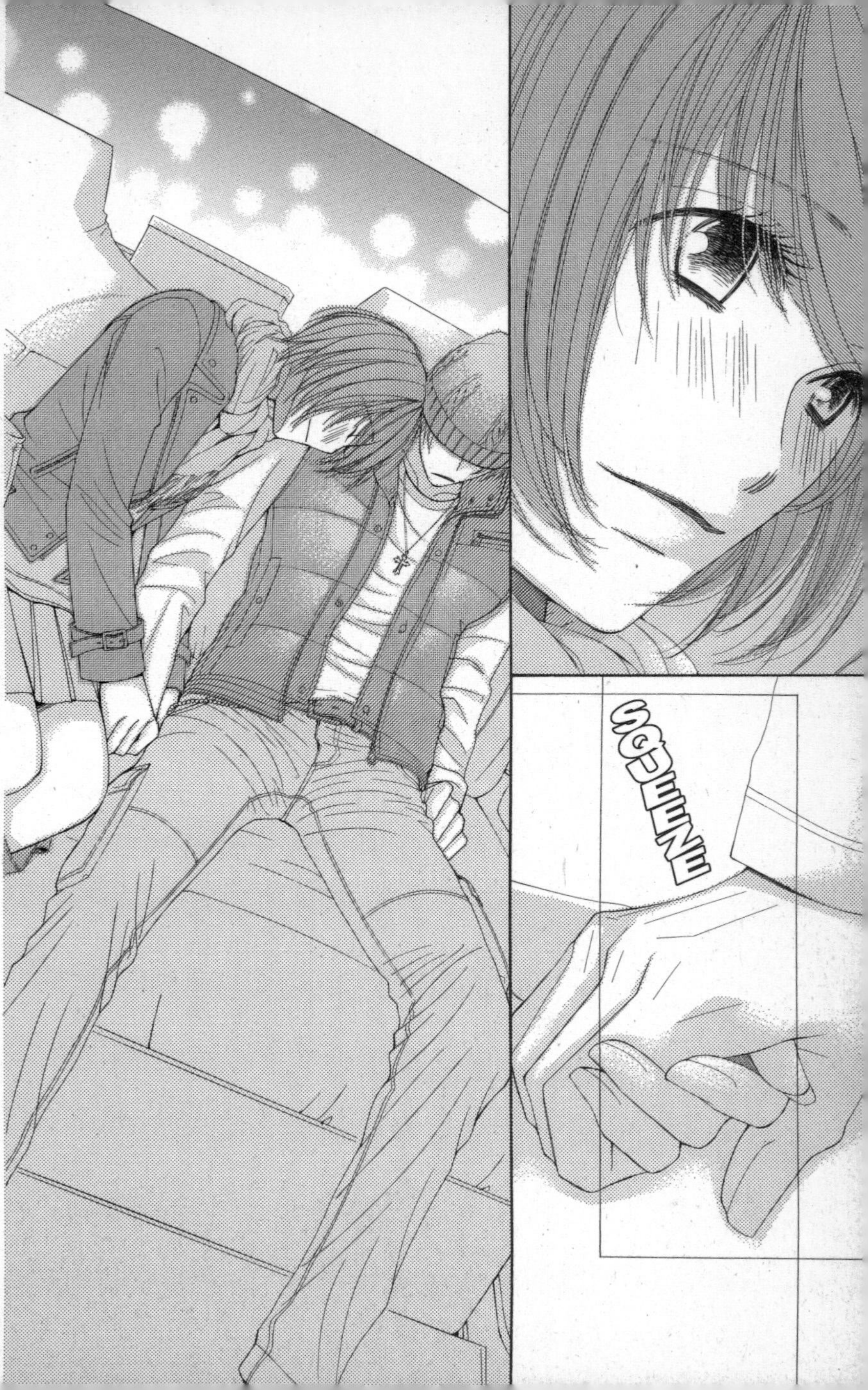
SQUEEZE

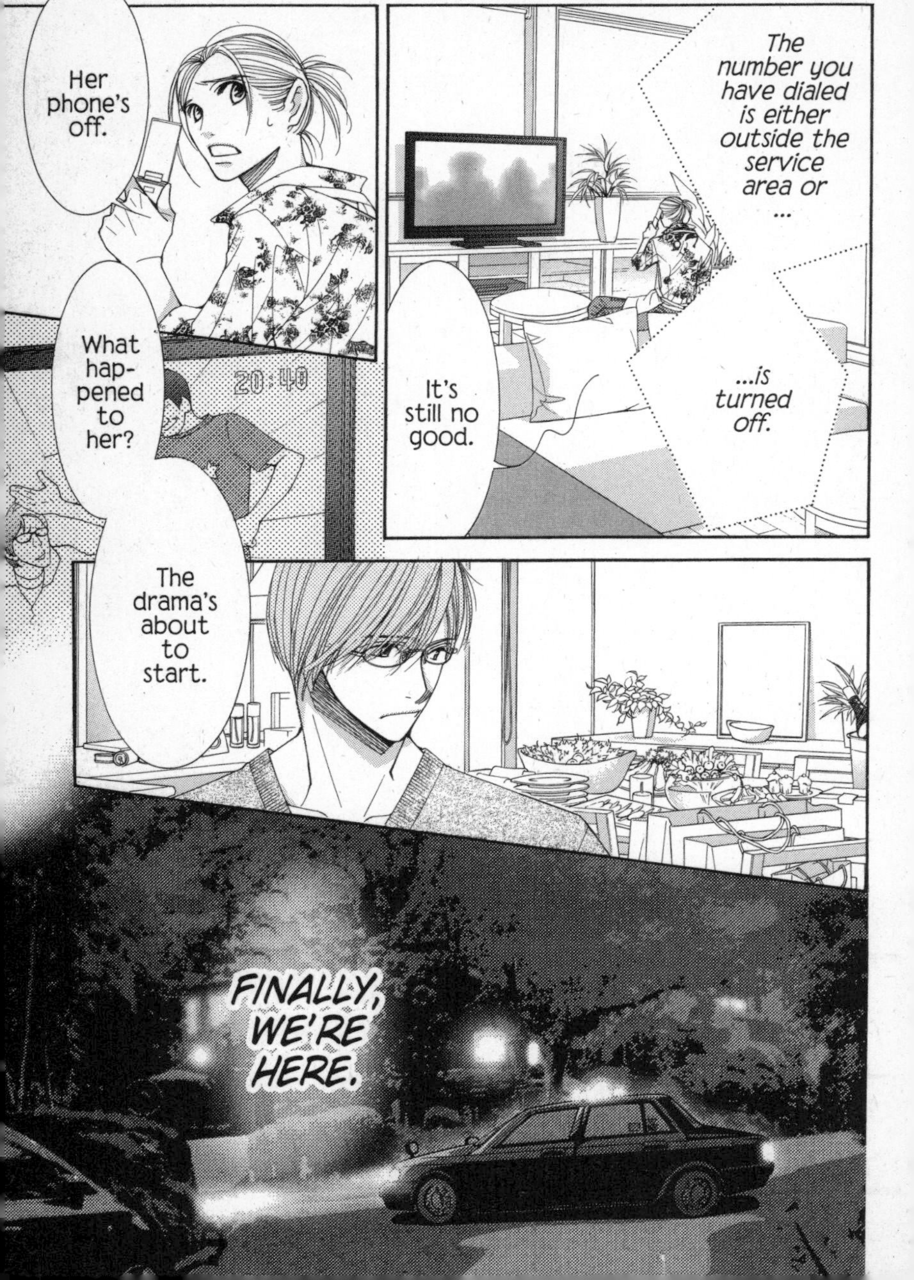
The number you have dialed is either outside the service area or ...
...is turned off.
It's still no good.
Her phone's off.
What hap-pened to her?
The drama's about to start.
FINALLY, WE'RE HERE.

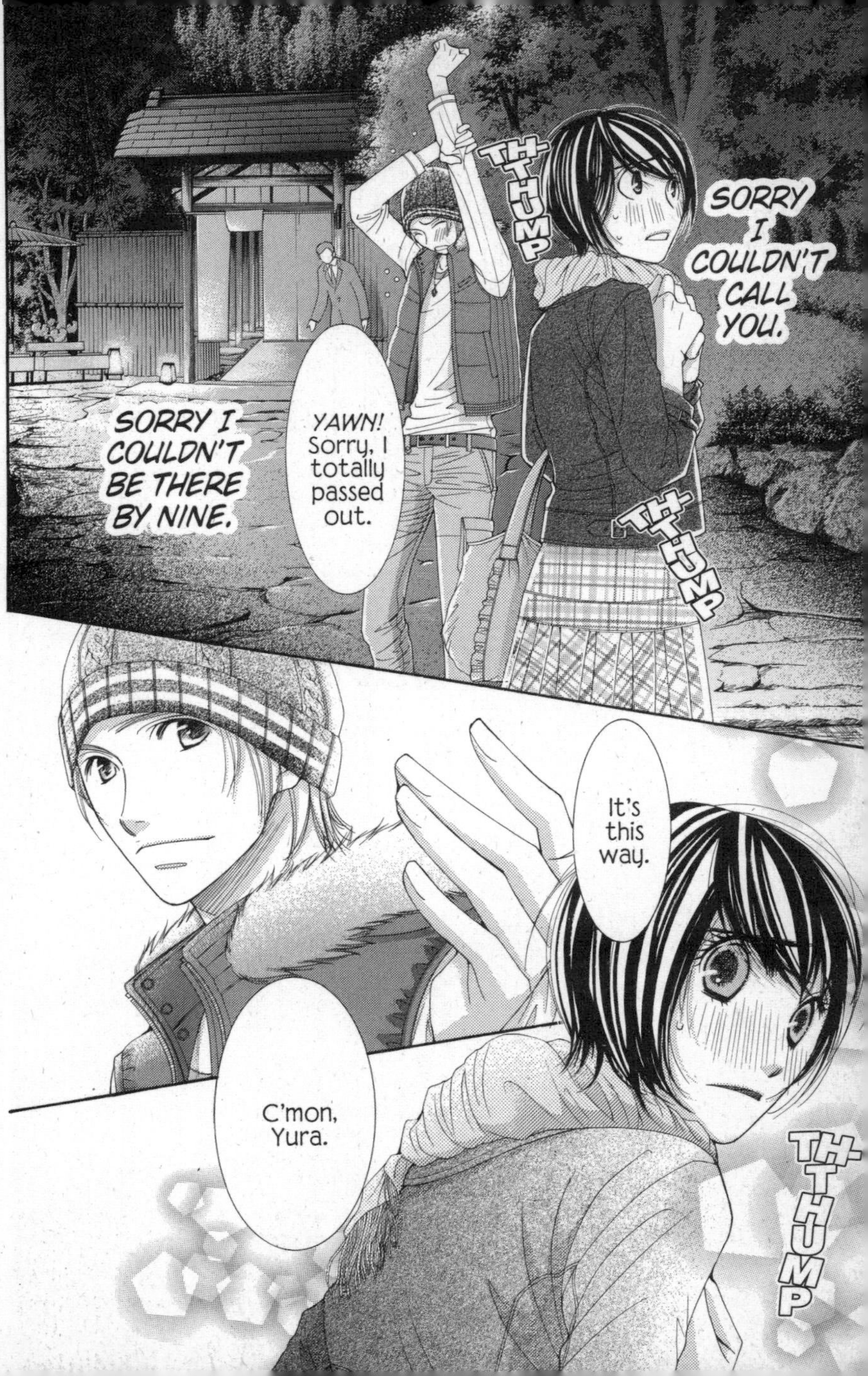
SORRY I COULDN'T CALL YOU.
TH-THUMP
YAWN! Sorry, I totally passed out.
SORRY I COULDN'T BE THERE BY NINE.
TH-THUMP
It's this way.
TH-THUMP
C'mon, Yura.

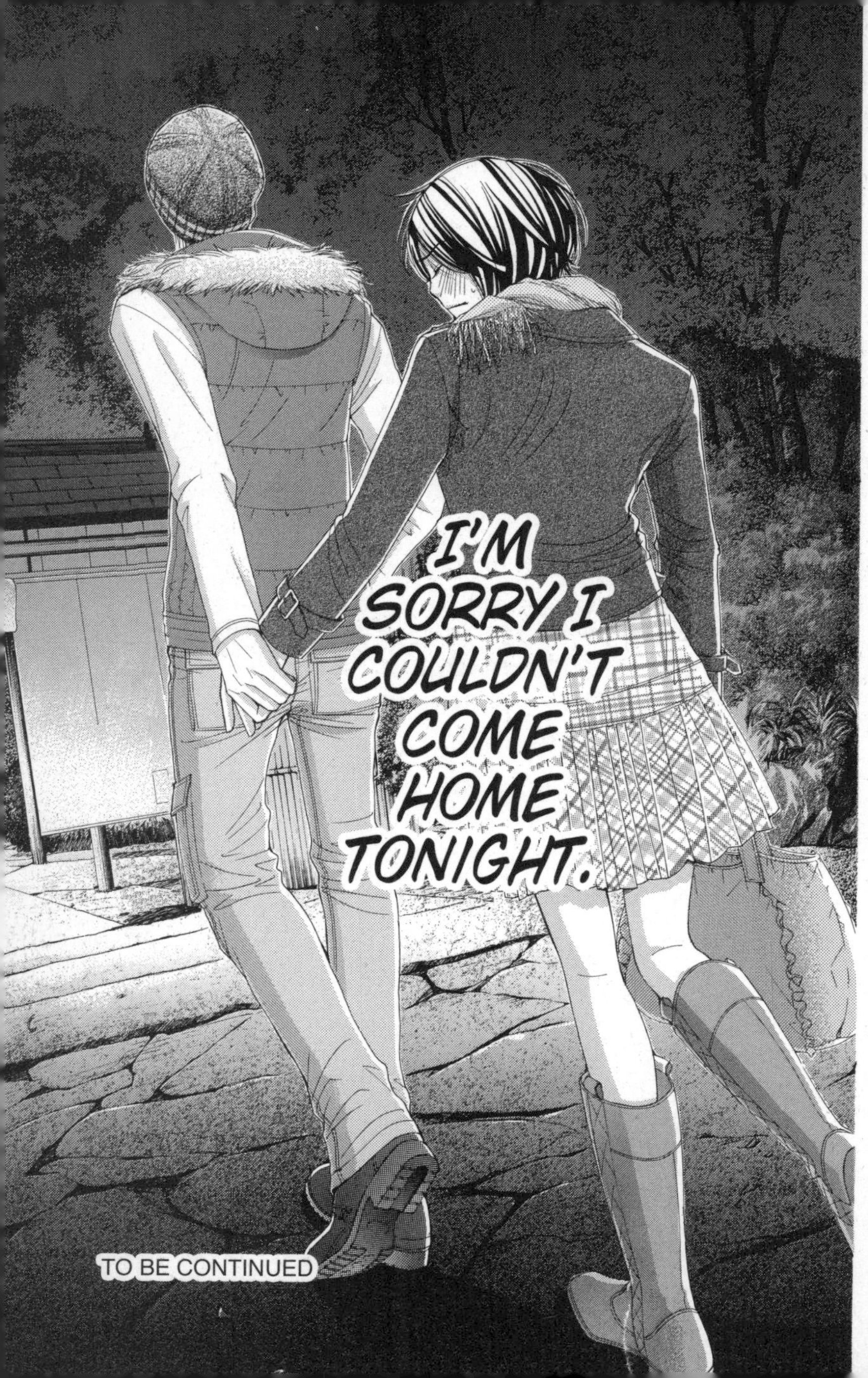
I'M SORRY I COULDN'T COME HOME TONIGHT.
TO BE CONTINUED

thank you
for reading.

● **Send correspondence to:**
Miki Aihara/Honey Hunt
c/o VIZ Media, LLC
P.O. Box 77010
San Francisco, CA 94107

● **E-mail**
miki_aihara@livedoor.com

● **Blog**
http://mikimiki.net (from PC)
http://mikiniki.net/m/ (from phone)

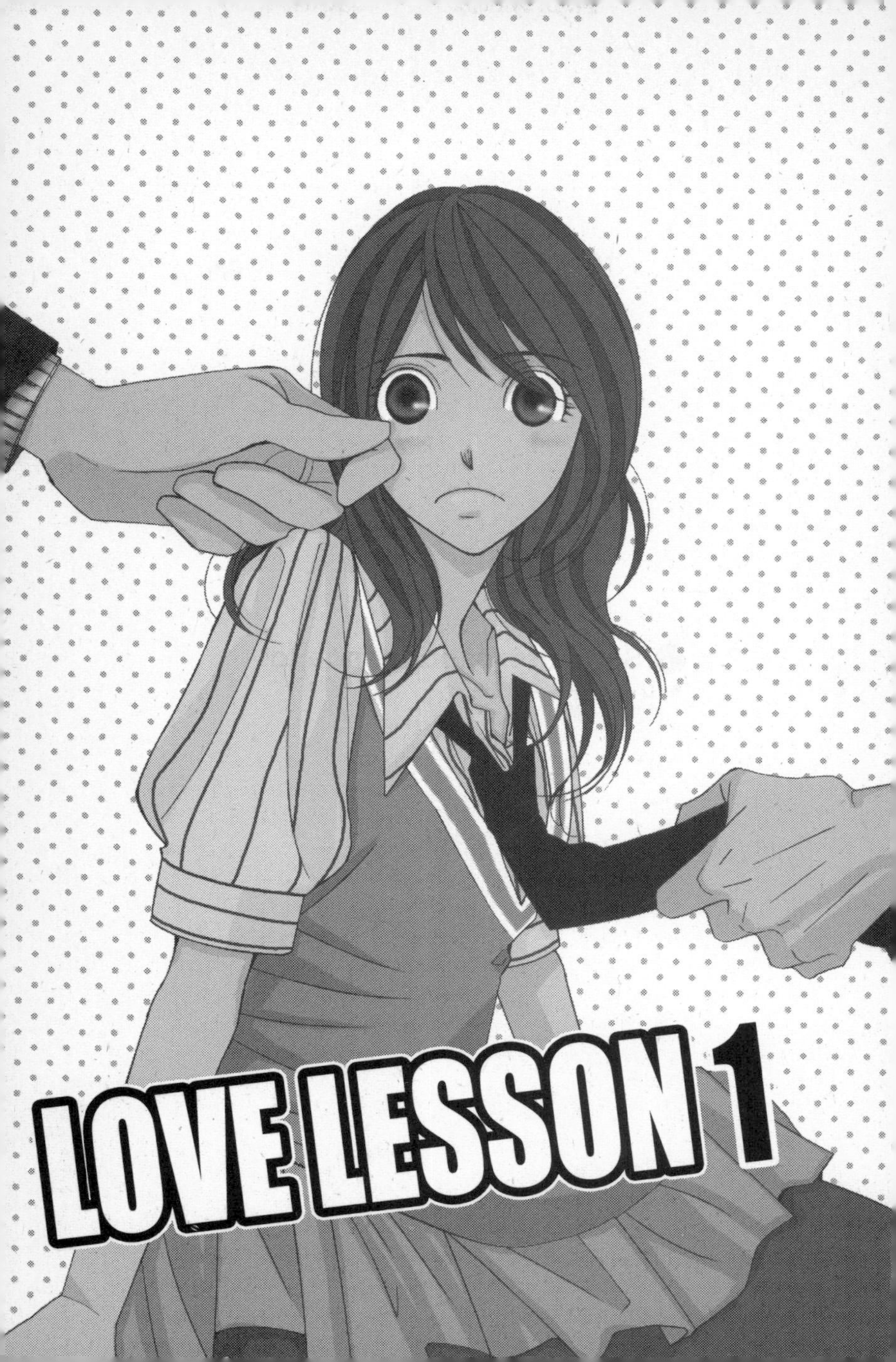
LOVE LESSON 1

Director: Maki Todo. Starting Monday nights in April at nine p.m. Cast: Mizuho Nitta, Shin Kitagawa (KNIGHTS)
Honey Teacher
LOVE LESSON 1
Hiroto Uehara (KNIGHTS), Yura Onozuka, Toshi Fujikawa,
Shoko Maeda, Izumi Ogiwara, and Kazuhiro Watanabe (guest appearance)

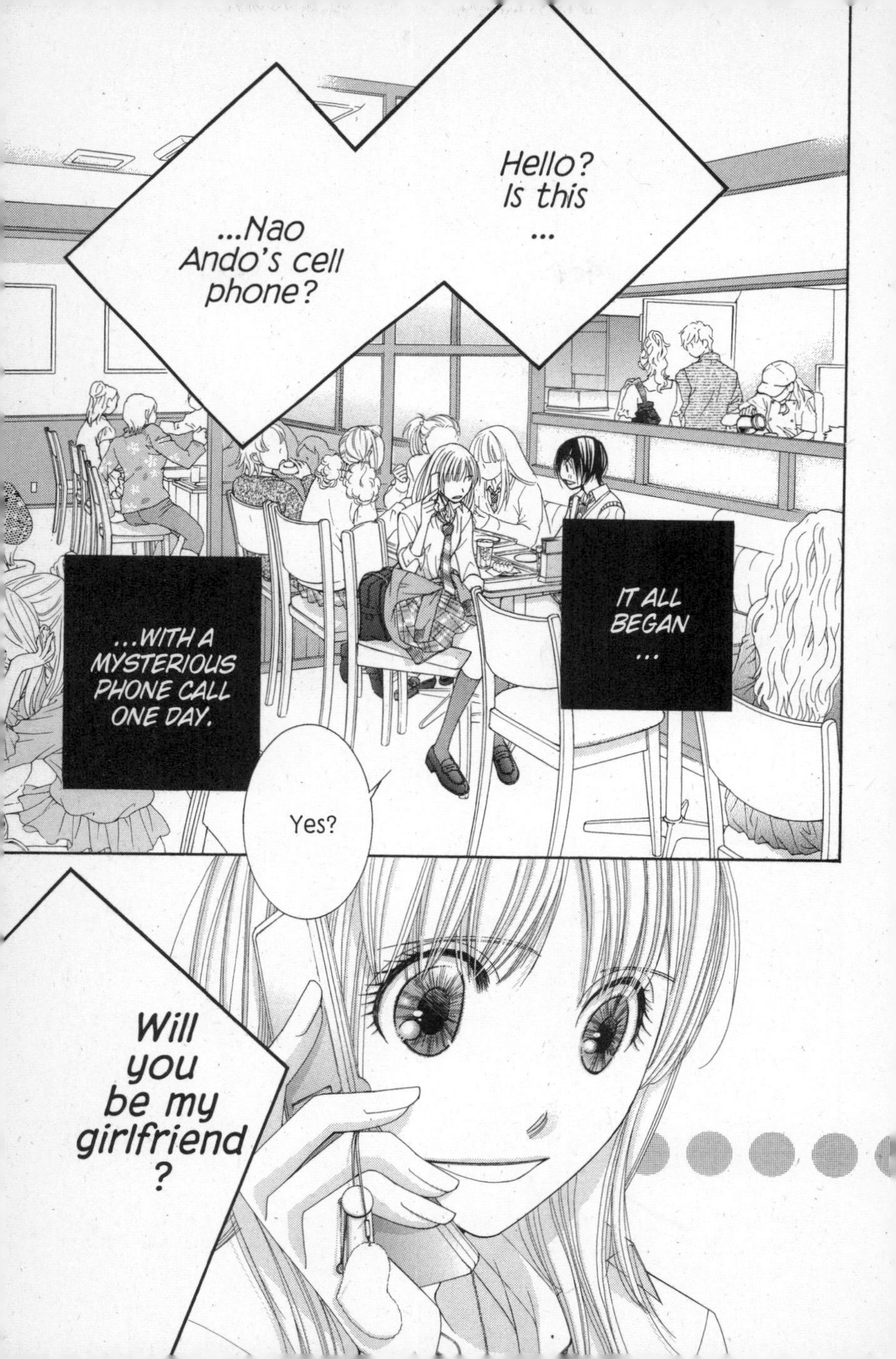
Hello? Is this ...
...Nao Ando's cell phone?
IT ALL BEGAN ...
...WITH A MYSTERIOUS PHONE CALL ONE DAY.
Yes?
Will you be my girlfriend ?

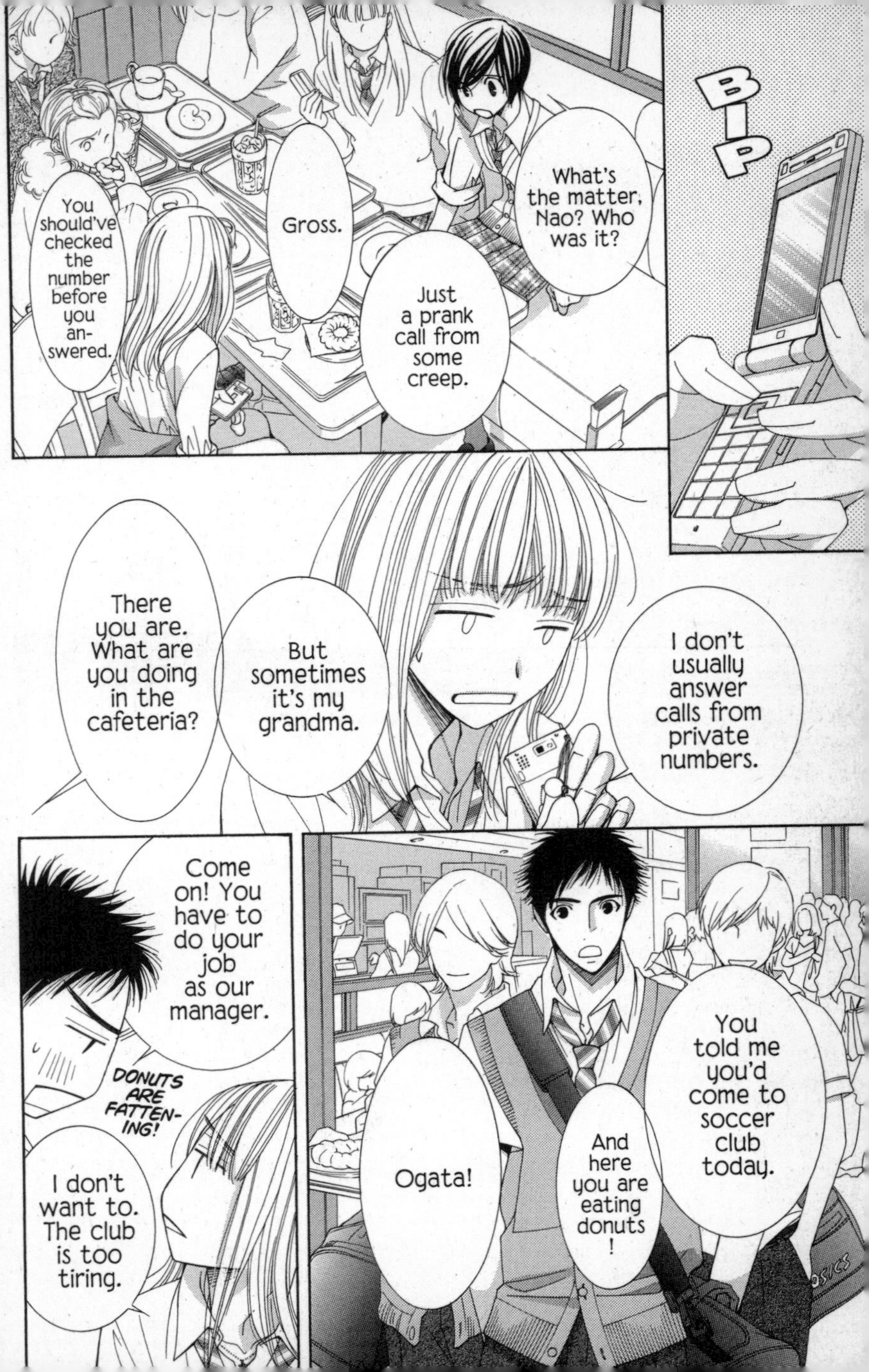
BIP
What's the matter, Nao? Who was it?
Just a prank call from some creep.
Gross.
You should've checked the number before you an-swered.
I don't usually answer calls from private numbers.
But sometimes it's my grandma.
There you are. What are you doing in the cafeteria?
You told me you'd come to soccer club today.
And here you are eating donuts!
Ogata!
Come on! You have to do your job as our manager.
DONUTS ARE FATTEN-ING!
I don't want to. The club is too tiring.

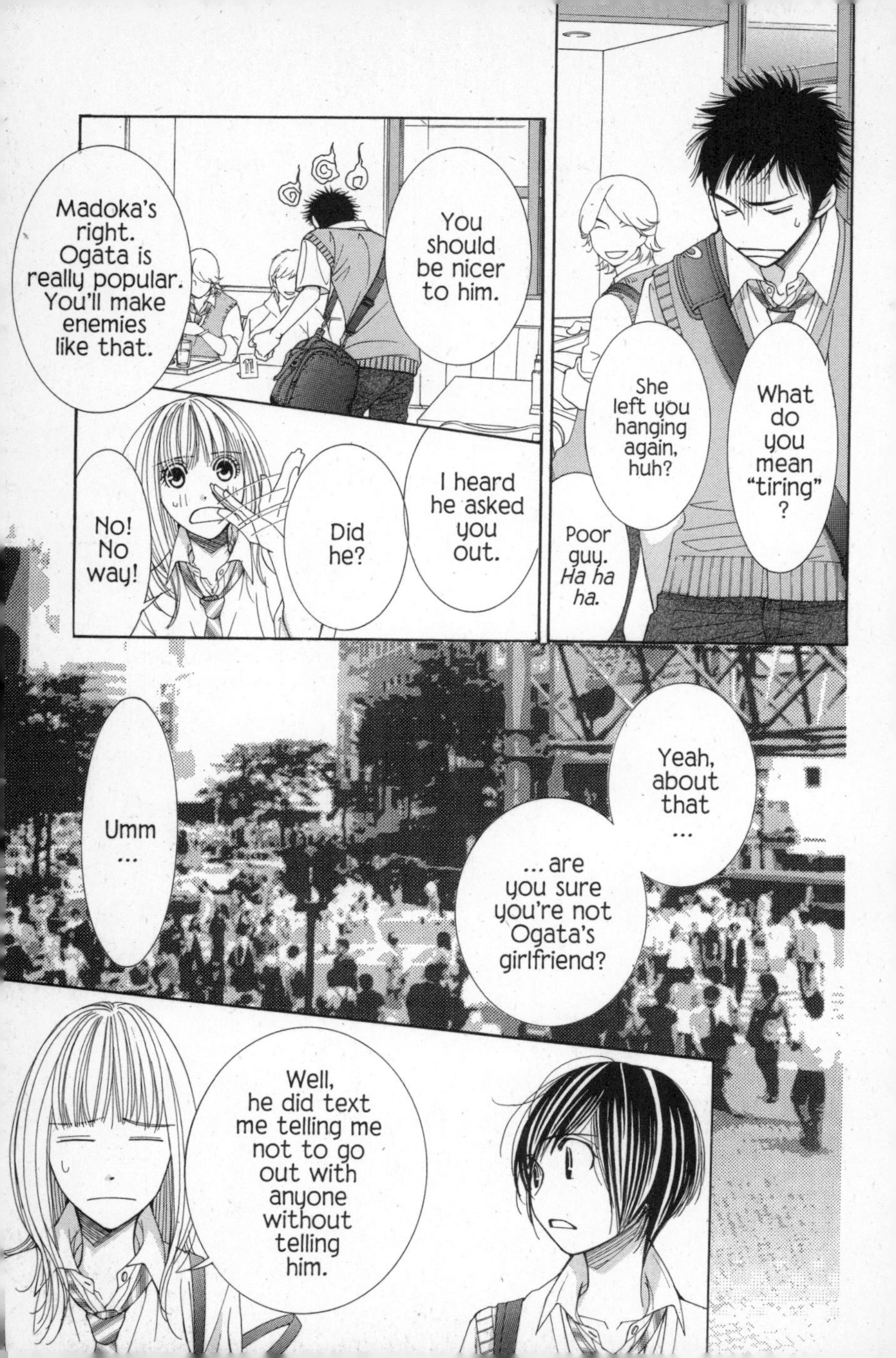
What do you mean "tiring"?
She left you hanging again, huh?
Poor guy. *Ha ha ha.*
You should be nicer to him.
Madoka's right. Ogata is really popular. You'll make enemies like that.
I heard he asked you out.
Did he?
No! No way!
Yeah, about that ...
... are you sure you're not Ogata's girlfriend?
Umm ...
Well, he did text me telling me not to go out with anyone without telling him.

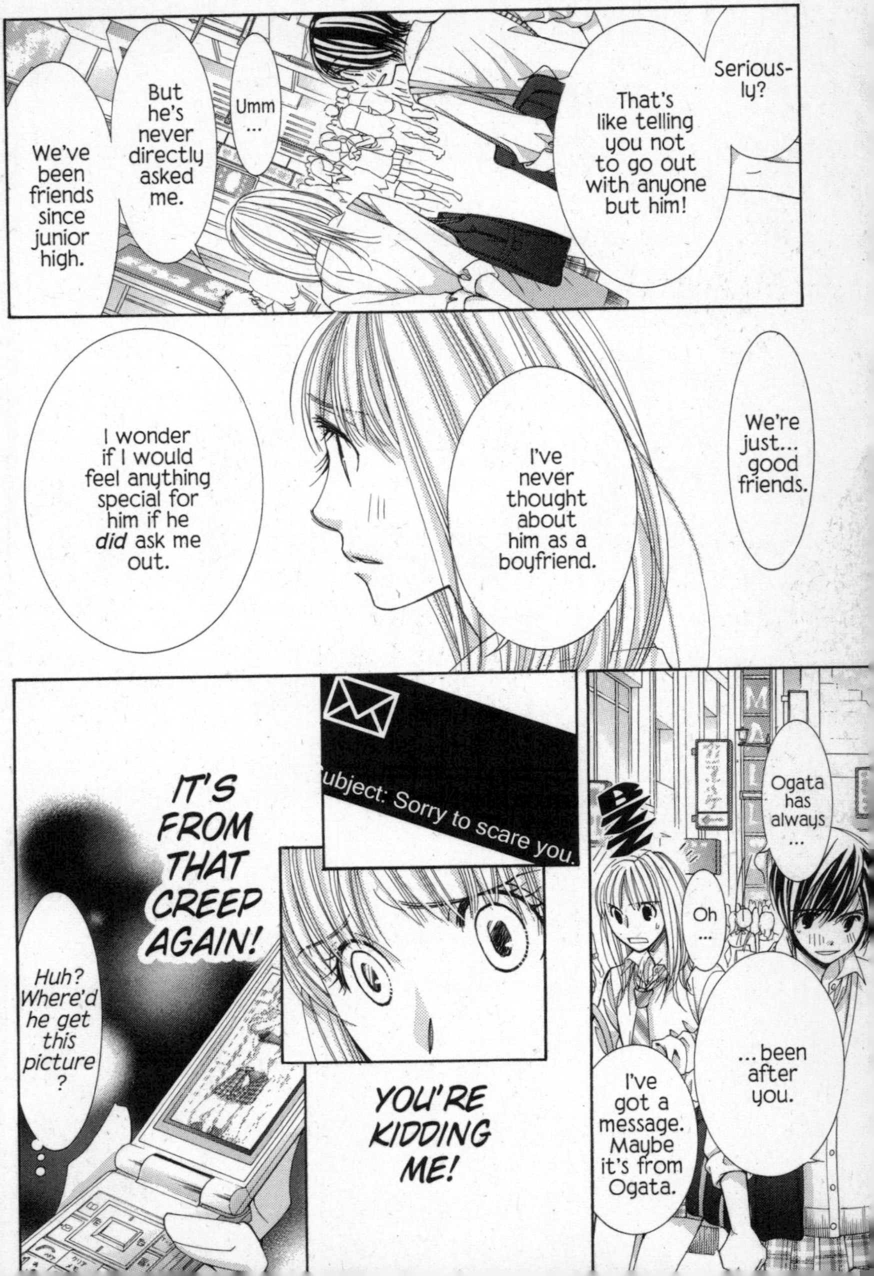
Serious-ly?
That's like telling you not to go out with anyone but him!
Umm...
But he's never directly asked me.
We've been friends since junior high.
We're just... good friends.
I've never thought about him as a boyfriend.
I wonder if I would feel anything special for him if he *did* ask me out.
Ogata has always...
Oh...
...been after you.
I've got a message. Maybe it's from Ogata.
Subject: Sorry to scare you.
YOU'RE KIDDING ME!
IT'S FROM THAT CREEP AGAIN!
Huh? Where'd he get this picture?

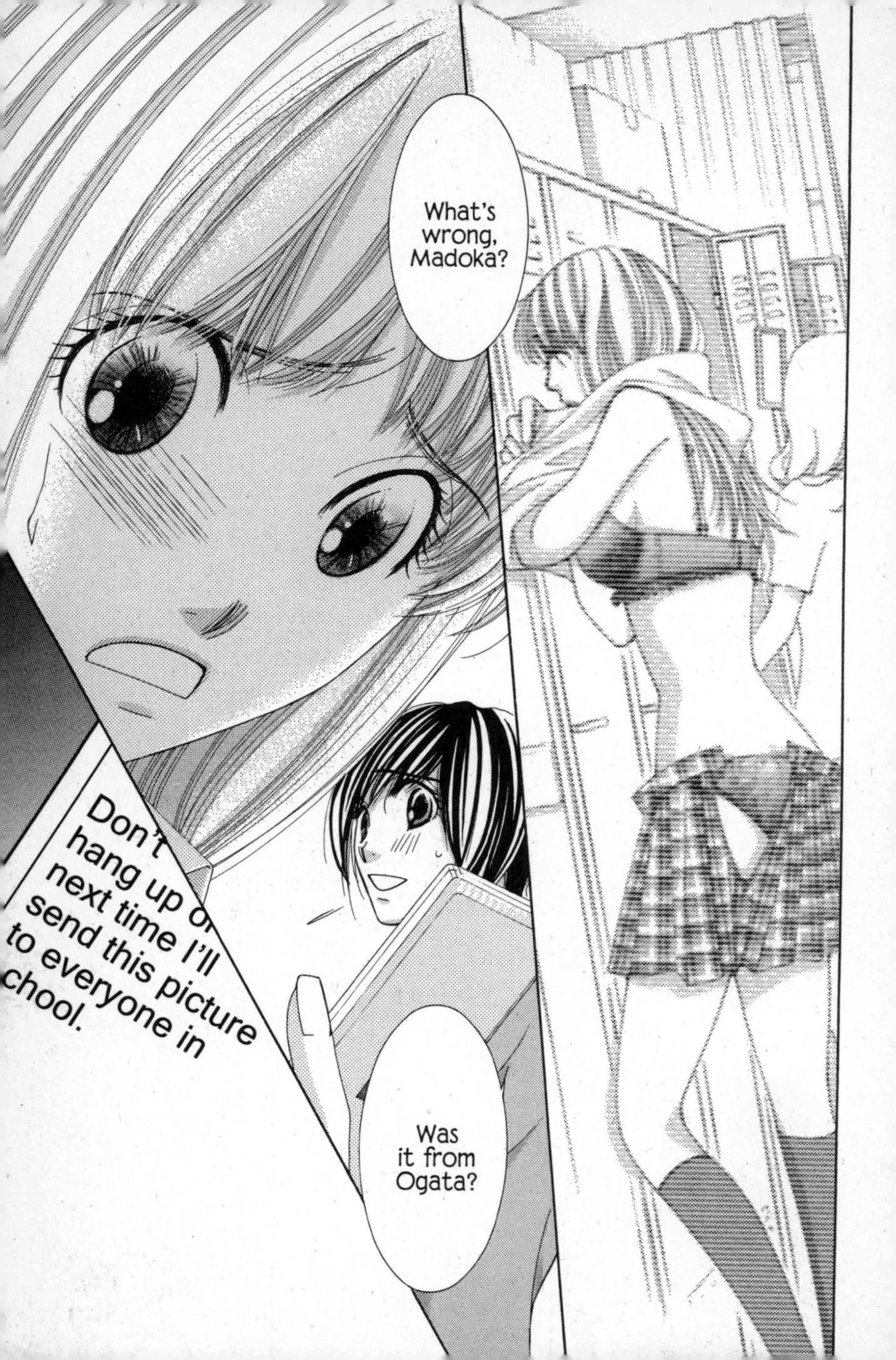
What's wrong, Madoka?
Was it from Ogata?
Don't hang up o next time I'll send this picture to everyone in chool.

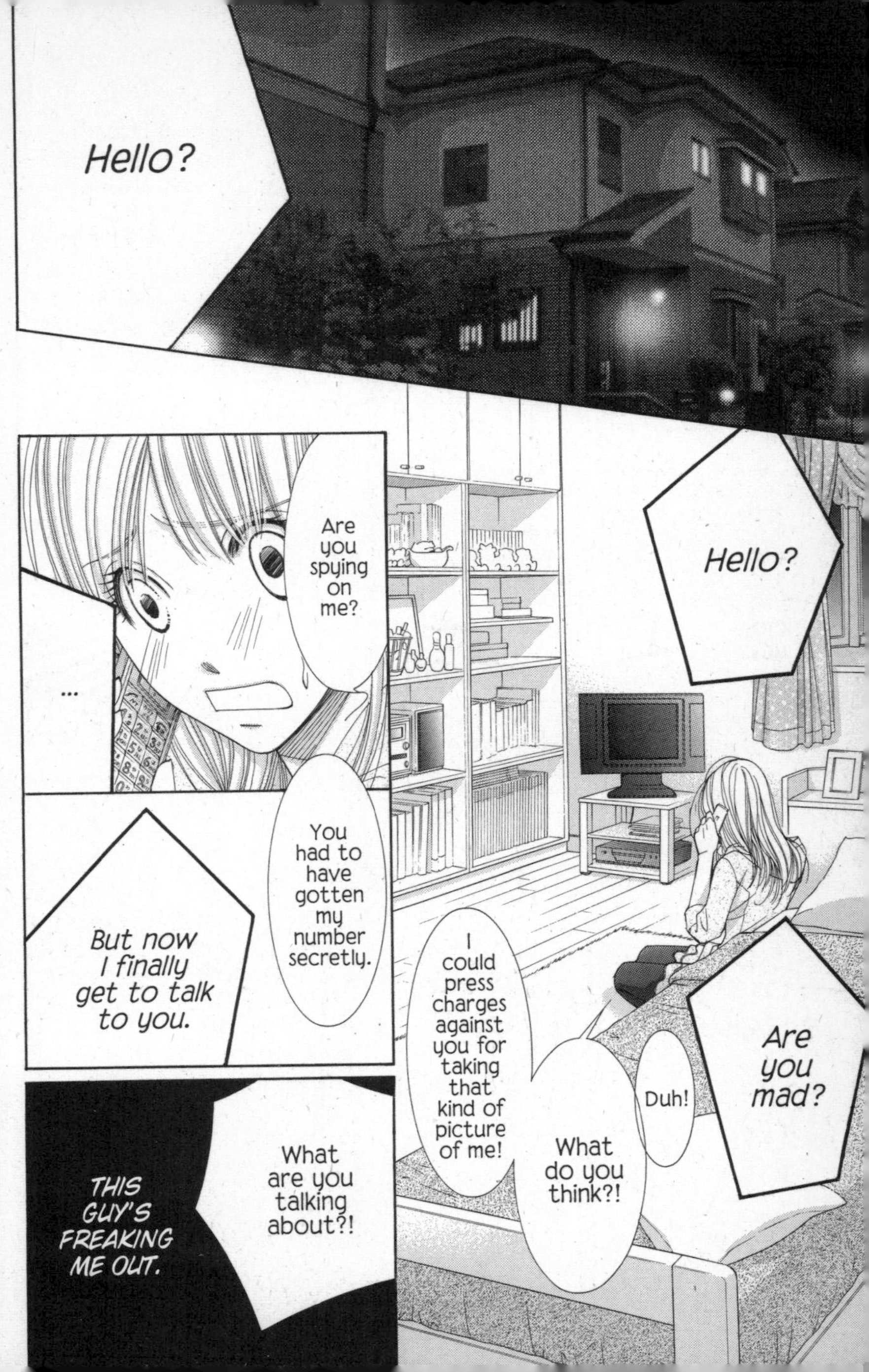
Hello?
Hello?
Are you spying on me?
...
You had to have gotten my number secretly.
But now I finally get to talk to you.
I could press charges against you for taking that kind of picture of me!
Are you mad?
Duh!
What do you think?!
What are you talking about?!
THIS GUY'S FREAKING ME OUT.

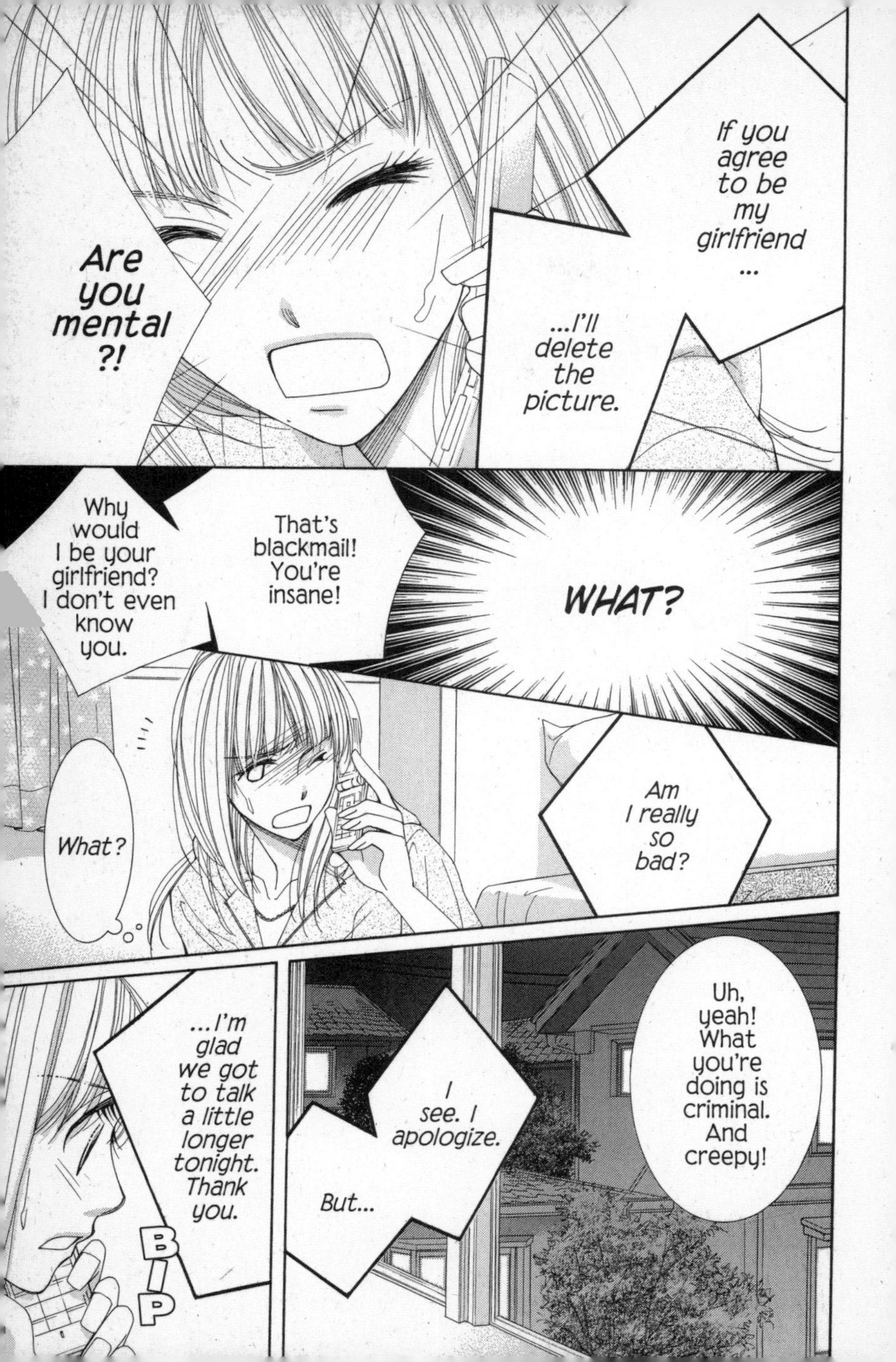
If you agree to be my girlfriend ...
...I'll delete the picture.
Are you mental ?!
WHAT?
That's blackmail! You're insane!
Why would I be your girlfriend? I don't even know you.
Am I really so bad?
What?
Uh, yeah! What you're doing is criminal. And creepy!
I see. I apologize.
But...
...I'm glad we got to talk a little longer tonight. Thank you.
BIP

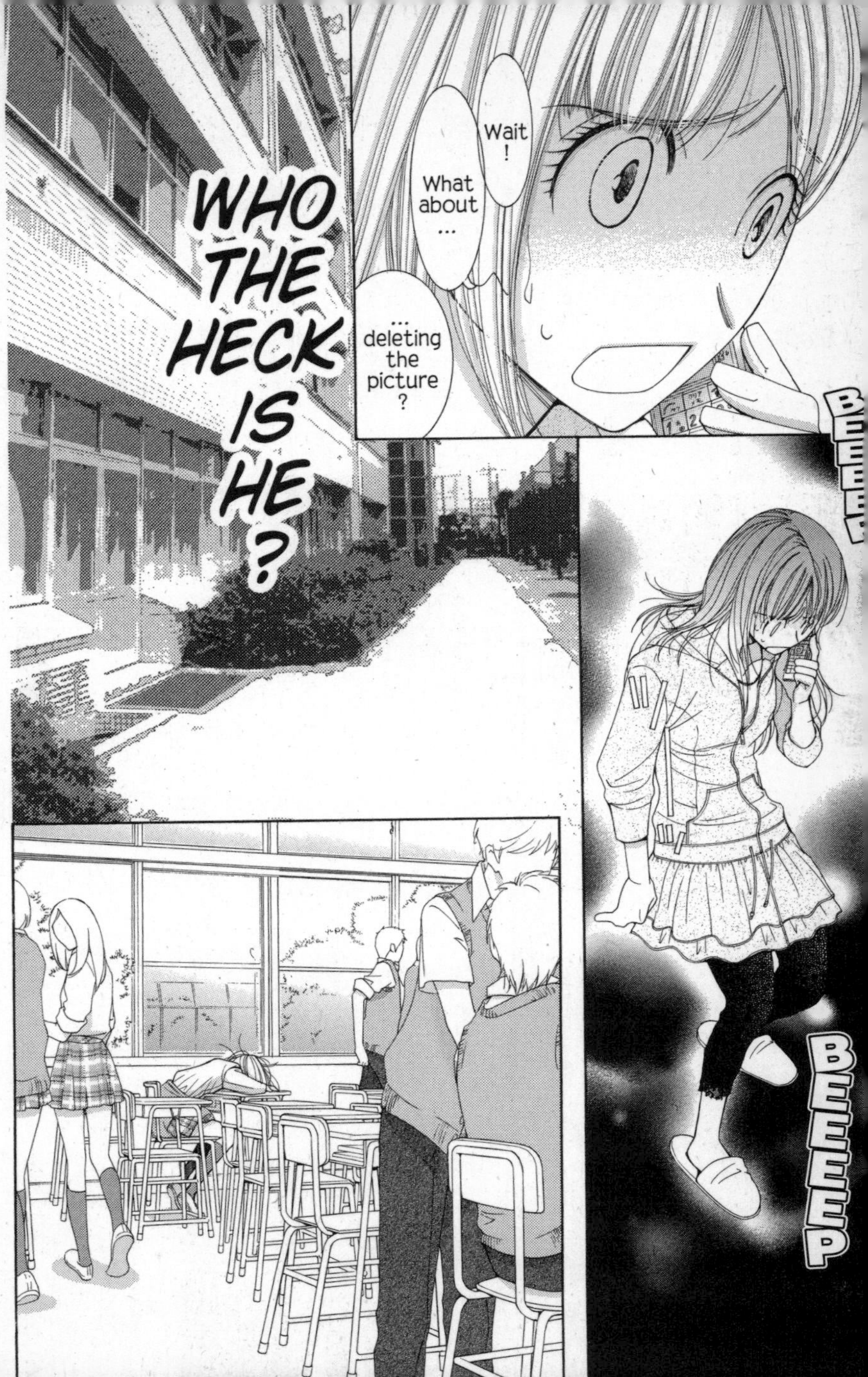
Wait!
What about...
...deleting the picture?
BEEEEP
BEEEEP
WHO THE HECK IS HE?

IF THAT PICTURE GETS OUT, MY LIFE WILL BE OVER.
SHOULD I REPORT THIS TO THE POLICE?
NO, NO, NO.
HE WOULD PROBABLY GET BACK AT ME IF I DID THAT.
I DON'T KNOW...
You scared me!
What do you want? How long were you standing there?
Are you okay?
You've looked upset ever since this morning.
What happened?
N...
Nothing.

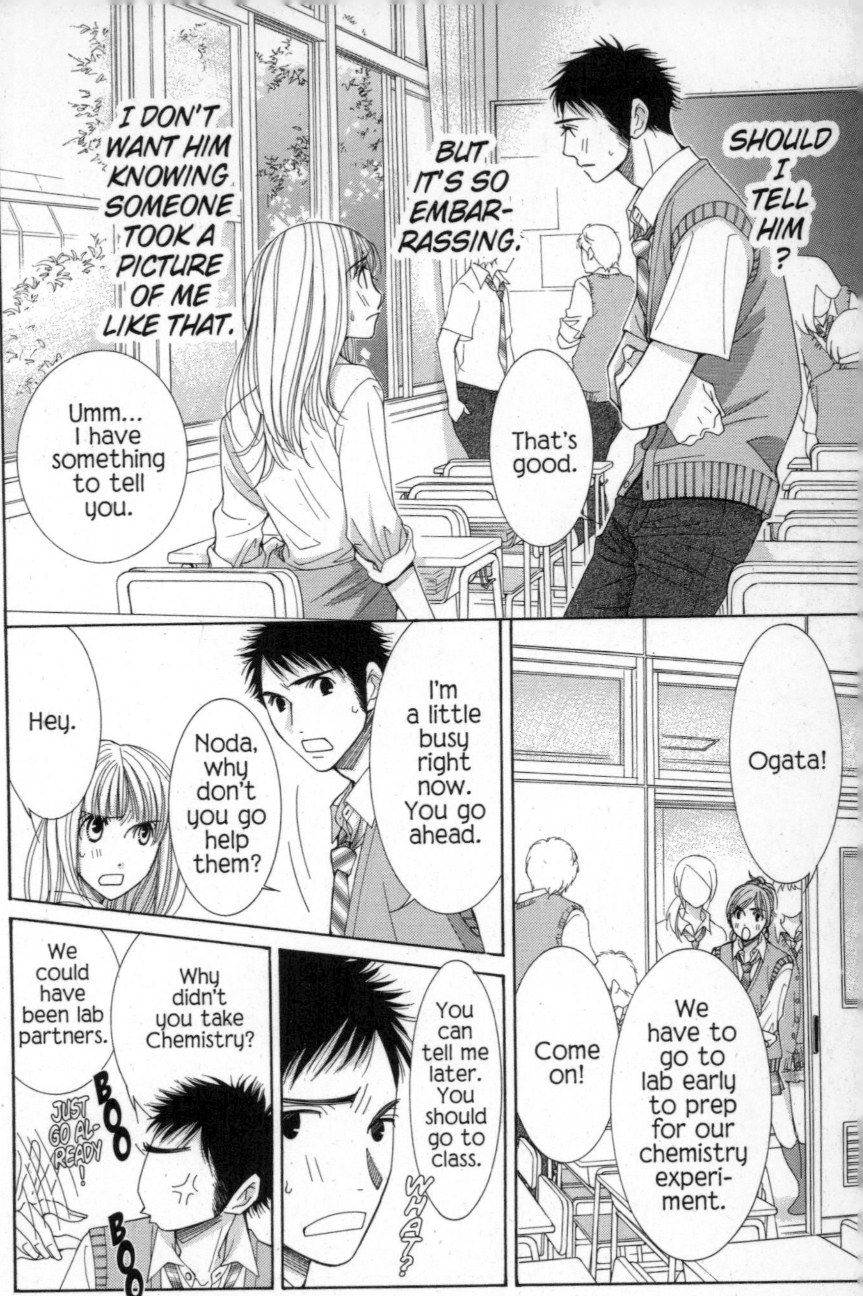
SHOULD I TELL HIM?
BUT IT'S SO EMBARRASSING.
I DON'T WANT HIM KNOWING SOMEONE TOOK A PICTURE OF ME LIKE THAT.
That's good.
Umm... I have something to tell you.
Ogata!
We have to go to lab early to prep for our chemistry experiment.
Come on!
I'm a little busy right now. You go ahead.
Noda, why don't you go help them?
Hey.
You can tell me later. You should go to class.
WHAT?
Why didn't you take Chemistry?
We could have been lab partners.
BOO
BOO
JUST GO ALREADY!

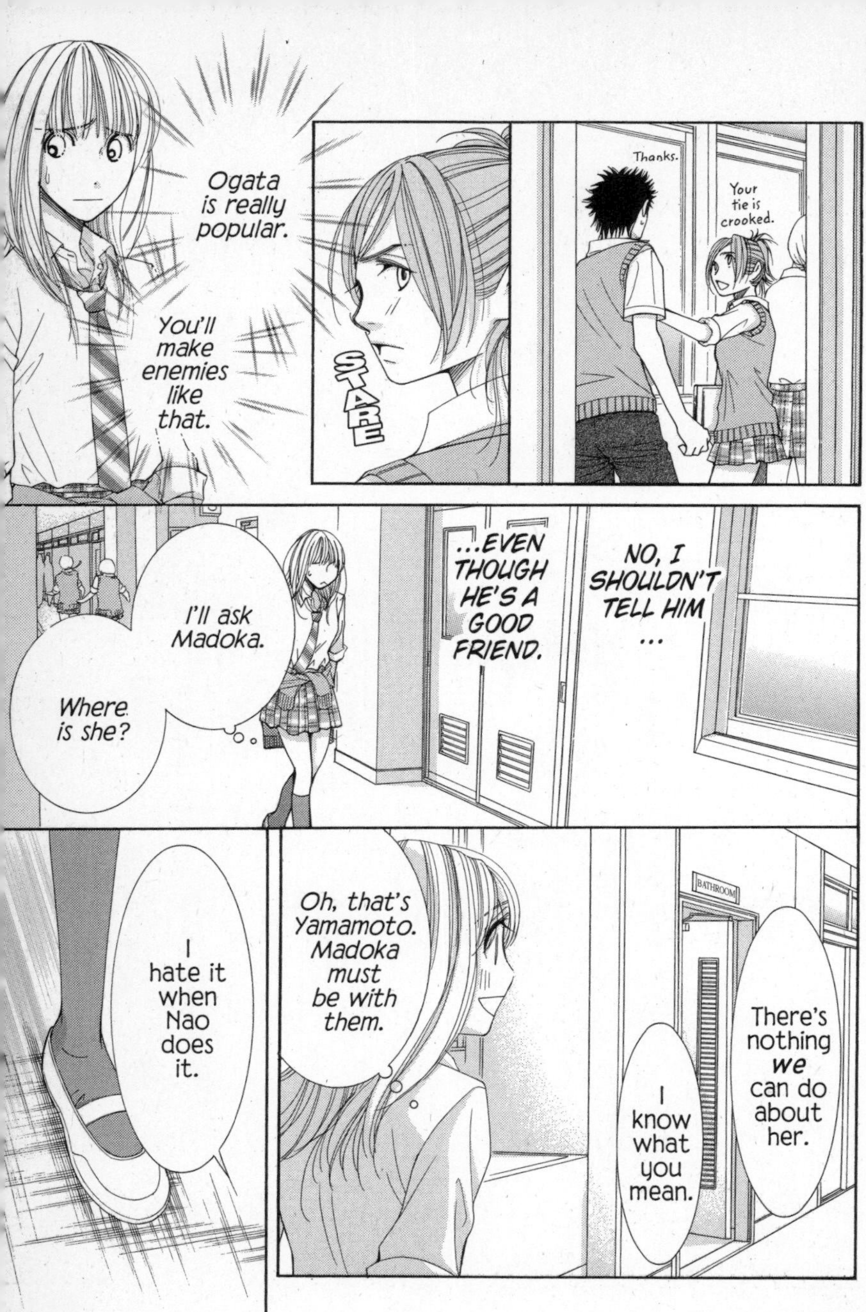

Your tie is crooked.
Thanks.
STARE
Ogata is really popular.
You'll make enemies like that.
NO, I SHOULDN'T TELL HIM...
...EVEN THOUGH HE'S A GOOD FRIEND.
I'll ask Madoka.
Where is she?
BATHROOM
There's nothing *we* can do about her.
I know what you mean.
Oh, that's Yamamoto. Madoka must be with them.
I hate it when Nao does it.

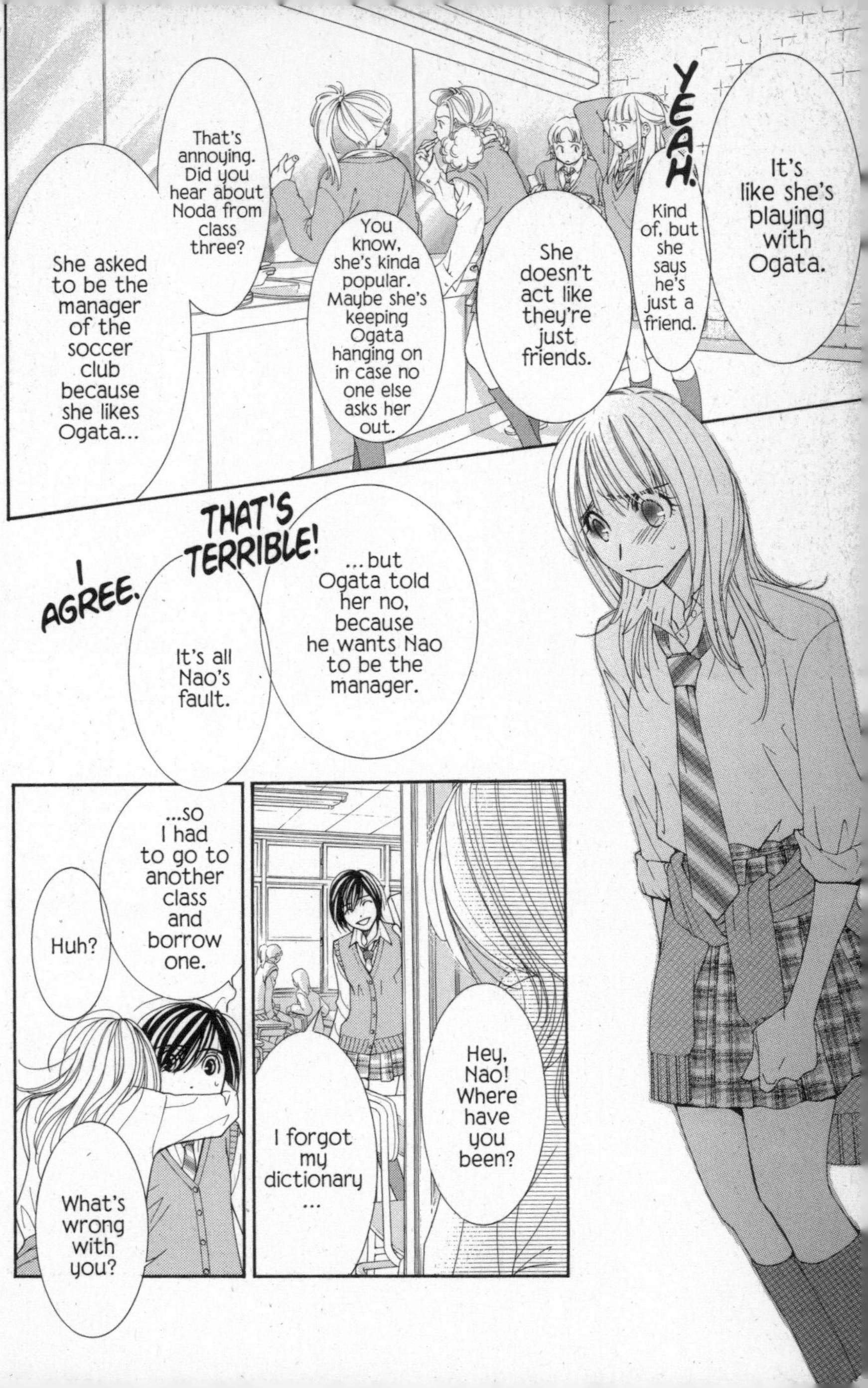
It's like she's playing with Ogata.
YEAH!
Kind of, but she says he's just a friend.
She doesn't act like they're just friends.
You know, she's kinda popular. Maybe she's keeping Ogata hanging on in case no one else asks her out.
That's annoying. Did you hear about Noda from class three?
She asked to be the manager of the soccer club because she likes Ogata...
...but Ogata told her no, because he wants Nao to be the manager.
THAT'S TERRIBLE!
It's all Nao's fault.
I AGREE.
Hey, Nao! Where have you been?
I forgot my dictionary...
...so I had to go to another class and borrow one.
Huh?
What's wrong with you?

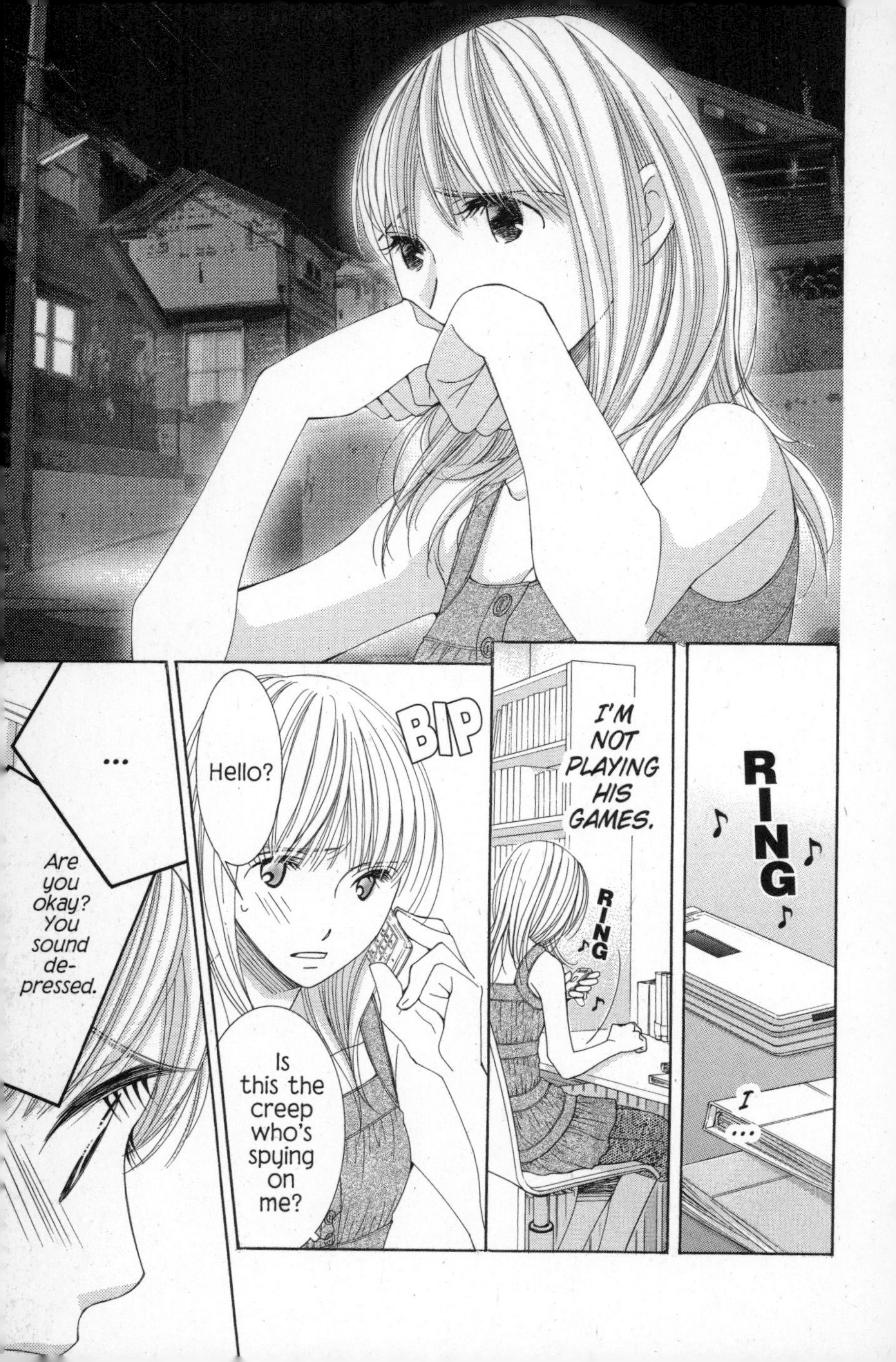

RING
I ...
I'M NOT PLAYING HIS GAMES.
RING
BIP
Hello?
Is this the creep who's spying on me?
...
Are you okay? You sound de-pressed.

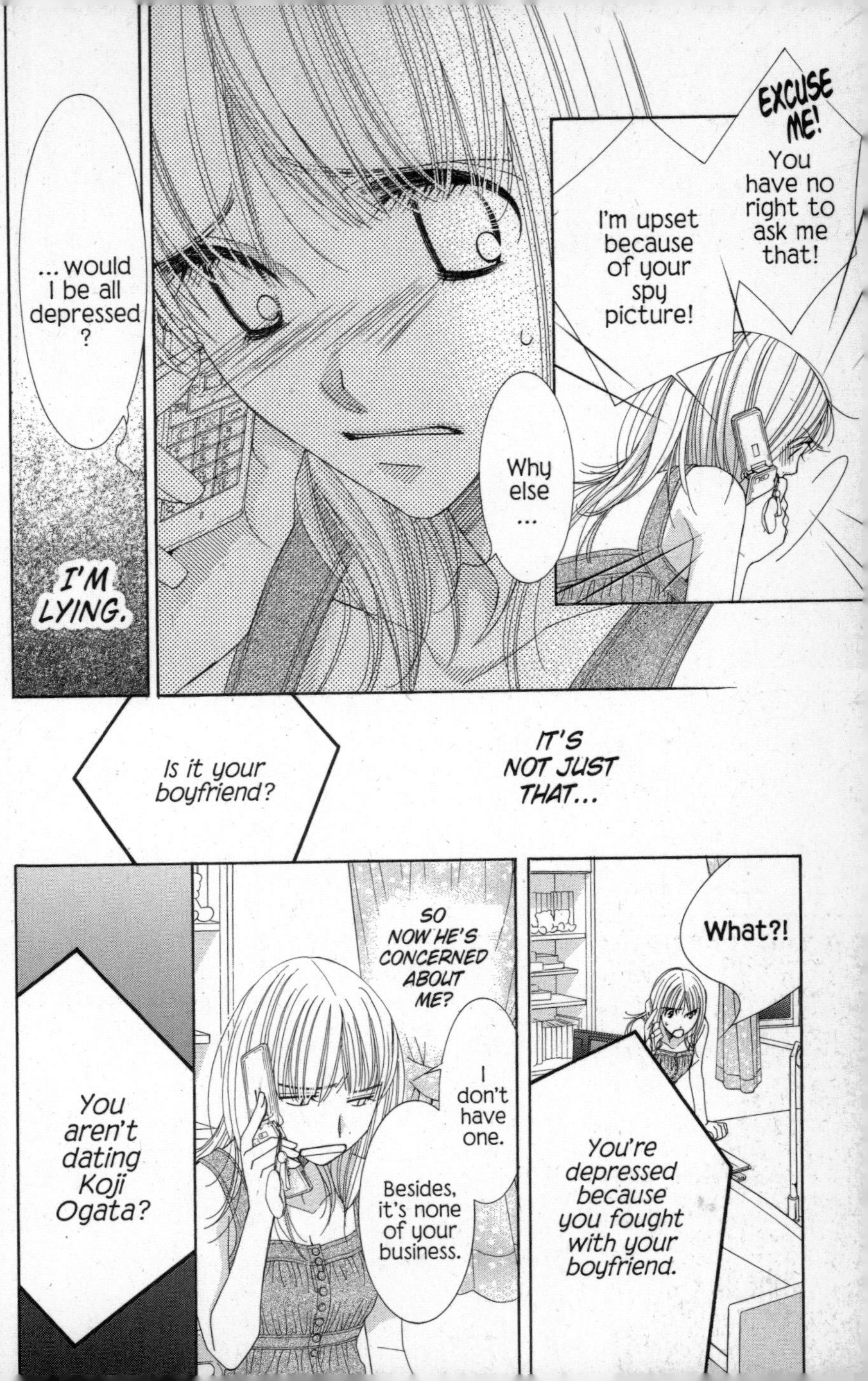
EXCUSE ME!
You have no right to ask me that!
I'm upset because of your spy picture!
Why else ...
... would I be all depressed ?
I'M LYING.
IT'S NOT JUST THAT...
Is it your boyfriend?
What?!
You're depressed because you fought with your boyfriend.
SO NOW HE'S CONCERNED ABOUT ME?
I don't have one.
Besides, it's none of your business.
You aren't dating Koji Ogata?

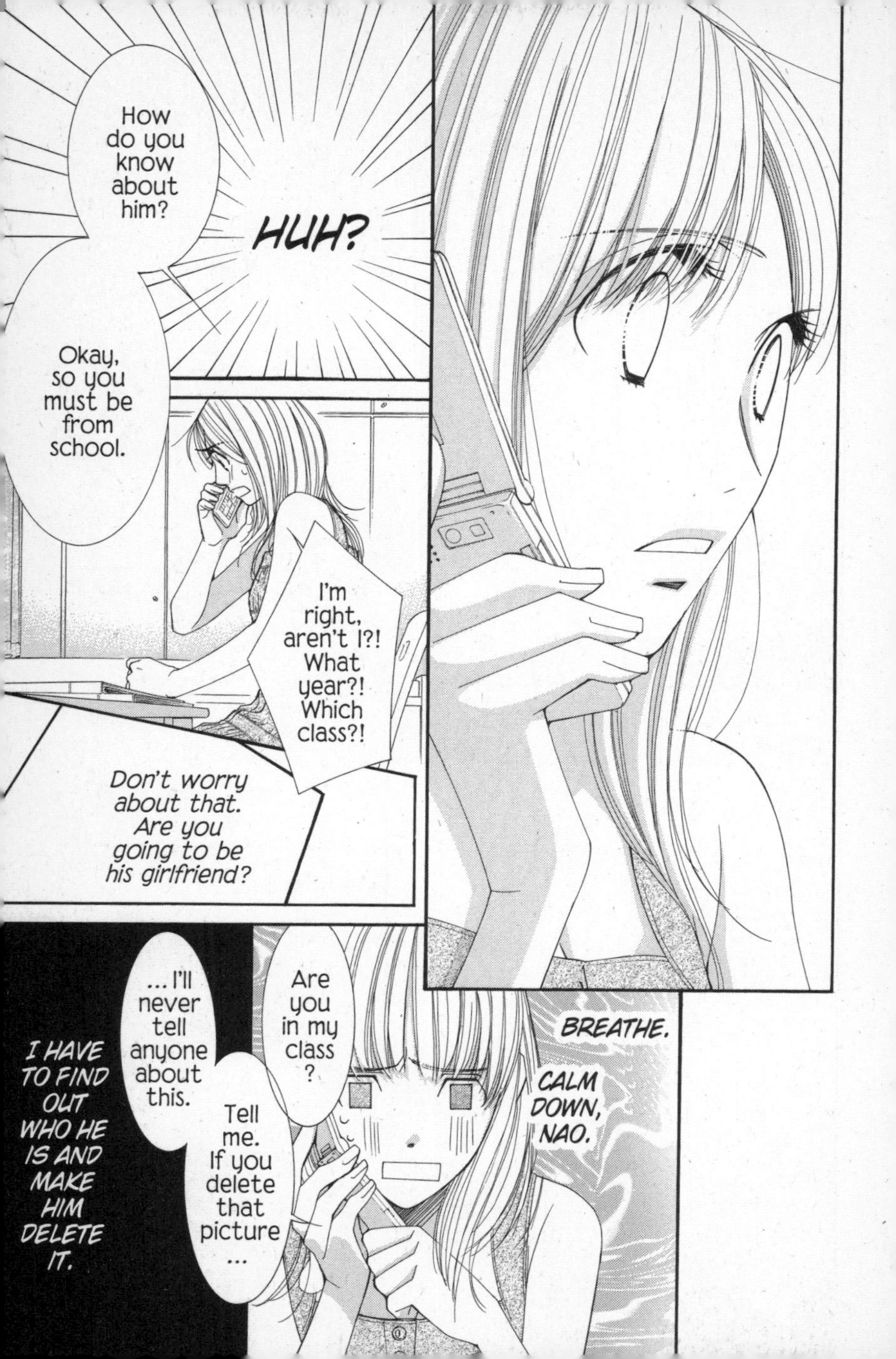

How do you know about him?
HUH?
Okay, so you must be from school.
I'm right, aren't I?! What year?! Which class?!
Don't worry about that. Are you going to be his girlfriend?
BREATHE.
CALM DOWN, NAO.
Are you in my class?
... I'll never tell anyone about this.
Tell me. If you delete that picture ...
I HAVE TO FIND OUT WHO HE IS AND MAKE HIM DELETE IT.

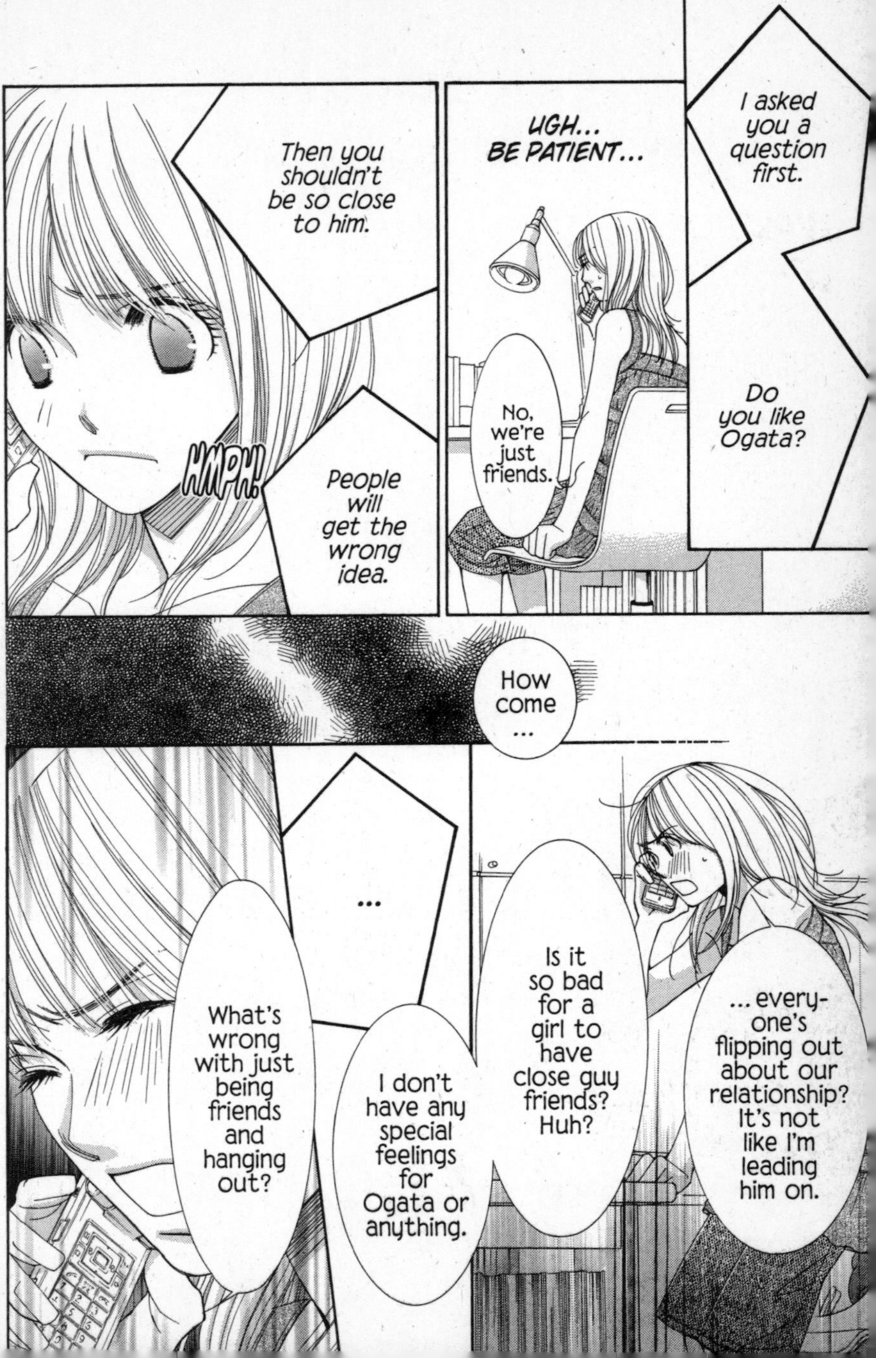
I asked you a question first.
Do you like Ogata?
UGH... BE PATIENT...
No, we're just friends.
Then you shouldn't be so close to him.
HMPH!
People will get the wrong idea.
How come ...
... every-one's flipping out about our relationship? It's not like I'm leading him on.
Is it so bad for a girl to have close guy friends? Huh?
I don't have any special feelings for Ogata or anything.
...
What's wrong with just being friends and hanging out?

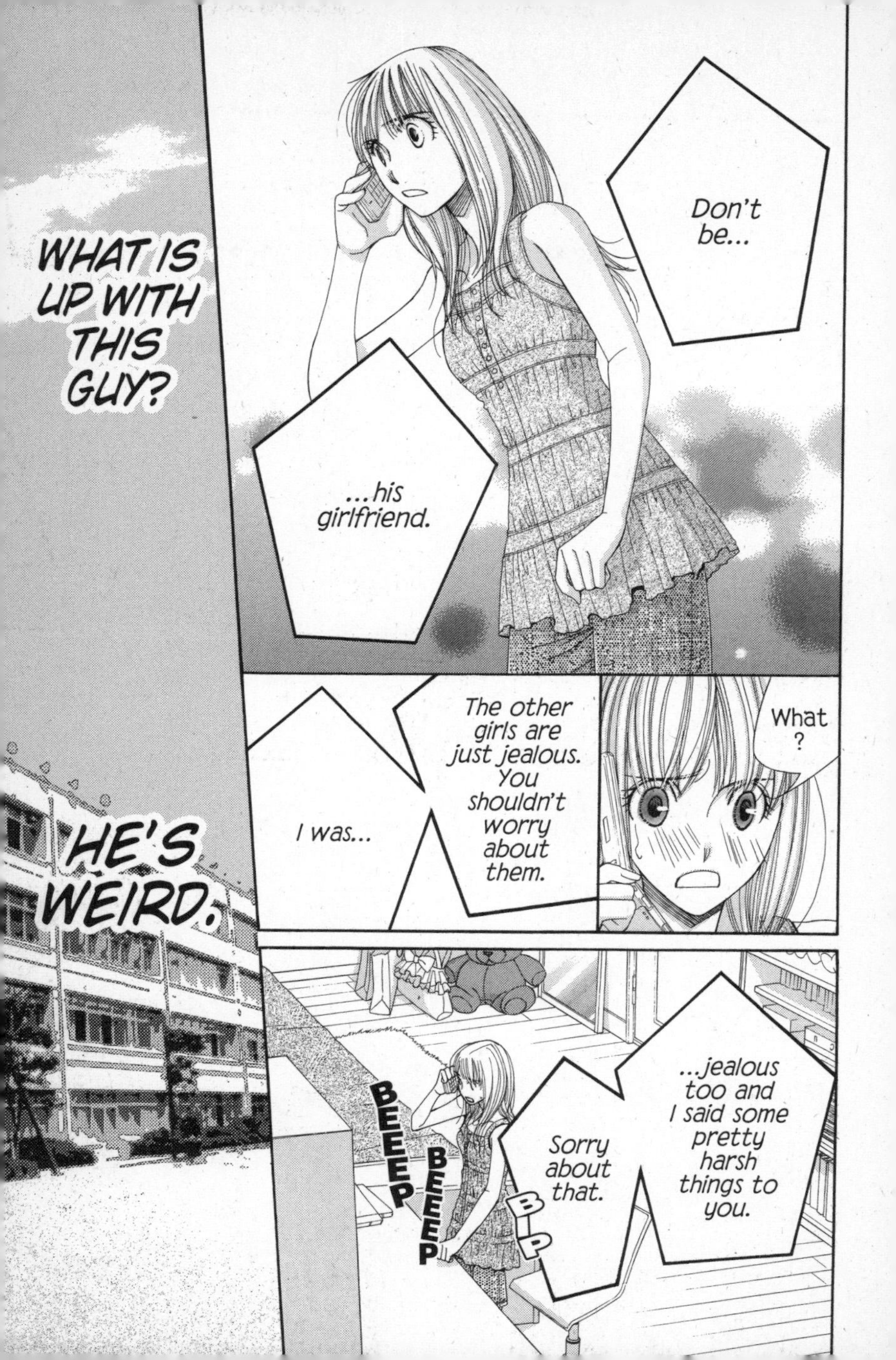
Don't be...
...his girlfriend.
What?
The other girls are just jealous. You shouldn't worry about them.
I was...
...jealous too and I said some pretty harsh things to you.
Sorry about that.
BIP
BEEEP
BEEEP
WHAT IS UP WITH THIS GUY?
HE'S WEIRD.

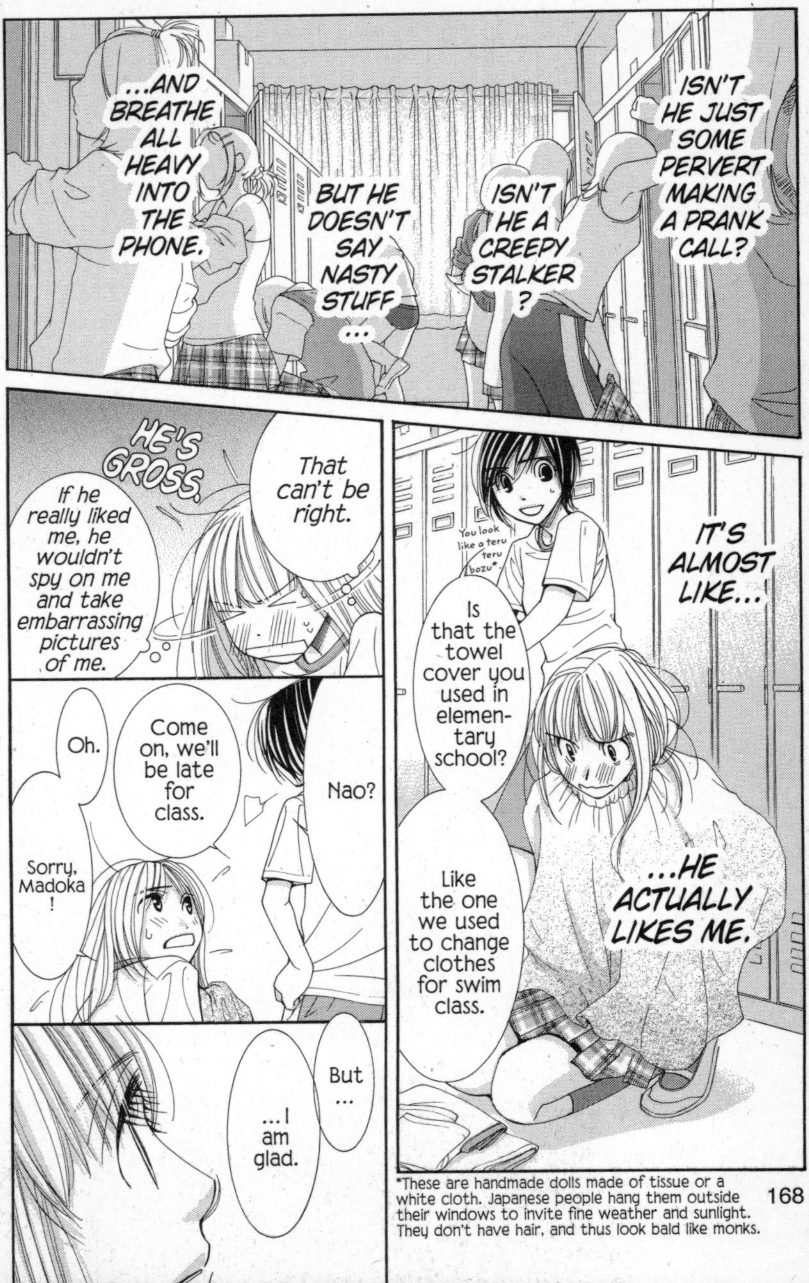
ISN'T HE JUST SOME PERVERT MAKING A PRANK CALL?
ISN'T HE A CREEPY STALKER?
BUT HE DOESN'T SAY NASTY STUFF...
...AND BREATHE ALL HEAVY INTO THE PHONE.
IT'S ALMOST LIKE...
You look like a teru teru bozu*.
Is that the towel cover you used in elementary school?
Like the one we used to change clothes for swim class.
...HE ACTUALLY LIKES ME.
That can't be right.
HE'S GROSS.
If he really liked me, he wouldn't spy on me and take embarrassing pictures of me.
Nao?
Come on, we'll be late for class.
Oh.
Sorry, Madoka!
But...
...I am glad.

*These are handmade dolls made of tissue or a white cloth. Japanese people hang them outside their windows to invite fine weather and sunlight. They don't have hair, and thus look bald like monks.

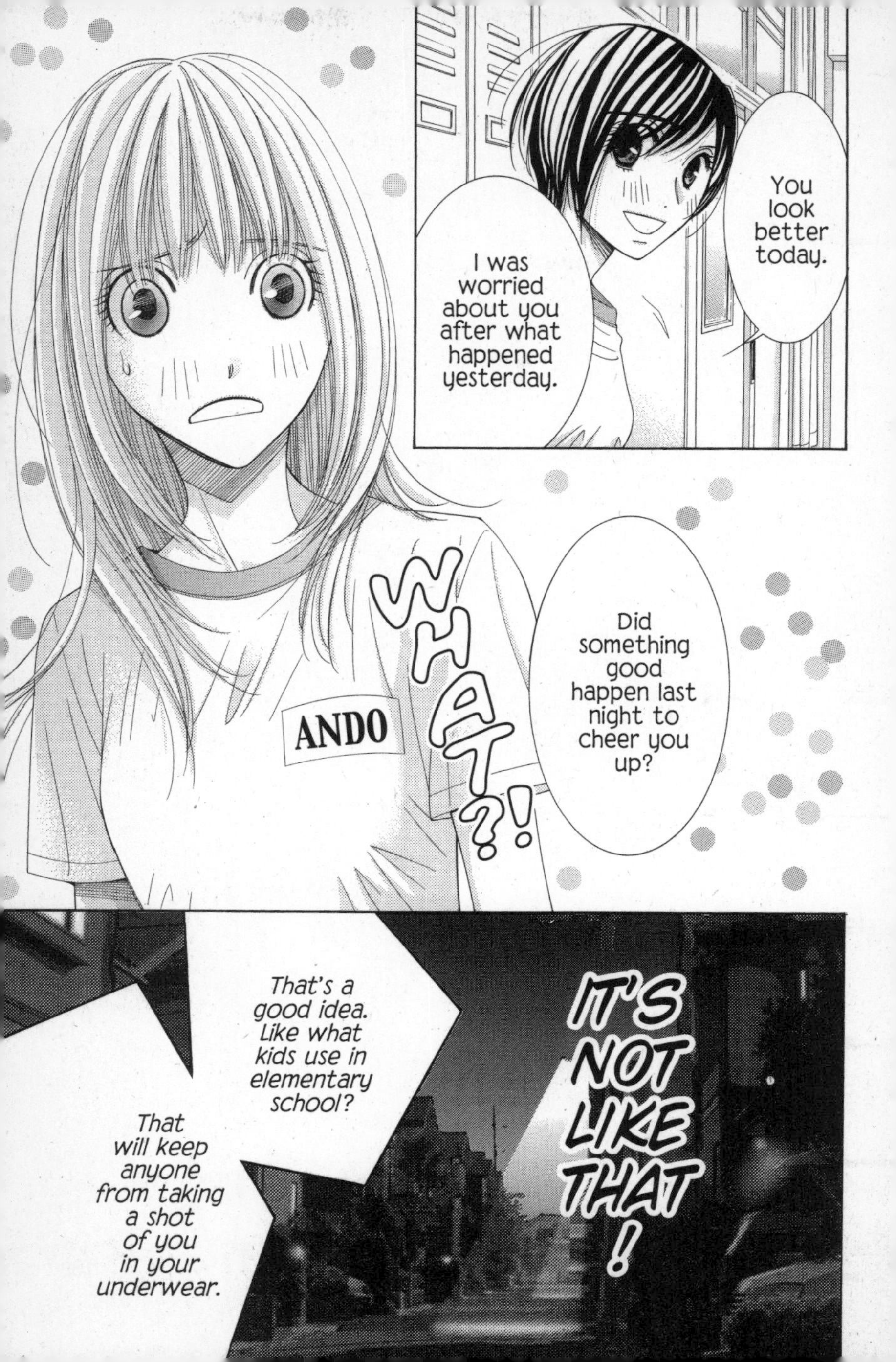
You look better today.
I was worried about you after what happened yesterday.
Did something good happen last night to cheer you up?
WHAT?!
ANDO
IT'S NOT LIKE THAT!
That's a good idea. Like what kids use in elementary school?
That will keep anyone from taking a shot of you in your underwear.

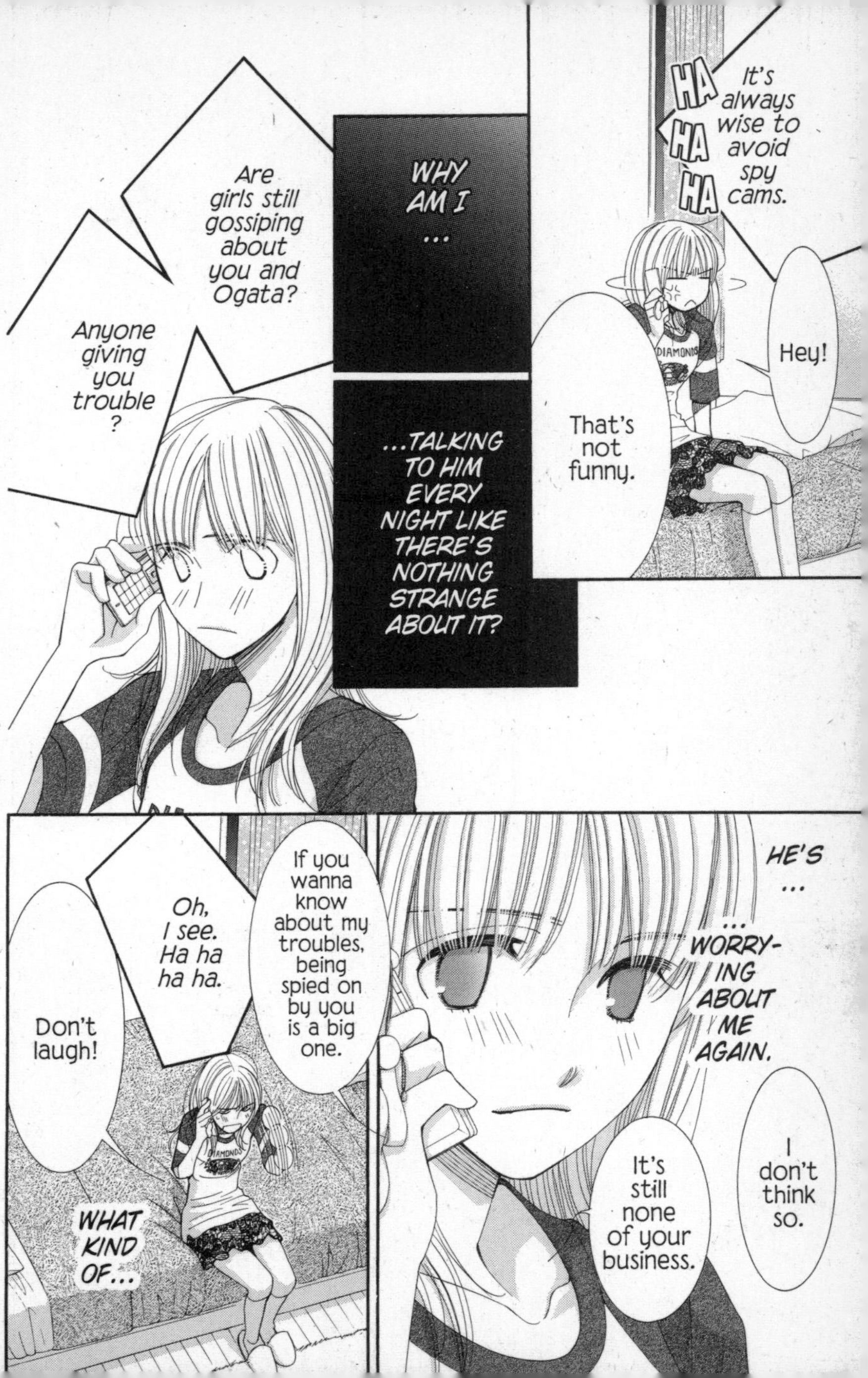
It's always wise to avoid spy cams.
HA HA HA
Hey!
That's not funny.
Are girls still gossiping about you and Ogata?
Anyone giving you trouble?
WHY AM I ...
...TALKING TO HIM EVERY NIGHT LIKE THERE'S NOTHING STRANGE ABOUT IT?
HE'S ...
... WORRY-ING ABOUT ME AGAIN.
I don't think so.
It's still none of your business.
If you wanna know about my troubles, being spied on by you is a big one.
Oh, I see. Ha ha ha ha.
Don't laugh!
WHAT KIND OF...

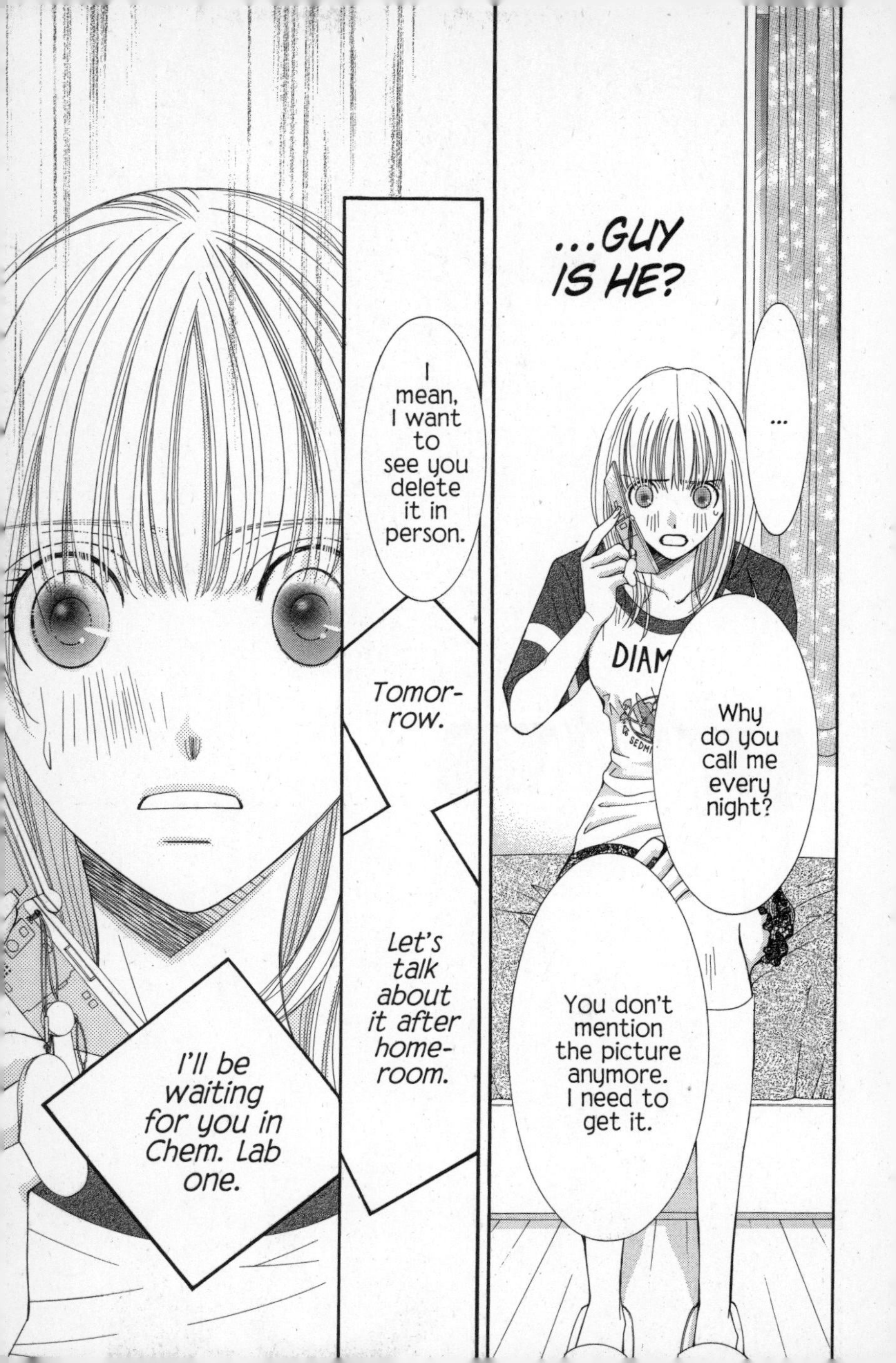
...GUY IS HE?
...
Why do you call me every night?
You don't mention the picture anymore. I need to get it.
I mean, I want to see you delete it in person.
Tomorrow.
Let's talk about it after homeroom.
I'll be waiting for you in Chem. Lab one.

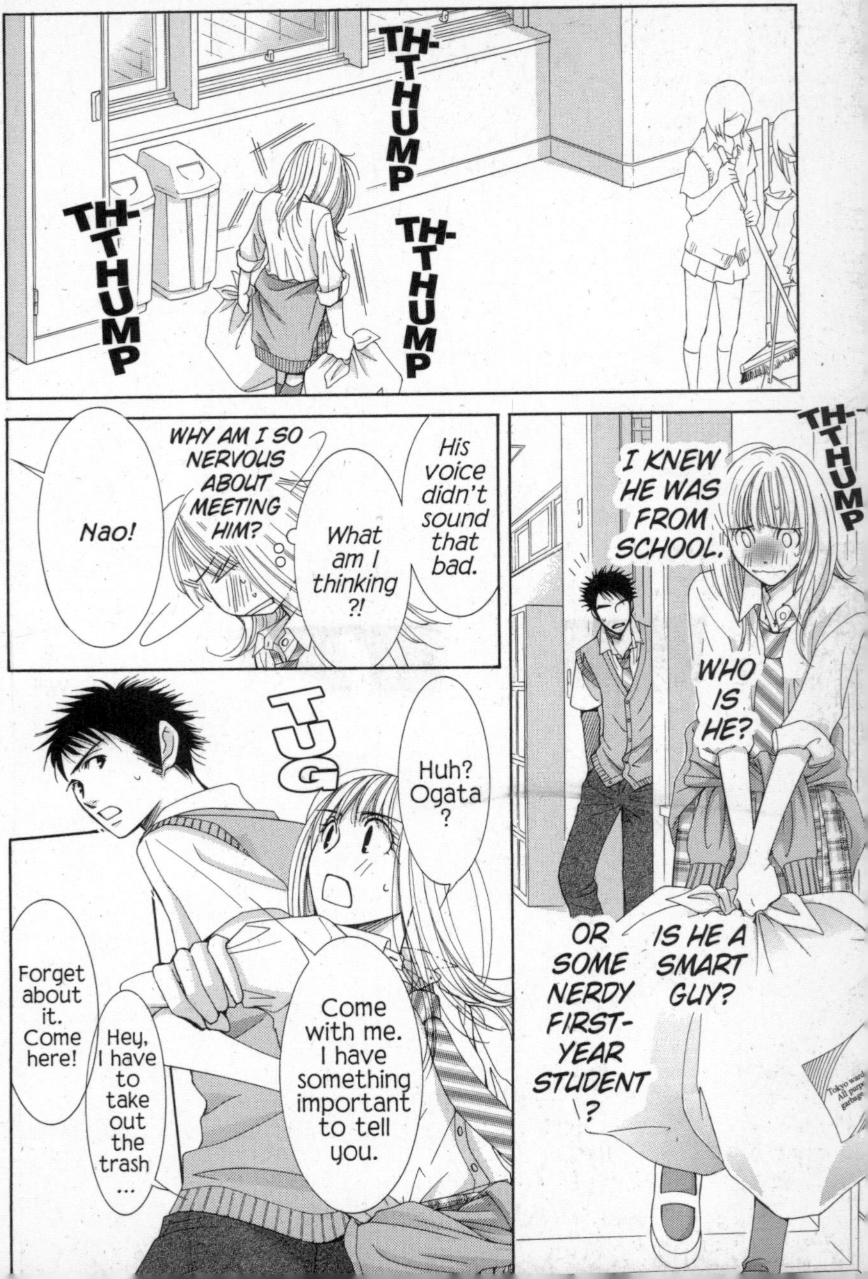
TH-THUMP
TH-THUMP
TH-THUMP
TH-THUMP
I KNEW HE WAS FROM SCHOOL.
WHO IS HE?
IS HE A SMART GUY?
OR SOME NERDY FIRST-YEAR STUDENT?
His voice didn't sound that bad.
What am I thinking?!
WHY AM I SO NERVOUS ABOUT MEETING HIM?
Nao!
TUG
Huh? Ogata?
Come with me. I have something important to tell you.
Hey, I have to take out the trash...
Forget about it. Come here!

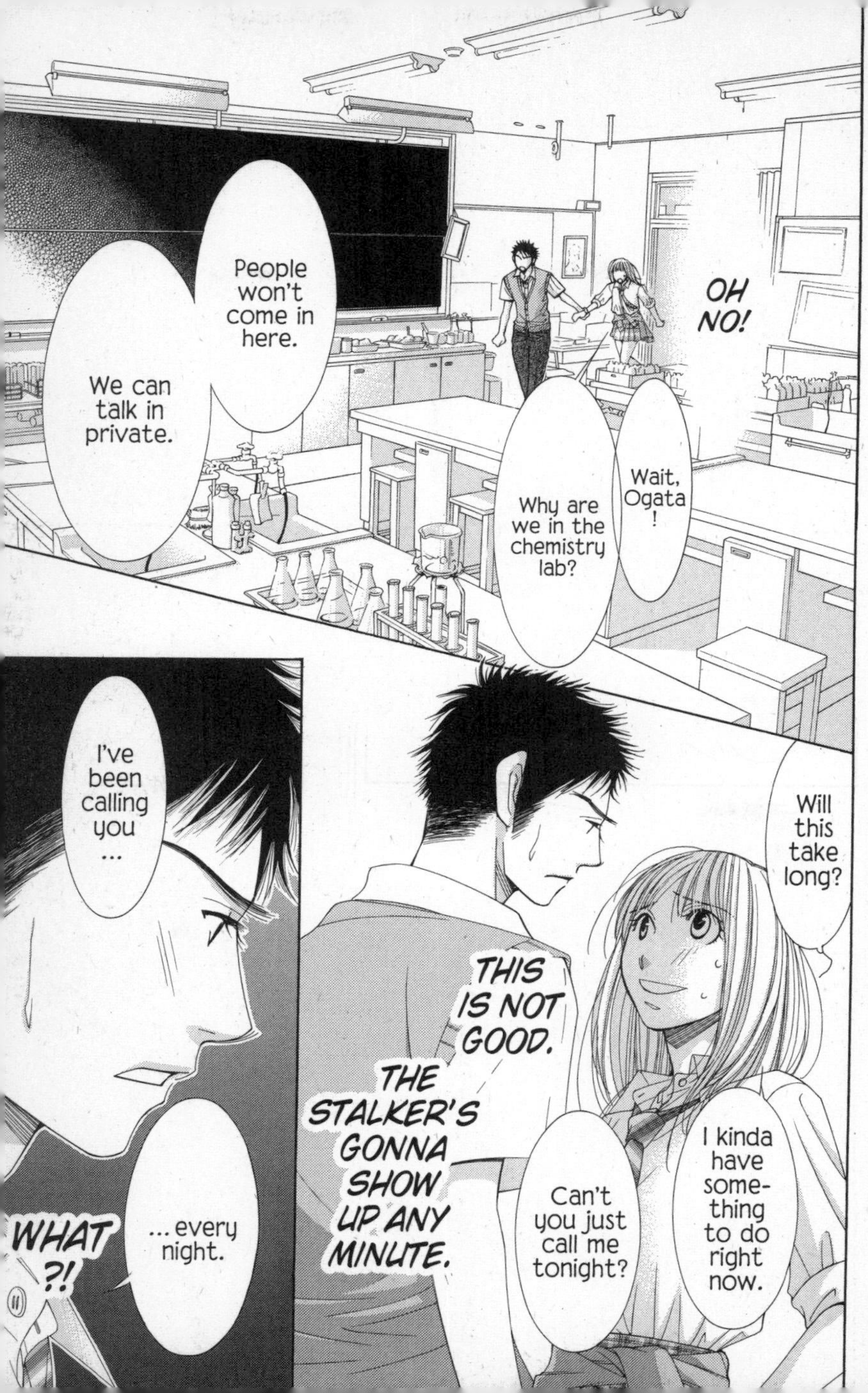
OH NO!
Wait, Ogata!
Why are we in the chemistry lab?
People won't come in here.
We can talk in private.
Will this take long?
THIS IS NOT GOOD.
I kinda have some-thing to do right now.
Can't you just call me tonight?
THE STALKER'S GONNA SHOW UP ANY MINUTE.
I've been calling you ...
... every night.
WHAT ?!

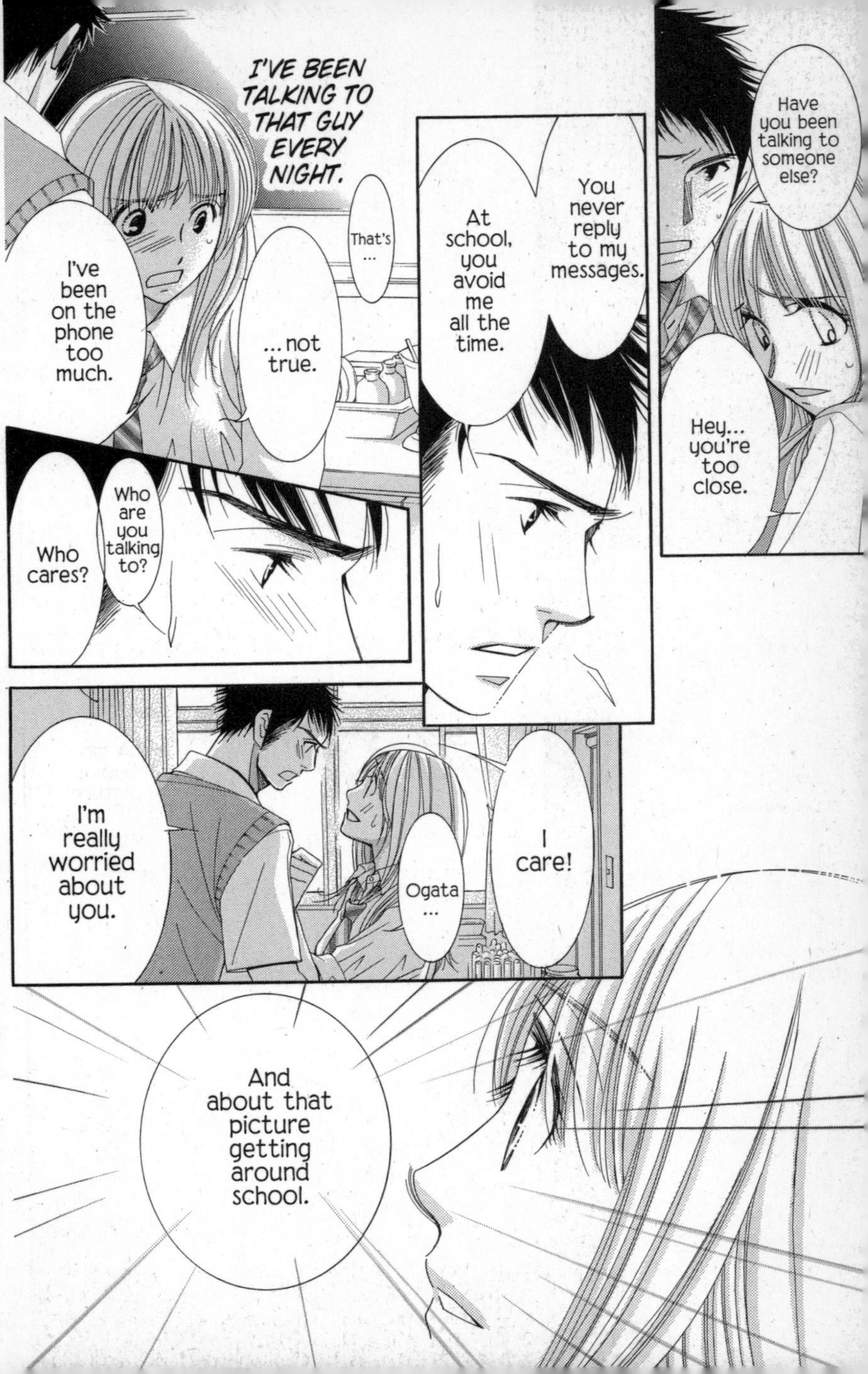
Have you been talking to someone else?
Hey... you're too close.
You never reply to my messages.
At school, you avoid me all the time.
I'VE BEEN TALKING TO THAT GUY EVERY NIGHT.
That's...
...not true.
I've been on the phone too much.
Who are you talking to?
Who cares?
I care!
Ogata...
I'm really worried about you.
And about that picture getting around school.

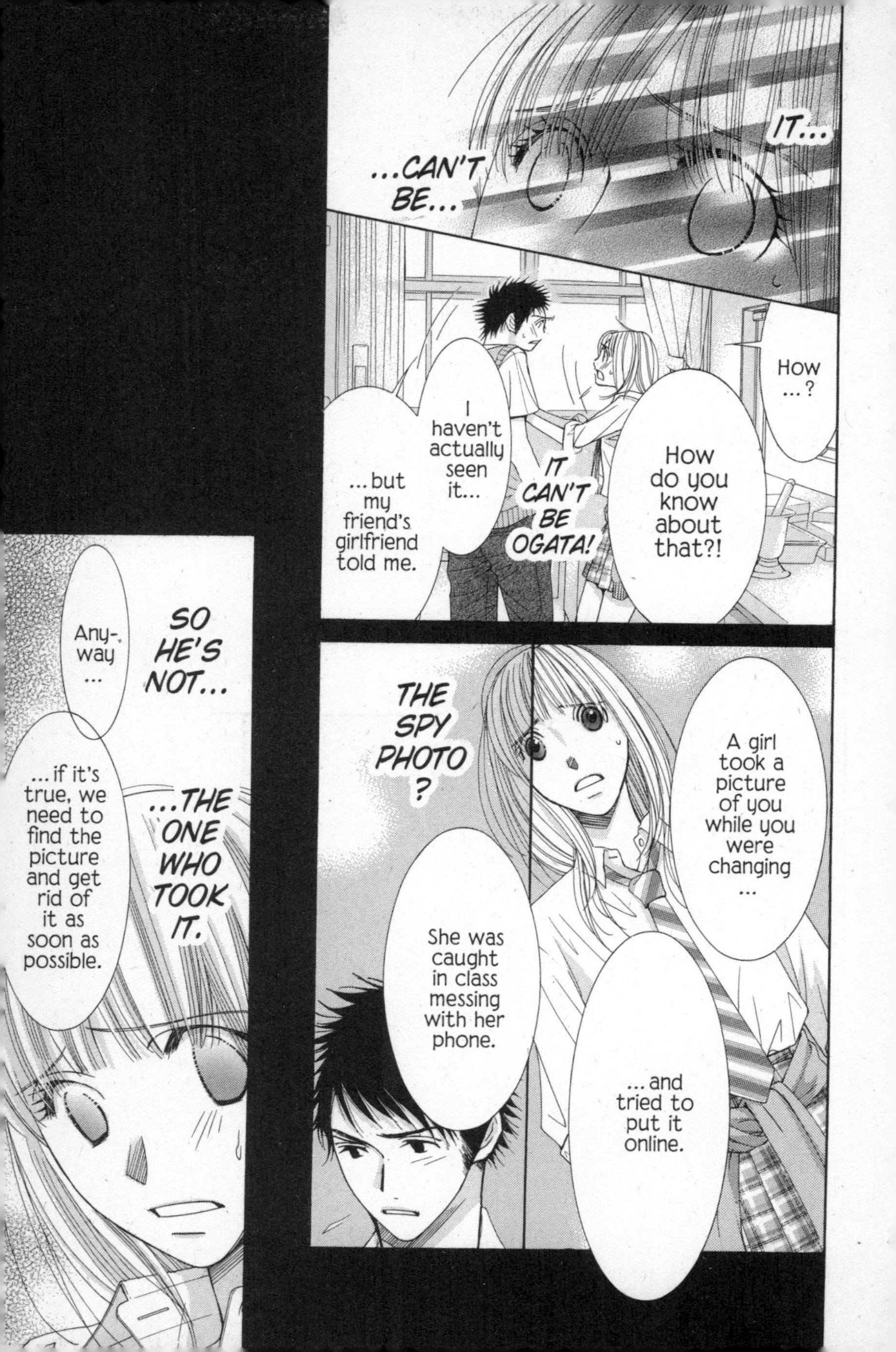
IT...
...CAN'T BE...
How ...?
How do you know about that?!
IT CAN'T BE OGATA!
I haven't actually seen it...
...but my friend's girlfriend told me.
A girl took a picture of you while you were changing ...
THE SPY PHOTO?
...and tried to put it online.
She was caught in class messing with her phone.
SO HE'S NOT...
Any-way ...
...THE ONE WHO TOOK IT.
... if it's true, we need to find the picture and get rid of it as soon as possible.

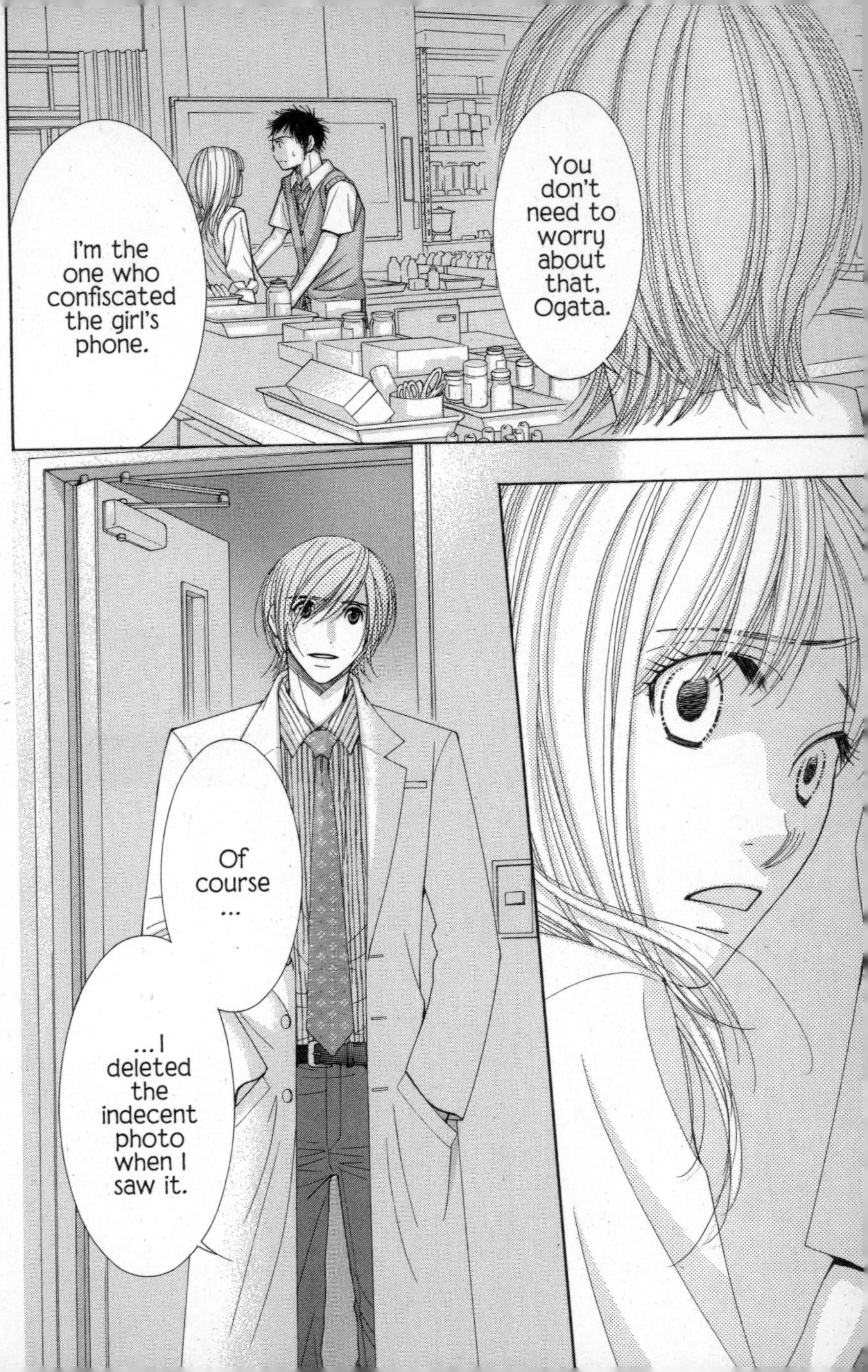
You don't need to worry about that, Ogata.
I'm the one who confiscated the girl's phone.
Of course ...
...I deleted the indecent photo when I saw it.

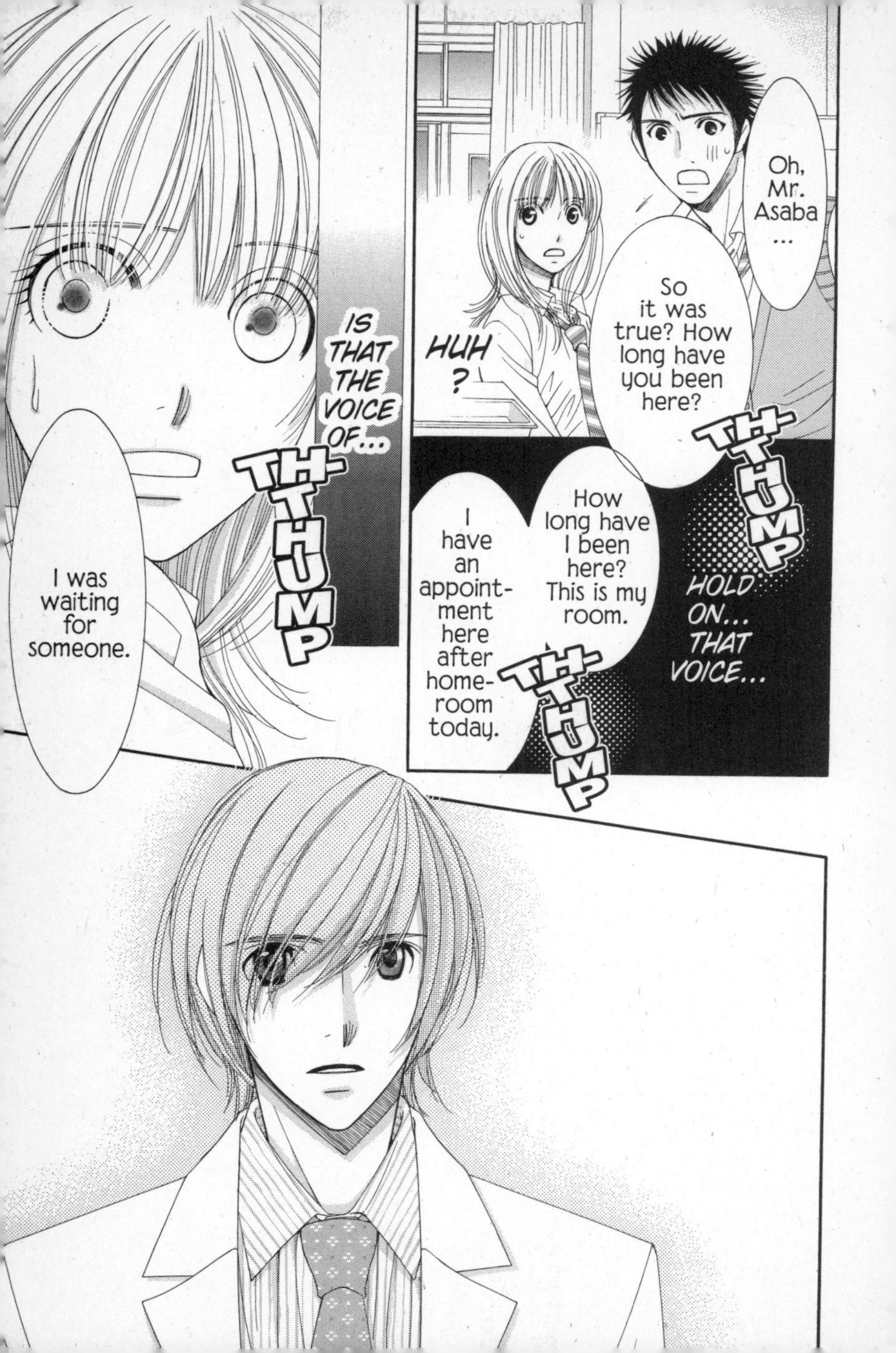

Oh, Mr. Asaba...
So it was true? How long have you been here?
HUH?
TH-THUMP
HOLD ON... THAT VOICE...
How long have I been here? This is my room.
I have an appointment here after homeroom today.
TH-THUMP
IS THAT THE VOICE OF...
TH-THUMP
I was waiting for someone.

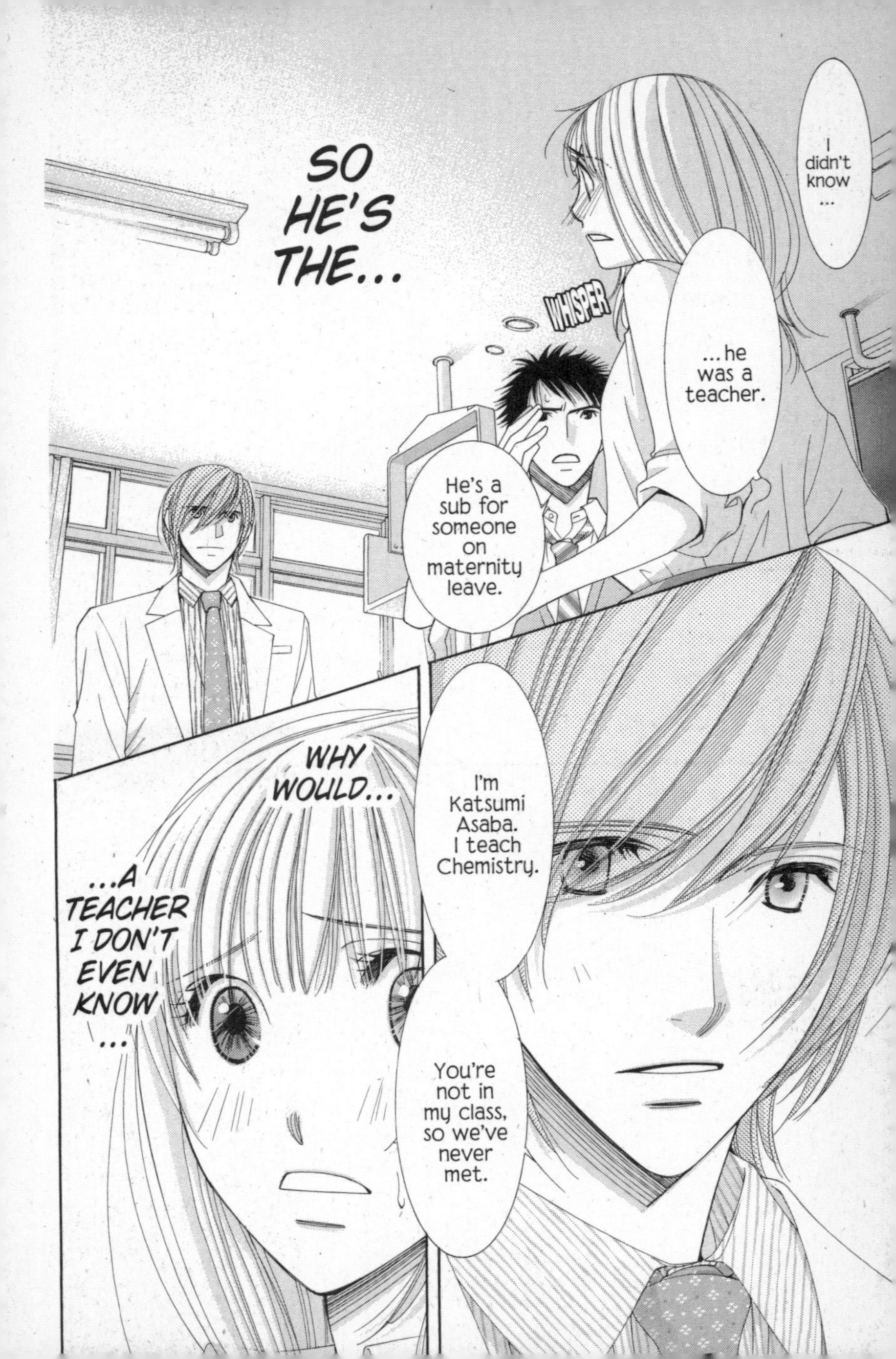
I didn't know...
...he was a teacher.
WHISPER
He's a sub for someone on maternity leave.
SO HE'S THE...
I'm Katsumi Asaba. I teach Chemistry.
You're not in my class, so we've never met.
WHY WOULD...
...A TEACHER I DON'T EVEN KNOW...

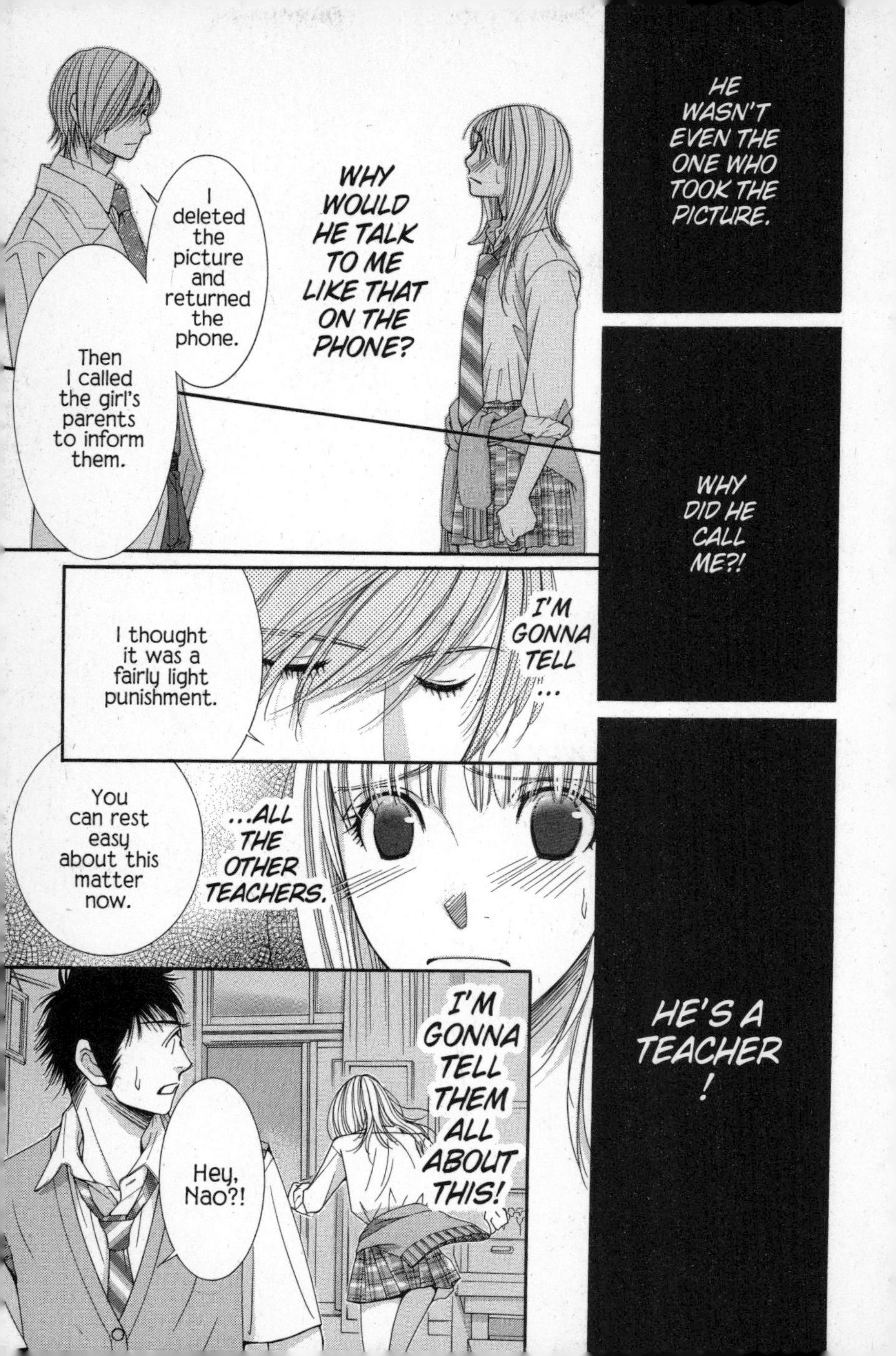
HE WASN'T EVEN THE ONE WHO TOOK THE PICTURE.
WHY WOULD HE TALK TO ME LIKE THAT ON THE PHONE?
I deleted the picture and returned the phone.
Then I called the girl's parents to inform them.
WHY DID HE CALL ME?!
I'M GONNA TELL...
I thought it was a fairly light punishment.
...ALL THE OTHER TEACHERS.
You can rest easy about this matter now.
HE'S A TEACHER!
I'M GONNA TELL THEM ALL ABOUT THIS!
Hey, Nao?!

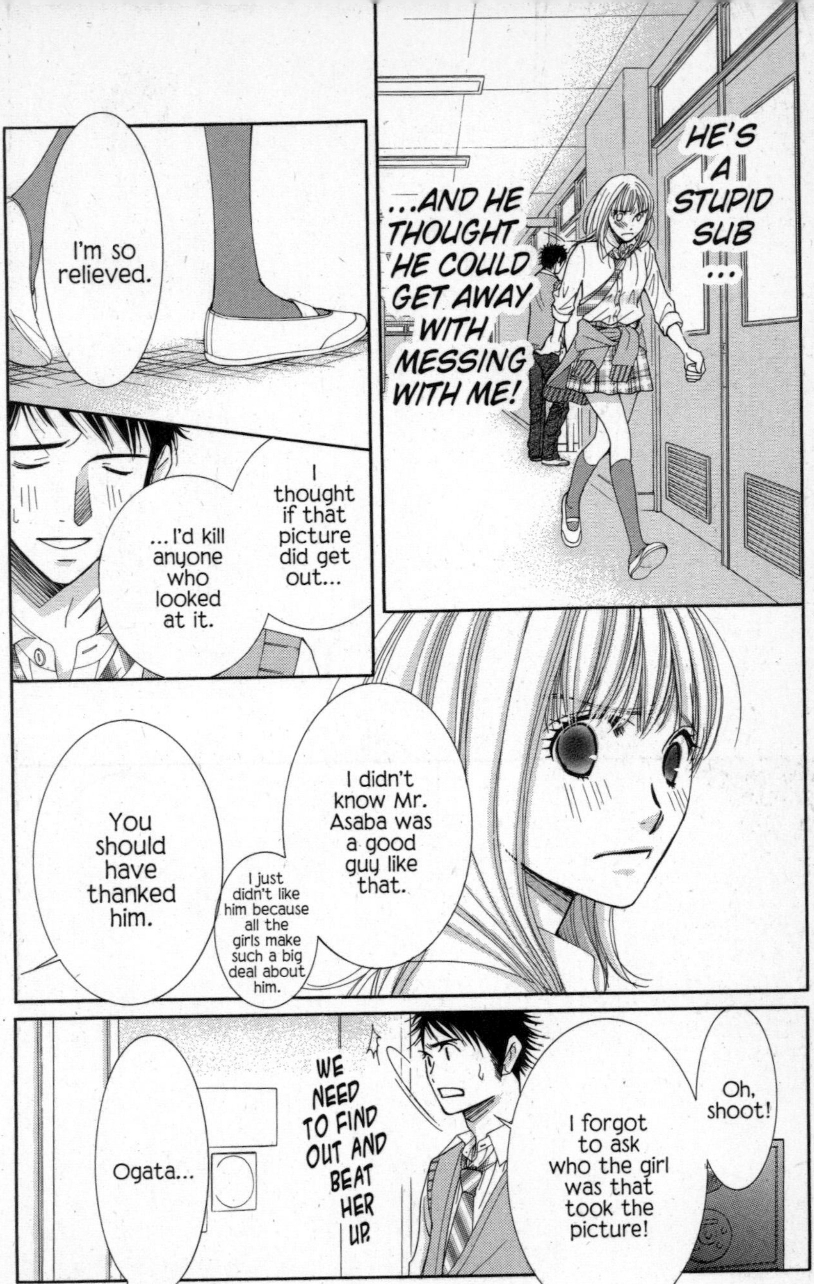
HE'S A STUPID SUB...
...AND HE THOUGHT HE COULD GET AWAY WITH MESSING WITH ME!
I'm so relieved.
I thought if that picture did get out...
...I'd kill anyone who looked at it.
I didn't know Mr. Asaba was a good guy like that.
I just didn't like him because all the girls make such a big deal about him.
You should have thanked him.
Oh, shoot!
I forgot to ask who the girl was that took the picture!
WE NEED TO FIND OUT AND BEAT HER UP.
Ogata...

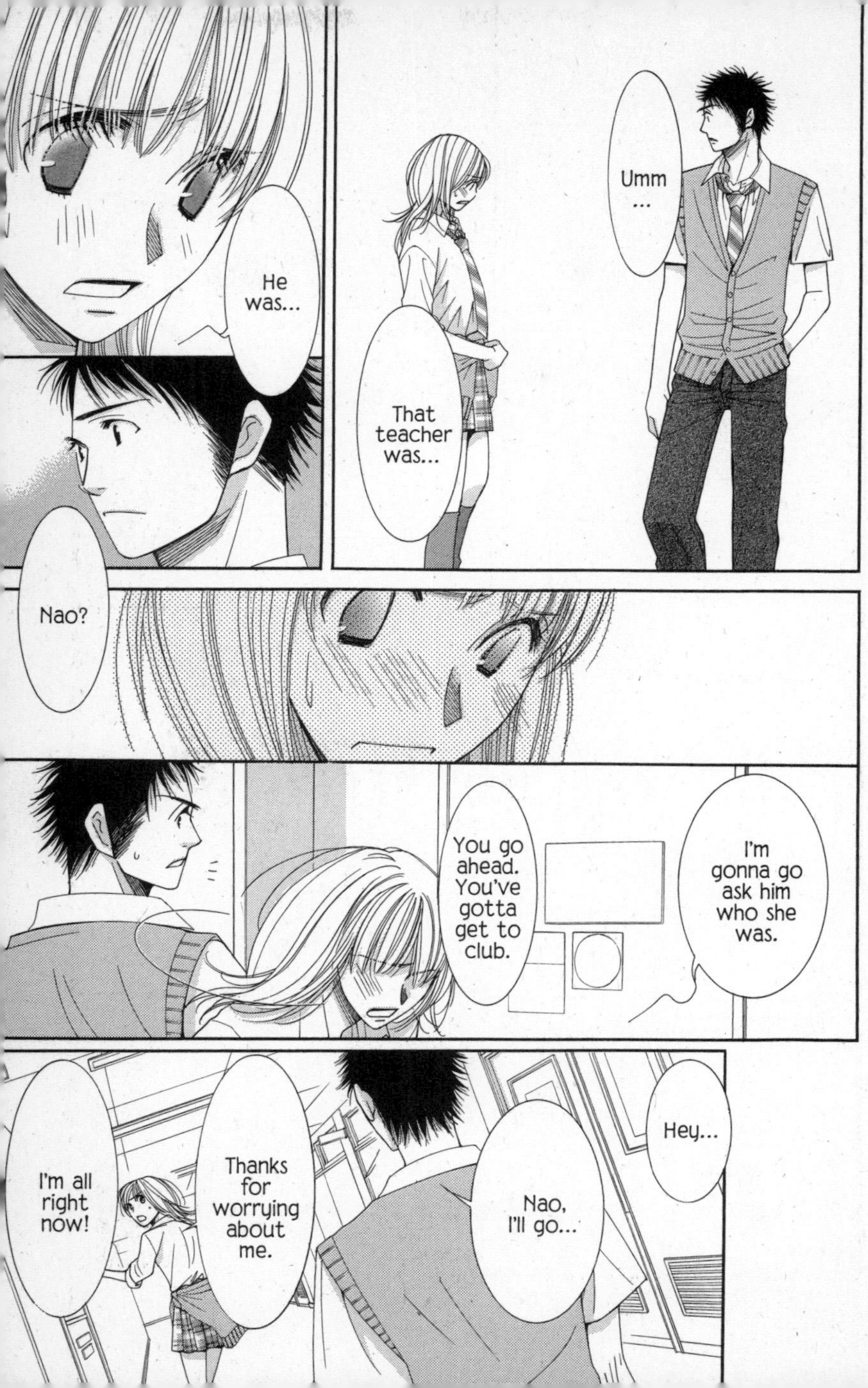
Umm ...
That teacher was...
He was...
Nao?
I'm gonna go ask him who she was.
You go ahead. You've gotta get to club.
Hey...
Nao, I'll go...
Thanks for worrying about me.
I'm all right now!

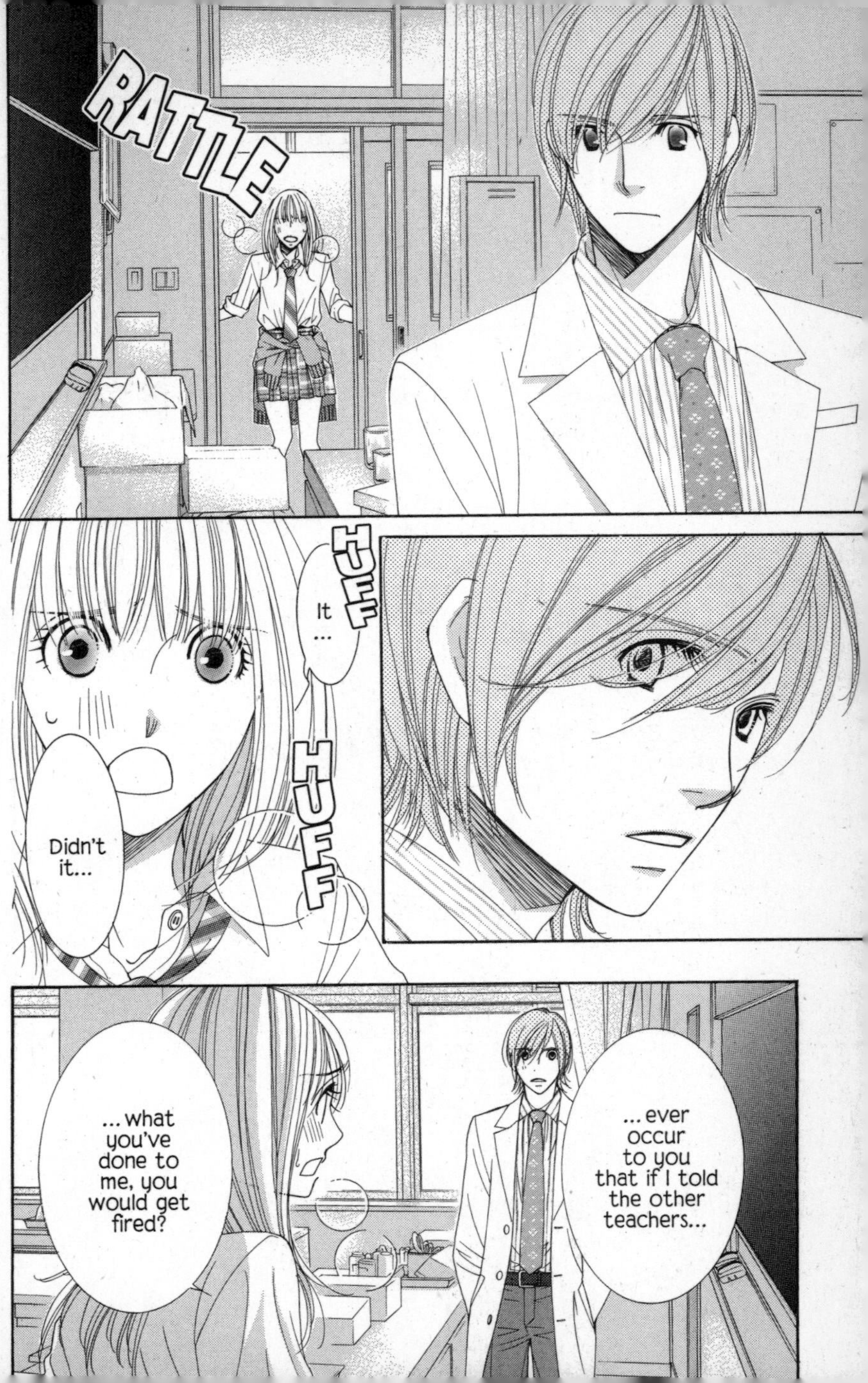
RATTLE
HUFF
It...
HUFF
Didn't it...
...ever occur to you that if I told the other teachers...
...what you've done to me, you would get fired?

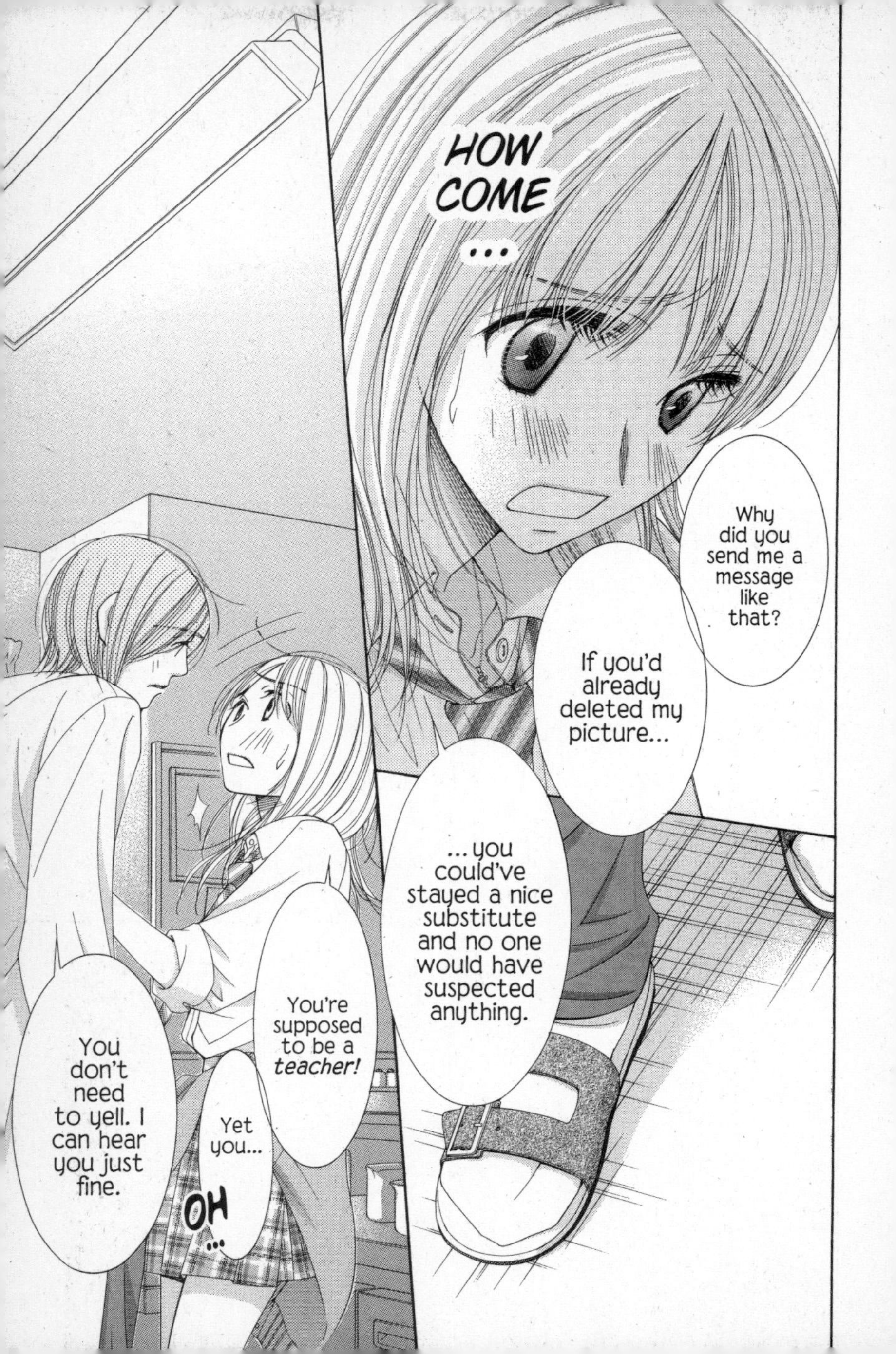
HOW COME ...
Why did you send me a message like that?
If you'd already deleted my picture...
... you could've stayed a nice substitute and no one would have suspected anything.
You're supposed to be a *teacher!*
Yet you...
You don't need to yell. I can hear you just fine.
OH ...

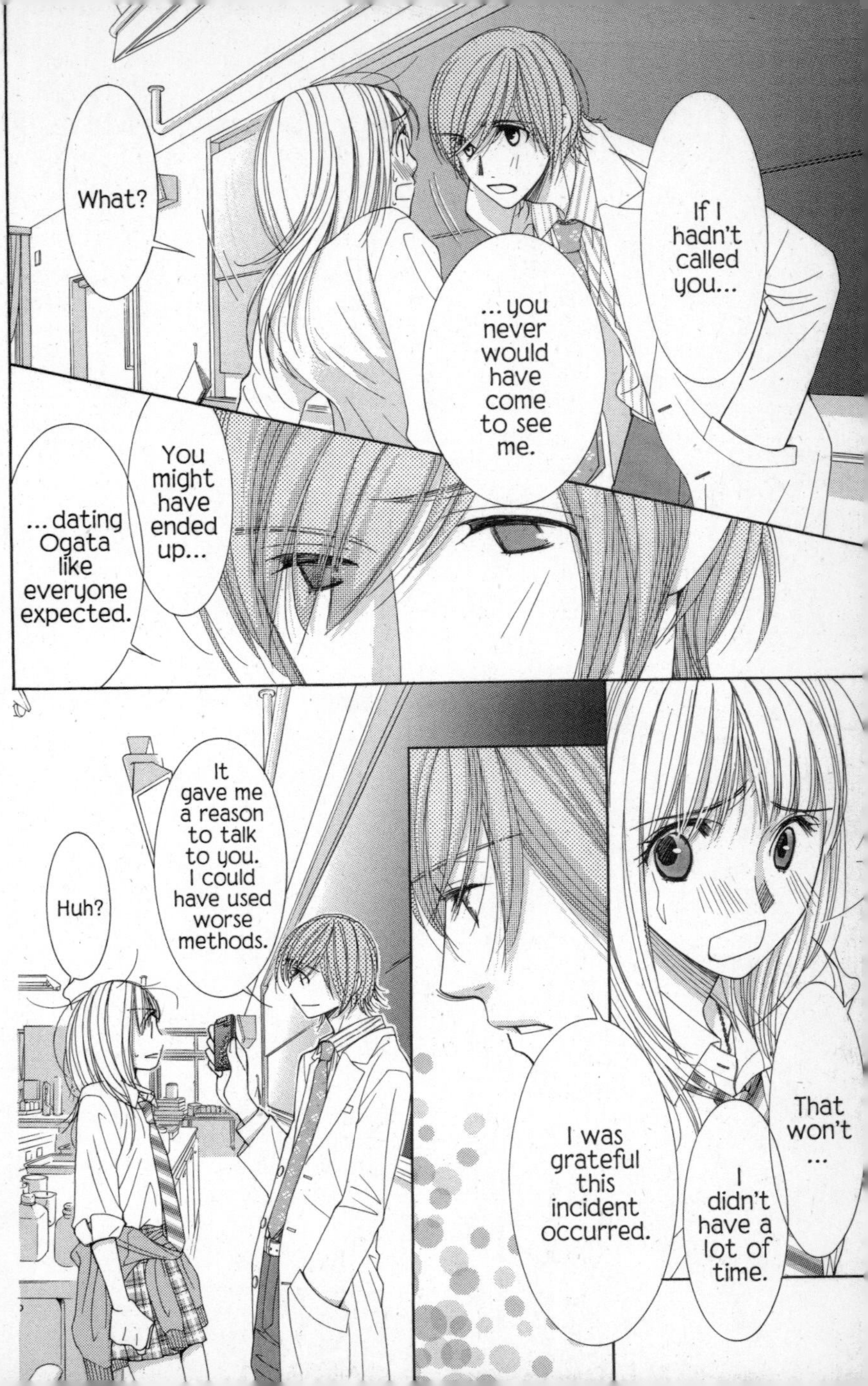
If I hadn't called you...
...you never would have come to see me.
What?
You might have ended up...
...dating Ogata like everyone expected.
That won't ...
I didn't have a lot of time.
I was grateful this incident occurred.
It gave me a reason to talk to you. I could have used worse methods.
Huh?

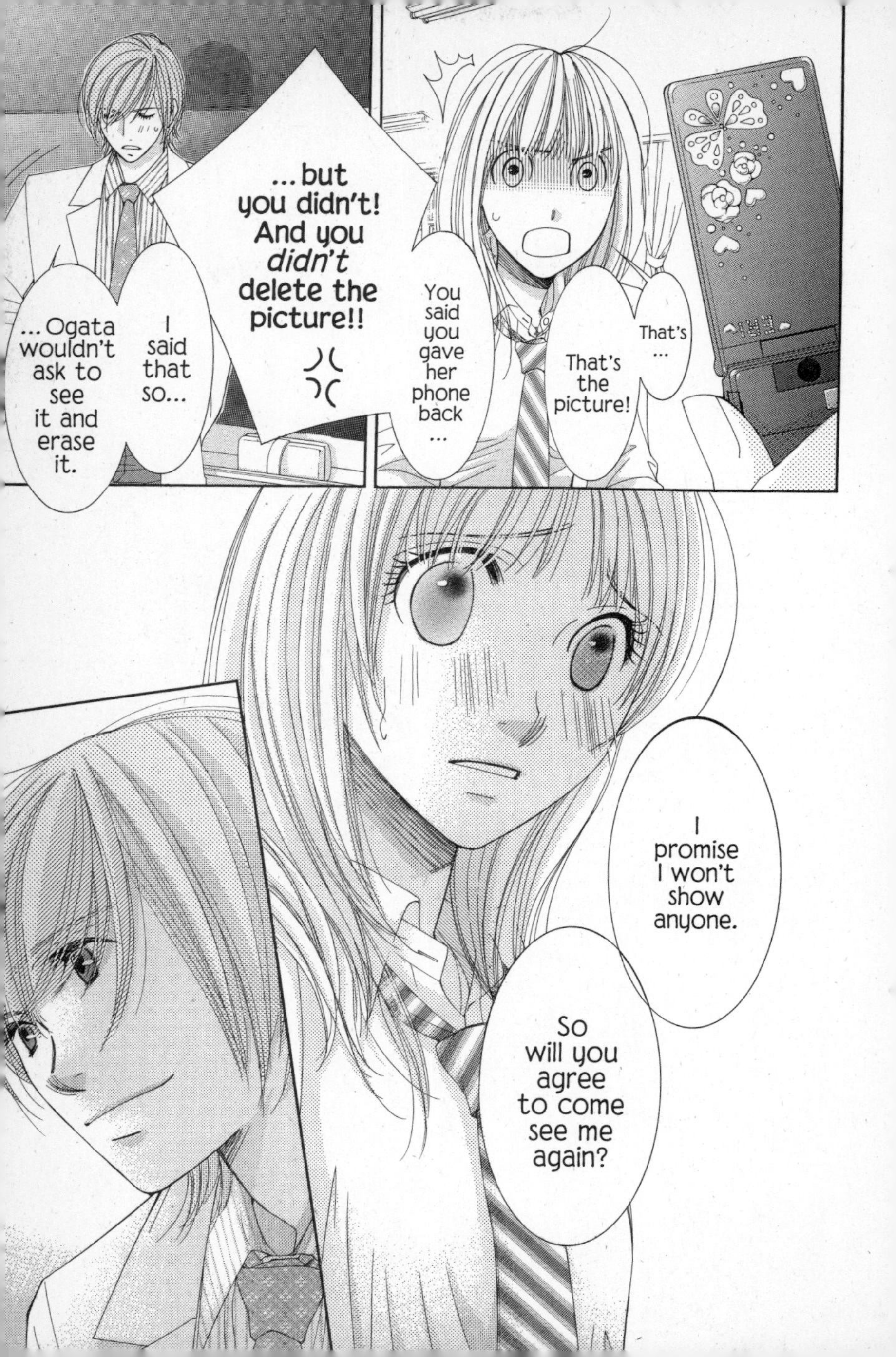
That's ...
That's the picture!
You said you gave her phone back ...
... but you didn't! And you *didn't* delete the picture!!
I said that so...
... Ogata wouldn't ask to see it and erase it.
I promise I won't show anyone.
So will you agree to come see me again?

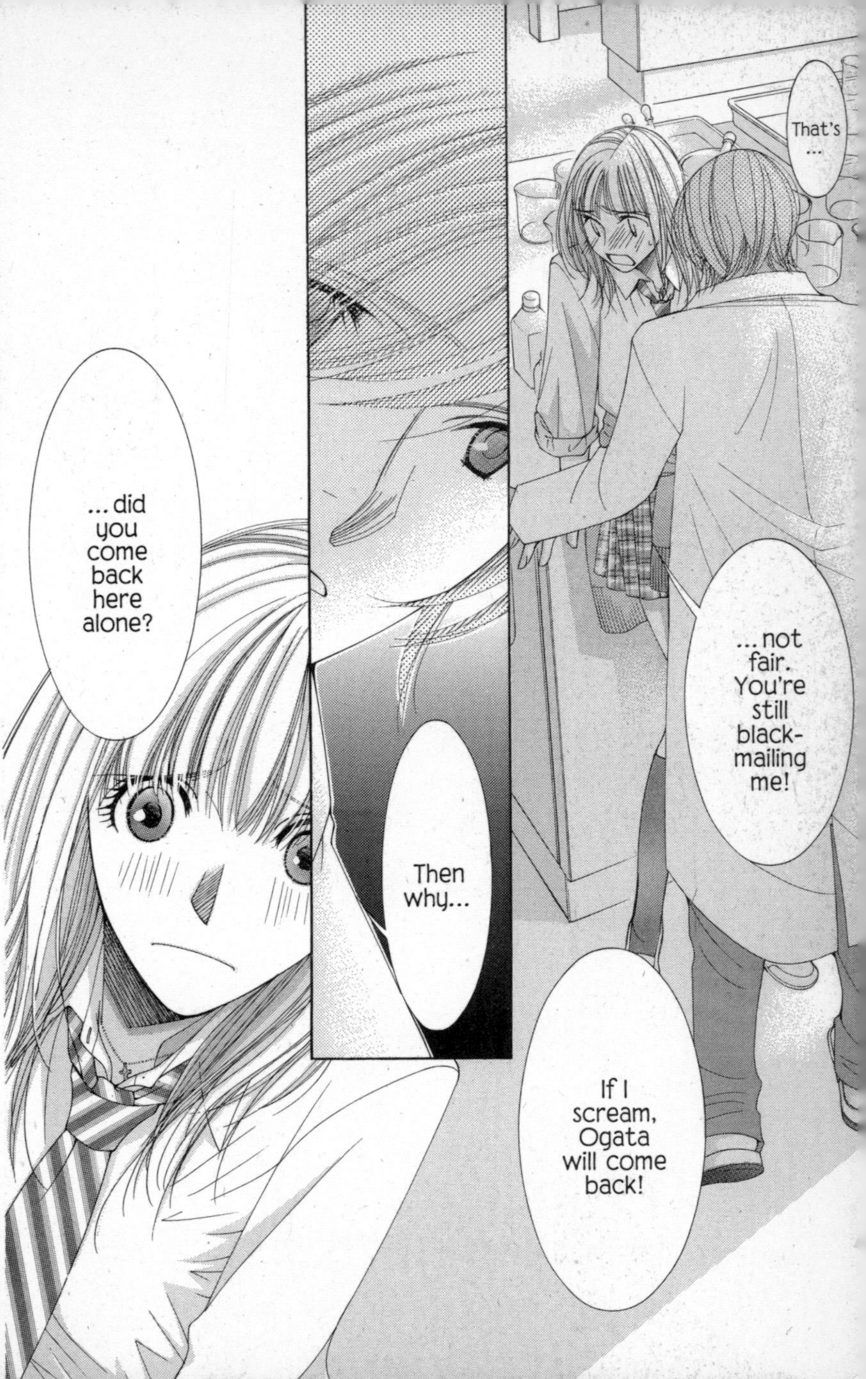
That's ...
... not fair. You're still black-mailing me!
If I scream, Ogata will come back!
Then why...
... did you come back here alone?

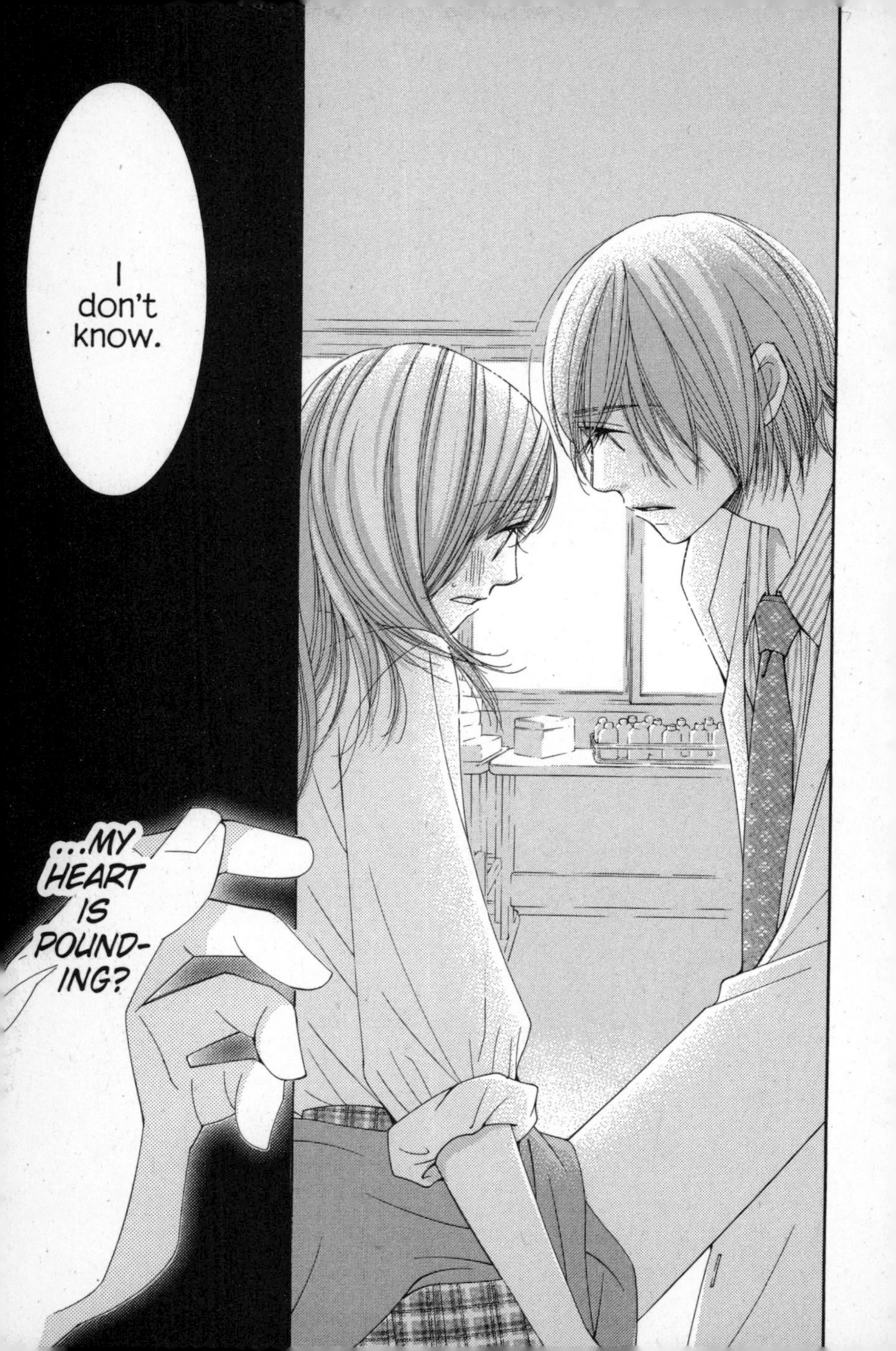
I don't know.
...MY HEART IS POUND-ING?

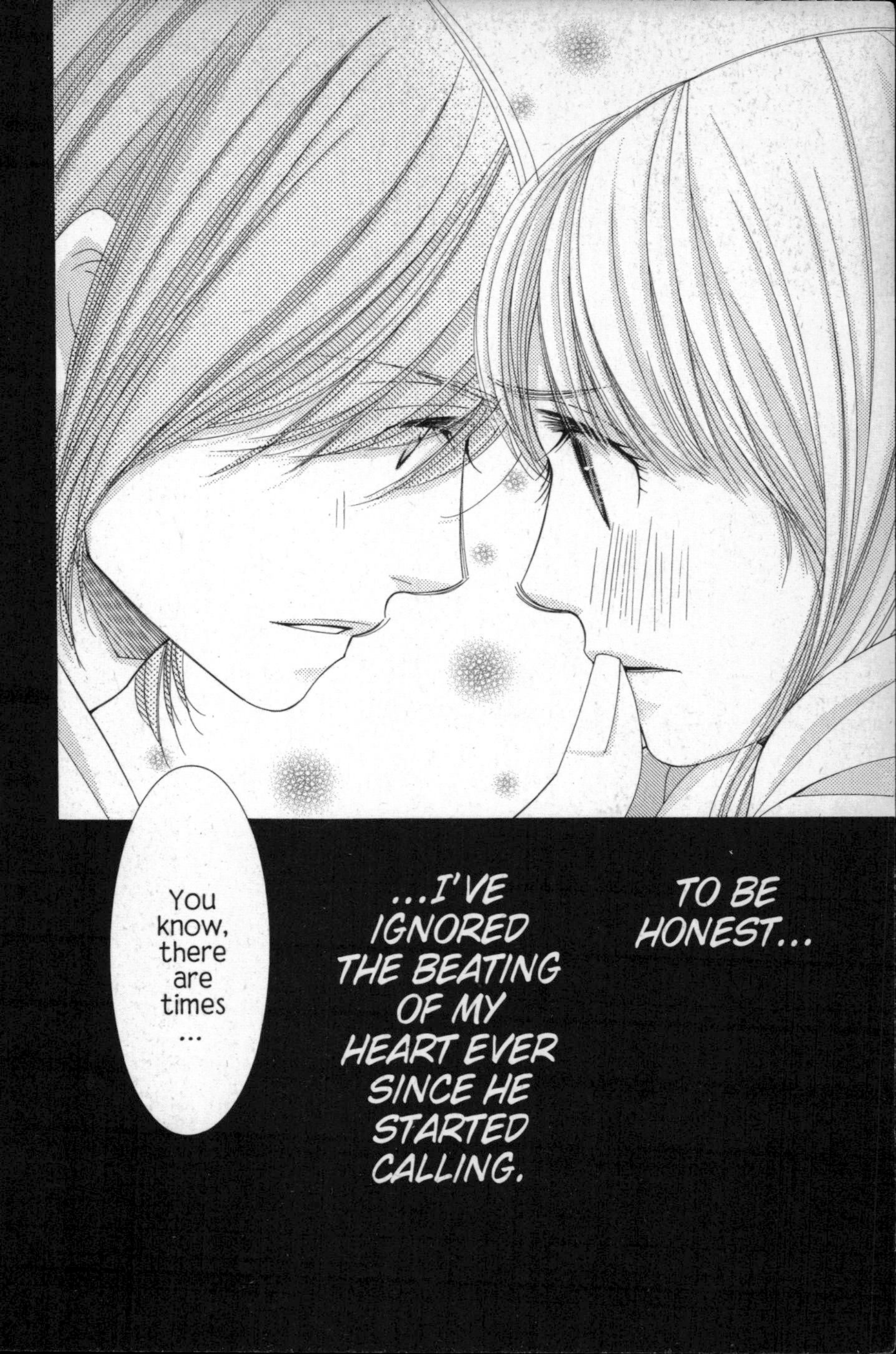
TO BE HONEST...
...I'VE IGNORED THE BEATING OF MY HEART EVER SINCE HE STARTED CALLING.
You know, there are times ...

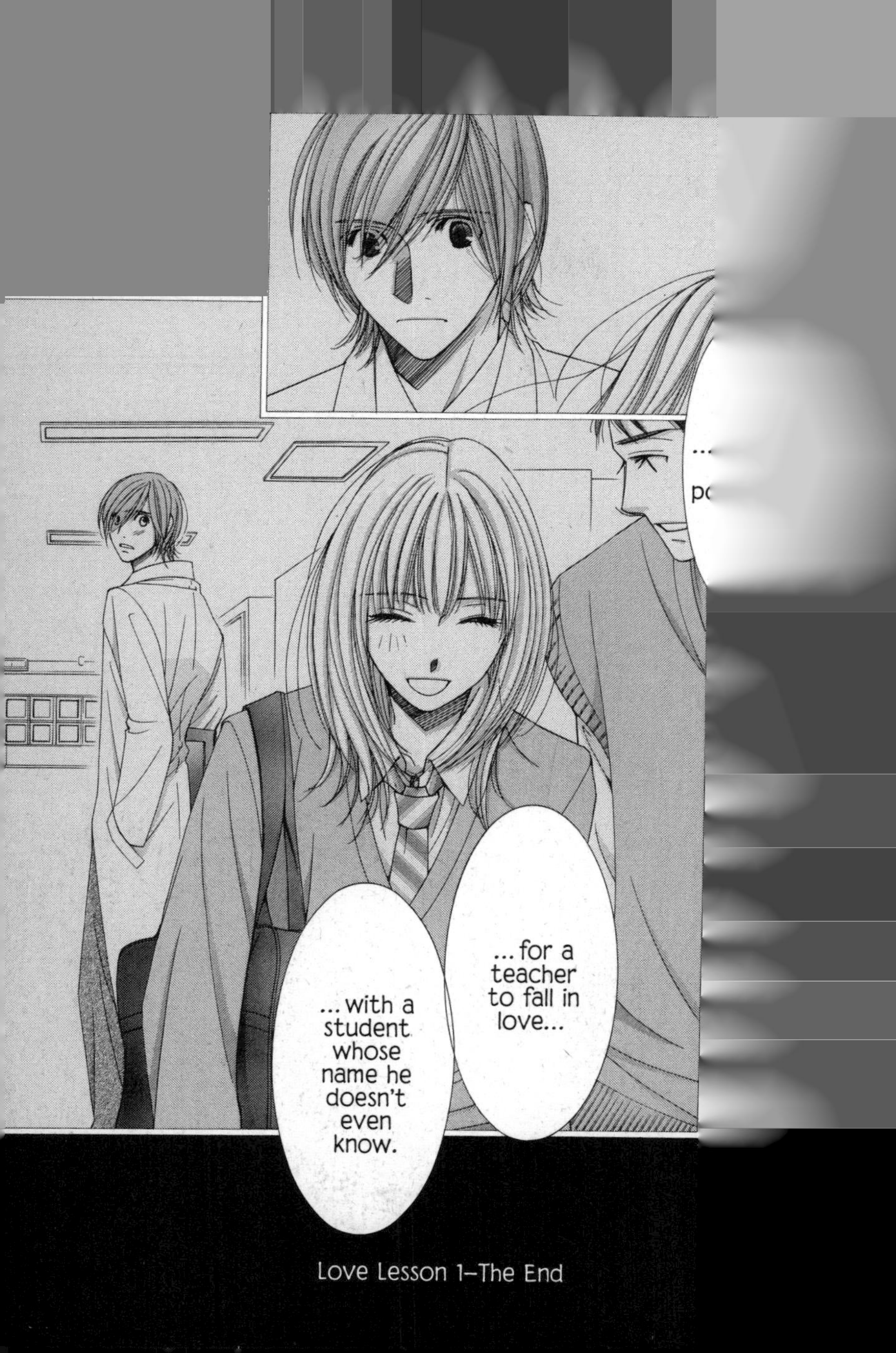
...for a teacher to fall in love...
...with a student whose name he doesn't even know.

Love Lesson 1—The End

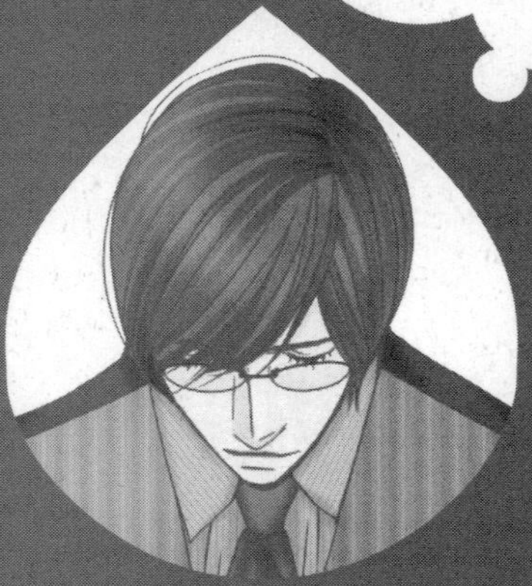

MIKI AIHARA

Here we go with the fourth volume! For readers who noticed (in the Japanese magazine version), there's a second masked character in chapter 17. That's Knights member Uehara, who accompanied Haruka to visit Yura. I apologize that for pacing reasons, I wasn't really able to show him more. FYI: The masks are of professional Japanese baseball players M and the H Prince.

Miki Aihara, from Shizuoka Prefecture, is the creator of the manga series *Hot Gimmick*. She began her career with *Lip Conscious!*, which ran in *Bessatsu Shojo Comic*. Her other work includes *Seiten Taisei* (The Clear, Wide Blue Sky), *So Bad!*, and *Tokyo Boys & Girls*. She's a Gemini whose hobbies include movies and shopping.

HONEY HUNT
VOL.4

Shojo Beat Edition

STORY AND ART BY MIKI AIHARA

© 2007 Miki AIHARA/Shogakukan
All rights reserved.
Original Japanese edition "HONEY HUNT" published by SHOGAKUKAN Inc.

English Adaptation/Liz Forbes
Translation/Ari Yasuda, HC Language Solutions, Inc.
Touch-up Art & Lettering/Rina Mapa
Design/Ronnie Casson
Editor/Alexis Kirsch

VP, Production/Alvin Lu
VP, Sales & Product Marketing/Gonzalo Ferreyra
VP, Creative/Linda Espinosa
Publisher/Hyoe Narita

Printed in Canada

Published by VIZ Media, LLC
P.O. Box 77010
San Francisco, CA 94107

10 9 8 7 6 5 4 3 2 1
First printing, April 2010

www.viz.com   www.shojobeat.com